JR MOORES is the resident psych-rock columnist for *The Quietus* and *Record Collector*, and his work has also appeared in *The Wire*, *The Guardian*, *Bandcamp Daily* and *Vice*, among many other places.

'A depth-charge exploration to the bloodied heart of heavy. Essential, energetic writing – JR Moores is the netherworld guide we always needed.'
– HARRY SWORD, author of *Monolithic Undertow: In Search of Sonic Oblivion*

'JR Moores is that rarest of things, a genuinely funny writer – unforced, with mighty panache.'
– LUKE TURNER, *The Quietus*

'*Electric Wizards* is entertaining as hell and not without its controversial claims, which are bound to stoke some fires.'
– *Electronic Sound*, Best of 2021

'The landscape of heavy music is vast, its existence is ever evolving. There is no better person to explore its dynamic terrain than JR Moores.'
– MATT BATY, Pigs Pigs Pigs Pigs Pigs Pigs Pigs

'JR Moores covers a rich landscape of sounds . . . What's more, he achieves a rare feat in rock criticism of saying something fresh and interesting about The Beatles.'
– DAN FRANKLIN, author of *HEAVY: How Metal Changes the Way We See the World*

T0042947

'Over the course of its 400-plus pages, this volume that speaks volumes about volume serves up a tasty and easily digestible smorgasbord of delights, nicely flavoured with personal insight, anecdote and wit.'
– *BUZZ*

'Writing about british band hey colossus, moores suggests their early material "sounded like mad max trying to grunt his way out of a giant bowl of rice krispies." Don't tell me you're not going to go straight onto google to check.'
– *The Herald*, music books of the year

'This book will open a wormhole in your brain.'
– JOE THOMPSON, Hey Colossus

Electric Wizards

A Tapestry of Heavy Music

1968 to the Present

JR MOORES

REAKTION BOOKS

Published by
Reaktion Books Ltd
Unit 32, Waterside
44–48 Wharf Road
London N1 7UX, UK

www.reaktionbooks.co.uk

First published 2021
First published in paperback 2022
Copyright © JR Moores 2021

Printed and bound in Great Britain
by TJ Books Ltd, Padstow, Cornwall

A catalogue record for this book is available from the British Library

ISBN 978 1 78914 653 0

For Stephanie
(she's so heavy)

CONTENTS

PREFACE

In July 2001 the British monthly music magazine *Q* published its rundown of 'The 50 Heaviest Albums of All Time'. The front cover of this issue featured Fred Durst, singer of nu-metal group Limp Bizkit, flanked by two blonde models in cheerleader outfits. Even at the height of their spectacular commercial success, Limp Bizkit failed to earn the respect of many – if not most – of their peers. As mentioned in *Q*'s interview feature, Metallica, Nine Inch Nails, Marilyn Manson and Pantera were just a handful of the acts to publicly scorn the band.[1] Ever since his rise to fame, Fred Durst has remained an enduring symbol of the calamities that can arise when heavy music goes more than a little awry.

This particular edition of *Q* hit newsagents' shelves during what I see as heavy music's weakest and bleakest era (for more detail on that sorry period, fast-forward straight to Chapter Fifteen). In spite of this, the magazine's list stands up pretty well to scrutiny, especially for one printed in such a mainstream publication. From its foundation in 1986 to the final issue of September 2020, *Q* was not known for its extensive coverage of heavy, experimental or boundary-pushing artists. One of its editors, Andrew Collins, said it was '*Smash Hits* with a mortgage'.[2]

Sandwiched between the Limp Bizkit interview and a feature on the AWOL-at-that-time Axl Rose, the list in question was introduced with the following caveat: 'Heaviness isn't just a kind of music: it's a state of mind.' One of the most impressive things about *Q*'s list is that the compilers' tastes were quite so eclectic, with their selections spanning multiple genres. I have my own quibbles with some of its entries and absences, as any reader would. But as much as they raise people's hackles, articles of this nature don't really purport to offer the last word on the subject; they are intended to initiate spirited debate. Overall, it's heartening that *Q*'s list does not exclusively champion albums from the world of heavy metal and its plethora of subgenres. It also makes ample room from the fields of blues, jazz, rock, prog, post-punk, goth, industrial, shoegaze and grunge. What's more, there are hip-hop, trip-hop and electronic records included in the rundown, plus the original soundtrack to Oliver Stone's *Natural Born Killers*. Personally, I wouldn't have put that last entry in there, and nor would Suicide's debut album make the cut. Its sound is too thin and tinny, people! And where are Dinosaur Jr, Melvins and Bad Brains? We could argue over this all day long. That being said – and here's a sentence I wasn't expecting to write – the book that you currently hold in your hands embraces a similar spirit, if not content, to the '50 Heaviest Albums of All Time' as printed in 2001 by *Q*.

Let's make the agenda clear from the outset. This book was never intended to be a comprehensive chronicle of *all* heavy music. What single volume could accomplish that feat? Naturally the topic is highly subjective, and the definition of heaviness itself is open to many interpretations. What does or does not constitute 'heavy music', what it is and what it is not: these matters are in constant cultural flux and are likewise deeply personal. The ensuing pages offer my own version of the evolution of heavy music. Yours could be quite different. It would be a bit weird if we shared the exact same views, although I hope I can convince you of certain matters. This will by no means be the final word on the subject.

It barely needs mentioning that there are countless heavy bands and tons of undeniably heavy albums that could stake their claim at inclusion and yet, mainly for the purposes of space and continuity, do not appear in this book. Yes, I have heard of Iron Monkey, Shit & Shine, Converge and Pantera. I agree they are all heavier than a beached blue whale. It pains me almost as much as it does you that there is no passage on each of those bands.[3] The same could be said of numerous other acts whose output has more than earned its place in the canon of heaviness. Needs must, however, and difficult decisions had to be made.

I have tried to home in on noteworthy acts whose work has stood – and is likely to continue to stand – the test of time. These range from household-name practitioners to obscurer cult heroes and heroines of the form. The overriding idea is to extol those who did things differently, who introduced something fresh, new and exciting into the world of heavy, whether by calculated design, slight accident or sheer chance. Often these developments involved taking an approach that ran counter to conventional thinking and popular trends. For that reason, many of the artists covered here took a while to catch on. Others are still waiting for the wider appreciation they properly deserve. Some of these acts made their breakthroughs by combining formerly segregated elements and ideas. Others took known heavy methods to their even heavier logical conclusions. At the same time, then, I plan to show how each successive phase in heaviness was forged by what came before and to join the dots between musicians whose connections may at first seem distant or perhaps a little surprising.

In doing so, it is my hope to broaden the scope of what we mean when we talk about heavy music, and which kinds of music and musicians are merited for inclusion in such a category. Many histories of heavy metal and its subgenres have already been published, ranging from the slapdash to the enlightening. This book does not concern itself with repeating the same patterns, stories, ideas and timelines. There is more than one alternative to the official, well-charted map of heavy music. Another way of navigating this journey might well begin in the same place, and perhaps even end at a similar juncture. The route we will be embarking on, however, will not be that recited in your average history of heavy metal. That classic tale might go from the blues and The Beatles to Black Sabbath, Led Zeppelin and Deep Purple, before taking in the leathery sights and meticulously recorded sounds of Judas Priest, Iron Maiden and Metallica, and maybe from there explore thrash metal, death metal, black metal, glam metal, groove metal and other later developments. We'll be taking another route altogether. You might say it's the scenic or more colourful one. I'll let others be the judge of that. It begins with The Beatles, sure, and specifically their most incredibly heavy track. And, yes, it absolutely has to embrace Black Sabbath. From there it will spiral outwards and delve deep into . . . well, let's not spoil the fun. With any luck, this more open approach will help to highlight the work of artists neglected, or else mentioned only in passing, in other tomes.

Having made a case for eclecticism, and despite there being some mention of more 'electronic' or computer-aided methods of heavy-making, I have opted to keep things more or less restricted to material that is, at root, guitar-based. Much as I would have liked to tumble further down the rabbit hole to explore genres like techno or drill 'n' bass, we'll have to save those delights for another time.

What is 'heavy' and where did it come from? 'Where will you start? Wagner?!' as the writer Rob Chapman asked, or perhaps advised, when this book was in its infancy. Erm, no. Sorry, Rob. I decided it was best to begin at some point after the invention of amplification in the twentieth century. Before it was applied to rock music, 'heavy' was a common term in hippie slang. It is not true, as band manager Charlie Greene liked to claim, that heavy only became something other than a measure of weight after his own savvy marketing of the debut album by Iron Butterfly (1968's *Heavy*).[4] The hippies inherited it from earlier Beat writers and jazz musicians. The word was used to indicate profundity or depth, something that was especially thought-provoking or meaningful, or else it could refer to potency in terms of feelings or sentiment. When John Lennon of The Beatles sang the words 'she's so heavy' in infatuation with Yoko Ono, he was not referring to his partner's weight as calculated by the couple's white bathroom scales. The connotations of 'heavy' could be both positive and negative. 'Whoa! Dr Leary's lecture was heavy, man!' enthusiastic hippie students might have said to one another after having their minds blown by the celebrity LSD-proselytizing professor. When the same hippies' commune had imploded because of relationship tensions born of free-love complications and internal power plays, members might then have fled the sorry situation, bemoaning how 'The scene had got too heavy, dude!'

The term 'heavy rock' emerged in the 1960s in reference to bands that used loudly amplified electrical guitars, which usually had a distorted tone, and were backed by noticeably hard-hitting rhythm sections. Judging from the examples of music journalism in the *Rock's Backpages* digital archive, 'heavy' was initially only used to describe the most physically demanding instrument, the drums (as in 'a heavy beat').[5] There is also talk of 'heavy' acting roles and cinematic plotlines from musicians who starred in films or scored for the movies.[6] 'Rock and roll with a heavy beat is pretty much gone,' claimed singer Bobby Vee towards the end of 1961 without knowing how wrong he would be. 'I don't believe people are aware of the change. What we do now is still called rock 'n' roll but it's much less raucous.'[7] In 1963 The Beatles were more likely to be described as suffering from heavy colds (as reported at least twice that year in the *New Musical Express*) than dabbling in heavy music.[8] The following year, Brian Poole of The Tremeloes described a couple of his band's new numbers as 'beaters with a fairly heavy rock sound, but a nice melody'.[9] As the decade progressed, 'heavy' was used to describe other individual musical aspects besides those made by drummers. Pete Staples of The Troggs seemed to stand out for his 'heavy', 'uncompromising' and 'thunderous' bass playing.[10] With the rise of other raucous acts (sorry, Bobby Vee) like The Yardbirds and The Who, the term 'heavy rock' became common, often used interchangeably with 'hard rock'.

The term 'heavy metal' only emerged later. The genre's most important originators, Birmingham's Black Sabbath, were for some time referred to as a heavy rock band like any other. In Sabbath's early years, people were even happy to lump them in with the contemporary prog rock scene,[11] something that would be considered an act of categorical madness nowadays. (Although it's true that Black Sabbath were mates with Yes, and guitarist Tony Iommi did play a couple of gigs in a short-lived line-up of proggy flute-botherers Jethro Tull.)

Back then, as at any time thereafter, 'heavy' (without the 'metal' appendage) was open to interpretation. In 1969, for example, *Melody Maker* hailed The Nice as 'Britain's heaviest group', repeating the claim that future Emerson, Lake & Palmer member Keith Emerson was 'the Jimi Hendrix of the organ'.[12] Could such a prospect come anywhere near the heaviness of Hendrix himself, who back then was still alive and gigging frequently? Jimi Hendrix: the Jimi Hendrix of the guitar! Only two-thirds of The Jimi Hendrix Experience were English, of course, but where other rival domestic groups were concerned there were plenty around at that time whose heaviness could equal and surpass the proto-prog stomp of The Nice. In the summer of 2020, one of the readers of *Record Collector* wrote to the magazine's letters page to insist that Steve Marriott's Humble Pie, back in the early 1970s, were 'by far the LOUDEST band' he had ever seen, surpassing the admirable efforts of AC/DC or Deep Purple.[13] It's worth bearing in mind that while any kind of music can be played at an excessive volume, the surplus power of heaviness relies on other factors as well. There are lots of different ways for musicians to make heavy music. As we shall see, whether it remains packaged within verse-chorus-verse structures as in the style of the 'ear-bleeding country' band Dinosaur Jr or breaks free of structure entirely as in the abstract work of Earth, heaviness tends to be about the *sound* rather than the song.

Let's not pretend that my own tastes, age, location and personal prejudices haven't influenced this book's content. As someone who fell in love with music after the 1990s grunge explosion had supplanted the MTV-centric image-consciousness of the previous decade, and from there having buried myself deeper into the endless subterranea of what might broadly be called 'alternative music', I have been unable to shake my dislike of a reliance on posturing or theatricality when it comes to our heavy music makers.

There is little need to get too bogged down in who does or does not 'keep it real' (whatever that means), and there are many who would argue that the avoidance of posture is simply another form of posture. Journalist Michael Hann insists that rock is never 'all about the music' (man). 'One of the things it's about is image', he writes. 'Every decision every band makes about how they appear onstage has been calculated to one degree or another. The group who amble on in their grubby T-shirts and ill-fitting jeans have chosen to do that. They have chosen to reject costume, just as the group in ridiculous silver and golden outfits have chosen to embrace it.'[14] There's definitely some truth to that, and its sentiment can be extended from costume to posture and other forms of exhibitionism. When push comes to shove, however, I usually cannot help but side with the modest dressers over the flashy golden-suited brigade, who are probably trying a little too hard to catch the eye when they should be putting more effort into catching the ear. Those bands that have calculated such matters to a lesser degree and who tend to concentrate more on what comes naturally, or at least give the impression of doing so, are the ones I'd typically stick up for, with the odd exception here and there.[15]

One of my more recently acquired heroes is Joe Thompson, a professional postman and bassist in the casually dressed and ever-evolving noise rock outfit Hey Colossus. When I met up with him for an event at Birmingham's Supersonic Festival in 2019 to discuss his book about life as an underground musician, Thompson happened to mention that he has a severe dislike of any band that performs in masks. 'That's marketing', Thompson sighed. On the whole I tend to agree. Mask-wearing is perhaps an extreme example, but it is representative of the way in which certain gestures and artistic choices tend to distract from, rather than enhance, the overall heaviness. This extends to the music itself, where stylistic decisions – often at the more showboating end of the scale – can cause similar obfuscations. Virtuoso technique, in this case, can act as a metaphorical mask to conceal the artist's lack of more genuine, sincere and interesting creative ingenuities.

Inevitably, some of the musicians featured in the following pages are able to play others under the table. Nobody can be completely incompetent and still make music, as anyone who formed a band at school will tell you. Melvins' Dale Crover, for instance, is to all intents and purposes one of the best drummers of all time, yet he is never ranked as highly as more famous drummers, such as those two dudes from Foo Fighters. As explained by J. J. Anselmi, a drummer himself and the author of a history on the sludgier end of heavy metal, Crover's style can sound somewhat 'sloppy, dumb, and even out of control' to the untrained ear. The thing is, it's intentional: the awkwardness of the unusual timings and changes in rhythm, joined with the off-kilter beats and drum fills, a semblance of sloppiness and even moments of temporary silence all serve to enhance the harsh, rough, dirty and generally unhinged nature of Melvins' music.[16] It increases their heaviness.

Two artists working in wildly different areas were jazz titan Miles Davis and post-punk avatar Mark E. Smith of The Fall. Each one developed the habit of regularly replenishing his band's personnel with fresher-faced and less professionally experienced musicians, many of them still teenagers when recruited, in the knowledge that a healthy amount of musical naivety could help circumvent the pitfalls of complacency, avoid any overreliance on well-worn formulas, and keep the music moving ever forward and thus constantly regenerating. That kind of shake-up helped to keep those band leaders on their toes as well. As it happens, each one's music grew heavier as they aged. That's just one way of doing it. Paul McCartney, who as we shall see composed The Beatles' heaviest moment, never bothered to learn to read music. 'I'm one of the least technical people you're likely to meet,' he insisted when interrogated by *Bass Player* magazine.[17] This is the man who fought with George Harrison when the latter, as lead guitarist, tried to play too many 'dang-diddle-da-da' parts on 'Hey Jude'. McCartney doesn't like it when songs grow overly wordy or are overburdened with too many chords and is delighted by Duke Ellington's unexpectedly basic one-finger piano solos on the song 'Duke's Place'.[18] Heaviness requires intensity, yes. But it is often accompanied by a complementary looseness.

Speaking of heroes old and new, even the subjective and personal nature of heaviness is prone to constant modification. In my youth I could barely make it through the more severe tracks on Nirvana's *In Utero* without reaching for the skip button. When listening to the same songs with a more mature aural palate, they seem a lot tamer than some of the more extreme material that has crept its way into my collection. This happens to artists too. In his liner notes to the Big Black compilation CD *The Hammer Party*, Steve Albini wrote that 'time puts everything into weird perspective. What sounded wild then sounds timid now thanks to the numbing effect of the myriad trends we've been subjected to since. We were proud of this shit though. It was pretty good then.'[19] It is not the aim of this book to determine what the heaviest music ever created may be by the use of some elaborate points-based system. It's more about the journey. There *is* a chapter on Napalm Death, mind. They would easily rack up one of the most competitive scores. Sections such as that one ought to placate the metalheads who are reading.

The content of *Electric Wizards* is presented in a broadly chronological manner, although it is arranged thematically, so there may be certain overlaps in terms of what happened when. It could be said, too, that there is an Anglo-American bias to the proceedings, despite the odd trip to other areas of Europe, as well as Japan and

Australia. I warmly welcome future work on unsung offerings from elsewhere around the globe.

The purpose of *Electric Wizards* is to tie more closely together a bunch of connected but seemingly disparate threads and, in doing so, weave a new tapestry of heavy music. Here and there it might also raise a smile or two. At the very least, it should encourage readers and listeners to increase the volume on the many heavy recordings we pass along the way.

Paul McCartney looking heavy: close-up of The Beatles' statue
at Liverpool Pier Head.

INTRODUCTION

L ike virtually every breakthrough in the history of recorded music, heaviness was invented by the greatest member of The Beatles. By his mid-twenties Paul McCartney had already achieved several world-changing accomplishments. He had come up with the fully formed melody to 'Yesterday' literally in his sleep. He had been chiefly responsible for his beat combo's innovative use of tape loops. He was the first person to have conceptualized the concept of the concept album. He had introduced his friend John 'the experimental one' Lennon to the transatlantic avant-garde art scene. Having achieved all that and more, it was then time for McCartney to forge a new kind of tonality: heaviness, which he did with *The Beatles'* (aka the *White Album*'s) 'Helter Skelter' in 1968.

The story goes that when casually flicking through a music magazine, McCartney stumbled across an interview in which Pete Townshend made the bold claim that his group, The Who, had just finished making the 'raunchiest, loudest, most ridiculous rock 'n' roll record you've ever heard'.[1] Never one for resting on his laurels while the competition flexed its muscles (and certainly not in his fiercely ambitious Beatles days), McCartney set about creating what was truly the most raunchy, loud, ridiculous and noisy rock 'n' roll track yet recorded. The result would out-heavy The Who by a significant margin.

For various spurious reasons, several Beatles scholars have treated this monumental track with contempt. When he listened to 'Helter Skelter', Ian MacDonald heard McCartney 'shrieking weedily' over 'out-of-tune thrashing', the sum total being nothing more credible than a 'literally drunken mess'. On this 'clumsy attempt' at squaring

up to The Who, the Fab Four had 'comically overreached themselves', MacDonald concluded. As he saw it, The Beatles' intuitive
strengths lay in the subtler arts of 'balance, form, and attention to
detail'. This reading might be expected from a critic who dismissed
heavy metal – in its entirety – as 'more a sonic contact sport than
a musical experience',[2] yet MacDonald was not alone in his inability to respectfully engage with the elephantine majesty of 'Helter
Skelter'. In *The Mammoth Book of the Beatles*, it is listed under the
White Album's roster of 'failed experiments' and reprimanded for its
inclusion of 'what must be the only instance of terrible bass playing
by Paul on record'.[3] Other writers have singled out its bassline as one
of the track's most crucial elements, its 'gnarled timbre' located so
high in the mix and with McCartney striking his strings with such
force that it creates a percussive, near-slap-bass effect through which
the instrument begins to resemble an additional rhythm guitar or
even a lead one.[4] At the boisterous and, yes, rather inebriated recording session, both McCartney and Lennon contributed bass parts.
Still, McCartney can be credited with conceiving the tune in the
first place before guiding it towards fruition. John Lennon would
go on to disown 'Helter Skelter' by saying it belonged to Paul 'completely'. Lennon also claimed he had 'never listened to the words,
properly, it was just a noise'.[5]

It is erroneous to believe The Beatles' heavy endeavours were
uniformly absurd and embarrassing, as MacDonald viewed them.
It might be fair to say that Lennon's own attempt to 'do' heavy on
the same double album's 'Yer Blues' doesn't quite succeed in transcending the grade of half-jokey pastiche. In contrast, McCartney's
'Helter Skelter' sits on a higher plane entirely, not to mention a
step above the rock templates that preceded it. It is taken from
an album that is, in fact, rich in pastiches and parodies, or at
least tracks that take pastiche as their starting point before being
sprinkled with some original Beatles magic. 'Helter Skelter' is not
one of those compositions. McCartney was competing against a

description of heaviness and what that might sound like in his mind, rather than lampooning or paying homage to any specific prior songs or artists. This is one of the signifiers that, on an album that flirted with calypso, doo-wop, music hall and other musical bricolage, 'Helter Skelter' pointed forward instead of concerning itself with the past.

The track's originality was apparent in the trouble that reviewers of the *White Album* had in describing and categorizing 'Helter Skelter'. The anonymous reviewer in *Record Mirror* cited the 'screaming pained vocals' and 'ear splitting buzz guitar' among the song's 'general instrumental confusion, but rather typical pattern'. The ending sounded 'like five thousand large electric flies out for a good time', wrote he or she (probably he).[6] Some reviewers got it: Geoffrey Cannon of *The Guardian* extolled the virtues of listening to the stereo rather than mono version of the double LP, whereupon 'Helter Skelter' transformed itself from mere 'nifty fast number to one of my best 30 tracks of all time'.[7] In the *International Times*, counterculture writer Barry Miles called it 'probably the heaviest rocker on plastic today'.[8]

There were those who compared it to the style of acts such as Cream or The Jimi Hendrix Experience, but 'Helter Skelter' pushed beyond the boundaries of its blues and hard rock forebears. Just as The Beatles had done earlier with the innovative feedback intro to 'I Feel Fine' and the radical riff that opened 'You Can't Do That', 'Helter Skelter' marked the beginning of a new era in heaviness. Another stepping stone in the direction of McCartney's breakthrough moment was 'It's All Too Much', written by George Harrison. Although the public didn't get to hear this *Yellow Submarine* track until after they'd been introduced to the *White Album*, it had been recorded earlier, in the spring of 1967. The recording conditions were similar to those of 'Helter Skelter'. In George Martin's absence, the musicians ran riot. Lennon tore craggy noise out of his guitar, perhaps paying homage to Hendrix. Harrison slapped and prodded dingy chords out of his damp-sounding organ, singing about his experiences of tripping. McCartney provided a rolling bass track, and Starr was his usual modestly marvellous self at the drum kit. The Fab Four were basking in the group sound, and not so much in Harrison's song itself, around which the cacophony was hung, and the recording makes it seem as though they could have kept on playing it through the night and into the early morning. They are jamming, which is not something The Beatles did very often on record. The album version ends at the six-and-a-half-minute mark, but the band clearly played on for longer before editing it down for the sake of their less patient listeners. 'It's All Too Much' irritated those puritans who thought The Beatles' main function was to produce concise pop symphonies. But that was never their job. That was Brian Wilson's. The Beatles were put on this earth to do a whole lot more than that. Ian MacDonald called 'It's All Too Much' a 'protracted exercise in G-pedal monotony . . . marked by hamfisted feedback guitar',[9] as if that's a bad thing. The result was not as intense as 'Helter Skelter', but The Beatles were certainly getting there.

When 'Helter Skelter' did arrive, the song had such potency that it became an obsession of the white supremacist Charles Manson, who misinterpreted its lyrics as prophesizing a near-apocalyptic war between the races, after which he and his followers would emerge from their hiding place and take over the world. Manson's cult members wrote the words 'Healter [sic] Skelter' on a refrigerator door using the blood of their murder victims. Having said that, the same gang of homicidal buffoons were equally inspired by the George Harrison composition 'Piggies', which can hardly be labelled as particularly heavy given its jaunty baroque harpsichord accompaniment and orchestral string arrangement.

Released in 1988, U2's *Rattle and Hum* opens with a live rendition of 'Helter Skelter'. It is introduced by their singer with the following words: 'This song Charles Manson stole from The Beatles. We're stealing it back.' Little did Bono realize that rock 'n' roll had already reclaimed the number long before *Rattle and Hum*. By the time U2 got their sticky fingers on it 'Helter Skelter' had already been covered by artists including Aerosmith, Siouxsie and the Banshees, Hüsker Dü, Mötley Crüe and Pat Benatar. So while the song would remain inextricably tied to Manson in the popular imagination, it isn't as if he'd commanded any exclusive hold over the title.

Notwithstanding the undeniably powerful 'song' part of the composition, a key element of the genius of 'Helter Skelter' is that almost half the track's running time consists of the prolonged 'outro' and numerous false endings. Where a more traditionally minded blues rock outfit like Cream, for example, might have instinctively used that extra space to shred out some technically proficient solo or instrumental flourishes, The Beatles took the more uncompromising and avant-garde route of wallowing in weird noises, brassy skronk work, wild screams and enraptured riffing, all of it some distance removed from the 'rather typical pattern' described by *Record Mirror*.

In a rare moment of youthful insight, Noel Gallagher of Oasis once remarked that 'Helter Skelter' marked the beginning of punk. Its attitude and aesthetic, Gallagher argued, was absorbed by MC5 and The Stooges, whose debut albums were both released in 1969, a year after the *White Album* went on sale. 'They sound exactly like that record,' Gallagher informed the *Addicted to Noise* website in 1995. Ergo, 'Helter Skelter' equals 'the birth of punk rock as we know it'.[10]

Punk would have a critical role to play in the history of heaviness, even though – as will be discussed in a later chapter – punk is not an especially heavy genre itself. In fact, the impact of 'Helter Skelter' stretches far further and wider than is implied by its proto-punk credentials. The Who and rival hard rock outfits were required to up their game accordingly after 'Helter Skelter' had revealed compositions like 'I Can See for Miles' (the track Townshend had been referring to in the quote above) to be relatively timid.

In 1969, along with The Rolling Stones' disastrous Altamont concert and the presidential election of Richard Milhous Nixon, the Manson murders that 'Helter Skelter' and 'Piggies' unintentionally inspired comprised one of the events that were taken to symbolize the end of the hippie era and the beginning of a more pessimistic, cynical, dark and morbid time. This was a cultural mood that loyal Beatles devotees Black Sabbath were able to tap into and capitalize on in a more potent and seismic way than any of their contemporaries.

The Beatles–Manson association would become even more pronounced after the 1974 publication of Vincent Bugliosi and Curt Gentry's book on the murders, appropriately titled *Helter Skelter*. Even before the book's publication, The Beatles' track had already indicated a wider shift towards darkness, uncertainty and futility. As Gerald Carlin and Mark Jones put it,

> Caught on the cusp of emergent heavy metal, and with its ambiguously frivolous/ominous 'coming down fast' lyric, 'Helter Skelter' perhaps seems far more synoptic of the slide from revolutionary optimism to disillusionment and crisis than other, more overtly political, tracks of the period.[11]

Taken literally, the lyrics might at first appear daft, childish and playful; a description of going up and down a slide. McCartney later explained that the words were also intended to symbolize the inevitable collapse of all empires: 'the fall, the demise, the going down'.[12] Such subject-matter, as Chris Butler of heavy music website *Invisible Oranges* has pointed out, has since been the focus of entire albums by countless metal bands, from Megadeth to Lamb of God.[13]

'Helter Skelter''s significance does not end there. Musically speaking, the song's reliance on power and groove, and its confrontationally nonconventional and spontaneously arranged structure, share much with the later tropes of noise rock as well as the higher-brow subgenre of post-metal. The guitar scrawl and experimental brass racket that occurs at around the three-minute mark could have come straight out of a later no wave or post-punk track. The absence of a traditional pop/rock arrangement in favour of minimalist instrumental repetition and the idea that talented musicians could retreat back to playing in a more primal way – one that emphasized texture and feeling – were techniques that would be echoed by the agendas of the 1970s krautrock scene. The thirteen-minute take of 'Helter Skelter' that finally saw the light of day thanks to the 2018 deluxe edition of the *White Album* is even more krautrock-like. It is softer and calmer than the original but wallows gloriously in repetition, anticipating the ideas of Can, who formed in Cologne in the same year as the *White Album*'s release.

What's more, Ringo's yelp of 'I got blisters on my fingers!' anticipates the snippets of in-studio chitchat that, in the late 1980s, heavy engineer extraordinaire Steve Albini would include in the gaps between tracks on records such as Slint's *Tweez* and Pixies' debut album *Surfer Rosa*. That burning desire of Paul's to create the loudest and most ridiculously raucous music ever recorded, and to push his drummer to the physical limits in doing so, shares the spirit and intentions of 1980s grindcore pioneers Napalm Death, whose heaviness has rarely been exceeded.

Choosing not to fill one whole side of an LP with the longest take of 'Helter Skelter' was a missed opportunity. Imagine how perfect the *White Album* could have been if The Best Beatle had been bold enough to put his foot down by trimming away some of the double album's weaker contributions, such as the genuine failed experiment of 'Revolution 9' (a clumsy homage to Karlheinz Stockhausen cobbled together by John Lennon and Yoko Ono). For now, that near mythical 27-minute take remains locked away in the Abbey Road vaults, so we can only speculate on its nature. Does it take the form of an epic stoner jam that resembles the doom, drone and sludge rock subgenres that would slowly evolve out of the mere four-minute, thirty-second embryo of 'Helter Skelter' via Black Sabbath and various mutations thereafter? Had the extended version of 'Helter Skelter' been released in 1968, we might have witnessed records like those made by Earth, Sleep and Electric Wizard crawl out of heaviness's primordial soup much earlier than the 1990s.

A wild and intoxicated session that resulted in a single track that ran for nearly 30 minutes. Blood splattered across the drum skins, spilled from the blistered digits of a drummer who was instructed to 'just beat the shit out of the drums; just kill them.'[14] A lead guitarist who was running around the studio holding a flaming ashtray atop his head in impersonation of Arthur Brown.[15] While that unhinged revelry was occurring, the singer was recording a succession of increasingly frenzied vocal takes. A bass (or two) that sounds as if it's trying to trepan its way through the listener's skull. A quartet trying to recapture the magic of playing live music together as a bona fide rock band, having retired from concert performances because they couldn't hear themselves over the screams of their fans. A group that was moving away from the studio experiments of their mid-1960s LPs in favour of capturing a more rough-and-ready feel to their recordings. (And it doesn't get much rougher, more ready, more live-feeling than 'Helter Skelter'.) This went beyond blues and blues rock, beyond hard rock, and into other places entirely.

Admirers ranging from Killing Joke's Youth to Soundgarden singer Chris Cornell have said that Paul McCartney's genius on the *White Album* lay in his ability to veer from 'one of the best scary vocals ever recorded' (as Youth described that incendiary 'Helter Skelter' performance) to more 'beautiful and fragile' moments like the same album's 'Blackbird'.[16] The two could also be fused, of course. Cornell, as early as age nine, would marvel at McCartney's straddling of the extremes: 'The Beatles did whatever they wanted. This is a band that did "Helter Skelter", "Yesterday" and "Penny Lane". No one said, "Hey, they can't do that!"'[17] If anyone did have the gall to object, it seems The Beatles wisely ignored them. Cornell put that fearlessness to good use in his grunge band Soundgarden, whose own material encompassed heavy metal, hard rock, elements of psychedelia, occasional acoustic balladry and an unlikely cameo from a street performer who played the spoons.

As a principle to govern the succeeding chapters of *Electric Wizards*, our definition of heavy will be this: a combination of sonic power and sincere emotion, of all kinds and within various genres, performed by those who value texture and density of sound above conventional technical prowess. While the world of heaviness is vast and varied, it tends to be about riffs, thickness of sound (often via distortion), deep and bassy. It's almost always made by an ensemble, be this two people or more, who create their sound as a cohesive unit, not as a conduit to underscore the talents of one spotlight-hogging star singer or player.

Music that relies too much on virtuosity and showboating, it will be argued, risks losing, obscuring or diminishing the purity and soulfulness of its heaviness. There is, to be fair, a thin line between rapturous, transcendental solo and showing-off solo. Between shamanism, if you like, and emotionally empty onanism. And yes, the difference is fairly subjective. For me, guys (and it is usually GUYS) like Dave Gilmour, Jimmy Page and Joe Satriani allow themselves all too often to sink head first into the latter category. On the other hand, Dinosaur Jr's J Mascis, Eddie Hazel and Michael Hampton of Parliament-Funkadelic, Carrie Brownstein from Sleater Kinney and Neil Young & Crazy Horse are the real deal. A useful example is Dean Ween, who often appears in lists of 'most underrated guitarists'. This is because he plays in the oddball band Ween, known for their Zappa-like parodies, eccentric humour and eclectic straddling of musical styles. Deaner (real name Michael Melchiondo Jr) is an accomplished player, but Ween are also followers of the demon god Boognish and are advocates of what they refer to as 'the brown sound'. This is roughly defined as 'fucked-up in a good way'. For Ween producer Andrew Weiss, the 'brownness' of sound often rises from unorchestrated 'glorious mistakes' such as the strangled tone a distortion pedal might croak out when its battery is fading.[18] In the early days of recorded music, distortion itself was initially viewed as a sonic aberration, a mistake that needed to be contained, corrected and eliminated in order to achieve as crisp and clean a sound as was humanly and technically possible. That was until people cottoned on to the fact that distortion sounds really, really cool. This aural smudge, this happy side effect, this leaking wrongness became a defining element of, first, the electric blues and, subsequently, rock music as a whole.[19]

In terms of showing off, anybody who, without irony, places their foot upon the stage monitor, thus raising their knee and inviting the doting audience to gawp upwards at their godlike crotch, should be treated with suspicion. The most technically proficient grunge guitarists – Jerry Cantrell, Kim Thayil, Mike McCready – were just about humble enough (and eager to distance themselves from the indignities of the 1980s cock rock scene) to avoid such phallic posturing. Often sheer ignorance can help, as in the case of the Stooges-worshipping Seattle band Mudhoney. In 1991 when Duff McKagan was invited to join Mudhoney onstage, the Guns N' Roses bassist asked what key the song was in. 'What's a key?' replied Mudhoney's Matt Lukin.[20] Paradoxically perhaps, guitar players who are less technically accomplished can have the edge over more experienced and dexterous musicians. Steve Turner has also said that having grown gradually but noticeably better at playing the guitar from years of touring and recording, he now battles with trying to unlearn what he knows so that Mudhoney don't risk losing their shambolic rawness. 'I was always under the idea that progress on the guitar was the enemy of good rock 'n' roll,' he explained to *Plan B* magazine. 'So I never tried to be a better guitar player. But you can't help but get better and, by playing so many acoustic shows by myself, I know I have done. With Mudhoney, I try and forget most of my knowledge . . . I just try and dumb it down, and I don't mean that cynically. It's great to get lost in the sound and not think about it too much.'[21] Get lost in the sound. Don't get lost in technique. Thrash metal millionaires Metallica may have been searching for something similar when, in one of their regular bouts of identity crisis, they recorded 2003's *St Anger*. Uncharacteristically for Metallica, this album featured zero guitar solos. The reception was mixed, although favourable critics found it captured the band sounding groovier, more stripped back and pissed off, than they had in years.

Whether related to guitar solos specifically or broader musical qualities and artistic decisions, the point is that heaviness is a form of expression that runs deeper than drawing attention to one's exemplary talents as a composer and performer. This is why Sabbath are heavier than Led Zeppelin and 'Helter Skelter' is heavier than any precious Pink Floyd composition. It also means that – counter-intuitively – artists that traditionally have been understood to be heavy are arguably not. It's also true that artists who were never truly heavy were once considered so. Check out *Kerrang!*'s '100 Greatest Heavy Metal Albums of All Time', printed in 1989, and gasp at its inclusion of *Reckless* by Bryan Adams. Heavy metal's name implies heaviness by definition, but certain bands from the naffer end of that genre can barely compete in the heaviness stakes. Artists from other categories, like Butthole Surfers or Mogwai, can out-heavy Def Leppard or Queensrÿche with the greatest of ease. With their shiny production intended for mass consumption and maximum radio play, and their reliance on codified norms and standardization, the latter offer only a simulacrum of the truly heavy.

Real heavy music typically has a 'low art' grubbiness and a rawness to it. Relatively cheaply made and ramshackle in nature, it glories in its own messiness and imperfections. Its artists are usually averse to glossy, clean, overly manipulated and archly commercial production and live-mixing techniques. They give the impression of searching for something intangible, mystical, in the rehearsal, recording and recital of this music – catharsis, release, meditation, freedom, whatever it may be – rather than simply wishing to attract adoration, applause and riches. They are, as Julian Cope would have it, 'on a prolonged shamanic search for sonic obliteration'.[22] They are not the Electric Mechanics, Electric Brain Surgeons or Electric Cirque du Soleil Acrobats.

They are the Electric Wizards.

1

THE PREHISTORY

The gravestone of McKinley 'Muddy Waters' Morganfield in Restvale Cemetery,
Westmont, Illinois.

You get a more pure thing out of an acoustic but you get more
noise out of an amplifier.[1]

MUDDY WATERS

Spoiler alert. There is a brilliant moment that occurs in the very closing moments of 1977's *Interface*, the sixth album by the cult Parisian space rock combo Heldon. The album concludes with its title track, one that is so long it fills the whole of the LP's second side, just as 'Helter Skelter' should have been allowed to do. With such room to play with, 'Interface' builds up gradually into a roaring tornado of mutating drum patterns, effervescent synthesizer noises and guitar licks that wail into the atmosphere like an abandoned astronaut. Eventually, after around nineteen minutes of futuristic-sounding, avant-garde and alien-like music, this ultramodern cacophony finally fades out and is replaced, to near comic effect, by a final few seconds of traditional blues rock guitar. 'We were finishing the track, the tape was rolling, and I started to play a normal boogie or whatever,' recalled Heldon leader Richard Pinhas when interviewed for the album's 2020 reissue. 'I think it was a good idea to keep it. It just came naturally, at the end.'[2]

Sounding incongruous on first listen, the contrast between the track's main racket and its brief call-back to the blues reminds us just how far rock 'n' roll had transformed – how the original blueprint had been jolted and nudged down all kinds of unexpected avenues – since its earliest days. By the time Heldon were operating, the genre had branched out into several different mutated forms, and it wasn't likely to stop there. Rock 'n' roll had given rise to contorted clones and had shifted into unrecognizable shapes, akin to some extraterrestrial creature from one of the science fiction tales that were so fondly admired by Richard Pinhas himself.

Heldon, as we shall see, represented one of rock 'n' roll's most distant relatives thanks to Pinhas's inventive fusion of abstract rock sounds and weighty Moog pulsations. At the same time, the surprising way in which Pinhas decided to sign off *Interface* with those trad blues licks reminds us that so many of the records we listen to today, however modern-sounding or fused with electronic elements, all have their roots in earlier genres. This message had already been imparted on Heldon's earlier third album, a double LP released in 1975. It combined heady synth throbs with expressive blasts of spacey guitar in a decidedly radical fashion, with noticeable similarities to krautrock. Pinhas named the album *It's Always Rock 'n' Roll*.

Waters, Wolf and Tharpe

Paul McCartney may have taken heaviness to a whole new level with 'Helter Skelter', but it would be churlish for us to neglect the prehistory. As part of his adventures for compiling the Archive of American Folk Song project for the Library of Congress, Alan Lomax had already recorded the likes of Woody Guthrie and Lead Belly when, in 1941, he arrived in Mississippi, where he hoped to record the legendary blues guitarist Robert Johnson. When Lomax got there, he was informed that Johnson had died two years earlier. Lomax was lucky enough to come across McKinley Morganfield, however, who was otherwise known as Muddy Waters. Then 26 years old and living on the Stovall Plantation near Clarksdale, Morganfield was surprised by how great he sounded when he heard Lomax's recordings played back to him. His confidence given a vital boost, Morganfield moved to Chicago in 1943 to properly pursue a career in music. With the help of fellow bluesmen including Big Bill Broonzy, Memphis Slim, Sunnyland Slim and Sonny Boy Williamson, Muddy Waters broke into the Chicago scene. The first thing he wanted to do was to get an amplifier. In the crowded, bustling, boozy venues of Chicago where fights and arguments broke out frequently, it was hard for audiences to hear acoustic blues music over the cacophony of their own making. When Waters got hold of that sought-after amplifier, his ensemble would make its name as the first electric blues band. While Muddy Waters may have been the named leader of the group, all members contributed to the overall harsh and energy-emanating sound. This was, in essence, the first rock band, and music would never be the same again.[3]

Hot on the heels of Muddy Waters, although actually three years his senior, came Chester Arthur Burnett, aka Howlin' Wolf, who moved to Chicago in 1952. Although Howlin' Wolf was initially welcomed to town by Waters, the two men become rivals, keeping a close eye on one another's activities and occasionally luring away each other's band members. Thanks to a vocal style that managed to out-growl Muddy Waters, and with the assistance of Willie Johnson's raucous guitar playing and signature distorted guitar sound, Howlin' Wolf has been cited as the most direct connection between the old blues, hard rock and heavy metal.[4]

Given his inclination to repeat the tale, Muddy Waters must have been proud of the fact that when he first toured Britain in 1958 the audiences there were apparently unprepared for his electrified take on the blues. According to trad-jazzman Chris Barber, who arranged Waters' visit and thus played his own crucial part in the history of heaviness, rumours that the music was too shockingly loud for the British crowds were greatly exaggerated, not least by Waters himself. The jazz critic James Asman may have retreated to the back of the audience before fleeing out the door in flamboyant objection to Waters' racket, but Asman's complaints were not a reflection of the broader reception. For one thing, the year before Waters' appearance Barber had booked an artist who had been considerably louder than Muddy Waters. That person was Sister Rosetta Tharpe. 'She played a very nice Les Paul with a big combi amp and she was louder than my entire band,' recalled Barber. 'And nobody complained!'[5] Of this godmother of rock, it is said that 'Nobody – not Chuck Berry, not

Scotty Moore, not James Burton, not Keith Richards – played wilder or more primal rock 'n' roll guitar.'[6] The people wanted heavy, even if James Asman didn't. Soon enough, bands like The Animals, The Rolling Stones, The Yardbirds, Led Zeppelin and Cream were basing their repertoires around these electric blues pioneers.

Surf's Up

Even those who broke away from the blues in a more inventive fashion had to acknowledge its significance as source material. In 1964 Ringo Starr commented that music by black musicians comprised 'ninety percent of the music I like' and described The Beatles' music as 'secondhand versions' of it.[7] When they landed in the United States, The Beatles expressed their desire to catch performances of Muddy Waters and another of their rock 'n' roll heroes, Bo Diddley. 'Muddy Waters,' asked one reporter, 'where's that?' The Beatles, laughing, lambasted the Americans for ignorance of their own famous – that is, most important – people.[8] It's an amusing anecdote, albeit one that should be taken with a pinch of salt. Just as James Asman's dislike of Muddy Waters cannot be said to be representative of other members of the British public, it's likely that this Beatles anecdote tells us more about one reporter's obliviousness to Muddy Waters than it does an entire nation's. Muddy Waters and Bo Diddley did both express gratitude to The Beatles for boosting their popularity with a younger crowd, but they weren't exactly unheard of.[9] For the writer Rob Chapman, 'the oft-propagated notion that English beat groups reintroduced America to its own black-music heritage is cultural colonialism taken to new delusory heights of condescension.'[10] Chapman points to early garage band records and American surf music of the late 1950s and early '60s as evidence of pre-Beatles American-grown rock music that was full of blues, soul and R&B influences. The garage rock staple 'Louie Louie', popularized by The Kingsmen's ragged and rocked-up version, was originally written in 1955 by the African American musician Richard Berry.

It was later performed by, well, almost everybody. The Kinks. An early incarnation of Pink Floyd. The Troggs (whose 'Wild Thing' was also fundamentally a 'Louie Louie' rewrite). The Sonics. Led Zeppelin. The Doors. Flamin' Groovies. MC5. The Stooges (Iggy Pop also recorded it as a solo artist). Lou Reed. Patti Smith. Johnny Thunders. The Clash. Jon the Postman (a cult figure in the Manchester punk scene, who would jump onstage at the end of gigs and perform 'Louie Louie' either a cappella or with friendly accompaniment from bands like Buzzcocks and The Fall). Motörhead. Black Flag. The Gun Club. Sisters of Mercy. Smashing Pumpkins. Mudhoney. The list goes on. Name any band and they have almost certainly covered 'Louie Louie'. And if they haven't covered it in an official capacity, they'll at least have jammed around its chords during rehearsals or soundchecks, just as The Beatles did during the *Get Back* sessions. Although the ever contrary Frank Zappa claimed to consider The Kingsmen's shambolic version to be a bit of a farce, he still maintained that it was impossible to underestimate the impact of 'Louie Louie'.[11]

Alongside garage rock, instrumental surf music also helped to set the scene for future heaviness. While this genre is vast, the music of Link Wray stands out as a particularly crucial prototype. The sound made by this Native American Korean War veteran could get particularly dark and moody, and pre-dates heavy metal in occasionally drawing on scary movies as well as real-life cases of terror. Take the suitably spiky, ominous and unpredictably violent sound of 'Jack the Ripper'. As schlocky as it is with its bursts of theatrical evil laughter, 'The Shadow Knows' anticipates Black Sabbath's fixation with horror movies and the desire to transfer the atmosphere of what they saw on screen into the grooves of a rock record. Although he was a dexterous enough player, Wray understood the power and capacity of simplicity. Simultaneously astute and innate,

Wray's grasp of elements like tone, distortion, volume and space had a potent effect on the emotions of his listeners. A well-placed chord that rang out for perhaps longer than it should have done, Wray knew, could have a much more intoxicating effect on the heart and mood of a listener than a busy succession of notes that might take up the same space on a track. Neil Young has been called 'the godfather of grunge', especially for his output with Crazy Horse. For his own part, Young traces 'the beginning of grunge' all the way back – before metal, punk, post-hardcore and noise rock – to the achievements of Link Wray.[12]

Wray's 1958 'Rumble' was an especially important track. Helping to popularize the power chord, it would resonate down the ages, providing both direct and filtered-down inspiration to successive generations of riff-centric rock 'n' rollers, punks, hard rockers and metalheads. When recording 'Rumble', Wray dirtied up its sound by physically damaging an amplifier, poking holes in its speaker cone to achieve a fuzzier and more distorted tone, preceding Dave Davies on The Kinks' 'You Really Got Me' by several years. Pete Townshend said that he would never have picked up a guitar in the first place if it wasn't for Link Wray and that particular seminal track.[13] Despite it being solely instrumental, when 'Rumble' became popular some U.S. radio stations refused to air it for fear that its violence-alluding title and brooding, malevolent sound would incite juvenile delinquency and gang warfare. They weren't actually that far off, especially where one notable future delinquent was concerned. When asked about the single most important influence on his own musical career, Iggy Pop pinpointed Link Wray. 'One day I was in the student union of this major university,' he remembered, 'and I heard this music – Duh! Duh! Duuuuh! It was called "Rumble" and it sounded *baad*. I left school, emotionally, at that moment.'[14] Unruly, hedonistic and never knowingly beshirted, the proto-punk trailblazer didn't look back.

2

SABBATH PHASE I:
BLACK SABBATH

Only the beginning: *Black Sabbath* by Black Sabbath.

We're only here for a short time. We know that. In three years' time or even next week, they could be saying 'Who the hell are Black Sabbath?' We'll be tomorrow's Tremeloes. You've got to do it while you can.[1]

OZZY OSBOURNE in 1972

Classical music goes back several hundred years, and electric music only goes back maybe 60 years, so were we able to live long enough, we'd probably see in a few hundred years that those first four Sabbath records are comparable to Beethoven or Mozart.[2]

AL CISNEROS (SLEEP/OM)

Download Festival, Donington Park, Derby, June 2016. There is torrential rain for much of the weekend. Perhaps thunderclouds are an appropriate accompaniment to Black Sabbath, who are headlining on Saturday night. The main stage has been temporarily renamed The Lemmy Stage, in honour of the recently departed Motörhead leader. Mortality has never been far from the Sabbath mindset, and by this point there is a real sense of an ending. The black-clad original members of the band will soon be septuagenarians. In early 2012 guitarist Tony Iommi was diagnosed with lymphoma, after which the band's tour dates had to be arranged to fit around his medical treatments. The Download date is part of Sabbath's final tour, which the band has christened 'The End'. Singer Ozzy Osbourne has already been diagnosed with Parkin syndrome. In a few years' time he will discover he has Parkinson's disease. At the Download performance Osbourne is his usual self: a walking emblem of fragile defiance. Unlike some of the more desperately pumped and overtly macho singers who front other bands on this weekend's bill, Osbourne resembles a wide-eyed schoolboy who's found himself trapped inside the body of a slightly feminine old man, as if the plot to the Tom Hanks film 'Big' has gone rather awry. Bassist Geezer Butler's hair is lighter than it was in his youth and, in sharp contrast to his dark outfit, his beard is turning white. It is a shame that his original rhythm section partner is absent from the event. As thrashed out in a number of disgruntled Facebook posts, drummer Bill Ward has failed to see eye to eye with the other members of Sabbath. Ward claims the deal he was offered to tour with them was a joke. Osbourne will later write that Ward's excuse of being presented with an 'unsignable contract' was a smokescreen for the fact *that his health wasn't up to it: Ward simply wasn't capable (anymore?) of performing 'a two hour set with a drum solo every night'.*[3] *In Ward's place sits young pup Tommy Clufetos. He's in his late thirties and seems to find no trouble in bashing his way through the fourteen-song setlist. If we're being honest, though, it doesn't sound quite the same as the distinctive beats that can be heard on Sabbath's classic recordings. There is something missing here, and that something is Ward.*

You would think that a festival such as this, headlined by this legendary act, would provide a sense of the torch being passed on. With Iommi and Butler cranking out their iconic, timeless riffs and Osbourne doing his best to howl away the ominous clouds, all of them very much living in the present, the event is more like a widely panned photograph of a vastly extended family. The ageing patriarchs are surrounded on the line-up by younger generations of musicians who, were it not for Black Sabbath, probably wouldn't be doing what they do at all, or at least not in the same way. And boy are these children, grandchildren, great-grandchildren, cousins and distant cousins a diverse bunch of folk. The two other headliners are theatrical industrialists Rammstein and New Wave of British Heavy Metal conquerors Iron Maiden. Elsewhere on the bill are surviving representatives of the 2000s nu-metal scene in the form of Korn and Deftones. Although their fusion of thrash metal and sugary J-pop has been treated as suspect by purist metalheads in the less tolerant corners of the Internet, Tokyo's Babymetal are greeted like newfound heroes by the open-minded audience. Despite this ostensibly being a metal festival, not every act slots into that category or even one of its various subparts. Veteran eccentrics Jane's Addiction slink up onstage to do their arty alt-rock thing. There are melodic punky offerings from California's Pennywise and NOFX. Back at the weightier end, the grindcore contingency is led by Napalm Death. Even Kim Wilde, the pop-star-turned-celebrity-gardener, turns up to provide surprise guest vocals for Ravenshead's anarcho-grindcore pranksters Lawnmower Deth. She helps out on their punked-up cover of her 1981 hit 'Kids in America'. To Wilde's immense credit, she also knows all the words to 'Egg Sandwich' and 'Watch Out Grandma Here Comes a Lawnmower'.

Although it may be diverse in its way, a line-up such as this gives only a scant impression of the countless varieties of heaviness that have branched out from Black Sabbath. Besides the mortal fortunes of Sabbath themselves, this wasn't really the end, because there never will be one, not while musicians are still around to churn out heaviness and cement-mix different parts of it together in new and novel ways, and not while fans who need heaviness in their lives are still around to hear it.

In the grand scheme of things, this could still be the beginning.

There's a Darkness on the Edge of Birmingham City Centre

The Vietnam War (1954–75) had a profound and traumatic impact on America's psyche, and on its young people in particular. In his autobiography Bruce Springsteen wrote with sorrow and restrained anger about his friends and acquaintances who had been conscripted to fight in the war. The young Springsteen harboured no intention of joining them. He managed to avoid the draft by employing the widely shared tactic of making a deliberate hash of the required forms and staying awake all night before the physical exam. Under assessment, Springsteen pretended to be high on LSD. The relief at having avoided the same military fate as so many of his fellow countrymen was accompanied by its fair share of guilt and shame. As he grew older, Springsteen often wondered what had happened to whoever had been sent to fight in his place.[4] He would speak of this at his concerts: 'A lot of guys went, and a lot of guys didn't come back. And the lot that came back weren't the same anymore.'[5] One of his best-known songs, the sometimes misinterpreted 'Born in the USA' (1984), was written about soldiers returning home from the war who now felt alienated from their country of birth. The single's less famous B-side, 'Shut Out the Light', acts as a secondary narrative about a Vietnam War veteran. This time, the tale is rendered in a much more haunting and downbeat manner than its deceptively bombastic flip-side.

Springsteen was by no stretch of the imagination the only musician to address the Vietnam War in popular song, and he was certainly not the first. If every example were to be compiled, the resulting mixtape would be longer than the director's cut of *Apocalypse Now* and in certain places a darn sight more harrowing. On their *Monster* album of 1969, Steppenwolf addressed America's barefaced global immorality. Its second track, 'Draft Resister', championed the plight of those who had been imprisoned and branded as dishonourable for refusing to go to war. Its lyrics posited that the politicians in Washington and military tacticians in the Pentagon were the real deserters, morally speaking. These men were, in essence, traitors to humanity. That same year, Creedence Clearwater Revival's protest song 'Fortunate Son' climbed to number three in the U.S. charts.

The fact that the United Kingdom managed to avoid sending any troops to Vietnam did not prevent the conflict from having significant impact on its own artists. This is particularly true when it comes to Black Sabbath. Recorded and released in 1970, Sabbath's second album opened with an eight-minute pacifist anthem. It was given the name 'War Pigs'. This had been the intended title of the album as well. In the end, Sabbath were pressured by their label to name the LP after a different track, a snappier number with greater radio potential. The album became *Paranoid*. No one bothered altering the artwork: a blurry photograph of a semi-futuristic and semi-ancient warrior, leaping around in a gloomy forest and aggressively waving a curved sword. Written by the band's bassist and primary lyricist Geezer Butler, the words to 'War Pigs' were inspired by the concerts Black Sabbath had played at American military bases in Germany. When visiting these, the band members heard at first hand stories about the atrocities of the Vietnam War. They were also made aware of the lack of support for conscripts and veterans, and of the heroin and other mind-numbing substances that were consumed by soldiers and ex-soldiers in order to ease the trauma that had been carved into their psyches.[6] While 'War Pigs' was directly inspired by Vietnam, it spoke too of war in general, as echoed by the often derided but actually rather apt figure prancing around on the album's cover, historically vague as he appears. Sung in Ozzy Osbourne's default tone of utter dismay, Butler's lyrics envision Old Testament-style vengeance on the cowardly leaders who have hidden in their ivory towers while ordering the poor to their deaths as though partaking in a game of chess. The music itself has an apocalyptic sound to match. It may not have been as sprawling as the forty-minute embryonic version that Sabbath had dished out to unsuspecting listeners when the band were cutting their teeth at the Star-Club in Berlin. Even so, the slow, sparse, deep, rumbling and lengthy album opener is the very definition of epic rock music.

The album's second longest track, 'Hand of Doom', addresses the same military theme. This time it was scaled down to a case study of an individual soldier who returns from the front hopelessly addicted to drugs. The veteran frequently and repeatedly presses the needle into his skin, destroying himself in the process. Its narrative is not dissimilar to 'Shut Out the Light', especially the early and unreleased version of Springsteen's song in which the character's drug habit is spelled out in more explicit terms. Incidentally, in 1970 Springsteen's early band Steel Mill had played a gig opening for none other than Black Sabbath. 'Hand of Doom' was on the setlist that night.

Paranoid's 'Electric Funeral' broadens out the imagery to describe the nuclear holocaust that many people at that time suspected to be lurking just around the corner. 'The Cold War was at its height,' remembered Butler. 'Everybody thought they were gonna get blown to bits any second. So it was just all about real life and what was going on.'[7] Had the UK bowed to the imbalanced obligations of the 'special relationship' and capitulated in sending its own troops to Vietnam, the members of Black Sabbath could well have been among those who were enlisted. 'We were four working-class people in the most industrial part of England, and all we had to look forward to was dead-end jobs in factories,' explained Butler. 'And we thought at any second we'd be called up to drop in to the Vietnam War, because it looked like Britain was going to get involved in it as well. So there wasn't much future in anything for us.'[8]

Their lives had also been shaped by conflicts past. Each person who would end up in the original line-up of Black Sabbath had been born a few years after the end of the Second World War. This was in a country now deep in war debts to the USA, where rationing would remain in place until 1954. Having been bombed extensively by the Luftwaffe, Birmingham's already drab industrial landscape had been left in a state of rubble-laden disarray. Children would use the city's abandoned bomb-damaged buildings and the huge empty craters that had been created by the Blitz as makeshift playgrounds.

Countering the gloom, remembered drummer Bill Ward, was a real closeness between families. It existed in the culture because the city – and country – had lost so many people. When Ward was growing up, his jazz-loving parents would celebrate the end of the war every Saturday night by obtaining kegs of beer and hosting parties. Ward's mother played the piano. His father sang. Their neighbour, a drummer, would bring his kit to the parties. The drum set would usually still be downstairs the following morning, waiting to be collected by its owner, who had stumbled home drunk. When the adults were busy nursing their Sunday hangovers, young Ward would tinker with the drums. This started at age five. By eight or nine he had made his decision to become a drummer.[9]

Along with jazzy keg parties, the spirits of the post-war working classes were lifted by the success of The Beatles. 'They took me away,' Ozzy Osbourne told music journalist Mat Snow in 1991. 'Those four guys who came from a similar kind of background to me: the industrial town. Theirs was docks and mine was factories. I was surrounded by factories where I lived and it was a real miserable shithole of an area. It wasn't pleasant at all.' Covering the young Osbourne's bedroom wall were any pictures and posters of The Beatles that he could get his hands on. When he wasn't imagining what it would be like to be a member of his favourite band, Osbourne fantasized that one of his three sisters might marry a Beatle. 'It would take me away from the misery,' he said.[10] When asked by David Gans who he'd listened to as a kid before The Beatles came along, Osbourne replied with a firm, 'Never anybody. The Beatles gave me everything. Especially Paul McCartney. I adore him.'[11]

The rise of The Beatles was equally revelatory to Geezer Butler: 'It was like four people from exactly the same background as where I was from, being able to rule the world. It gave everybody that was from the working classes in England some hope. So that almost took over from religion, and became a religion in itself.'[12] Perhaps John Lennon's controversial quip about The Beatles being more popular than Jesus wasn't so far-fetched after all. As well as having hailed from ordinary northern backgrounds, The Beatles' nationality demonstrated that it wasn't just American artists like Elvis – or his ropey domestic imitators – who were able to storm the hit parade. From 'Love Me Do' onwards, people like Osbourne and Butler realized that home-grown musicians could develop their own unique sound and, furthermore, take their music into hitherto unimagined places.

Osbourne once claimed that there was nothing left to do after The Beatles. They had already done so much, done everything, and done it so well.[13] It was a fair point. Yet there was still more to be done, especially where heaviness was concerned. Black Sabbath may not have invented heaviness. That was Paul McCartney, of course. What Black Sabbath did manage to do was to make heaviness even bloody heavier.

Just like The Beatles, Black Sabbath would never have achieved what they did if those four specific individuals had not been drawn together at precisely the right moment in time and in precisely the right place. Without each vital piece of that puzzle, the jigsaw would have been rendered incomplete, the outcome would never have been quite the same and history would have ended up quite different. As with John, Paul, George and Ringo, each one of the Sabbath contingent added their own distinct ingredients to the magic formula, making a group that was much more than the sum of its parts.

Terry 'Geezer' Butler had initially been a rhythm guitarist until he saw Jack Bruce playing in Cream and felt the urge to swap to bass. Raised a strict Irish Catholic and originally harbouring the ambition to become a priest, Butler had dabbled in the occult as a youth. A few years later he was put off it for good when he awoke one night to see an eerie black-clad figure at the end of his bed. It has been speculated that this may have been Ozzy wandering about in his dressing gown.[14] Demonic or not, this ungodly encounter was enough to steer Butler away from the whole black magic business for good. To be on the safe side, he tore down the inverted crosses and devil posters from his wall and began wearing a crucifix at all times. As the band's principal lyricist, Butler wrote about Satan lurking around the corner not in celebration of the Devil, as many assumed, but more out of fear. Having said that, the band *were* dedicated fans of horror films and science fiction. This fuelled one of their great ideas. The decision was made to create rock music that could match the scariness of the movies, literature and comic books that thrilled them so. Beatles fixation aside, when listening to the other sugary pop coming out of the wireless when he was growing up, Ozzy would gaze down at the ragged clothes he wore and his bare, shoeless feet. He would think to himself, 'There's so many fucking people out there, talking how wonderful the fucking world is, and there's so many of us fuckers that ain't got nothing.'[15] Audiences would pay good money to experience the ghastly happenings that occurred in the era's popular horror movies, Black Sabbath realized. Why wouldn't such people enjoy a scarier style of rock music that wallowed in a bleaker outlook? 'People feel evil things, but nobody ever sings about what's frightening and evil,' said Butler when promoting 1972's *Vol. 4*. 'I mean the world is a right fucking shambles. Anyway, everybody has sung about all the good things.'[16]

Down, Down, Deeper and Downer

Singing about the shambolic state of the world may not have been an entirely groundbreaking phenomenon. Musicians had always soaked up and commented on such misery and chaos. The huge sound of Sabbath certainly suited the gloomy lyrics and gave them added gravitas and impact. Key to Sabbath's blood-curdling songs were the grinding riffs of self-taught, left-handed guitarist Tony Iommi, whose musical career was almost halted at the age of eighteen when two of his fingertips were cut off in the sheet metal factory where he worked. After doctors informed him he would never play again, Iommi spent a month feeling so forlorn he considered suicide. When his old factory manager gave him a record by Django Reinhardt, the Romani jazz guitarist who had overcome a similar injury, Iommi realized that all was not lost. Iommi fashioned makeshift thimbles out of Fairy Liquid bottle caps to help him press down on the guitar strings without it causing too much agony. Because he could no longer play in a conventional way, Iommi also began experimenting with fatter chords that required fewer fingers to master.

Reviewers of Black Sabbath made no concessions regarding Iommi's impairment. If truth be told, they often mocked his playing outright. To them, his style seemed primitive in comparison to guitar gods like Eric Clapton or Jimmy Page. They could not know that Iommi's techniques would prove to be prescient. Covering a concert in Glasgow, Pete Silverton of *Sounds* complained that 'Iommi's guitar work, especially on his one long solo, always sounded like he had difficulty in finding the right notes in time to keep up with the beat.'[17] Sabbath's fans, however, such as this seventeen-year-old interviewed by *NME* in 1972, insisted that

Tony Iommi is just as good a guitarist as people like Beck or Clapton, but he never gets the credit he deserves playing in Sabbath. I read some of the musical papers and I've always thought they've had a rotten deal from the critics, because they are not playing for the benefit of reporters – they're playing to us.[18]

In fairness, there were some writers who could appreciate the splendour in what Iommi was doing. *The Rag*'s Mike Saunders saw Sabbath as channelling the same spirit of 'crude unrefined street clatter' that had defined all great rock 'n' roll music from Little Richard to the more recent racket of The Stooges. Where Cream's and Jeff Beck's 'egomania and interchangeable ten-minute jerk-off guitar solos' went unchecked, Saunders could identify no equivalent superfluity in Iommi's group. Reviewing 1971's *Master of Reality*, he wrote, 'Black Sabbath grind out riff after riff after unrelenting riff; even the guitar leads are riffs, and there isn't one excessive uncalled-for guitar lead on their whole new album.'[19] As if Sabbath's sound wasn't heavy enough in the first place, it was on this third LP that Iommi began to downtune his guitar, the looser strings making it even easier for him to play. Butler tuned his bass down to match. The result made Black Sabbath's music even deeper and more thunderous than before.

To keep up with the two guitarists' increased heaviness, Bill Ward began playing with double bass drums and added some extra pieces to his kit. A bit of a Ringo Starr when it comes to rarely earning the same level of respect or admiration as flashier and busier contemporaries like Ginger Baker or Keith Moon, Ward could hit those skins as hard as the best of them. He was also, crucially, one of those drummers who really *listens*. When introducing jazzier or fancier elements, Ward would do this sparingly and shrewdly in order to enhance rather than distract from the overall feel. Such moments may not occur every four seconds or so, but, much like

Ringo's, when one of Ward's instrumental flourishes do suddenly spring out of the speakers, it can be one of those leap-out-of-your-seat moments. Ward explained that his distinctive drumming style had its roots in his youthful nights of lying awake listening to noises emanating from the nearby local metalwork factories. By tapping his fingers on the headboard of his bed, Ward would add his own fills to the pulsating and repetitive sounds that he could hear.[20]

One element that didn't deepen in concurrence with Iommi's downtuned strings was the pitch of Osbourne's vocals. Ozzy's voice remained quite the contrast to the Sabbath musicians' deep and fearsome rumblings. Despite their desire to make scary music and the accusations of Satanism that were routinely thrown in their direction, these crucifix-wearing Brummies didn't celebrate evil. They condemned it and trembled in the face of it. This fear emerges in its most apparent form in Osbourne's voice. It is a high, quivering embodiment of fragility – mental, physical, even vocal – but in such a soulful way. A more appropriate term, perhaps, might be lost-soulful.

If Philip Larkin is to be believed, sexual intercourse was invented in 1963. Six years later, when Black Sabbath released their self-titled debut album, a cultural post-orgasmic comedown was under way. The explosion of erotic excitement that had accompanied the Summer of Love had been replaced by the equivalent of lying in a wet patch in a state of sober existential regret. Free love, it turned out, wasn't always what it was cracked up to be. The 'physical act of making love', as General Ripper puts it in Stanley Kubrick's *Dr Strangelove; or, How I Learned to Stop Worrying and Love the Bomb* (1964), was followed by a 'profound sense of fatigue, a feeling of emptiness'. In his madness, Ripper misinterprets this sensation, and this leads him to instigate an ultimate 'wargasm' in the form of the kind of nuclear apocalypse described in Sabbath's 'Electric Funeral', the result of which would be the biggest comedown of all: the end of life as we know it. All pleasure is temporary. You can climb right back up to the top of the ride, however momentarily, but you'll always come crashing down to earth with a thud.

When Black Sabbath were busy fashioning their sound, some were of the opinion that the radical ideas of the 1960s had been neutered by the nefarious forces of capitalism and conservatism. Others pointed out that the hippie lifestyle had only ever been available to an affluent and privileged few who happened to reside in hotbed areas like London or San Francisco. The situation elsewhere, for most people, was still defined by black-and-white post-war drudgery, such as in the working-class areas of Black Sabbath's home city. Either way, a sense of disillusionment had set in. The 'wave', as Hunter S. Thompson put it in 1971, had broken and rolled back.[21]

In this respect, the 'downer rock' descriptor that was applied to Black Sabbath by American journalists in the 1970s still seems rather fitting. It denoted an outlook at odds with hippie optimism and with a focus on bleaker subject-matter, both in the spiritual and material senses. It implied the tranquillizing effects of depressant drugs – 'downers' (Quaaludes, opiates) rather than uppers (stimulants like amphetamines and cocaine) – which matches Sabbath's music thematically speaking, even if those individuals who were making it, not to mention many of its listeners, may have been experimenting with intoxicating substances at every end of the spectrum. Downer rock implied a comedown – from drugs or sex or political romanticism, or simply sliding down from the top of a fairground ride. The Beatles' 'Helter Skelter' had already hinted that the age of flower-power optimism was over. Originally flare-wearing longhairs themselves, Black Sabbath took this idea further than it ever could have been taken by Paul McCartney, who, however much he tries, no matter how hard he rocks out, can never fully suppress his innately upbeat, thumbs-up joie de vivre. 'Most people are on a permanent down, but just aren't aware of it,' noted Bill Ward. 'We're trying to express it for the people.'[22]

If reviewers of The Beatles' *White Album* couldn't quite fathom how to categorize the unkempt sound of 'Helter Skelter', critics had an even harder time figuring out what to do with Black Sabbath. Who can blame them? Those writers could hardly foresee that they were witnessing the big bang that would birth heavy metal and, besides that, countless other forms of heaviness. Several American reviewers likened Sabbath to other 'downer' bands, like Michigan's Grand Funk Railroad, a more traditional hard rock outfit who as it happens also had a track named 'Paranoid', but who Ozzy Osbourne hadn't even heard about until his band toured the United States for the third time. Even then, Grand Funk didn't really do anything for Ozzy.[23] Jim Esposito of U.S. biweekly rock mag *Zoo World* argued that the first four Sabbath albums were completely indistinguishable from one another, and that anybody who had the nerve to suggest otherwise was a barefaced liar. Esposito proposed that instead of comparing the music contained in the band's LPs, some sort of weight measurement system needed to be devised whereby it could be determined which Sabbath album was heaviest.[24] The allegations of one-dimensionality and brutal monotony were reiterated frequently in the music press. A review of *Vol. 4* claimed listeners could leave the room for ten minutes at a time without missing anything important.[25] At this time, groups like Yes and Emerson, Lake & Palmer were hailed as heroic intellectual innovators because they were seen to be on a mission to elevate rock music to a higher plane, one that promised to compete with the esteemed intricacy and sophistication of classical music. In such a climate, the scruffy Sabbath boys were accused of using sheer volume to compensate for a lack of musical talent. It was an indictment they hardly denied themselves. Sabbath's first U.S. tour was promoted with posters boasting the promise 'Louder than Led Zeppelin'.[26] They never claimed to be better, just louder.

As musicologist Andrew Cope has analysed, while the music of both Led Zeppelin and Black Sabbath had its basis in the blues, the former remained much more firmly rooted in those origins, as well as steeped in folk conventions, even if they were blended with eclectic stylizations, sheer volume and developments in production techniques. When writing the track 'Black Sabbath', argues Cope, Tony Iommi did not fall back on his own past of playing in blues covers bands. Rather, he 'drew on a unique synthesis of multi-sectional design, unresolved tritones and aeolian riffs'.[27] Sabbath's employment of downtuned guitars; their angular riffs based on modal forms, use of power chords over standard chords and of pentatonic minor lead scale (similar to a blues scale but one that sounds very different – again, it was easier for Iommi to play); their interest in timbres more common to those found in classical music and film scores; and the overall use of space in their songs: these all illustrate how Black Sabbath broke from the past. Cope concentrates on how these innovations essentially invented heavy metal, but Sabbath also influenced a whole lot more besides that.[28]

The rock and prog elite's condemnation of Sabbath acted as a precursor to those same criticisms that would be used to condemn punk rock at the later end of the 1970s. By that moment in time, the original incarnation of Black Sabbath had started to subside, buckling under the strains of excessive drug use and financial problems that had arisen from mismanagement, legal fees and tax debts. Although actually quite fun to listen to if you don't take the material too seriously, 1976's *Technical Ecstasy* and 1978's *Never Say Die!* do seem lacklustre, plagued as they were by indecision and a lack of focus. The band were getting on less well on a personal level, too. And to make matters worse, their popularity appeared to be diminishing, especially in light of the contrasting twin threats of the punk rock movement, which had transformed the music scene more than Sabbath could ever have imagined, and up-and-coming bands who were keen to up the antes of theatricality, virtuosity and polish in the realm of rock music (ideas that would soon dominate the 1980s rock and metal scenes). In 1978 Black Sabbath's support act was Van

Halen. With their athletic frontman and shredding guitar style, these sprightly Californian upstarts were seen to be upstaging Black Sabbath night after night and were clearly responsible for a hefty chunk of the tour's ticket sales.[29]

Osbourne was finally booted out of Black Sabbath in 1979. The singer would enjoy a successful solo career, though it hardly matched up to the music he'd made with the band. Black Sabbath would limp on without Ozzy. Despite the continued efforts, the battle had been lost. Never again would either party hit the dizzy heights of the first five or six Black Sabbath albums. Both would resort to looking over to Van Halen for pointers on what exactly the kids now wished to purchase with their pocket money. Nevertheless, the seeds they had sown together would continue to spread out into the infinite. Black Sabbath represent the birth of heavy metal and are thus the starting point for the sprawling plethora of heavy metal subgenres as well: post-metal, symphonic metal, trap metal, math rock, melodic metalcore, alien deathcore, blackened crust . . . the list is endless. Sabbath would also be a direct influence on successive generations of heavy music makers, who would look back to those 1970s albums long after Sabbath and Ozzy had gone off the boil. Grindcore bands, industrial rockers, the Seattle grunge scene, drone rockers, doom rockers, desert rockers, stoner rockers, noise rockers – all had their fair share of committed Sabbath-heads among their ranks.

A teenager when punk spilled forth, the writer Garry Mulholland felt it his duty to despise all heavy metal bands and the associated 'dinosaurs of rock' whose extinction had been promised by the latest youth movement. Fair enough, thought Mulholland. Most of those musicians wore appalling outfits, had flogged the blues rock horse to death, possessed laughable deific pretensions, sang in faux-American accents and were unashamedly misogynist. Try as he might, however, Mulholland could never curb his love of Black Sabbath. A guilty secret it may have been at a time when music subcultures were more tribal than they are today, 'Paranoid' was Mulholland's favourite song of all time. After purchasing The Clash's debut album, the next record on his shopping list was 1973's *Sabbath Bloody Sabbath*. Sabbath's problem, identifies Mulholland, was that 'there was always this other band from down the road in Birmingham', namely Led Zeppelin, who carried themselves with greater confidence, flair and pomp than Sabbath could ever muster. 'But, even after all these years,' Mulholland wrote in 2009, 'I admire Led Zeppelin – while I feel real warmth and affection toward Black Sabbath. They were silly and clumsy and misguided and ultimately doomed to fail. How, as a provincial punk rocker, could one fail to relate?'[30]

Mulholland may have kept his Sabbath worship to himself, but he wasn't the only punk to have been touched by the band's dark magic. Johnny Rotten considered 'Paranoid' to be one of the greatest singles ever released. It was 'a stonker', he said, 'from start to finish'.[31] When Rotten's post-Sex Pistols band Public Image Ltd launched their debut album in 1978, one of the many tracks to which Nick Kent's *NME* review took objection was 'Religion II', particularly its 'jarring Black-Sabbath-on-Largactyl [*sic*] riff'.[32] The Fall's Mark E. Smith claimed to have held zero interest in music as a child: 'Then at 14, all at once, I went through it all, really quick: Pink Floyd? Crap! T.Rex? Rubbish! Paul McCartney? Urrgh! Black Sabbath, "Paranoid"? Great! Know what I mean?' It was the first single Smith ever bought.[33] The same song was covered by The Dickies, the LA punk band whose repertoire included an abundance of cover versions because, they admitted, it took less effort than having to write a greater number of originals. As Dickies singer Leonard Phillips saw it, 'Paranoid' was a punk rock song that predated the existence of any identifiable punk rock scene. It's what he and his friends would listen to when they were in their early teens. He identified 'a certain minimalism' and 'a certain energy' to 'Paranoid' that was 'very punk-ish'.[34] It wasn't just Black Sabbath's faster numbers that appealed to punk and post-punk musicians.

Black Flag were devotees of Sabbath, and the Californian punk band's influence became ever more pronounced as they progressed from purveyors of breakneck hardcore to experimenting with misanthropic dirges of the decidedly slow and sludgy order. In the same interview in which he sang the praises of 'Paranoid', Mark E. Smith boasted that The Fall were working on an 'Ozzy Osbourne parody' based around a 'dead slow' riff similar to Sabbath's 'Iron Man'. Steve Pringle, author of the highly recommended Fall-based blogs *The Fall in Fives* and *You Must Get Them All*, believes that particular Fall track must have been left on the cutting-room floor, although he points out to me that 'Fol De Rol' from the band's final album, *New Facts Emerge* (2017), shamelessly pinches its main riff from Sabbath's 'Zero the Hero'. When promoting 2013's *Re-Mit*, an album with which he hoped to 'terrify people', Smith declared, 'I want my music to be as punchy and aggressive as Black Sabbath. I don't want it to be something simpering that sounds like Jarvis Cocker.'[35]

The affinity between Sabbath and punk isn't particularly far-fetched, as Osbourne himself recognized at the time. He lamented some of the more elaborate studio facilities and orchestral treatments in which Sabbath had indulged themselves. Such extravagances were more suited to Yes and ELP, said the singer, while he reiterated Sabbath's origins as a 'backstreet' band. 'I'm not saying we were before punk,' he explained, 'but in our own way we were what the punk groups are now: a people's band.' He didn't necessarily want to jump on the bandwagon, he noted. But he enjoyed listening to 'the new wave' because 'you don't have to be a brain surgeon to listen to it. It's just a simple, down-to-earth music that people can tap out on a tin lid.'[36]

David Hepworth is misguided when he says that Black Sabbath's 'imaginative world' had no relation to real life in the slightest; that it did not reflect the worldly experiences of its audience. 'With Sabbath,' claims Hepworth, 'we move from the recognizable world of teenagers and teenage concerns, from dating and dancing and driving cars and learning how to fit in with your fellow man, to an entirely confected world of gloomy castles, passing bells and white-faced figures of foreboding.'[37] Surely this says more about Hepworth's own teenage years than anybody else's. Spare a thought for those who didn't go out dancing all that much, either through lack of confidence or opportunity, or who couldn't afford to drive a car to pick up their date. What about those who took their dates to see horror films? Or those who went to see such movies with friends, or on their own? Moreover, be they literary or filmic, the best science fiction and horror stories tell us more about the times in which they were written than they do about their purported imaginary worlds. The truly great ones also manage to resonate down the ages by appealing to generations way further along the line. The same could be said of the music that such stories have played their part in inspiring. Whether Hepworth likes it or not, science fiction, horror, existential angst, mistrust of the establishment, paranoia and fear in general, especially since the first atomic bomb was dropped, are as much an eternal component of teenagehood as courting, canoodling, dancing and driving.

The fear that they might be shipped over to Vietnam at a moment's notice. The empathy with those who had been forced to fight in the conflict. The anger at those who were responsible and their domestic counterparts. The threat of nuclear apocalypse. The pleasures and dangers of drugs. These were very real terrors and moral choices that Black Sabbath – and their fanbase – were required to ruminate on seriously and to navigate as best they could. This was something pointed out by American music critic Lester Bangs, who had initially written off the first Sabbath LP as a worse version of Cream. By 1972 Bangs had come around to the idea of Black Sabbath as 'moralists' who were up there with other heroes of his like Bob Dylan, William Burroughs and John Milton as 'artists trying to deal with a serious present situation in an honest way'.[38] Only on the most superficial level did Sabbath's material hinge upon spooky graveyards and creeping devils. Certain Sabbath-derived groups later down the line may have grown a little overly obsessed with scaled dragons or sexy witches. Sabbath themselves, as Osbourne pointed out, were extremely down to earth.

That being said, while Sabbath are arguably the epitome of heavy, it's hard to deny that they are also a key source of many of the platitudes – the bottles of liquor and crucifixes, the daft stage props and big hair – that distinguish those artists who aspire to heavy and the ones who truly embody it. The band itself became objectively farcical in its unstable post-Osbourne years, and there are countless rock snobs who continue to view Sabbath as a pitiful joke that went on way too long. Black Sabbath did, after all, provide direct source material for Spinal Tap. Antics including the Osbourne family's reality television show in the early 2000s did little to raise their reputation, even if it was useful in boosting their fame. Still, the Sabbathian mode is an absolutely necessary recurring motif than runs through the history of heaviness; a deep seam that holds together the disparate threads of our serious tapestry. While the subjects of some of the following chapters are more manifestly indebted to Black Sabbath than others (a clearer line can be drawn from Sabbath to grunge than from Sabbath to funk, for example, although there are links to the latter too), the sections in this book dealing with the different 'phases' of Sabbath will put the spotlight on those milestone records, bands or scenes where outright Sabbath acolytes have lifted the blueprint virtually wholesale – the slow tempos, the deeply distorted and frequently downtuned riffs, some of the lyrical obsessions – and pushed it to its outer limits (Earth, Sleep) and/or laced it with a few new eccentricities of their own (Melvins, Pigs Pigs Pigs Pigs Pigs Pigs Pigs). This shows how the precedent set by Sabbath has been passed down the ages in its most potent form and adapted by successive generations of riff-worshippers for their own peculiar purposes.

3

ACID ROCK AND BEYOND

The Jimi Hendrix Experience: admired by virtuosos and skronkers alike.

there are some basic grounds for outlawing LSD, DMT, STP – it can take a man permanently out of his mind – but so can picking beets, or turning bolts for GM, or washing dishes or teaching English I at one of the local universities. if we outlawed everything that drove men mad, the whole social structure would drop out – marriage, the war, bus service, slaughterhouses, beekeeping, surgery, anything you can name. anything can drive men mad because society is built on false stilts.[1]

CHARLES BUKOWSKI

If Black Sabbath were inspired to make rock music that was more doom-ridden than ever before, the acid rock movement of the late 1960s and 1970s provided a more 'colourful' way to experiment with heaviness. The best stuff still had a dark and threatening edge to it, but there was also room for greater exuberance and the absorption and splattered regurgitation of a broader range of musical styles than you would find in Sabbath's blueprint. The Beatles, again, were pivotal in spreading this new kind of heaviness far and wide.

When The Jimi Hendrix Experience played London's Saville Theatre on 4 June 1967, the leader of the band opened the set with a warning to his audience: 'Watch out for your ears! Watch out for your ears! Watch out for your ears! Okay?' His trio then launched into an electrifying version of the title track from *Sgt. Pepper's Lonely Hearts Club Band*. In the audience that night were Paul McCartney and George Harrison of The Beatles. Their album had been released just a few days earlier. During his rambunctious solo, Hendrix attacked his strings with such verve that by the end of that first number he had managed to bend his guitar drastically out of tune. He then asked if Eric Clapton, who was also hiding somewhere in the crowd, would be kind enough to come up to the stage to assist in retuning the instrument. Clapton refused.

With Hendrix's powerful English rhythm section backing him, the Experience were the power trio to beat all power trios. This was especially true where live performance was concerned, even if the band was not always quite so righteous studio-wise. Hendrix's bleeding guitar really did seem like an extension of his own body, mind, spirit and soul. Just watch virtually any footage of him play-ing it. No matter how Hendrix strums, picks, strokes or smashes it, waves his instrument around casually, attacks it with his teeth or mistreats it in other ways, that guitar and its amplifier always seem to ring out with a range of almost otherworldly noises. Be they melodic or discordant, pretty or less so, rehearsed and recog-nizable or dished out spontaneously, it all sounded magical. This, surely, is why Hendrix proved so inspirational to such a wide range of talent, including those with little of it themselves. For all the technicality that seemed far beyond the capabilities of so many of Hendrix's idolizers, it didn't take years of hard practice to turn the amplifier up as loud as it would go to recreate the shimmering feed-back and earth-shaking dissonance of Jimi at his messiest. Hence Hendrix's echoes can be found in the output of highbrow guitar heroes and minimalist, unpolished krautrockers alike, and much more in between. This helped change the game.

It has even been suggested, by the writer and comedian Stewart Lee, that there is a connection between the arrival of Hendrix on the rock scene and the racist views that the ex-Cream guitarist Eric Clapton would reveal, some ten years later, when onstage in Birmingham. Praising Enoch 'rivers of blood' Powell, the drunken Clapton raged against foreigners, immigrants and non-whites. He did this using the foulest language and most bigoted terms in the English vocabulary. 'I used to be into dope, now I'm into racism. It's much heavier, man,' Clapton claimed during his hateful rant.[2] Back in the mid-1960s, during the guitarist's tenure in The Yardbirds and John Mayall's Bluesbreakers, the phrase 'Clapton is God' had appeared in graffiti across London and New York, and presumably other locations too. Once The Jimi Hendrix Experience had turned up to blow everybody's minds, Clapton's crown had been usurped. As Lee puts it, this left Clapton 'a seething Salieri to Hendrix's soaring Mozart'.[3] Whether the two events, which did happen a decade apart, are so intimately connected or not, it's easy to see why the resentful Clapton wasn't eager to jump up to tune the emergent prodigy's guitar in front of The Beatles and others, and so be demoted from musical deity to mere mortal roadie in one fell swoop.

At his more recent concerts, Paul McCartney has recited the anecdote about Hendrix's hastily thrown-together cover version after playing not the Beatles song in question but, rather, Wings' 'Let Me Roll It' from 1973's *Band on the Run*. At the end of this downtempo, bass-heavy, Hammond organ-laden rocker, McCartney and his backing band segue into a brief rendition of Hendrix's 'Foxy Lady'. At the time of *Sgt. Pepper's*, McCartney was still a couple of years away from forging 'Helter Skelter'. The album did contain hints of the hardness that was around the corner, however, something Hendrix must have picked up on. That attention-grabbing title track – and its reprise that follows later in the album – is defined by its hard bass tone, spiky-sounding riffs, distorted guitar sounds and Ringo's pounding beats, interspersed with his typically smashing drum fills. McCartney's voice has a manic enthusiasm that, on the verses at least, threatens to escalate into a startling bark. 'Keep the bass drum loud. Bam! Yeah!' McCartney can be heard saying on Take 8 of the 'Reprise' that was included in the 2017 deluxe edition of the album. In contrast to the bold studio experimentation that is said to define that middle era of The Beatles' career, 'Sgt. Pepper's' has a live and lumpy feel. Hendrix's rendition may well have pushed McCartney into fulfilling that heavy direction. While McCartney's contribution to studio-based innovation cannot be understated, he was also always the Beatle who most missed going out on tour to prove his group still had the chops.

After The Beatles retreated into the recording studio, it was up to other groups to take psychedelia to the stage. Psychedelia's bastard sibling, acid rock, would join Black Sabbath as a critical influence on doom, stoner rock, desert rock, grunge and other heavy genres. With their eyes dilated and arms a-writhing, many of the key pioneers sprang from San Francisco's Bay Area. They benefited from the brief window when LSD was still legal and found themselves egged on by Timothy Leary's 'Turn on, tune in, drop out' motto and the Acid Test antics of Ken Kesey and his Merry Pranksters. Harder and louder than the good-natured trippy beat combos or folk-tinged hippie troubadours who were also knocking around at that time, acid rock groups were able to explore the stranger, more unpredictable, erratic and negative aspects to the psychedelic experience, or at least had the semblance of doing so. The acts in question tended not to have the same financial backing, levels of patience or studio nous of The Beatles. As such, many of them were known to perform better on the boards than in the studio – just like Cream and Hendrix – and did so with plenty of fuzz, wah-wah, feedback and other freaky sonic effects. Albeit unconvincingly, Marty Balin of Jefferson Airplane tried to deny that The Beatles had any influence whatsoever, deeming the Liverpudlians' output to be too complicated and studio-oriented to have much relevance to him and his San Fran contemporaries. Another, unnamed member of Jefferson Airplane added that Brian Wilson's work with The Beach Boys was 'fine' but lacked 'balls'.[4]

No Going Back

As a term, 'acid rock' may be a something of a misnomer. For a long time after it was created – by Albert Hofmann in a Swiss laboratory in 1938 – lysergic acid diethylamide was considered largely in visual terms, because of the hallucinations it caused. 'Would a naturally gifted musician hear the revelations which, for me, had been exclusively visual?' asked Aldous Huxley in *The Doors of Perception* (1954), but, as Rob Chapman points out in his history of psychedelia, until the mid-1960s, nobody did.[5]

What's more, tripping affected different people in vastly different ways, even when two people imbibed the same dose from the same batch of the stuff. Whereas Huxley used hallucinogenic drugs to think deeply about the nature of existence, stare in wonder at his own trousers and not get too carried away, for Timothy Leary LSD offered the chance to upturn the whole nature of society and become an outrageously famous celebrity in the process. Arthur Koestler, meanwhile, decided to stick to his preferred social stimulant of alcohol after experimenting with other drugs like hallucinogenic mushrooms while at Harvard with Leary. 'They produce a temporary therapeutic psychosis,' he informed Leary while sipping a Scotch on the rocks. 'But there's no wisdom there. I solved the secret of the universe last night, but this morning I forgot what it was.' Koestler's solution to the predicament was to stick to the whisky. Leary's was to take more drugs but also to take more notes, if not to remember the secret of the universe exactly then at least to have a more reliable account of the effects that various mind-altering substances had on him and his associates.[6]

The popular perception, or perhaps caricature, of acid's effects revolves around bright and contrasting colours, globular shapes of the variety you'd see inside a lava lamp, and wobbly pink elephants appearing before your very eyes. 'What they don't tell you about acid is it's dull, it's really dull,' insisted Bill Bailey in his stand-up show *Part Troll* (2003). The comedian recounted taking LSD at Glastonbury Festival and spending the next few hours buzzily mesmerized by the suddenly fascinating angle of a table leg. Scolding TV writers for constantly misusing the phrase 'on acid' as lazy and unimaginative shorthand for 'wacky', Bailey proposed that '*Terry and June* . . . on acid!' would actually consist of Terry examining the floral pattern on a plate for four days while going, 'That's quite interesting, that's quite interesting, that's quite interesting.' This is not to knock the LSD experience, though. As something that can reveal the magic that is hidden in what usually appears to be mundane, it could help explain where much of heavy music's obsession with repetition and minimalism comes from.

The Beatles were pioneers of psychedelic rock music, but the four members' experiences of LSD differed wildly. John Lennon and George Harrison embraced acid with cheery gusto. Paul McCartney, on the other hand, never seemed to shake his fear of overdoing it, lest he mangle his brain or run into other sorts of mishaps. He was the final Beatle to try it out. Afterwards, Paul remained more faithfully committed to his earlier love: marijuana. While it has been said that Paul's penchant for pot comes across in his warm, kind-hearted and laid-back compositions, weed has its darker side just as acid does. Marijuana's less euphoric effects can include paranoia and psychosis, and this negative edge can perhaps be heard in 'Helter Skelter', as it can in Sabbath's 'Sweet Leaf' and the entire stoner rock movement. Lennon had a personality that was more in line with that of Tim Leary. He adapted Leary's writings for the lyrics to 'Tomorrow Never Knows', and on 'Strawberry Fields Forever' would go on about nothing being real. McCartney's corresponding composition on the flip-side to that single, 'Penny Lane', uses a Liverpool location as its starting point too, and is also tinged by The Beatles' acid experiences. Yet the lyrics to 'Penny Lane' do not drift off into cod-mystical philosophy. McCartney's blurred vision remains fixated on the scenes directly in front of him, much like Bill Bailey staring at some camping furniture in a Glastonbury field. The local barber. A banker and his motorcar. A group of children. A nurse selling poppies. It is all 'very strange', but LSD has helped reveal to McCartney the beauty and wonder of everyday life that is so often unseen or taken for granted. He is less Leary than Huxley, with a touch of Koestler, staring not at the amazing creases in his trousers but at the people and places around him or, at least, his memories of them.

Always the most down-to-earth Beatle, even less psychedelic than Paul, Ringo Starr said that drugs had helped widen the scope of his group's music and lyrics but he would never condone them as a requirement for making decent music. As Starr was quick to point out, 'The Troggs haven't [taken drugs], so they tell me, and they're doing all right.'[7] The culturally ravenous McCartney didn't need mind-altering drugs to be drawn towards the avant-garde arts scene, the work of experimental composers and all the other fascinating happenings that whirred around him in the 1960s. Likewise, Harrison was always going to nudge his bandmates towards the exciting sounds of India, whether drugs helped them get into the right mindset for a spiritual raga or not. Before Harrison was even born, as biographer Joshua Greene notes, his mother used to tune in to the programme *Radio India* in the hope that 'the exotic music would bring peace and calm to the baby in her womb'.[8] By the early 1970s Starr had begun insisting that he'd only ever taken about nine trips in his entire life, and those he partly regretted. 'Like, I wish I had got to that stage without it,' he said. 'I really think it opened my eyes a bit, opened a few passages in my brain, but I wouldn't advise anyone ever to touch it. I would never touch it again. You see, once you've taken it there's no going back.'[9]

The Troggs weren't the only ones to hold off. Big Brother & the Holding Company preferred speed and booze to LSD, and their singer, the ill-fated Janis Joplin, 'remained avowedly, unrepentantly unpsychedelic'.[10] For his own part, Hendrix could've dropped all the acid the Western world had to offer. If it wasn't for crucial technical innovations in equipment like effects pedals and amplifier units, he'd have really struggled to make music that was anywhere near as loud, colourful and brash as his fancy scarves. Hendrix didn't think of his music as acid rock. Around the time of 1968's *Electric Ladyland*, Hendrix had started referring to his style as 'electric church music'. Afterwards, he predicted his next step would be influenced by Strauss and Wagner and could take the form of 'sweet opium music'. 'You'll have to bring your own opium,' he added. 'You know the drug scene came to a big head. It was opening up things in people's minds, giving them things that they just couldn't handle. Well music can do that you know, and you don't need any drugs.'[11] A fortnight after that interview's publication in September 1970, Hendrix was dead, having choked in his sleep after binging on alcohol and barbiturates.

Frank Zappa certainly subscribed to the idea that you don't need drugs to create weird and wonderful music, acid rock or otherwise. Zappa had no time for recreational drugs or the hippies who took them, sardonically mocking The Beatles, their followers and associated hippie happenings on *We're Only in It for the Money* (1968) by The Mothers of Invention. Zappa clarified his thoughts in a CBC interview three years later. Drugs completely drained people of their ambition, he insisted. He saw sad acid burnouts to be turning up more and more frequently. Pre-teens and young teenagers should consider themselves lucky that their older siblings had done all the recreational experimenting before them, he argued. They got to see their brothers and sisters stumble around making all the mistakes, without having to get involved in such counterproductive misadventures themselves.[12] Zappa's output offered plenty of evidence that you didn't have to take acid to make out-there music, even if there is an emotional coldness to much of his oeuvre.

It hardly needs to be stated that the bands who ingested the greatest quantities of the most potent psychedelic drugs did not necessarily make the best psychedelic sounds. Those who made the most out-there music did not necessarily lead the most hedonistic or exploratory lifestyles. What's more, the music made by the big-name burnouts of the acid scene – Syd Barrett of Pink Floyd and Roky Erickson of The 13th Floor Elevators – has overshadowed the equally impressive and often superior output of those who didn't become mysterious recluses with juicy back stories that could fill the pages of a million music magazines. Erickson sure does unleash some rapturous howls on the Elevators' garage rock classic 'You're Gonna Miss Me', but is that track significantly superior to the selections offered by some of the less well-remembered acts on Lenny Kaye's famous compilation *Nuggets: Original Artyfacts from the First*

Psychedelic Era? That album also includes Blues Magoos' 1966 rendition of 'Tobacco Road', for instance, with its primal, proto-glam rock riffing and hypnotic instrumental mid-section wig-out that, halfway through, seems to get bored of trying to invent zz Top and settles instead on anticipating Wipers' 'Youth of America' as if covered by French space skronkers Heldon.

As any music journalist will tell you, the reality of the profession is that editors demand angles, hooks and spicy stories, and these gatekeepers will not buy 'good band makes good music' as a strong enough reason to commission a feature. Every band has a story. With some artists, you have to look a bit harder for it. But the fact of the matter is that bands with debilitating drug issues in their personal histories often win out and hog the spotlight. This means that shambolic beshaded drug abusers float to the top of the public's attention while better, less hedonistic musicians remain floundering in the toilet circuit below. Since the mid-1990s Andrew Falkous has headed two excellent and underrated bands – Mclusky and Future of the Left – and he summed up this whole situation in characteristically withering terms when he posted on Twitter: 'The band take the drugs, the band take the drugs, eee-iiii-the-whatever-the-fuck, and now you've got something to write about.'[13] The point I'm trying to make is that it's best not to think of acid rock as something that was created, wholesale, by psychedelic adventurers who were always mashed off their heads on LSD. Rather, acid rock at its best should feel like it's having a warping impact on the mind of the listener, even when the strongest substance that's been ingested that day is half a can of unpeppered cream of tomato soup.

Magic Bands, Big Organs and Soft Machines

The Grateful Dead were tie-dyed-in-the-wool acid proselytes, but their output was rarely as fierce or otherworldly as was promised by their gnarly skeleton-based logos and colourful record sleeves.

As Rob Chapman has said of the Dead's 1967 eponymous debut, anyone who placed the needle down expecting to be subjected to 'the full-on Kesey Kool-Aid experience' would have most likely been 'bemused by the absence of mind-blowing experimentation'.[14] Never truly shaking their origins as a blues-based jug band, the Grateful Dead remained – even at their wildest – a frustratingly cosy prospect, shuffling along comfortably, noodling away into the sunset. Better, at least initially, were Jefferson Airplane, who were moodier, edgier and less predictable. Their music was uplifting and rapturous on the one hand; on the other, it could be unsettling and a little scary. Nor did they always conform to people's expectations. In spite of the hippie credentials, for her joint album with Airplane bandmate and then partner Paul Kantner, Grace Slick penned 'Silver Spoon': a vegetarian-baiting ode to cannibalism written to antagonize the sanctimonious 'hairy-armpits, no-work, bake-your-own bread' brigade.[15] Perhaps by that point in time Zappa had rubbed off on Slick. Later, though, she converted to veganism.

The same year that The Jimi Hendrix Experience performed 'Sgt. Pepper's' and unveiled their own apparently druggy milestone, 'Purple Haze' (a term more likely lifted from literature, specifically Philip José Farmer's sci-fi novel *Night of Light*, though it also appears in Charles Dickens's *Great Expectations*), Jefferson Airplane released 'White Rabbit', a paean of sorts to hallucinogens, albeit one that owed a significant debt to *Alice's Adventures in Wonderland* (as did The Beatles' 'Lucy in the Sky with Diamonds', also in 1967). The track was written by Grace Slick, who had already performed it with her previous band, The Great Society. Slick said she came up with it after a long LSD trip, and the song would go on to become a de facto anthem of the acid era with its talk of the shapeshifting properties of pills, the wild coda that instructed listeners to feed their heads and the way it seems to conjure up both the euphoria and the darker side of tripping. There was more to the song than druggy imagery, however. Slick had been listening to Miles Davis's *Sketches of Spain* (1960) for 24 hours straight when she penned it, and the slow and atmospheric bassline was inspired by Maurice Ravel's *Boléro* (1928). For Slick, the subject-matter was less about the experience of drug-taking itself than the hypocrisy of the older generation who had once filled their children's imaginations with the vivid imagery found in bedtime stories and then wondered why their offspring had taken so eagerly to drug culture. 'Parents were saying, "Why are you taking all these drugs?"' Slick told Mark Paytress in 2002,

> Well, they say the most important time in a child's life is between the ages of zero and five. Everybody reads their kids *Alice in Wonderland*, and there are drug references throughout it. Eat Me! Alice gets literally high, too big for the room. Drink me! The caterpillar is sitting on a psychedelic mushroom smoking opium. Peter Pan? You sprinkle some white dust – could that be cocaine? – on your head and you can fly! In every one of those stories you take some kind of chemical and have a great adventure.

The repeated coda in 'White Rabbit', Slick insisted, was as much about the importance of educating oneself with valuable information as it was to do with fuelling your brain with mind-altering substances.[16]

More abstract, jazzier and prone to being pelted with fruit by hostile audiences than Jefferson Airplane were Soft Machine, from Canterbury. They were tour mates of The Jimi Hendrix Experience and rivals of the rather more whimsical Pink Floyd. Soft Machine admired the radical free jazz of Ornette Coleman, had a keyboard player who'd long grown 'sick of guitarists having all the balls',[17] and quickly learned to offset the din of booing audiences by segueing each of their 'songs' into the next. The band's original members were a mismatched crew from the off. Alongside keyboardist Mike Ratledge, there was Kevin Ayers, who at some point discovered

Sufism and was eager to explore repetition and drone but found himself scuppered by bandmates who felt compelled to add extra elements, much to Ayers's frustration.[18] For a concert in St Tropez in 1967, however, Soft Machine did unleash an hour-long version of the Ayers-penned 'We Did It Again'. 'Your best ideas happen when you're naive,' said Ayers later, reflecting on that performance. 'There was something magical about that early band . . . Later on, you become more sophisticated and competent but the content is rarely better.'[19] Feeling his simplicity was boring the other members, harbouring no interest in playing in crazy 19/7 time signatures, and exhausted after touring on a self-imposed macrobiotic diet ('You can't do a two-hour gig on a green apple, a glass of water and a bowl of rice'[20]), Ayers quit Soft Machine the next year, after the first album. That was longer than guitarist Daevid Allen lasted. He formed the beguiling Gong straight after that European tour. Singing drummer Robert Wyatt would also leave as Soft Machine's jazz fusion direction became ever more pronounced. It is generally accepted that Soft Machine peaked somewhere between forming in mid-1966 and the departure of Wyatt in August 1971, although there is little consensus beyond that agreement. For some the group peaked live, before even entering the studio to record that first LP. Others see the debut album as the apex. Or they might plump for later recordings such as the handful of mammoth tracks that make up 1970's *Third*. The one thing that's for sure is that somewhere along the line, Soft Machine's psychedelic edge and the spirit of naivety identified by Ayers vanished altogether.

Back on the other side of the Atlantic, Frank Zappa's chum Don Van Vliet forged his own unique brand of heaviness under the alias Captain Beefheart and his rotating cast of musicians billed as The Magic Band, whose best performances were coerced out of them by Vliet's various methods of verbal, mental and sometimes physical abuse. 'All great psychedelia, I think, has a hint of menace,' says Stuart Maconie of BBC 6 Music's *Freak Zone*.[21] The Grateful

Dead's general lack of menace is surely one of the factors that helps to explain why they in particular seem to attract the strongest disapproval from punk rockers, more so than any other hippie group, including The Beatles and Pink Floyd. In the lyrics to the NOFX song 'August 8th', the sight of hippies in tears is taken as a signal that it's a beautiful day. 'I wrote this song about Jerry Garcia dying, cuz I fucking hate the Grateful Dead,' explained songwriter Fat Mike while having the honesty to admit he actually got the date wrong. The recorded date of Garcia's death was 9 August 1995. 'Whoops. I guess I'm lame,' added Mike.[22] In stark contrast to the complacent boogie-woogie of the Dead, Captain Beefheart's material contained more than its fair share of menace. His music with The Magic Band had its roots firmly planted in the blues, but Van Vliet was determined, to a degree of practical lunacy, to push this into truly strange territory. Their *Trout Mask Replica* of 1969 has to be one of the most widely purchased avant-garde rock albums of all time. For a looser, far less stiff and more transcendental experience, check out the expansive jams of offbeat acid rock at its finest that can be found on *The Mirror Man Sessions*, recorded in 1967 and released in a variety of forms thereafter.

Like The Magic Band, The Doors were based in California. Unlike Beefheart's crew, however, The Doors were never especially heavy. For one thing, they had no bassist. It isn't entirely impossible to be heavy *sans* bass player, but in order to compensate for the absence you're going to need more than a spot of organ-fondling with the left hand. You could also do with a singer blessed of convincingly shamanic credentials like Van Vliet, rather than a posturing frontman with poetic pretentions whose whole raison d'être was an assault on his Pentagon-payrolled parents.

More interesting than The Doors were an obscurer group of organ-wielding and bass-happy plodders who didn't luck out by having their singer die young only for Val Kilmer to then play him in a biopic. Success and posterity in the music business has never had an awful lot to do with meritocracy. Galumphing along in the grooviest possible way, and indicative of that general dark turn that art and music took in the late 1960s, The Maze were a bit like The Doors if they'd collectively suffered a bout of fatigue. Summing up the mood of 1969 and hinting at the San Fran band's future (or, rather, lack thereof), The Maze's sole album was titled *Armageddon*. So trudging is this record's tempo that the whole band and all of their instruments sound as though they are slurring in unison. Some mystified listeners would surely have wondered whether the record was spinning at the correct speed. The dominating organ tones and minimalist basslines are subterranean and ominous. When given their chance to shine, the fuzzy guitar solos jab casually at the ears before slinking back down the nearest grimy alleyway. The almost chant-like vocals match the despondent misery of the lyrics. Granted, the shortest of *Armageddon*'s seven tracks is a love song called 'Happiness', and its lyrics pay lip service to cheerful concepts like joy and happiness. The Maze struggle to sound sincere about this, though. The track feels sarcastic and sneering, with happiness and love coming across as things that you'll succumb to and be plagued by, like a bad trip. One online music database dismisses *Armageddon*'s 'minor-key' lumberings as 'generic [and] at times tedious',[23] which raises the question of who else out there was recording such down-tempo and misery-laden psychedelia?

Perhaps the writer was thinking of Vanilla Fudge. The New York band had a similar approach and were knocking around earlier, although, unlike The Maze's original material, Vanilla Fudge's emphasis on cover versions awarded them extra novelty value and a sort of theatrical air as popular tunes were dragged down into the dirt and kneaded into dusty mulch. In Vanilla Fudge's hands, 'Eleanor Rigby' became four times as long as the original in order to really enter the slogging, barely beating hearts of all the lonely people described in McCartney's lyrics. Stripping Donovan's rumination on the changing mood of the times of any of its remaining lightness, 'Season of the Witch' was stretched out by Vanilla Fudge as if on a medieval torture rack to almost ten minutes in length.

Motor City Is Burning

We now find ourselves wandering further away from peace and love and understanding and into proto-metal and pre-punk territory, to which Michigan's garage rock scene made priceless contributions. The Amboy Dukes were formed in Chicago but later relocated to guitarist Ted Nugent's home state of Michigan. Alice Cooper would end up there too, after the group had failed to find much appreciation in Phoenix and Los Angeles. Put to the back of your mind what would become of them: Nugent in his latter-day role as the rifle-toting geetar hero beloved by right-wing nationalists; Alice Cooper (the band) being outlived by singer Vincent 'Alice Cooper' Furnier and his rise to golf playing, Republican-voting prominence. Before these transformations took place, for a little while both acts were part of a vibrant scene that made its mark on the history of heavy music.

In Detroit they discovered, as Mr Furnier put it, that 'You couldn't be a soft-rock band or you'd get your ass kicked.'[24] This was, after all, the home of MC5 and The Stooges. The former were radical communists who took a lot of acid (among other drugs) and spat out high-energy rock 'n' roll that, at its best, felt like it was constantly teetering on the brink of falling apart. The latter were a more nihilistic and pessimistic prospect. The antics of their provocative and danger-prone lead singer, James Newell Osterberg Jr, aka Iggy Pop, became notorious. However, it takes a lot more than rolling around in glass, vomiting all over the stage and antagonizing violent biker gangs to make an impression, not only on contemporaries but on future generations. The Stooges weren't widely appreciated in the 1970s, claimed drummer Scott Asheton, because the band was simply too heavy for its own time: 'I'd say the biggest reason that stuff didn't do well is because we were rocking too hard.'[25] That might sound like a generic and unenlightening rock-star boast coming from somebody else, but where The Stooges are concerned there was something in this.

For The Stooges, if a riff was deliciously nasty enough then it was worth repeating ad nauseam, even for an entire song. Tastefulness was for squares. The radical jazz of Sun Ra was something to aspire to, even if in execution the results sounded nothing like Sun Ra. A guitar solo wasn't a proper guitar solo unless it sounded like somebody was jabbing an assailant in the ear with a flick knife. There was no shame in coming across as a bunch of brain-dead bozos to those who had a hard time understanding the genius of what was perceived to be 'low art'. Rough-and-ready recordings were nothing to be scared or ashamed of. In fact, such aural grubbiness complemented the rawness of the emotions that inhabited their songs. Ugliness could be a beautiful thing. It is easier than prettiness for most people to relate to. A 'singer' didn't have to scrub up well. They could be a conduit for repressed primal urges, through which audiences could live out their fantasies of breaking free from society's chains and violently vent their frustrations in a vicarious manner. In Detroit, rock 'n' roll got a whole lot dirtier and more dangerous.

Drugs were rife in the city. This was a place in serious decline. Detroit's best days as motor-manufacturing centre of the USA were already behind it. Even the bleak prospect of factory work, similar to that which Sabbath's members in Birmingham had been desperate to avoid, was looking like a career 'option' that would soon disappear. Riots broke out. Young men were terrified of being drafted to Vietnam. Again, substance habits and penchants among the musicians there did vary. Not everybody partook. John Sinclair, manager of MC5, harboured a mistrust of Ted Nugent, who never got high. Nugent said he found rock 'n' roll to be inebriating enough in the first place. Besides, he couldn't bear the conversation of stoned hippies. Nor did he have any time for concert promoters of the hippie persuasion. When The Amboy Dukes were offered a spot on the Woodstock bill, the opportunity was turned down because Nugent predicted the event would turn out to be an utter shambles. He was vindicated by reports that Jimi Hendrix's set ended up being postponed until the early hours of the Monday morning. 'Are you shitting me? Who would do that to Jimi Hendrix? I'll tell you who would do that: an uncaring, inconsiderate, soulless, piece-of-shit, stoned fuck, that's who would do that,' said Nugent.[26] Other Detroit bands fell apart or succumbed to heroin habits, or both. One thing was for sure. The cuddly hippie dream was no more.

Making Hard Rock Harder

Elsewhere, blues rock was in the process of being tugged and twisted into other kinds of stranger shapes. Among the English contingency were The Groundhogs and Pink Fairies. The U.S. offered bands like Steppenwolf (reportedly the first band to sing the words 'heavy metal', though in reference to a motorcycle), Iron Butterfly (famed for their seventeen-minute proto-doom riffathon 'In-A-Gadda-Da-Vida') and Blue Cheer. Critics liked to sniffily compare these acts to what had gone before. A 1969 profile of Blue Cheer quoted one of the band's 'biggest fans', who'd been asked to explain the appeal: 'Sure they sound like Hendrix and are a bad imitation at that, but they're here and we only get to see Hendrix and the Cream maybe twice a year.'[27] Blue Cheer were mocked for their apparent ineptitude and sloppiness and for compensating for this clumsiness with sheer volume. Eventually people would begin to cotton on to the fact that this was actually a massive part of their appeal. Blue Cheer's music was like Led Zeppelin's but stripped of the folk inclinations that Zeppelin never truly managed to shake even at their heaviest, and without the fiddly complexity. For aspiring rockers in the years before punk opened the doors even wider, this was even more within reach than Hendrix. As discordant and seemingly replicable as Hendrix's moments of messy noise had been, they were always balanced by undeniable guitar prowess. Blue Cheer, on the other hand, operated at a 'sub-sub-sub-sub-Hendrix' level, as Lester Bangs enthusiastically identified, their 'guitar overdubs stumbled around each other so ineptly they verged on a truly bracing atonality'.[28]

Out of the rainier valleys of Wales trudged Budgie, formed in 1967, a hardworking but unlucky trio whose achievements have never really gained the respect they deserve. 'We might have had a pint before we went on stage,' recalled guitarist Tony Bourge in 2017, 'but the drugs and the sex was right out the window. To be honest, I freak out if I have to take an aspirin!' Bassist and singer Burke Shelley took the abstemiousness one step further, refusing even to eat any food after 3 p.m. so that his body was nice and empty come showtime, as he felt this made it easier to sing. Bourge was even eager to avoid the contaminating effect of other people's music, doing his best to avoid it.[29]

Budgie were never considered to be cool, and their fans even less so. 'Theirs is not exactly music to nibble artichokes to,' declared the *NME*. Rather, it was 'no doubt perfect mood music after five or six pints of Newcastle Brown on a Saturday night'.[30] This snobby summary fails to capture the appeal of Budgie's music and the clandestine intelligence of Shelley's lyrics, which were often rich in wordplay and tongue-in-cheek humour. (Budgie's supposed love songs included 'You're the Biggest Thing since Powdered Milk' and 'Hot as a Docker's Armpit'.) One of Budgie's few advocates in the music press was Simon Frith. His review of Budgie's second album, 1972's *Squawk*, for *Let It Rock* magazine opens with an account of the professional doors that would be slammed in the writer's face if he was naive enough to reveal his love of Budgie to a prospective editor. Having persuaded his bosses at *Let It Rock* to let him write about the Welsh band through 'a mixture of subterfuge, flattery and plain lying ("Hey, would you like a real *shitty* review of Budgie?")', Frith sneaked into the magazine's pages an assessment loaded with flattery and which, though breezy in style, contained a great deal of insight. Frith considered the bass guitar to be playing lead parts, whereas the lead guitar sounded like it was handling the bassline. As the singer was the bassist, the vocals – 'an after-dub' in Frith's words – were also 'constructed like bass runs'. Drummer Ray Phillips's style was described as 'a healthy mixture of inevitability and eccentricity – he sounds as if he's falling down endless stairs', an observation that could also have been applied to the great Ringo Starr or the mighty Bill Ward. *Squawk*'s two acoustic tracks, curiously sequenced next to each other, were the only downside. 'If I wanted that sort of thing, lads, I wouldn't be listening to you,' cautioned the reviewer. Frith came to Budgie for their heaviness, in which he saw a yearning eagerness and exhilarating innocence. As Frith put it, 'truly heavy groups don't bother with the superficialities of lyric and melody, sound and rhythm are what they're after – take care of the pulse and the crowds will take care of themselves.'[31]

Budgie's reputation never kindled to the same degree as Black Sabbath's. In 1997 the original Sabbath line-up reunited to headline two hometown shows at the NEC arena. When Budgie toured in 2008, in its umpteenth revived incarnation, the band were still traipsing to venues like rock club JB's in Dudley. A visit to the other side of the Iron Curtain in 1982 had secured Budgie a loyal and long-lasting following in Poland, mind. Plus, their heaviness has been certified by the range of bands who have covered them or cited them as a key influence, from New Wave of British Heavy Metal bands (Iron Maiden) to hair metal pioneers (Van Halen), thrashers like Metallica and Megadeth, and grunge acts including Soundgarden.

For the Russian linguist and music blogger George Starostin, Budgie managed to draw on the rock bands that had come before them without ever sounding 'like a bunch of pathetic rip-offs'. Writing that Budgie 'refused to pander to the lowest common denominator, making music that was complex and irony-laden both in the musical and the lyrical sense', Starostin still couldn't work out why Budgie never hit the big time alongside the likes of Blue Öyster Cult. He says that some of the band's proto-prog material seems to anticipate Canada's Rush, while other cuts are worthy of the unhinged psych-rock of early Flaming Lips. He also notes the similarities between Budgie's 1973 version of the blues standard 'Baby, Please Don't Go' and AC/DC's version, which would not be released until two years later. On their rendition, Budgie manage to 'kick ass without sucking out all of [the song's] bluesy evil'. While it has been speculated elsewhere that AC/DC may have been drawing on Them's 1964 cover version, Budgie seem to be the more likely source. There are similarities in the chugging nature of the tempo and groove. The fact that both Budgie and AC/DC added additional riffs between the verses cannot be a coincidence, concludes Starostin, unless Budgie had already pinched the idea from another unknown group.[32]

From the mid-1970s onwards, AC/DC would rock like no other band (alleged Budgie-borrowing aside). Among their fans the Australian group would count heavy musicians as broad as Alice in Chains, Anthrax and Steve Albini (and that's just at the start of the alphabet). It's a testament to AC/DC's appeal that they also have a host of admirers from other, more surprising fields. Alan Sparhawk of moody slowcore harmonizers Low remembers *Dirty Deeds Done Dirt Cheap* being one of the first records he ever owned, when he was yet to turn thirteen. He reckons he can still sing all the songs word for word.[33] Stuart Murdoch, leader of the polite Glaswegian indie group Belle & Sebastian, says that nothing gets much heavier than *Back in Black*. He would fall out of love with other bands from his youth, Whitesnake and Saxon, but would never give up on AC/DC.[34] Tabloid-pin-up-turned-pop star Samantha Fox is a fan of the same album and would encourage her touring guitarist to mimic Angus Young's stage moves.[35] Like The Beatles or Black Sabbath, AC/DC manage to hook in huge numbers of fans from each successive generation. Those listeners tend be won over during adolescence or thereabouts, at an age when one can be more forgiving of a group whose major lyrical concerns are big testicles, hot girls and hell. Yet as they grow older those fans remain faithful, so there must be something that keeps followers loyal to the end.

For one thing, it's practically an exercise in postmodernism for a rock band to have quite so many songs about, simply, rocking. 'Rocker', 'Rock 'N' Roll Singer', 'R.I.P. (Rock In Peace)', 'There's Gonna Be Some Rockin'', 'Let There Be Rock' . . . the list goes on. Their critics claim that AC/DC churn out what is essentially the same (or very similar) stripped-back, riff-based, no-nonsense rock song over and over again to fill up whole albums, which, early on, were released at a rate of two per year. There must be more to it than that. Or perhaps that's the key to it. AC/DC's formula is so base, so straightforward and free from any kind of highbrow pretentions or ornamentation, its appeal so primal, that you don't have to think about it. Just let the undeniable spirit of rock wash over you.

At the same time, if you do want to think harder about it, the slate is so clean to begin with that almost anything can be scratched into it. Countering claims that AC/DC have never really changed, music writer Julian Marszalek divided the band's career into six distinct phases. Even Angus Young himself had confessed, 'A lot of people say we've made the same album eleven times, and really they're lying because it's actually the twelfth time.' For Marszalek, there were AC/DC's 'Glam Rock Years' (lasting from the band's formation in 1973 to 1976's *Dirty Deeds Done Dirt Cheap*), the 'Punk Rock Years' of 1977's *Let There Be Rock*, the 'Disco Years' (1978 to 1981), the 'Mullet Years' (1983 to 1990) and the 'Britpop Years' (when AC/DC noticed that many new bands had a throwback sound and so opted to become 'a tribute to themselves'), and this made the way for the final 'Heritage Years'.[36]

Others have homed in on one particular album as evidence of AC/DC's malleability. Singling out the band's most 'experimental' album, Michael Hann writes that on 1978's *Powerage*, singer Bon Scott replaced the previous 'seaside postcard bawdiness' with grimmer observational material that read more like Jim Thompson short stories. Musically, the old 'bluesy shuffles' dropped out completely. '*Powerage* is the most extreme AC/DC record,' argues Hann. 'It's the least flashy, the most gritty, the least concerned with its audience, and the driest: one wouldn't be in the least surprised to be told Steve Albini had spent his entire career as an engineer/producer/recorder trying to capture its sound.'[37] We'll hear more on that topic from Albini himself in a later chapter.

'In a way it was AC/DC's *Sgt. Pepper's*,' said *Powerage*'s engineer Mark Opitz.[38] It's a funny analogy to make because on that album, their prior ones and those that would follow, AC/DC are about as psychedelic as corrugated cardboard. Perhaps that's one reason why they were one of the older established rock acts that punks felt they could enjoy. *Let There Be Rock*, claims Jaz Coleman of Killing Joke, was 'the only metal album that all the punks used to play. Every punk loved this album but it was metal, so it went beyond genre because it was so bloody good and there's no pretentiousness about AC/DC.'[39] AC/DC weren't, strictly speaking, an outright metal band, but you can see what Coleman is getting at. AC/DC's music is simple. It's direct. It does not dabble in fancy embellishments. You don't have to be Eddie Van Halen to imitate the Young brothers' coolest riffs. *RAM* magazine called AC/DC a 'street punk band' as early as 1975, lumping them in with New York Dolls, Iggy & the Stooges, MC5, The Troggs and The Sweet.[40] When the style we now consider to be punk emerged, AC/DC were less than impressed. 'They're not punk, they're just shite,' Young would say of the UK scene. As for New York's Ramones, they were dismissed as 'trying to do a Small Faces thing . . . but they can't play'.[41]

Writing about the title track to 1980's *Back in Black* but also the magic of the band in general, Michael Hann had this to say:

You might say 'Highway to Hell' was AC/DC's greatest riff. But then you hear 'Back in Black'. So simple, but there's so much going on. The descending spiral at the end of the first reading of the riff, the little musical hiccups at the end of the second. And, as on all the best AC/DC songs, feel the space that allows those details to be so evident. Great songs leave things out, rather than adding them.[42]

While some bands achieve their heaviness through sheer sonic density and multiple layers of instruments, effects and overdubs, others manage it in a way that makes room for space and gaps in the sound. AC/DC are definitely in the latter category. In this respect they help to join the dots between 'Helter Skelter', Black Sabbath and post-punk. 'There's space in *Unknown Pleasures*,' Dave Haslam wrote of Joy Division's debut album, 'like something's missing, some silence at the heart of the music, dragging the listener in.'[43] On first listen, AC/DC and Joy Division seem worlds apart. One came from sunny Australia and sang about shagging, drinking and rocking (a lot). The other wore thick coats in the cold arches of rainy Manchester and sounded in a permanent state of bookish, existential and celibate distress. Sometimes subtraction, a flaying of the sound, can be a more effective means of securing heaviness than the more instinctive habit of piling noise upon noise. Both AC/DC and Joy Division were masters of skeletal heaviness, achieved through the use of space in their stripped-back and minimalist sound. Something else they had in common was that rare thing of managing to sustain a long and fruitful career after the death of a lead singer: AC/DC by replacing the departed Bon Scott with Brian Johnson in 1980; Joy Division by renaming themselves New Order after Ian Curtis had died, also in 1980.

In Search of Space

London's Hawkwind were always less concerned with sonic space than with outer space and, unlike AC/DC, were more than happy to cloud the atmosphere with thick textures and sound effects galore. They fused psychedelia with science fiction, electronics, layer upon layer of distortion and liquid light shows, thus jump-starting the space rock movement. Jefferson Airplane would go rather awry when exploring their own sci-fi leanings and transforming into the increasingly cheesy and arena-friendly Jefferson Starship. In contrast, Hawkwind would keep ploughing their own furrow, swaying in and out of fashion and constantly updating their sound but never quite buckling under trends, birthing countless sister groups and losing members left, right and centre until Dave Brock was the only remaining original one. Hawkwind are still best known for their sole hit 'Silver Machine' (1972), a catchy little ditty that doesn't give the full impression of the immersive and hypnotic power of Hawkwind at their finest. A more appropriate starting point would be the double LP *Space Ritual*. Recorded in 1972 and released the following year, it is one of the handful of live albums that are actually essential to the shelves of any self-respecting record collector. The no-nonsense riffs chug along, with chord changes usually kept to a minimum for fully entrancing effect. Adding to the density of the guitar sounds are the swirling textures emanating from Michael 'Dik Mik' Davies and Del Dettmar's audio generators, ring modulators, synthesizers and other wired-up bits and pieces. Forcefully present in the mix is the bass of Ian 'Lemmy' Kilmister, who can be heard playing like a man possessed.

In the minds of some people, Hawkwind get lumped in with prog rock, perhaps on account of those lavish gatefold album sleeves boasting of strange and distant worlds. Added to that are the spoken-word passages that lesser hands would bungle. Some of their songs' lengths and the grooves that Hawkwind get stuck in can threaten never to end. Because of these things, and their association with the countercultural hippie movement, Hawkwind's reputation suffered under punk. They also triumphantly survived punk, though. John 'Johnny Rotten' Lydon had been a fan back when he was a long-haired teenager, and he never ceased singing their praises. When the reformed Sex Pistols returned once again to the festival circuit in 2008, they would encore with 'Silver Machine'. Hawkwind and The Damned shared the same music publisher, often bumped into each other at gigs and festivals, and soon became buddies. The two groups may have been on different drugs to each other but they bonded over their anti-establishment tendencies and the ability to make basic talent go a long way. As soon as Stranglers bassist Jean-Jacques Burnel heard the title track to Hawkwind's 1977 album *Quark, Strangeness and Charm*, he wished he'd written it himself and kept trying to convince his bandmates to cover it.[44] Hawkwind's trance-inducing repetition and mesmeric textures were rooted in simplicity, and at times their sound could also equal the licentious scuzziness of The Stooges. When Brock appeared in a documentary in 2020, his delight in his group's simple yet fruitful formula still hadn't waned: 'I mean, if you listen to "Opa-Loka" [from *Warrior on the Edge of Time*, 1975], basically it's just a rhythmic sort of drum beat and us just plonking away on the guitars behind it with weird sounds going on. In one key, I might add! We were good at playing in one key. You could play half an hour in the key of E and not be boring.'[45] Hawkwind could offer transport to far-off lands in the listener's mind, or else help to empty it completely as if in meditation. But what they offered was also in reach. *Space Ritual* was advertised as '88 minutes of brain damage'. Who wouldn't be tempted to try that out as a momentary escape from the humdrum reality of everyday existence? Drugs may have helped some listeners to reach that mental space, but they were by no means a prerequisite. *Space Ritual* was potent enough in the first place.

Made in Japan

If Western artists differed in their enthusiasm for substance use and abuse, plenty of Japanese acts remained suspicious or fearful of drug-taking on account of both cultural tradition and the strict legal penalties for possession in their country.[46] In no way did this prevent Japan's bands from creating some of the most far-out acid rock on the planet, much of which easily rivalled the West in terms of energy and inventiveness, even if it didn't attract the same amount of exposure. Roused by the late 1960s counterculture movement and the huge social changes that were occurring across the globe, pushing against the ultra-conservatives of the older generation and smitten with The Beatles (here the Yoko Ono connection had a particular and more positive impact), Japanese rockers put their own unique spin on the acid rock template by fusing it with elements from their own culture.

The near-mythical Les Rallizes Dénudés were formed at Kyoto University in 1967 by a bunch of communist-sympathizing, existentialism-studying Blue Cheer fanatics. Their original bassist, Moriaki Wakabayashi, was particularly committed to the cause. In league with other members of the Japanese Red Army Faction, Wakabayashi took part in the shambolic hijacking of a Japan Airlines flight in 1970 and ended up exiled in North Korea. After the Flight 351 incident, all longhair hippies came under suspicion from the authorities, but frontman Takashi Mizutani continued with the Les Rallizes Dénudés project despite the direct connection to the hijackers, albeit on his own obscurantist terms. If many of the Western world's acid bands felt more comfortable onstage than in the studio, Les Rallizes Dénudés took this to the extreme by never setting foot in a studio and refusing to put out any official releases. Unless you were ever lucky enough to catch them live, bootleg recordings have been the only way to experience Les Rallizes Dénudés. An article written in 2014 by Grayson Haver Currin illustrates just how difficult it is to unearth any concrete information on the band and its personnel. Currin found that some other Japanese underground musicians, like Kazuyuki Kishino (aka KK Null), claimed complete ignorance of Les Rallizes Dénudés' existence. It is said that Keiji Haino briefly played in a covers band with Mizutani that performed only early Blue Cheer numbers. Certainly, Mizutani's and Haino's guitar noise aesthetics are similar to one another. But Haino has much greater visibility than Mizutani, around whom a mystique has built up owing to his withdrawal from the public eye. For one thing, Haino actually bothers to release records. He also carries himself as a kind of 'international emissary' for the Japanese underground. It is even said that Haino becomes furious at the mere mention of his rival Mizutani and refuses to speak about Les Rallizes Dénudés.[47] Wrapped in fierce blizzards of distortion and feedback, anchored by colossal minimal-chord basslines, with aching amplifiers that sound as though they're at risk of melting at any moment, Les Rallizes Dénudés' free-form, drawn-out songs are like Hendrix at his most abstract, stuck in a time loop while battling The Velvet Underground or perhaps a hastily assembled Lou Reed backing band at their loosest and least tuneful. It is *Heavier than a Death in the Family*, as the title of one of those bootlegs puts it.

Another notable group from the vibrant Japanese scene were Tokyo's Flower Travellin' Band, who put all sorts of discordant, improvisational, expressive and unfettered twists on their inter-pretation of Western rock music. They also managed to clock the significance of Black Sabbath much earlier than most others and used this insight to their advantage. Featured on their debut album *Anywhere* (1970), Flower Travellin' Band's repertoire included a rendition of 'Black Sabbath', the first song from Black Sabbath's also self-titled debut album. This is no mere cover version of 'Black Sabbath', insisted Japanese rock expert Julian Cope: 'Instead, they let its tyres down and ride it across a ploughed field.'[48] The impressive thing about this track is that Flower Travellin' Band's 'Black Sabbath' is even more Sabbathian than Sabbath's game-changing original. In that respect, it anticipates – by decades, no less – later developments in the Sabbathian mode that would be undertaken by the likes of Melvins, Earth and Sleep, all crucial to the naissance of doom metal, sludge and drone, ambient metal, post-metal and other heavy mutations.

4

FUNK

The artwork to the *Funkadelic Finest* compilation, paying homage
to *Cheap Thrills* by Big Brother & The Holding Company.

George was known for always making the gig. Never late,
even if nobody showed up. I remember one time: me, Catfish,
and George showed up to a sold out, outside gig. We were
the only ones that showed up. George said, 'Well, we gotta
go on. We're here.' We went up, killed them for three hours.
No drummer or anything. Just a guitar, a bass, and George
singing. Killed them! The crowd loved it. Then again they were
all blitzed out of their minds.[1]

BOOTSY COLLINS

The word 'funk' might strike fear into some readers of a book about heaviness. It can, after all, have connotations of some decidedly light music: tunes that are best suited to the discotheque or beachside cocktail bar as opposed to the dimly lit and dingy venues of the city (and similarly shady avenues of the mind) where heavy music grows like a moss. Such judgements are understandable given that funk-pop superstar Prince, for example, was consistently much heavier in concert than he ever sounded on the radio. It should be remembered, as shown by Prince's repertoire and elsewhere, that funk is a very broad church. There is that which lies at the soulful end, like Marvin Gaye's 'Got to Give It Up' (1977) and the hits of Stevie Wonder. There is the cheerful disco-friendly material of Kool & the Gang and Chic. There is also the stuff that has earned its place in the canon of heavy.

It is too easy to fall into that segregated mindset where white musicians are playing rock music in one corner while black funk musicians sit in the opposite one. As is so often the case, the reality is more reciprocal and integrated. For instance, future funk star Rick James's early group The Mynah Birds, formed in Canada when James was on the run from the Vietnam draft, featured the 21-year-old Neil Young in one of its incarnations. It included other members who would go on to play in Steppenwolf. Before joining James's group, Young had struggled (and failed) to break into the somewhat conservative Toronto folk scene. While playing together, James convinced Young of the merits of The Rolling Stones' basic way of rocking (beforehand, Young had been firmly in The Beatles' camp). During his Mynah Birds stint, Young realized how much fun it could be to get locked into a funky live groove and to rock out without having to sing all the time.[2] It was a lesson that would remain with him, especially in his activities with Crazy Horse. Another of Young's backing acts, The Stray Gators, featured on bass Tim Drummond, who had played in James Brown's touring band. 'His singing was a little strange,' James would write of Young, 'but his facility on the guitar was crazy. He got all over those strings and showed me some shit I'd never seen before. Neil helped reshape The Mynah Birds into the band I'd been hearing inside my head.'[3]

Neil Young performed at the Woodstock Festival in August 1969 as a member of Crosby, Stills, Nash & Young. This being a supergroup, and one of the earliest and most successful examples of the phenomenon, there was much anticipation for the perform-ance. 'They represented the Woodstock sound, whatever that was or is,' said Grace Slick of Jefferson Airplane, also on the bill.[4] 'Woodstock was a bullshit gig,' Young would reflect. 'A piece of shit. We played fuckin' awful. No one was into the music.'[5] CSNY were never really edgy enough for Young. In the studio they were prone to indulging in too many precious overdubs, resulting in a sterile feel. It removed any sense of spontaneity, covering up any of those nice raw mistakes that Young tends to keep in his mixes to make them feel more alive. Onstage, the joint harmonies were too pretty for Young. Just as when the pair of guitarists had been in Buffalo Springfield together, Stephen Stills's habit of overplaying by dishing out the slick licks clashed with Young's more primitive and abstract methods of making a racket. While touring with CSNY in 1970, Young would seek solace from all the smoothness that surrounded him by listening to the wild free jazz of John Coltrane on a Sony cassette machine. At Woodstock, he'd felt his fellow musicians had been playing to the cameras rather than the crowd.[6]

Also on the Woodstock bill, and not stinking up the place like the CSNY ego vehicle, were Sly & the Family Stone. They went onstage at half past three in the morning. Theirs was said to be one of the better sets of the weekend, and perhaps the finest performance of the band's career. They had already triumphed at the previous month's Newport Jazz Festival, where Stone and his crew had been greeted so rapturously that the event's organizers had feared a riot might erupt. On a bill that also included The Who, Jefferson Airplane, Grateful Dead and Jimi Hendrix, Sly & the Family Stone's set was the pinnacle of the whole weekend, as Woodstock's founders wrote with no amount of understatement:

In this rightest of all places and times, here was the rightest man. Whether by accident, design, or instinct, his hand moved unerringly to the crowd's celebratory nerve. He wanted to take them where they wanted to go: Higher!

Prancing, dancing, coaxing, cajoling; an ecstatic daemon bathed sensual by the purple-filtered floodlights, Sly worked on his audience like a consummate hetaera on a young man's body. He offered pleasure. He demanded Dionysian abandon in return – and he got it. Bright flashes of exhilaration illuminated the hillside like fireworks: hands, faces, eyes, bodies, leapt into incandescence and were swept up into a bonfire of sound and feeling.

'I wanna take you higher . . .' Sly chanted, and the crowd answered him, 'HIGHER!!!' again and again, each time from a more rarefied eminence, until height and depth lost meaning and there was only the moment, the eternally transient Now of existence suffusing the mingled thousands with a sense of fruition, of communion, and of reward.[7]

That all sounds pretty heavy to me.

The greatest funk band of all time, Funkadelic, had close ties to the Detroit garage rock scene. They would tour with fellow locals The Stooges and each band would push the other into pursuing ever more outrageous ideas and antics. Funk bands would show rock musicians the importance of the bass guitar as something that was not just there to help keep the rhythm in check but was an instrument that had a centrality to the overall sound in its own right. Funk could help free rock musicians from pop-based verse–chorus song structures and the limitations of restricted running times. It could offer ways for rock musicians to take advantage of the longer LP format, without having to resort to going full-on prog or taking oneself too seriously in other ways. Funk music could get locked into long, repetitive grooves without it getting boring and while boring (in another sense of the word) its way into the conscious and opening up the mind to new possibilities. From there, further inhibitions and hang-ups could be shed. Free your mind, preached Funkadelic, and your ass will follow. That band's imagination knew no bounds, from guitar solos that actually had soul to inventing African American science fiction heroes and alter-egos, from thrusting black sexuality in the faces of their multiracial audiences to imagining an America in which people of all creeds and colours might live together in funky harmony. The impact of hard funk is not only identifiable in the work of musicians playing broadly in the same genre. Its lessons were also soaked up by post-punks, psych-rockers, noise rockers, stoner rockers and many others besides.

'Mommy, What's a Funkadelic?'

Funk is a vast genre with a long history. There is one person who can be credited with making it heavier than anybody else in the scene. Well, one person with the assistance of countless collaborators and enablers, who had several different projects running concurrently like spinning plates for a host of different record labels, with a multitude of alter-egos in tow, alongside alter-egos that possessed their own alter-egos. That man is George Clinton, aka Dr Funkenstein, aka Star Child, aka Maggot Overlord, aka Uncle Jam, aka the Ultimate Liberator of Constipated Notions and more.

If we take the meaning of 'funk' by its older definition, that of a 'foul stench', then George Clinton was literally born among funk, his mother having given birth to him on 22 July 1941 in the family outhouse. Growing up, the young George witnessed the murder of one of his friends and consequently made the astute decision to avoid being sucked any deeper into the gang life of New Jersey, where his family had moved from Clinton's birthplace of North Carolina. Instead, he immersed himself in the doo-wop scene and broke into the barbershop business.[8] He would soon outgrow doo-wop and grow out his hair. Clinton's group, The Parliaments, were rebranded as Funkadelic and later resurrected as Parliament. In the 1970s, both Funkadelic and Parliament were operating simultaneously using the same ever-changing and expanding line-up. The collective would also birth a host of splinter projects, including Bootsy's Rubber Band, The Horny Horns and Brides of Funkenstein. On the differences between his two principal projects, Clinton explained that Funkadelic utilized loud guitars to bring the rock, whereas Parliament made greater use of the horns. In all honesty, though, both sets of instruments appear on both incarnations' work, and Clinton's most imperative philosophy was to 'not be bound by no one particular thing'.[9]

Despite graduating in doo-wop and initially setting his sights on the Motown label, Clinton already possessed catholic tastes by the time *Sgt. Pepper's Lonely Hearts Club Band* was unveiled to the world. Even so, Clinton has credited that particular album with setting him on the path to becoming a polymathic funk-rock superhero. It was not just the psychedelic properties of *Sgt. Pepper's* that appealed to Clinton but also The Beatles' enthusiastic embracement of any style that took their fancy, be it rhythm and blues, classical Indian music or whatever else happened to catch their ears and spark an idea worth pursuing. From that point onwards, Clinton realized, any type of band from any kind of background could dabble in any form of music they wished to explore.[10] As the title to one

Funkadelic number would rhetorically ask, 'Who Says a Funk Band Can't Play Rock?', its lyrics also calling on jazz bands to play dance music and for rock bands to play funky. 'I'd bite off the Beatles, or anybody else,' Clinton explained to *Rolling Stone* in 2018 before expanding on his inclusive philosophies:

> It's all one world, one planet and one groove. You're supposed to learn from each other, blend from each other, and it moves around like that. You see that rocket ship leave yesterday? We can maybe *leave* this planet. We gonna be dealing with aliens. You think black and white gonna be a problem? Wait till you start running into motherfuckers with three or four dicks! Bug-eyed motherfuckers! They could be ready to party, or they could be ready to eat us. We don't know, but we've got to get over this shit of not getting along with each other.[11]

Clinton and his band(s) drew on Smokey Robinson and The Temptations as well as the multiracial and multi-gendered funk stars Sly & the Family Stone, an act Clinton admired but with whom he also wished to compete. Jazz was another influence, especially the Afrofuturist tendencies of Sun Ra. Clinton also appreciated the cheeky FBI-baiting naughtiness of counterculture oddballs The Fugs. He was into harder rock, too: Jimi Hendrix and Cream, of course, but also the less mainstream likes of Blue Cheer and Vanilla Fudge. Another epiphany was experienced when the latter band's equipment was borrowed by The Parliaments at a gig in Connecticut. With tall stacks of powerful amplifiers at their disposal, Clinton and his cohorts had their minds opened to the volume and power they could achieve were they always to feed their instruments through such apparatus. For the first time, young guitar whizz Eddie Hazel heard just how Hendrixian he could sound if he played through the right amplifiers. Within weeks of that concert, The Parliaments had acquired the same set-up as Vanilla Fudge.[12] The Fudge's tempo was another element that intrigued Clinton:

> rock & roll is energy, so it's easy to play loud and fast. But to play loud and slow? That's hard. You get bored and you lose your trail of thought. Otis Redding was one of the only guys I knew who could do that and yet Vanilla Fudge did it on a whole album. And that blew me away.[13]

Clinton's interest in slowness would filter down, as we will see, to the post-punk generation. John Robb of The Membranes was one such advocate. 'The thing with rock music is that the faster you play the more exciting it is, but the thing about funk is that the slower you play it the groovier it gets, and that's quite an alien language for a rocker,' he noted. 'But it takes you to a weird place where your body moves in a slow way like a slow fuck which is a great place for your body to be.'[14]

Other esoteric art forms helped fuel the transition from doo-wop to psych-funk, including science fiction, comic books, blaxploitation movies and their accompanying soundtracks. Clinton was also impressed by the conceptual ambitions of albums by The Who and Jethro Tull. A relocation to Detroit was also formative. The idea was to get a foot in the door at the Motown label. The result was an alliance with that city's hotbed of high-energy, proto-punk rock miscreants: MC5, The Stooges, The Amboy Dukes, Alice Cooper and others. The appearance of Funkadelic on the same bills as these artists would stimulate the formation of African American rock bands like Black Merda and Death. These were 'the true progenitors of punk', at least according to MC5's Wayne Kramer. 'We were three black brothers playing straight-up white rock,' said Death's Dannis Hackney. 'It was loud. It was hard-driven. After we had finished a song, instead of clapping and cheering, people would just stand there and look at us like we were weird.'[15] At first, Funkadelic faced similar obstacles. They were embraced and encouraged soon enough by local Detroiters. Audiences further afield took longer to win over, however. 'We was too white for the blacks, and we was too black for the whites,' observed Clinton. 'Whites could go for one black guy up there, but not ten. We was young enough to be as horny as hell, so all that shit that everybody was afraid of was there.'[16] Immersion in the Detroit scene gave Clinton the courage to be as outspoken, outrageous, controversial and provocative as he craved. That, coupled with a Herculean acid intake, certainly loosened up Clinton and his fellow Funkateers.

Loose Booty

George Clinton's music is often viewed as following in the footsteps of James Brown. Bass player Bootsy Collins was one of several musicians who would escape Brown's backing band to perform in an assortment of the outfits assembled by Clinton under the 'P-Funk' (Parliament-Funkadelic) umbrella. In Collins's experience, Brown and Clinton operated at opposite ends of the spectrum.[17] Brown's suited-up musicians were conducted under strict discipline from their perfectionist leader, who would deduct his players' wages if they made even the most minor musical mistake or committed some other oversight such as failing to polish their shoes before a performance. This strictness sometimes had the unintended consequence of instigating disobedience. Despite Collins's penchant for acid, he had made a promise to himself never to be on it during a gig. One day, Brown pestered the bassist so many times about avoiding acid that Collins took the drug just to spite him. The only thing that Collins could remember about the gig afterwards was that his bass had turned into a large snake. Brown was furious. He reprimanded Collins after the show and told the bassist that his playing was terrible even when acid was not part of the picture.[18] George Clinton's attitude towards drugs would prove rather more liberal, to say the least. Payments under Clinton could also cause problems, so haphazardly were they arranged, but his reign was far more benevolent. Clinton needed his musicians to feel comfortable and relaxed, in the interests of allowing unbridled creativity. Although Clinton was essentially in charge, with certain key members descending the P-Funk hierarchy, James Brown alumnus Fred Wesley recalled how 'Nothing that popped into anybody's mind was dismissed. Everything, no matter how crazy and unconventional, was considered.'[19] Under Brown, Wesley was always wary of making a mistake, with any creativity outside the strictly prescribed groove being virtually non-existent and firmly discouraged. Wesley had once been in the 55th Army Band. Being in the military, he felt, had been easier work than playing for the demanding Brown.[20] With Clinton's anything-goes attitude, Wesley was more worried that literally any piece of music he laid down in the studio could end up as a song or part of a song, whether Wesley would've liked it to or not.[21] 'If [the musicians] are feeling a certain way on a certain day then that's the way it's gonna come out,' said vocalist Calvin Simon. 'Basically, that's what Funkadelic is to me: what you feel and that. Sometimes it was really good. Sometimes it was real bad, but at least you had an opportunity to do it.'[22] Sly Stone's old mucker Neil Young operated under a similar philosophy. According to Crazy Horse guitarist Frank 'Poncho' Sampedro, when they were rehearsing and recording together, Young never told the band they were working on an album: 'Every once in a while Neil would say – and I remember it shocking us – "Hey man, I sent in a record." I said, "Oh yeah? What was on it?"'[23] Clinton may have shared James Brown's prodigious work ethic, yet their approaches to getting things done differed widely. Clinton would, for example, refuse to bathe until an album had been completed, with some of his musicians joining their leader in unwashed fraternity.[24] Funky indeed.

Where Brown's musicians had to adhere to a strict, smart uniform and stay obediently in place while performing, Clinton's ragtag crew could wear whatever they wanted, be it casual clothes, fancy dress, no clothes or, in the case of Gary 'Diaper Man' Shider, an adult nappy. Onstage they could wander about wherever they liked; Dr Funkenstein wouldn't mind. The Parliaments' 1967 debut at the Apollo Theater in Harlem had been an embarrassing shambles after which, rather than continuing to pursue slickness and smooth synchronicity, Clinton and the gang worked on embracing anarchy, chaos and impulsivity instead. In this pursuit they were egged on by The Stooges and others in the Detroit scene.

Clinton recruited undeniably talented musicians of whom there are simply too many in number to assess individual contributions or even name them all. They ranged from Bernie Worrell – a fan of Jimi Hendrix and Duke Ellington who also counted Chopin, Mozart and Schubert among his list of idols and whose sense of composition added a whiff of sophistication to the sonic chaos swirling around him – to a random drug addict who wandered into the studio to perform the guitar solo on 'Get Off Your Ass and Jam' before disappearing again with fifty dollars in his pocket before anybody could catch his name. However skilled his musicians, Clinton also preached the idea that 'The Funk' reveals itself the very first time anybody picks up their instrument. Thereafter they have to be careful not to lose that primitive edge as they inevitably begin to improve:

> When you first start playin' that groove, you're so glad that you got it, you play it for*ever*. And then as you start getting technical ability, it gets boring to you. So you have to be able to go back to that no matter what you learn, remember to always keep that in your repertoire. What you first started out doing? That's valuable.[25]

Even without possessing any prior knowledge of Brown's and Clinton's contrasting working methods, it would be possible to identify the differences in the two leaders' take on funk. As booty-shakingly infective as it is, Brown's music feels so much stiffer and more constricted compared to the looser and multidimensional melting pot that is P-Funk. As indicated by Calvin Simon's words above, the results could be less consistent than Brown's, while Clinton's open-minded approach to incorporating any form of music meant P-Funk material encompassed soul, R&B, disco, blues, even yodelling, and mongrel hybrids thereof. When they rocked out, which was often, Clinton's gang were heavier than any rival funk band.

Who Says a Funk Band Can't Play Rock?

Eddie Hazel seems to have earned his place in history as the guy who played what is considered by many to be one of the greatest guitar solos of all time. It is Hazel's solo that dominates the mostly instrumental ten-minute title track that opens Funkadelic's 1971 album *Maggot Brain*. After the rest of the band had laid down their parts, Clinton was mixing it when he realized the track would, paradoxically, sound even heavier if he faded everybody else all the way down in order to foreground Hazel's sizzling solo. Rumour has it that at the acid-fuelled session, Clinton informed Hazel that Hazel's mother had died, before revealing that the news wasn't true. The softer version is that Clinton instructed Hazel to play *as though* she had died. Whichever process was used, Clinton got a hell of a take out of Hazel. Hazel was another Hendrix fanatic, even going so far as asserting that he carried Jimi's spirit inside him. Such a bold claim would have looked more ridiculous had Hazel not been able to put his money where his mouth was. 'Maggot Brain' was recorded shortly after Hendrix's death, so it also acts as Hazel's requiem to his hero.[26] It certainly is a contender for the greatest guitar solo of all time. A far cry from the less relatable nature of many guitar heroes' moments in the spotlight, 'Maggot Brain' is a soul-bearing, pain-exorcising, utterly engaging gift from the gods that ebbs, dips and flows between darkness and light, delicate and dexterous in some places and fuzzy and cosmically slipshod in others, feeling as defiantly *alive* as the most powerful Miles Davis trumpet movements.

When Michael Hampton was recruited by Funkadelic during a year Hazel spent in prison for having drugs on a flight and assaulting the cabin crew, Hampton proved his chops by performing a perfect recreation of the 'Maggot Brain' solo. 'I knew Mike was going to be in the group then,' recalled Garry Shider, ''cause he played it note for note. Eddie couldn't even play it note for note.'[27]

As glorious as it is, 'Maggot Brain' has overshadowed not only Hazel's other moments of incredible lead guitar work but Funkadelic's propensity for coming up with the goods in terms the all-important riffs. The same album includes 'Super Stupid', on which Hazel also sang, his lyrics drawing on the experience of mistakenly buying and snorting what he thought was cocaine and turned out to be heroin. Again, Hazel solos away like a man possessed, but the track really earns its proto-metal credentials through its lurching rhythm parts and thick distortion. *Cosmic Slop* (1973) is another heavy Funkadelic album, featuring the helter-skeltering riffs of 'Trash A Go-Go' and its raucously soulful title track. As *The Wire*'s Joseph Stannard has argued, Funkadelic did always, and will forever more, have the edge over lesser so-called 'psychedelic adventurers' such as the Grateful Dead:

Not only do the former's leaps of crazy wisdom leave the latter's dazed, hazy lyricism in the dust, the command George Clinton's mob have over the anatomy is undeniable. Funkadelic understood that the separation between ass and mind was a false dichotomy and that both were crucial to the war against mediocrity. Crucially, they had riffs . . . Biomechanical constructions forged out of flesh, wood, metal, electricity, designed to control and release the listener, to subjugate them and set them free.[28]

These credentials are acknowledged on 'Hard as Steel', from 1996's *T.A.P.O.A.F.O.M.* by George Clinton & The P-Funk All-Stars, on which, despite the song mimicking the G-funk sound developed by Dr Dre in light of Funkadelic and Parliament, Clinton is credited with brandishing a 'heavy metal hard-on'. Sonically heavier was Michael Hampton's first proper solo album a couple of years later. It was called *Heavy Metal Funkason*, rocked as hard as Bad Brains meeting Hendrix in heaven, and boasted song titles including 'Sloppy Metal', 'Heavy Metal Funkadelic' and 'Club Metalfunkadelamack' (it also featured 'Chronic Reggae'). Coming back to *Cosmic Slop*, 'March to the Witch's Castle' ticks the Black Sabbath boxes on account of both its title and the fact that its subject-matter is not really about spooky happenings at all. Its topic is America's mistreatment of its military veterans who had returned home from Vietnam. This was by no means the sole reference in the P-Funk repertoire to that conflict and its awful consequences.

African Americans were drafted for the war in disproportionate numbers, often from poor areas where the idea of joining the army was sold to youths as a better option than going to prison. And while serving in Vietnam, they found themselves disproportionately punished. They received a higher percentage of non-judicial punishments and courts martial than their white comrades, were mostly assigned to combat units and were sent on the most hazardous missions. If these men were lucky enough to return, they often bore mental and physical damage. Many came home addicted to heroin, which had been readily available overseas. They also found that the conditions of black neighbourhoods were in an even worse state than they had been when the soldiers had shipped out.[29] 'It was about the heroin in Vietnam,' Clinton said of Funkadelic's 1972 double-LP concept album of soulful, progressive funk, the indignantly titled *America Eats Its Young*. 'That whole war was about heroin.'[30] This is perhaps the most glaring example, but it is just one of the darker themes to appear in the P-Funk repertoire. These were sometimes obscured by the jokey wordplay on display, the sheer uplifting energy of the music and the party-like-the-end-of-the-world-is-nigh atmosphere of their onstage Funkathons, which could rock on for three or four hours at a time. But those underlying themes were always present, feeding the groups' output and their sense of urgency. Ned Raggett put it well when he wrote that Funkadelic 'brought the party so well that too many people missed the forest for the trees and only saw the party'.[31] As one of the lines from Pedro Bell's artwork to *Cosmic Slop* put it, 'I have gazed upon the so-called highest life form on this planet with unbridled disgust!' It's a Sabbathian sentiment if ever there was one.

Get Off Your Ass and Jam

Funk was of paramount importance to foregrounding the power of writhing, body-shaking, hypnotic basslines and for breaking free of traditional song structure. Going from the smooth, smart and precisely arranged sound of Motown and doo-wop to embracing messier psychedelic rock tricks and melting disparate forms of music together was not only groundbreaking. For Clinton and his followers, it was an act of freedom. 'It was totally liberating with those first Funkadelic albums which really came out of our jam sessions onstage,' said George. 'We played these long psychedelic grooves, broken into different chants and freestyled over them. We knew how to structure a song. To be so unstructured was liberating for us.'[32] Outside Clinton's P-Funk empire and under the sway of disco, things would become softer once again and a lighter, diluted sound would emerge. Yet the rhythm-centric, bass-heavy, riff-wielding and abstract experiments of Clinton and his revolving set of collaborators would be passed down and dispersed across a range of genres. Clinton, naturally, was delighted by these developments. 'We came from Motown – we knew how to make a clean, straight record,' he told *The Quietus* in 2015,

> But we didn't want to. We wanted to be so loud that it hurt. My intention was to have things so loud that you could run your hand across the record and feel the bass. Public Image Ltd came along afterwards and they understood: bring the noise. They understood the concept of tearing the roof off.[33]

PiL and their free-form, post-punk, bass-happy brethren, which included The Pop Group, The Slits, Gang of Four and Killing Joke, are obvious examples. The P-Funk legacy does not end there. It also filtered into krautrock, such as the avant-funk of Can or the more robotic electro-funk of Kraftwerk (Detroit techno pioneer Derrick May would later describe his own genre as 'George Clinton and Kraftwerk stuck in an elevator with only a sequencer to keep them company'[34]). Hardcore punk band Minutemen were also paying attention to Clinton, along with the bass-centric goth scene (The Birthday Party, Bauhaus) and alternative rockers later on. As an obvious exemplar of Funkadelic's influence on the latter category, check out the searing version of 'Maggot Brain' on which Dinosaur Jr's J Mascis performs Hazel's part for ex-Minutemen bassist Mike Watt's 1995 album *Ball-Hog or Tugboat?* The same track has been covered by many others, including the extremely heavy Philadelphia psych-rock band Bardo Pond in 2013. Altering the formula more than Watt and Mascis's fairly faithful interpretation, Bardo Pond beefed up the rhythmic accompaniment, with Isobel Sollenberger reinterpreting some of Hazel's melodic guitar lines through her flute. '"Maggot Brain" is an archetypal tune for us,' explained guitarist Michael Gibbons. 'Its powerful architecture is something we aspire to. Through very simple means it achieves maximum effect. The tune incorporates minimalism, repetition (mantra-like in its flow) and aching emotional tones. These are elements that we try to put in our music.'[35]

By the middle of the 1970s even the great Miles Davis had decided to jump on the funk bandwagon. The Parliaments had ditched the respectable buttoned-up suits of the doo-wop band for a messier, more psychedelic image to accompany their wilder, rockier sound. In turn, jazz legend Davis swapped the plain suits of yore for bright, multicoloured garments for his next period as a jazz-funk-rock fusion artist. He was turned onto Hendrixian rock and Clintonian funk during his short-lived marriage to Betty Davis (née Mabry). Shortly after splitting from Miles, Betty would become one of the heaviest funk artists to grace the planet, although she unfairly remained a cult concern and has only recently had her hefty and freaky repertoire reassessed. She arranged all her music personally, making savvy use of her collaborators, who included members of The Family Stone, Santana and Hendrix's Band of Gypsys. The groove-oozing recordings she released in the first half of the 1970s contain a funk that is so slow, heavy, phat, fierce and full of feeling that it could persuade even a morgue full of corpses to resume shaking their booties.

A far cry from the polite, neatly dressed and submissive image of 1960s girl groups like The Ronettes, Betty Davis was a much more threatening prospect to the sensibilities of Middle America than even George Clinton, with his own penchant for nudity, sexually explicit material and lyrical fantasies of African Americans taking command of Washington DC. Davis delighted in writing 'anti-love' songs that extolled the virtues of casual sex, one of which opened with lines about how she used to beat her 'big freak' with a turquoise chain. With plenty of flesh on display, Davis's aggressively sexual live performances and outrageous lyrics were a long way ahead of their time, paving the way for artists like Prince, Madonna and Lil' Kim. She was proud that her onstage gyrations had the potential to scare men as much as anything. U.S. television stations, she said, wouldn't go anywhere near booking her.[36] Her music had a grinding, sweat-dripping, crotch-centric hard funk groove to match the carnal nature of the words, with Davis's vocal range stretching wildly across cooing, moaning, singing, shouting and growling. When Betty Davis truly roars, however momentarily it lasts, it suggests that instead of disappearing into reclusive obscurity she could have forged an alternative career as an authoritative death metal vocalist. 'If George Clinton waved his freak flag proudly,' wrote *Pitchfork's* Joshua Klein upon the re-release of her first two albums, 'Betty Davis wore it as underwear then rubbed your face in it.'[37]

While the albums created by Davis's ex-husband during that period are not the most highly regarded among his diehard aficionados, they are among his heaviest. Defending this so-called 'sell-out to funk' period, Julian Cope compared the outlandish recordings made by Miles Davis to experimental krautrock, improvised rock music from Japan, space rock, heavy metal and the sound you'd get if you played all the discs from The Stooges' seven-CD *Complete Fun House Sessions* at the same time on different budget ghetto blasters.[38] Needless to say, it is material that has enthused later practitioners of ugly, gritty, abstract music. In 2009 the drone metal act Sunn O))) named a track after Davis's 1975 double album *Agharta* (another of theirs is named after Alice Coltrane). Mika Vainio of the Finnish electronic act Pan Sonic called Davis's funk-derived material – along with John Coltrane's *Interstellar Space* and similarly intense works by Ornette Coleman, Charles Mingus, Don Cherry, Pharoah Sanders and Albert Ayler – a 'kind of grindcore jazz'.[39]

5

THE 1970S EXPERIMENTAL EUROPEAN UNDERGROUND

Faust IV.

Can are coming to Britain soon. I'm looking forward to their visit with guarded interest. They sound a weird bunch of geezers.[1]

MICHAEL WATTS in *MELODY MAKER*

The music, lyrics and artwork of Parliament-Funkadelic had plenty of recurring outer space, science fiction and alien themes. George Clinton's many alter-egos included the extraterrestrial Star Child. On the front of the Parliament album *Mothership Connection* (1975) he can be seen in the door of a spacecraft, wearing a silvery suit with matching knee-high boots, legs akimbo. The band would also commission a lifesize replica of the ship to enhance their spectacular stage shows. Claiming to be returning from space (the real home of Earth's black population) to reclaim the pyramids as their own, the lyrics were a carnivalesque extension of Marcus Garvey's idea for the descendants of the displaced slave population to return to Africa.[2] Clinton's sci-fi interpretations of the African American experience also drew on the work of experimental jazz composer and Afrofuturism pioneer Sun Ra, who insisted he was a peace-preaching visitor from the planet Saturn.

Other musicians have used space as a way of representing marginalized groups. David Bowie's Ziggy Stardust character, an outlandishly dressed bisexual and androgynous alien, resonated with a broad range of social outcasts. Hawkwind, those anti-establishment, commune-dwelling space rock loonies who frequented free festivals to preach joy and revolution, 'animated the provincial underground and became a rallying point for heads and freaks everywhere' (in the words of Joe Banks).[3] Such ideas were often developed in resistance to those of an older and more conservative generation. In 1970s Germany the older generation had associations far beyond what might be deemed 'conservative'. The timeless experimental music that came out of that country at that particular moment would be labelled 'krautrock' by foreign onlookers. Some of the musicians who made it preferred the native term *kosmische Musik*, meaning 'cosmic music'. Sometimes these groups were labelled 'space rock' and compared to Hawkwind, as in a piece on Can for *Sounds* magazine in which Martin Hayman asked, 'So what if they can't play rock and roll music?' (He also called them a 'pataphysical boogie band'.)[4] As krautrock expert David Stubbs points out, the name of Can's recording studio was Inner Space, 'which encapsulated the vast introversion of their sound. While the Americans were busy penetrating the outer variety and attempting to colonise the moon, it was Europeans like Can who held sway in the mental regions of the aesthetic beyond.'[5]

There have always been problems with the term krautrock. First and foremost is its employment of the 'kraut' prefix, what with its derogatory connotations that came to particular prominence during the First World War and have continued to thrive in the British and American lexicon thereafter. It remains unclear who first coined 'krautrock' as a catch-all phrase for the experimental German bands of the 1970s. Some say it was initially uttered by John Peel on his radio show. Others have attributed it to Ian MacDonald during his time at the *NME*. Richard Williams is fearful he might have been responsible for its creation during his service at *Melody Maker*.[6]

Another issue is that most of the artists grouped under the krautrock umbrella sounded wildly different from one another, with many of them possessing different agendas. The acid rock wig-outs of Ash Ra Tempel or Amon Düül II contrasted with the more propulsive motorik material of Neu![7] The confrontational harshness of Kluster gave way to the prettier sound of Cluster. Cologne's Can thought of themselves as expressionists and would eventually struggle to adjust to new technologies, their later work dampening under the introduction of multitrack production. This meant the once consolidated unit were no longer playing as one and were less able to bounce musical ideas off one another in real time.[8]

Düsseldorf's Kraftwerk, on the other hand, embraced technology so wholeheartedly that they were almost successful in their mission to transform themselves into robots. Kraftwerk were precise, detached, deliberate, sober, orderly perfection-seekers. They would come to be defined through their determination not to rock. Stubbs considers them to be the 'anti-Springsteen', noting Ralf Hütter's frequent use of the word 'little' in conversation and his group's mission to keep on making everything smaller and smaller, including the equipment they used, in an ongoing exercise in self-emasculation.[9] Yet even the withdrawn Kraftwerk made a huge mark on future practitioners of heavy. This can be seen most obviously in the thumping electronic music and beat- and loop-driven backing tracks of hip-hop. Guitar wielders, too, paid attention, for instance those who would combine rock music with electronic equipment to create industrial rock. Given recording engineer Steve Albini's preference for a live-sounding and hard-rocking production style, you would think he'd feel happiest over in the Can camp. He was impressed by Kraftwerk's lack of ego, though. Big Black, Albini's 1980s noise rock band whose industrial credentials included using a drum machine in place of a human drummer, recorded a crunching cover of Kraftwerk's 'The Model' for their final album, *Songs about Fucking* (the title itself mocking the principal lyrical concern and preferred leisure-time activity of rock 'n' rollers across the ages).

It's unsurprising that most of the German musicians lumped together into this supposed genre did not take the term 'krautrock' seriously. Many wanted nothing to do with it. John Weinzierl of Amon Düül II seems to have been as offended by the 'rock' part of the equation as he was by the derogatory opening prefix.[10] It implied that Germans were still trying to follow in the footsteps of British and American traditions, whereas the mission of the artists involved was to break away from such formulaic conventions or even wind the musical clock back to year zero and begin anew. The Beatles' global impact had had particular potency in Germany, given that it was in the clubs of Hamburg that the Liverpool band had once learned their chops. Coupled with The Beatles' subsequent world-wide fame, this had resulted in the rise of groups who strived to be Germany's answer to Merseybeat through a process of close replication. It would have been a better idea to embrace the true spirit of The Beatles, which was to innovate rather than merely imitate. As for American music, Irmin Schmidt of Can expressed admiration for blues musicians but was in no way willing to appropriate their style. Were Can to go down that route, he decided, they would be lying to themselves and their audience.[11] To help break away from Anglo-American cultural dominance, Can soaked up music from Spain, Morocco, Africa, India, Turkey, Vietnam, Iran and elsewhere. Schmidt had visited America, mind, where he did pick up a few ideas from the minimalist composers based there, as well as The Velvet Underground and the Fluxus movement. Schmidt was also a big fan of Jimi Hendrix, who he felt was the Charlie Parker of the electric guitar.[12] Not that jazz pointed the way forward either. Schmidt's bandmate Jaki Liebezeit had been an accomplished drummer on the German free jazz scene until he reached the conclusion that the supposed freedom offered by that style was itself trapped by its own restrictions and clichés. Ironically, perhaps, Can found liberation in stricter repetition. A strange 'freak' (in Liebezeit's words), who was probably out of his mind on LSD at the time, approached the drummer after one jazz gig and imparted the wide-eyed wisdom that 'You must play monotonous[ly]!'[13] This was the breakthrough Liebezeit was searching for. He ruminated further on the suggestion, and then never looked back.

Other German bands tried to reclaim 'krautrock' as their own, or at least repurposed the phrase in a mocking manner. 'Krautrock' is the name of the first song on Faust's 1973 album *Faust IV*. It also happens to be one of the heaviest tracks in the krautrock canon: a wavering, wobbling, glorious monolith of an instrumental dirge. For Ian MacDonald, Faust were 'the most extreme of the

German experimental bands' by a significant margin. Their output, MacDonald declared in the *NME* in 1973, would prove to be as significant as The Beatles' most daring attempts to push the envelope of rock music, if not more so.[14] Faust were fans of The Mothers of Invention, whose *We're Only in It for the Money* had lampooned the Fab Four. As commune-dwelling hippies, Faust did not share Frank Zappa's zeal for discipline, nor his penchant for snide pastiche or virtuoso superiority. Faust used drums, organs, guitars, bass and sax, showing little interest in actually mastering their instruments. Inanimate objects that happened to be lying around were utilized too, and they 'played' construction tools like cement mixers and jackhammers. They also enjoyed manipulating their equipment to make it sound nothing like it was supposed to. In this they were assisted by sound engineer Kurt Graupner. Like a Jamaican dub producer or, indeed, The Beatles with the assistance of George Martin, Graupner used the basic studio equipment he had at his disposal to manipulate Faust's collective racket. This added additional echo, texture and a general wrong-sounding strangeness. Graupner also custom-made mysterious metre-long black Perspex boxes covered with white buttons, referred to as 'sound generators'. These allowed the members of Faust to mix and manipulate their own as well as one another's sounds in real time, adding further spontaneity, unpredictability and sonic depth to Faust's music.[15]

If the members of Black Sabbath thought they had it bad when living among Birmingham's Blitz-shattered streets, imagine what the situation was like for young Germans. Besides all the rubble, they couldn't help but notice that, as John Weinzierl of Amon Düül II did, the country still had 'bloody Nazis around, all over the place'.[16] These elders could be grandparents, parents, teachers, judges – all kinds of people who had been involved to some degree or other in the Nazis' activities but would never agree to talk about such matters. There was, as Faust's Jean-Hervé Péron explained, 'not only a physical vacuum, with all these areas being bombed, all these anti-spaces – there was also an intellectual and emotional emptiness which needed to be filled'.[17]

As David Stubbs has written, if there was anything that the separate krautrock groups shared it was the anti-fascist and egalitarian nature of the different artistic adventures on which they embarked. The rejection of the older generation's actions and beliefs was present in the krautrock musicians' personal politics, but it also determined the methods used to conduct their operations and compose their music collectively. There was no hierarchy in Faust, no clear leader, no task-mastering Zappa figure. Nor was there in Can, a band that split all their payments equally and credited the compositions to, simply, 'Can', whoever happened to be in the line-up at the time. Although they did become more professional with time, early performances by Amon Düül would involve the idealist practice of handing instruments to their audience and encouraging them to play along; a tradition that has been adopted by the modern-day experimental noise band Sly & the Family Drone, whose on-the-floor performances usually end with drums, cymbals and sticks being passed into the surrounding audience, who join in with the din until an appropriate climactic – or even anticlimactic – endpoint can be reached. Krautrock had singers, but it had no individual stars. Nobody was allowed – or would even have had the gall – to be the central focus of attention. Some tracks had vocals, others remained instrumental, depending on necessity and whether it was appropriate. The overall sound was of far more importance than the actual 'song' itself. Krautrock was, as Stubbs tells us, 'predominantly about texture, rather than text'.[18] It's an attitude that is shared by so many of our earlier and later electric wizards.

Krautrock was progressive, yet in an extremely different manner to prog rock. In many ways, it was prog's complete antithesis. Progressive rock was grounded in meticulous forethought and detailed extravagance. Its cerebral stars thought of themselves as arch composers who had the talent and intellect to lift rock music, once the sound of the dirty backstreets, to the cherished and respectable heights of the classical canon. Holger Czukay and Irmin Schmidt of Can had studied under Karlheinz Stockhausen. Other krautrockers learned how to play as they went along. The stars of prog rock were known for rarely missing an opportunity to show off their musical chops. The krautrockers who had chops in the first place, like Can, felt the urge to repress, deny, disregard or repurpose such skills in order to unearth a sound they suspected would have greater profundity, purpose, impact and groove. Technical ability, declared Schmidt, was 'a political term' and 'an old value'. For Can, it was an obsolete idea to believe that one had to meet a certain technical standard before being able to create music of worth. 'If somebody wants to express himself he doesn't need to study eight years to learn how to play quickly,' explained Schmidt. 'To me, somebody who is the fastest on the guitar may well prove to be the most alienated to the guitar of all. His guitar doesn't have anything to do with his life. His aim is just to be a fast guitarist.'[19] Furthermore, anybody could get involved. Damo Suzuki was a nomadic busker who was enlisted as Can's vocalist after being spotted in the streets. His first gig with Can, in 1970, was performed without any rehearsal at all. Krautrock mischievously embraced monotony, though few of the resulting works were a genuinely monotonous experience. It celebrated impulsiveness, welcomed mistakes and happy accidents, and thrived on happenchance. It's little wonder that punks, or perhaps more specifically post-punks, held such reverence for krautrock. Johnny Rotten was a fan, as would become clearest in his post-Sex Pistols project Public Image Ltd. The Fall took up repetition as their modus operandi and would record a song called 'I am Damo Suzuki', packed with musical and lyrical references to the Can mystique.

Vive la Révolution

The relationships between children and parents were changed radically. It was the beginning of the anti-authority education, there was a big revolution in France, De Gaulle had to go, and also we were not happy being a deluded echo of what went on in the music scenes of England and the States.[20]

JEAN-HERVÉ PÉRON (FAUST)

It ought to be noted that, as well as taking inspiration from areas far outside Germany and removed from the usual culturally dominating Anglo-American tradition, there was an international presence in krautrock membership. Faust's Jean-Hervé Péron was born and raised in France, for example. His bandmate Rudolf Sosna was part Russian. Can singer Malcolm Mooney was an African American expat. His replacement, Damo Suzuki, came from Japan.

Unable to identify very closely with the American rock canon's bombastic anthems about jumping in a Cadillac with your baby in the passenger seat and burning down Route 66, Kraftwerk's response was the gently propulsive sound of 'Autobahn' (1974). It was inspired by the motorways in their native country and the pastime of trundling along them in an unglamorous Volkswagen Beetle. Not only did this have little in the way of the heroic, orgasmic release offered by phallocentric U.S. rock, 'Autobahn' threatened to go on forever. It probably would have done, too, had Kraftwerk not run out of the minutes available on a 33 rpm record. Just a couple of years later, the same band felt the need to assert their European identity. They began working on the album that would turn out to be called *Trans-Europe Express*. Along with the title track, the record's other centrepiece was 'Europe Endless'. Just how German was krautrock anyway?

As Kraftwerk may have been implying, another problem with the 'krautrock' term itself is that it overshadowed the experimental music that occurred at the same time in other areas of Europe. Focus has remained fixed on the German acts of the 1970s, with interest in them stoked on a regular basis by the publication of books like Julian Cope's *Krautrocksampler* and, more recently, David Stubbs's *Future Days*, not to mention the juicy articles that can be churned out whenever one of the well-known krautrock records hits an anniversary with a nice round number ('30 Years On: What Cluster's *Zuckerzeit* Taught Me about Comorbid Insomnia!'). Krautrock was not particularly popular, certainly in its native country, at the time most of this hodgepodge of eccentric musicians were creating their most vital and groundbreaking work. Because so many people now know all about it, we can look back and feel a sense of superiority to all the philistines from the olden days who were preoccupied with purchasing the Osmond family's singles from Woolworths instead of mail-ordering a first pressing of *Känguru* by Guru Guru.

Future generations would be justified in laughing at us for our brazen disregard of the vibrant work that has survived from nearby countries too, much of it similarly dismissed at the time and still, broadly speaking, neglected to this day, certainly in comparison to the key German bands. Nowadays, even the most casual music fan will nod in recognition if Neu! crop up in conversation, if only because that bloke from LCD Soundsystem keeps ripping them off. Try mentioning Heldon or Lard Free, however, and the very same person could just stare back at you as blankly as a sports personality on *Celebrity Mastermind*.

Krautrockers including the anarchic Faust, a Frenchman among their ranks, had been impressed by the May '68 movement in France. Richard Pinhas, leader of Heldon, had personally participated in the Paris riots. In 1974 he was awarded his PhD, supervised by Jean-François Lyotard at the Sorbonne. Philosophers like Michel Foucault, Jacques Lacan and Gilles Deleuze were like rock stars to the young Pinhas, but they were also accessible to him. Deleuze became a friend as well as a mentor; the transcendental empiricist's voice can even be heard on a handful of Pinhas's recordings. Science fiction was important to Pinhas too, particularly writers like Norman Spinrad and Frank Herbert. The name Heldon was lifted from Spinrad's alternate-history novel *The Iron Dream* (1972), a book that satirized the way fascist ideologies were projected and perpetuated in science fiction as well as in popular culture and Western society more generally.

From the music world, Pinhas admired Jimi Hendrix, Miles Davis and Philip Glass, among others. The hero he looked up to the most was Robert Fripp, whose cultural significance Pinhas declared was right up there with Béla Bartók and Richard Wagner. Pinhas saw a direct connection between these three figures, adding that Fripp was the most important composer of the bunch.[21] King Crimson can stake a decent claim to being the heaviest prog band of all, at least outside the heinous world of prog metal, a mongrel genre that succeeds in being tougher to love than Damien from *The Omen*. For all their dizzying time signatures and generous use of woodwinds and violins, King Crimson rarely let too much ornamentation get in the way of a cracking riff. As the 1970s wore on, their sound only grew heavier, culminating in 1974's *Red*, which was recorded as a power trio and, for a short moment, threatened to be King Crimson's aggressive final statement. In a cordial joint interview with punk icon Joe Strummer that was conducted in 1981, Fripp recalled that although he had once been on the road to becoming a classical guitarist, he could hear Hendrix hit one single chord and it would speak to him more than the entire canon of classical guitar. Unlike many of his prog rock contemporaries who felt threatened by punk and chose to turn up their noses at such insolence, Fripp welcomed punk's passion and sincerity. He admired the iconoclastic attitude towards the debonair prog elite, who Fripp agreed had become bogged down in middle-class aspirations and superfluous feats of 'facile technique'.[22]

Richard Pinhas was not just enamoured with Fripp's output with King Crimson. The 'Frippertronics' techniques showcased on

(No Pussyfooting), Fripp's 1973 collaborative album with Brian Eno, made a further impression on the Frenchman. Pinhas always liked to cite his sources, just as he was required to do in his academic papers. Heldon's second album opened with a track called 'In the Wake of King Fripp', and another number was dedicated to Fripp and Eno. Heldon transcended the sum of its influences, however. The early Heldon albums exhibited a distinctive merging of spiralling space rock guitar and analogue electronics that conjured in the minds of its listeners the alien worlds and parallel universes that nestled in the pages of the science fiction literature Pinhas enjoyed reading.

Heldon also grew heavier as Pinhas's project progressed. The heaviness became particularly pronounced on Heldon's concluding trio of albums, beginning with *Un rêve sans conséquence spéciale* in 1976. It was named, appropriately enough, after a King Crimson bootleg. By this time, Heldon had gained access to a professional recording studio, no longer having to make do with Pinhas's apartment and the equipment hoarded within. Heldon had also managed to get their hands on a rare and rather cumbersome Moog synthesizer that had once, believe it or not, belonged to Paul McCartney. Its acquisition helped strengthen Heldon's sound and direct it down the heavier route it was to take. Pinhas's rotating company of collaborators had also started to solidify into something resembling a regular line-up, with François Auger on drums and Patrick Gauthier on synthesizers. Didier Batard would frequently drop in to lay down some bass.

All this enabled Heldon to produce material that was darker, denser and more intense than before, something that Pinhas had envisioned for his project from the very beginning. *Un rêve sans conséquence spéciale* kicks off with 'Marie Virgine C', which sounds like Pinhas has taken an axe to Robert Fripp, hacking him into bloody chunks in Thurston Moore's basement. Drummer Auger is the star of 'Elephanta', in all its Moog-assisted polyrhythmic glory.

On side two, 'MVC II' offers six minutes of sinister dystopian squelch rock. Next comes 'Toward the Red Line'. Lasting a quarter of an hour, this piece conceivably serves to connect the dots between Hawkwind's most free-form passages and the Detroit techno innovations of the coming decade.

Building on those advances, and no matter how abstract at times, there is a cheerful underlying funkiness to 1977's *Interface*, implying that Pinhas's wig-outs had become less indebted to Fripp and were now sharing something in common with various Parliament-Funkadelic luminaries. That's not to say *Interface* doesn't sustain the proto-industrial harshness that had been building in Heldon's work. As one five-star customer review on the Amazon website insists, an alternative title for this album could have been 'INYERFACE'.[23]

'Bolero' from 1979's *Stand By* has a colder and more robotic feel, echoing the parallel progress that film-maker John Carpenter was making in the field of sci-fi and horror scores. The hazmat-suit-clad alien or astronaut-like figure on *Stand By*'s sleeve could have walked right out the frame of such a movie. The mood of the record remains urgent throughout, its title track flaunting a scuzzier stoner rock swagger for its first five minutes before spiralling into full-bore space-prog territory and then having its handbrake yanked back into position again.

The spooky vocals on 'Bolero' were provided by Klaus Blasquiz of French group Magma. Blasquiz and Pinhas had once played together in the considerably less progressive Blues Convention (the clue is in the name), prior to Blasquiz joining Magma in 1969. Magma's Stella Vander and Christian Vander were, respectively, cousin and cousin-in-law to Pinhas, so there was a family connection as well. 'A lot of musicians from Magma came to Heldon, and vice versa,' recalled Pinhas in 2019. 'We were two bands that everybody hated because of the music we played. We didn't do rock 'n' roll. We didn't do blues. Still, after fifty years they only remember bands like Magma and very few others.'[24]

Magma's credentials are a little more purely prog than Heldon's output, although some would argue that lumping them in that category does a disservice to their idiosyncrasies. Magma's busy line-ups contained a greater number of personnel than Heldon's. There was a more orchestral, grandiose feel to their cosmic rock operas, which ended up somewhere between Stravinski and Sun Ra, with added rock crunch. Christian Vander called this style of music 'Zeuhl', which has become a fruitful subgenre in its own right, and one that boasts disciples as distantly separated in time, space and style as Potemkine (a Toulouse act whose debut album, *Foetus*, came out in 1976) and the complexly aggressive Japanese power duo Ruins, led by vocalist and drummer Tatsuya Yoshida, who first made waves in the late 1980s. 'It's sort of like what the Supreme Court said about pornography,' offered Steve Feigenbaum of the Zeuhl-friendly label Cuneiform Records when asked to define the style, 'I know it when I hear it.'[25] The word Zeuhl comes from Kobaïan: the constantly evolving made-up language in which most Magma lyrics are sung. This is the native tongue of the people of Kobaïa, a distant planet dreamt up by Magma's leader. Based in part on the scat singing of the jazz greats, this language, claims Vander, allowed him and the other Magma vocalists to express themselves more purely and honestly than doing the same thing in French. It's an idea that subsequent bands took to as well. The aforementioned Tatsuya Yoshida sings in his own made-up language. Alongside Ruins, his other Zeuhl projects include Kōenji Hyakkei. Formed in 1991, the eclectic Finnish experimental rock band Circle have their own equivalent tongue, known as 'Meronian'. Most of the material sung by Reykjavík-based post-rock band Sigur Rós is written in 'Hopelandic'. Pieter-Paul Devos shouts, screams and sings in an imaginary language when fronting the Belgian noise rock band Raketkanon. Magma got there before them.

Like many of the krautrockers, Magma's experiments weren't exactly embraced in their homeland, and especially not at first. 'They didn't believe Frenchmen could play like that,' said Vander in 1995. 'And they found the music too violent, aggressive . . . too hard.'[26] Sharing something of King Crimson's jazzy skronk-rock leanings, Magma certainly had the aptitude to sound rather more berserk than their competitors.

Magma and Heldon are just two of the better-known names from the French underground scene. Delve a little deeper and you'll find a treasure trove of strange and often heavy music waiting to be unearthed, absorbed and celebrated anew. Take Nyl's self-titled and sole LP, for example. It emerged the same year as *Un rêve sans conséquence spéciale*, was released by Pinhas's Urus imprint and had the words 'THANKS HELDON' printed in full caps on its sleeve. *Nyl's* bright artwork gave a suitable impression of what to expect. It featured various runic symbols surrounding a figure who could be a redheaded vision of the mythical Andromeda, freed from her chains with arms outstretched in an invitation to partake in some mysterious hallucinatory odyssey. That's pretty much what guitarist Michel Peteau achieves with the help of his troupe of saxophonists, vocalists, keyboardists and rhythm-setters. At least one specialist prog blog out there describes it as a 'messy album,'[27] but that is actually one of its finest attributes.

Along with the usual methods of digging through crates in record shops and scouring the listings on the Discogs website, listeners can discover further French underground treats by tuning in to Warren Hatter's *FrenchRockSampler* programme on Resonance FM. Hatter accepts that the French scene can't compete with krautrock in terms of the latter's more clearly traceable impression on hiphop, film soundtracks and modern-day bands. No French act can match the magnitude of Kraftwerk's fame, he says. However, Hatter remains convinced that the best fifty or so albums that came out of the French underground scene of the 1970s 'more than matches' the output produced by German artists in the same era. 'So I'll keep banging the drum for this music,' he says, 'whether or not we find a better name for it than "French Krautrock".'[28]

Richard Pinhas's activities seem to have had particular resonance among heavy music makers in Japan, a fact that Pinhas himself has difficulty explaining. Heldon's 1970s output was lapped up by Masami Akita, aka Merzbow, who launched his own career as master of noise music at the end of that same decade. Ruins' Tatsuya Yoshida is another fan. So too is Kawabata Makoto of Acid Mothers Temple, known for their far-out psychedelic jams. It's not just in Japan, either. *Interface* is a particular favourite of Nate Young from the Detroit noise unit Wolf Eyes.[29] All these acts, in a later stage of Pinhas's life, have had the opportunity to collaborate with their hero.

So maybe we just need to look further afield, or delve a little deeper, to properly determine the French scene's legacy. Just don't, whatever you do, call it Frogrock.

We Need to Talk about Sweden

We wanted to play what nobody else did. Find our own voice.[30]

KENNY HÅKANSSON (BABY GRANDMOTHERS)

The conflict that ravaged Europe and so many other countries from 1939 to 1945 wasn't called a world war for nothing. In its wake, the urge to begin again from scratch was not confined to nations as central to the conflict as Germany and France. In the late 1960s and early '70s, as the world began to recover from the fallout, avant-garde and experimental music flourished in all sorts of locations, not least in Sweden, which had remained neutral during the Second World War, though hardly in a condition of tranquil isolation. Sweden had traded with both Britain and Germany, including the extensive export of the iron ore that was of such value to Adolf Hitler's weapons industry. It provided arms, supplies and thousands of volunteer soldiers to assist Finland when the Soviet Union attacked in November 1939. Sweden was pressured into allowing the secret transportation of Nazi troops through its territory. It also took in more than 50,000 Norwegian refugees and provided asylum for almost all of Denmark's Jews.

After such turbulence, you can see why Sweden's young natives might have been roused to rip it up and start again. Having not been involved directly in the fighting, Sweden had an advantage in that its industrial and economic infrastructure was left in a relatively healthy condition at the end of the war. This made it one of the few European countries able to offer worthwhile remunerations to musicians from the u.s. who wanted to tour overseas. The production and importation of vinyl also recovered as the austerity of the war years faded into the distance.[31] As Jim Weir noted in *The Wire*, Sweden at the end of the 1960s, with its 'polity grounded in welfare liberalism and sufficiently unawed by the Soviet Union to welcome anarchist and libertarian politics like nowhere else in Europe', had become 'a mecca for draft-dodgers, bail-jumpers and other square pegs'.[32]

There seems to have been little direct connection between the Swedish 'progg' movement (not to be confused with British progressive rock) and the German experimental scene, although they shared some of the same ideas and methodologies. There was a utopian and egalitarian agenda, symbolized most obviously in that several of these progg bands liked to hand out instruments to audience members to emphasize that anybody and everybody could get involved.[33]

The term 'progg' was not coined until 1973, although the scene's emergence pre-dates that. Earlier names for it include the 'Alternative Music Movement' or simply the 'Music Movement'.[34] The scene was nationally oriented in the sense that it felt the need to resist u.s. cultural imperialism. Much of the singing was done in Swedish, although not exclusively. Certain American artists still proved important to the progg musicians, however. As with krautrock, admiration was shown for Jimi Hendrix. He performed at

Stockholm's Filips club, the brief four-month existence of which did not prevent its significance to the development of the progg scene. As well as hosting Hendrix, the club nurtured native acts including Baby Grandmothers, who played there twice weekly, and Hansson & Karlsson. The Swedes' respect for Hendrix was reciprocated. Baby Grandmothers got to support Hendrix on his Scandinavian tour of 1968. The same year, The Jimi Hendrix Experience began covering Hansson & Karlsson's 'Tax Free', often opening their set with it and stretching the song out for over fifteen minutes.

Again, there was hardly a great deal of coherence between the style of one progg band and the next. Some were jazzy, others were grounded more deeply in folk. Many were resistant to the increased commercialization of music in their homeland and the creeping influence of the capitalist music industry. The commercial aspect of the music business would quickly become epitomized by the stratospheric rise of ABBA, who, it's safe to say, were perceived as a cultural enemy.

Guitarist and music student Bo Anders Persson was galvanized to form Pärson Sound after his involvement with Terry Riley's performance of the minimalist milestone *In C* (1964) that took place in Stockholm in early 1967. Over time, the project would evolve into other incarnations: International Harvester, Harvester, and Träd, Gräs och Stenar.

Persson's project didn't get around to officially releasing anything when it was still operating as Pärson Sound. A double CD of archive recordings that came out in 2001 gives us an idea of how radical they were. Its opening song is called 'Tio Minuter', meaning 'ten minutes', and ploughs on for the length of time indicated by its title, a mesmerizing swamp of cyclic double bass, slurred chanting, misty guitar sounds, tape loops and expressive drum beats that sound almost out of time with everything else. The creaking, aching strings of Arne Ericsson's electric cello feel like Scandinavia's answer to John Cale's viola work for The Velvet Underground. A couple of other tracks on the compilation are longer and even heavier. Twice the length of the preceding track, 'From Tunis to India in Fullmoon (On Testosterone)' adds a howling saxophone to the mix. It's a whirling, droning space-jazz black hole that's situated somewhere between the planets of Hawkwind and Sun Ra and looking to suck them both inside. 'Skrubba' lasts almost thirty minutes. One blog writer calls this track 'a painful half an hour jam that is based on the second idea in "Let There Be More Light" from Pink Floyd's *A Saucerful of Secrets* . . . This has none of the sophisticated construction of Floyd's piece, however . . . [It] is too long by about 25 minutes and adds nothing to music's canon.'[35] Quite the contrary, such an unsophisticated deconstruction based on hypnotic repetition had much to add to the canon, especially considering it was recorded a couple of years before most of the krautrock bands got going.

The partly affectionate iconoclastic progression continued, both directly and indirectly, in Persson's subsequent projects. At 2 minutes, 41 seconds, International Harvester's 'There Is No Other Place' (1968) might be considered to be pop music compared to Pärson Sound's lengthier movements, but its stomping nature suggests a missing link between early Pink Floyd and the repetitively abrasive and nihilistic no wave scene of the late 1970s. Harvester's 'Nepal Boogie' (1969), meanwhile, is as if The Rolling Stones had pinpointed the most potent, booty-shaking seven seconds of music they ever recorded and then decided to perform a repetitive jam based around that tiny section for eight minutes instead of moving on to the verse and chorus.

A 1972 live recording of Träd, Gräs och Stenar covering the Stones classic 'Last Time' finds the Swedes drawing the song out for seventeen minutes, a glorious example of how a group can bend, twist and, most of all, stretch another act's song into a barely recognizable reclamation. Community, DIY culture, audience participation and live performance were all central to Träd, Gräs och

Stenar's unwritten manifesto, and the band are remembered for having performed better in concert than on record. Radical cover versions aside, their original material, especially the live recordings, are equally impressive. These could range from short acoustic chants to half-hour bass-driven psych-rock improvisations. 'The thing was that we learned to listen to rock in a new way,' said Thomas Tidholm of the creative process, 'and to be captivated by separate elements, instrumental bits, the beat, a few heavy riffs.' These riffs or phrases were sometimes invented by the band themselves, sometimes they were pinched from other acts such as The Rolling Stones (no strangers to plagiarism either). 'That's the core of rock, and of what we were looking for. We took it and modified it and repeated it a thousand times in the same tune.' Traditional music from India and Africa, Swedish folk music, polyrhythms and ragas were also added to the equation. 'We talked about making the music stop and stand perfectly still. And that did happen sometimes. We never let go of the drone. We hardly make any key changes and never changed chords,' Tidholm explained. The tape loops that had been heard in Pärson Sound were dispensed with, but their guidance remained apparent. After losing the tape recorders, the band concentrated on coming up with their own loops and figures, 'a sort of riff', as Tidholm calls them. 'I guess you could say, incredibly simple phrases, but they produced music that you could listen to on different levels. That's how you could describe it: several different structures arose in the music simultaneously.'[36]

Earlier, David Stubbs identified one coherence in the krautrock scene being that there were no leaders, no stars, no single member of any band hogging the spotlight. The same could be said of this lot. 'As for lyrics, I guess I had certain ambitions,' said the multi-instrumentalist and non-exclusive vocalist Tidholm. 'But there was never really room for that. And you couldn't hear them anyway, the times we tried having lyrics. I could stand there singing at the mic, but it just came out like noises . . . the words were indistinguishable in the overall sound. Usually I didn't even sing words, just some kind of syllables. It didn't matter.'[37]

Although both scenes shared some of the same political and creative ideals, in the late 1970s and early '80s the rise of punk in Sweden exacerbated the decline of the progg scene. More recently, there has been a gradual renewal of interest in and appreciation of progg's achievements. Collectors of ephemeral music who had already soaked up much of what krautrock had to offer yet remained hungry for more often ended up plunging themselves down a Swedish rabbit hole. Before his death in 2012, Thomas Gartz of Pärson Sound noted that the rise of rave and techno culture had benefited the proggers' reputation. Although working with different equipment and in a different medium, these electronic scenes also revelled in extended track lengths and the joy of repetition.[38]

A host of reissues and archive releases has stoked interest in Swedish progg music, and some bands have even resumed activities. With a line-up of Bo Anders Persson, Torbjörn Abelli, Thomas Gartz and Jakob Sjöholm, Träd, Gräs och Stenar toured the United States in 2004. This coincided with the rise of 'New Weird America'. Groups such as Jackie-O Motherfucker, No-Neck Blues Band, Excepter and the countless psych- and freak-folk projects that have thrived in their wake share the same enthusiasm for emancipated musical explorations as the Swedish originators. In 2018, Jakob Sjöholm released an album with Träden, another mutation that can be dated back to Pärson Sound. The same year, Baby Grandmothers re-emerged with an album of new material called *Merkurius*. Save for the odd moment of enraptured chanting, the record was mostly instrumental. It ran the avant-rock gamut from frantic and scuzzy (opening track 'Peloton'), through hazy astro-prog ('ADHD'; 'Dojjan'), to weighty minimalist sprawl ('Kraftverk') while remaining phat and playful from beginning to end. There isn't a single dull moment across the album's seven tracks, which is a lot more than can be said about many veterans' revival efforts. By this time, Baby Grandmothers were certainly not spring chickens but, by golly, they could teach a thing or two to the plethora of younger so-called psych musicians who attempted to compensate for the lack of fire in their bellies with a touch of reverb and vintage-store-bought flares. As a comeback record, *Merkurius* was as delightful as watching Gene Wilder do his somersaulting grand entrance in *Willy Wonka and the Chocolate Factory*.

6

PUNK ROCK:
THE NON-HEAVY GENRE THAT
WAS VITAL FOR HEAVINESS

Johnny Rotten is no more: Public Image Ltd's *First Issue*.

Punk was like a brilliant flash that was over in an instant but it dazzled everybody who saw it, and it cast really long shadows. All of us were there being dazzled by it and we're all walking in the shadows that were burned into the pavement. Punk happened, it was done, and everybody who was influenced by punk carried on with their lives having been startled and changed by punk. Punk as an idiom, a style, a format for music is fucking trivial. At this stage, anyone whose conception of music is so stunted that they have to play in an idiom really doesn't warrant serious consideration. But you can have been inspired by the things that devolved into a simplistic, idiomatic form and retain that inspiration without mimicking that form.[1]

STEVE ALBINI (BIG BLACK, RAPEMAN, SHELLAC)

owards the end of the 1970s, a movement that would come to be known as punk rock arrived and made older musicians – even those who were not yet particularly aged – look suddenly very old hat indeed. With its scruffy fashions, raw production, unrefined musicianship and 'Year Zero' chutzpah, punk promised to wash away hippies; prog musicians; album-oriented rock; most artists beloved by the older generation, including even The Beatles; and the establishment in general, including the British monarchy.

It didn't manage to do that in the end, and it could be argued that punk was actually more traditional than its advocates liked to believe. The emphasis on quick songs that lasted three minutes or less was a return, of sorts, to the way ephemeral pop music had been written, recorded and released before the album format had started to dominate. Punk's all-important DIY attitude, which helped to fuel the rise of homemade fanzines, independent labels, makeshift venues and new bands, had similarities to the impetuses behind skiffle or folk. Still, if you were there to bear witness to the punk explosion, as Steve Albini informs us above, it promised to have a life-changing impact.

It's fair to say that few of the original punk groups were especially heavy. Particularly for those of us who weren't around to experience that watershed moment at first hand, the recordings left behind by the punk rock originators do not have much to offer in the heaviness stakes. They are usually too hastily paced, resting towards the trebly end of the spectrum, with production that's often woefully tinny. Stylistically speaking, the Ramones were a rapid, amphetamine-enhanced rechannelling of the Phil Spector blueprint. Blondie were a similar deal, becoming increasingly ABBA-like in their wedding-disco power-pop palatability. As the proggiest of the CBGB crew, Television had ambitious ideas, but their high-pitched spirals of lead guitar interplay, coupled with the yelped affectations of Tom Verlaine, left little room for the bottom end to flourish. As confrontational as Suicide's performances are reputed to have been, the duo's debut album of minimalist electro-punk sounds pretty flimsy to modern ears.

As for the British contingent, The Damned slotted neatly into the fast, tinny and trebly mould. Besides, they considered themselves to be an old-fashioned rock 'n' roll outfit. Specializing in songs of unrequited love and adolescent frustration, Buzzcocks crafted exemplary DIY pop singles. The rhythmic chugging and Stooges-derived scuzziness of Steve Jones's guitar riffs certainly had something to offer in the oomph aspect, captured as it was on *Never Mind the Bollocks, Here's the Sex Pistols* by none other than Chris Thomas, the man who had once produced 'Helter Skelter' in the absence of The Beatles' usual studio partner George Martin. Thomas had also worked with Pink Floyd – Sex Pistols' symbolic nemeses – but his selection was preferable, so said Johnny Rotten, to 'some heavy metal noise merchant producer'. The latter option, in Rotten's view, would have been a disaster. Earlier sessions with the Pistols' regular live engineer had been abandoned after the band grew impatient with Dave Goodman's obsessive multi-take quest to 'make the heaviest song that had ever been in the universe'.[2] Goodman's dismissal, along with the band's appointment of a bass player too incompetent to even play punk rock properly, demonstrates the Sex Pistols' lack of commitment to true heaviness.

Punk rock's indifference towards the weightier end of the sonic spectrum can be attributed to the scene's desperation to distance itself from the older generation of 'dinosaur' rock stars and prog show-offs who had been dominating the album charts and pages of the music press. In spite of this antithesis, the message that punk dispatched, transmitted and hammered home – that anybody of any social class with little-to-zero talent and/or experience of music-making could pick up a cheap instrument and make a worthwhile hullabaloo – has served to inspire countless musicians down the ages, especially when it comes to practitioners of heavy. For people like Steve Albini, punk rock as a movement offered a smorgasbord of ideas before punk rock as an idea – or ideal – became regrettably regimented and formulaic. The Ramones, for instance, sounded nothing like the Sex Pistols, who were hardly comparable to The Clash, who had little in common with Wire.

The diversity of punk also appealed to Melvins, whose drummer Dale Crover was exhilarated by the differences between various 'brilliantly weird bands', from the frenzied-then-sludgy hardcore crew Black Flag to the more countrified twang of Meat Puppets. To Crover, punk rock meant musical freedom. His Melvins colleague Buzz Osborne agreed, having always preferred the small venues where punk rock and other strange and gritty music thrives to the soulless stadiums, designed for the purposes of sports events, where the connection between band and audience is lost along with any sense of immediacy or intimacy. At the same time, Osborne was wary that those who identify as punk rockers can be a dull, unadventurous and narrow-minded bunch, often overly concerned with dismissing the value of music that doesn't fit into the idiomatic parameters that Albini dismisses above. The first time in his life that Osborne heard the Sex Pistols, he was reminded of Aerosmith and Ted Nugent.[3] Mention that comparison in a room full of card-carrying, mohican-sporting purist punks and it's likely to go down as well as a fart at a funeral.

Melvins are just one example. Countless are the musicians who, inspired by the do-it-yourself and free-spirited nature of punk rock, started out playing something approximating that same style before spiralling off into other directions, often with greater heaviness in their sights. Even after stumbling down this path, some groups have continued to identify as punk while sounding nothing what-soever like a punk band. Two of the more outré examples spring to mind. First, the Chicago band Pelican, who have insisted they are some sort of misunderstood punk band despite specializing in loud and lengthy instrumental compositions of a distinctly post-metal nature.[4] Similarly, the constantly evolving output of the cult London/Somerset crew Hey Colossus has spanned a broad stretch of the alt-rock palate. Before incorporating melody among their walls of riffs, Hey Colossus released a cluster of records that were dirtier and more nightmarish. Hey Colossus bassist Joe Thompson was more bemused than anybody to find his band being offered slots at lots of psych-rock festivals as soon as Hey Colossus' recordings were being issued by the reputable Rocket Recordings imprint. 'We never thought of ourselves as being a psych-rock band,' reflected Thompson. 'It hadn't even occurred to us. We thought we were punk rock.'[5] Most musicians believe their work to be entirely unique to them. As such, they tend to object when they are lumped into any kind of classification system. The fact that punk appears to be the category into which they are most willing to be slotted is very telling indeed.

More Bass, Greater Freedom, Fewer Clichés

If in its earliest incarnations punk rock was a little lightweight, harder offerings and an even bolder sense of adventure were to be found in its bastard offspring that we now refer to as post-punk. It's a slightly misleading definition, given that some bands that have been labelled post-punk actually pre-date other punk bands. Cabaret Voltaire and Devo, for example, had been active for almost half a decade before The Damned, The Clash and Sex Pistols all released debut albums in 1977. Other post-punk groups formed with punky intentions only for their interests, creativity and circumstances to lead them down a different musical path. Fitting examples of this process are the bands that formed in the wake of the Sex Pistols' concert at Manchester's Lesser Free Trade Hall in 1976. The audience included future members of The Fall, Joy Division and Simply Red. Clearly the possibilities were endless, but let's not dwell on Mick Hucknall. Steve Hanley and Marc Riley, both of whom would play in The Fall, nipped out for a bag of chips towards the end of this legendary gig, catching only the first and final couple of numbers by the raucous headlining act. It wasn't so much the breathtaking brilliance of the Sex Pistols that encouraged these impressionable northerners to get their hands on some budget equipment, form bands, and start rehearsing and gigging as soon as was feasible. The band's enigmatic frontman notwithstanding, the pair were struck most by the Pistols' lack of talent. 'Surely we don't need some scruffy Londoners coming here to make a racket and scream abuse at us', thought Hanley, 'when the chances are we can do that ourselves.'[6]

Hanley would go on to be the longest-serving member of The Fall apart from their tenacious and cantankerous lead singer Mark E. Smith, famed for his maxim 'If it's me and your granny on bongos, then it's a Fall gig.' In a 1983 interview with *Melody Maker*, Smith suffered a rare bout of appreciation towards one of his colleagues by singing the praises of the bloke whose bass playing and songwriting duties were so crucial to The Fall. 'The most original aspect of The Fall is Steve on bass', Smith admitted. 'I've never heard a bass player like him in my life. I don't have to tell him what to play, he just knows. He is The Fall sound.'[7] The bassists who played in The Fall after Hanley's departure in 1998 made their own vital contributions to the band's discography, not least Dave Spurr, who was a consistent member of the group from 2006 until Smith's death in 2018. Yet all those who followed him were deeply indebted to the work of Hanley. A defining feature of his band's best-loved tracks and the inimitable Fall sound in more general terms, Hanley's basslines were both muscular and tuneful, never superfluously extravagant, with tricksy flourishes that were made all the more exciting because they happened only infrequently. Hanley's bass kept the Fall sound grounded, holding everything together, and even provided much of the melody that could be otherwise lacking whether surrounded by scratchy guitar parts, cockeyed Casio keyboard notes, pounding drums, amateur dancefloor electronics or a disorderly combination thereof, plus Smith's barked, yelped, chanted, spoken, garbled or gargled lyrical rantings. Hanley's bass parts also adhered to 'the three Rs' as taught by krautrockers like Can and prescribed in Smith's words to a certain agenda-announcing B-side: 'Repetition! Repetition! Repetition!'

Bass was also key to fellow Greater Mancunians Joy Division. Where Hanley's bass parts were deeply resonant, Peter Hook enjoyed moving his fingers the full length of his instrument's neck to hit its higher octaves. Shifting between intricate note patterns like a lead guitarist or else using full rhythm-guitar-style chords, Hooky developed this technique after being unable to hear himself over the din of rehearsals and, by his own admission, possessing an ego that prevented him from standing meekly at the back of the stage. In light of the punk 'revolution', Hook was also eager to distance himself from the rock star bassists of yore.[8] He achieved this detachment in a visual sense by holding his bass not at the traditional chest or waist height but having it dangling nearer to his knees. Hooky's high and melodic bass notes acted as a suitable foil for Ian Curtis's baritone vocals and intensely miserable lyrics. The dominating presence of the bass also contrasted with the other instruments: the simplicity of Bernard Sumner's raspy guitar and Stephen Morris's mechanical drumming. It was a sound made all the more desolate by the spaciousness provided by the band's perfectionist producer Martin Hannett, who enjoyed forcing the best performances out of his musicians by toying with them psychologically, convincing them to record in freezing temperatures, and sending them home early so he was free to manipulate the material without any interference from the pesky musicians who'd performed it.[9] Coming from a punk rock background, Joy Division were appalled by what Hannett did to their debut album, *Unknown Pleasures* (1979). Compared to their lively gigs, it first felt to them that the recordings lacked energy. This contrast worked the other way round too. The writer, future Haçienda DJ and Black Sabbath fan Dave Haslam had found himself enchanted by *Unknown Pleasures*, in the way it seemed to invert punk energy, in the 'iciness' and 'Gothic grandeur' of Hannett's mix. After falling in love with this intriguing album, when the young fan got to see Joy Division perform, Haslam was confused to find 'the band were a slightly chaotic blurred noise and the sound was a bit rushed.'[10] Despite their qualms, Joy Division must have suspected that Hannett had captured something special, as they used his services again on their second and final album, *Closer*, released shortly after Curtis's suicide in 1980. In his history of post-punk, Simon Reynolds compares Black Sabbath's 'Paranoid' to 'Digital' (one of the first recordings undertaken by Joy Division), for it was a similarly 'full-tilt dirge fusing pace and ponderousness'. Thereafter Joy Division came into their own when decelerating the pace and offering an equally downturned philosophy to that of Sabbath, albeit one that had spikier corners than the metal forefathers' dense lumbering.[11]

Speaking of blurred sounds and slow tempos, there was a shared affinity between the punk rock scene and dub and reggae culture, as we have been reminded by no end of radio and television appearances by Don Letts. This kinship between the two might seem unlikely, given the wide disparity between each of those musical styles, not to mention the warmness of the dub sound in contrast to Joy Division's frosty atmospheres. But dub offered punk rockers the opportunity to enjoy various elements that were not, at first, present in their own musical endeavours. Pioneered by Jamaican producers including King Tubby, Lee 'Scratch' Perry, Keith Hudson and Errol Thompson, dub came about thanks to the advent of multi-track recording technology. It began as the money-spinning exercise of remixing reggae musicians' tracks for quick and cheap B-side purposes. Dub then grew into a distinctive genre in its own right, characterized by its stripping back of vocals as well as parts of the instrumentation to emphasize the drum and bass patterns – the 'riddim'. It made extensive use of reverb, echo and other effects to create hazy and atmospheric textures that swamped and swarmed around the riddim almost as if by chance. King Tubby had one particular trick up his sleeve, known as the 'thunderclap'. From around 1974, it became one of the trademark sounds in the producer's repertoire. To create it, Tubby would physically pound his reverb coil. The resulting crashing sound could appear louder or softer on the recording, depending on how hard and quickly the equipment had been struck. Rather than necessarily fitting in with the rhythmic pattern of the track on which it appeared, the thunderclap could erupt at any time, randomly it often seemed, as if to suddenly wake up any (possibly stoned) listeners from their stupor.[12]

As it was elsewhere, dub was introduced to the UK by Caribbean migrants, and it liberated punks from clear, concise and precise songwriting. These were ancient pop traditions that this supposedly revolutionary genre had been clinging to nevertheless. Dub showed punks that not everything had to be played at amphetamine-enhanced breakneck tempos. It introduced them to vaguer, cloudier and more abstract structures. It brought to their ears a denser and thicker sense of aural texture. Most necessary of all, it showed them the irresistible power of the bass. It also provided an excuse for punks to indulge in the Rastafari herbal sacrament, ganja, while enjoying a distinctly psychedelic form of music – pastimes that had once been treated with suspicion on account of their association with the older hippie generation.

The Pop Group and The Slits were two groups who eagerly acquired the services of dub producer Dennis Bovell. The Slits, in just a few short years, blossomed from trading in a raw, rapid and primal rumpus with a beginner's proficiency to completely transcending the fetters of punk by hosting improvisational events in alliance with free jazz practitioners including Don Cherry and Steve Beresford. With its striking and provocative cover on which the band posed topless in loincloths, The Slits' debut *Cut* (1979) is the album that has graced a thousand listicles purporting to count down the 'Greatest Punk Albums of All Time'. Continued neglect has been the fate of the band's second studio LP, *Return of the Giant Slits* (1981). It's reasonable to assume, in fact, that some owners of the first Slits record have never even heard of its follow-up. On that second LP, The Slits really brought the myriad of jazz, African, Jamaican and other global influences to the fore, along with distinctly improved musicianship and, more importantly, an even greater spirit of adventure. To conservative Western listeners and purist punks alike who had never tuned their ears into international music or the avant-garde, *Return of the Giant Slits* sounded disagreeably messy and devoid of catchy tunes. The media were bamboozled by it too. *Record Mirror*'s Chas de Whalley, even in an otherwise broadly complimentary review, was forced to admit that *Return of the Giant Slits* 'often taxes the brain and squeezes the mind to the point of exasperation'.[13] The album pre-dated the coining of the term 'world music' and fused wide-ranging global influences with Western rock traditions before Paul Simon and Peter Gabriel introduced poppier forms of this approach to stadium audiences. 'It doesn't have any boundaries anymore,' said Tanju Boerue, who managed the late Slits vocalist Ari Up's solo career. 'They found a way to destroy rock 'n' roll. It died the moment it was released. And that's the big tragedy, basically, about The Slits.'[14]

Similarly broad-minded were the Bristol-based outfit who, in an apparently non-ironic but also wholly inaccurate gesture, decided to call themselves The Pop Group. When the band formed in 1977, none of its members knew how to play music. This did not dampen their aspirations to strive for originality and, in doing so, gnaw away at the ever tightening straitjacket of punk. Singer Mark Stewart would arrive at band practice clutching records by Parliament and hip-hop forefathers The Last Poets. He would listen to things like 'East River' by the Brecker Brothers and ruminate on how such vibrant energy and powerful basslines could be injected into his own group's music.[15] Even Stewart himself found that The Pop Group's attempts to channel both Funkadelic and Television made it sound like they were playing three different songs at the same time; a cacophony made all the wilder because they hadn't yet learned how to play their instruments properly. Stewart decided to keep shtum about it though, seeing as writers like *Melody Maker*'s Richard Williams seemed so excited by what The Pop Group were doing.[16] Their debut album, *Y* (1979), is still remarkable for its formless, spooky and liberated feel, with Stewart howling away like a caged animal snarling in vain at the corpse of its own neglectful mother.

Whereas The Slits would pose as mud-covered Amazonians for the cover of *Cut*, The Pop Group simply lifted a Don McCullin photograph of Papua New Guinea tribespeople for the sleeve of *Y*. 'It fits with the kind of general feel,' Stewart tried to explain, with drummer Bruce Smith adding, 'We're doing everything with the same approach, if you can call it an approach.'[17] As for Bovell's spacious and echoing mix, 'It actually sounds like it was made in a cave,' noted the *NME*.[18] The same reviewer, Paul Rambali, also complained about the record's indecipherable lyrics. Yet it was on the band's next album, when every element became all the more fathomable, that The Pop Group went off the boil. As with so many follow-up albums, 1980's *For How Much Longer Do We Tolerate Mass Murder?* would have fared better if it had appeared out of the blue like its predecessor. Following the radically amorphous *Y*, Stewart had taken a tighter control of the reins. The singer felt the world was in crisis thanks to the election of Margaret Thatcher, events in Cambodia and other pressing sociopolitical concerns. This fuelled Stewart's desperation to produce politically conscious art that had a clear and positive purpose. It's an admirable reaction to the world's problems, albeit one that doesn't always produce the most satisfying artistic results. Stewart's agitprop stance became increasingly didactic, sanctimonious even. Whether you agree with the sentiment or not, phrases like 'Nixon and Kissinger should be tried for war crimes for the secret bombing of Cambodia' are perhaps better suited to placards than as serviceable song lyrics. The album ended with 'Rob a Bank', a flimsy reinterpretation of Carl Sigman's theme tune to *The Adventures of Robin Hood*. In reality The Pop Group were feeling less and less like Merry Men. Their former gang (or tribe) mentality had waned considerably. Consequently, the instrumentation suffered too. In contrast to The Slits, The Pop Group became stiffer and less distinctive the more they managed to master control of their instruments.

If Stewart liked to arrive at rehearsals clutching Funkadelic LPs, Manchester's A Certain Ratio were no strangers to George Clinton's output either. They attempted to demonstrate this affection for Parliament and Funkadelic in their own music, even if it didn't come out in quite the right way. Unlike Throbbing Gristle, whose 1979 album was titled *20 Jazz Funk Greats* in order to trick unsuspecting members of the public into buying an album they wouldn't actually enjoy, A Certain Ratio were engaged in a sincere attempt to play jazz and funk. As their guitarist and trumpeter Martin Moscrop admitted, they just didn't have the musicianship to pull it off.[19] The results sounded all wrong and wonky – especially during the band's first year of activity, when they were bold enough to perform without a drummer – but their efforts were not without merit. Even after a drummer was recruited, Martin Hannett, producer of the band's first couple of albums, played his own part in wringing the warmth out of any funkiness ACR may have possessed, just as he did when manipulating the sound of Joy Division.

An hour or so up the M62 from A Certain Ratio and Joy Division's base, Gang of Four were a band formed by hard-drinking, widely read and chess-playing art students from Leeds University.

In the summer of 1976, singer Jon King and guitarist Andy Gill had the good fortune to visit New York City, where they spent a month sleeping on the floor of Mary Harron, who they had never actually met prior to their arrival in the United States. Now a successful film-maker and screenwriter, back then this friend-of-a-friend wrote for *Punk* magazine. Frequenting CBGB and similar venues in the evenings, King and Gill got to see and hang out with the Ramones, Television, Patti Smith and other luminaries of the New York punk scene. The pair returned to the home of Tetley's Bitter and Waddingtons board games with their heads brimming with ideas, spurred on by the thought that if those guys and gals in NYC could do it, then they could too. A rhythm section was sought out quickly. Not only did Hugo Burnham have his own drum kit, he also owned a transit van. This was such a precious find that King and Gill felt able to overlook Burnham's love of Queen and Elton John. They found one bass player who didn't assimilate very well with the others because, as Gill put it, 'he kept improvising, playing too many notes, so we found somebody else, who turned out to be Dave Allen.'[20] Even when Allen arrived, he was encouraged to play one bass note where he would usually be inclined to hit four. To the other members' love of the austere and jerky energy of Dr Feelgood, Allen brought the desire to play music that was 'like Stevie Wonder but heavy'.[21] Much of Gang of Four's heaviness, then, came from Allen's dominant bass tone. For his own part, Gill's choppy guitar work was heavy in an almost anti-rock respect. He reviled the idea of thickening his sound with distortion and other effects, choosing instead to concentrate on inventive rhythmic precision. He wanted an icy brittleness to seep out of the amplifiers, nothing that sounded fat or warm. The thought of playing guitar solos being another repulsive idea, the band instead wrote 'anti-solos' into their songs whereby Gill would simply stop playing for a few bars. With Gang of Four, every aspect of their compositions was calculated and analysed scrupulously. Nothing was jammed out. Bass, drums, guitars and voices were all considered equal and given the space to breathe while slotting together as one whole multi-angled unit. Despite the desire to avoid distortion and freestyling, Gill was a dab hand in the way he employed feedback and free-form noise, which were used to wash across the aural canvas like the thick smears of a Jackson Pollock brushstroke.

As you'd expect from their yearning to distance themselves from obvious and traditional rock practices, Gang of Four were similarly determined to avoid lyrical cliché. They may have had a guilty penchant for listening to the meat-and-potatoes hard rock records that Free had made in the 1970s, but Gang of Four were loath to write any boring songs about sexy babes with so much love to give. No, Gang of Four came up with songs like 'Damaged Goods', which considered the economic and financial constraints that push people into making certain decisions and thereby trudging down a particular path, even in terms of sex, love and relationships. This cynicism continued in 'Contract', its lyrics also exploring the transactional nature of all romance. Another track compared falling in love to being infected with anthrax. Elsewhere on their 1979 debut album *Entertainment!*, Gang of Four explored and often critiqued themes including the Troubles in Northern Ireland, the flawed 'great man' theory of history and the threat of nuclear war. In spite of their inflammatorily political name and post-Marxist credentials, there was an obliqueness to Gang of Four's material that distinguished it from the more heavy-handed nature of The Pop Group's second album. The lyrics asked listeners to question the cultural hegemony and to consider looking at life and society from a different variety of possible angles. Gang of Four avoided telling anybody outright exactly what they should think or do about any specific socio-political issue. They were subtler and cleverer than that.

There is a pleasing sense of reciprocality in that, having initially found the impetus to make a go of it thanks to that watershed trip to New York City, Gang of Four ended up influencing a whole host of American artists in turn, including hugely successful ones. REM is one example. Formed in Athens, Georgia, the band would eventually blossom into multi-platinum superstars. Earlier in their career, REM opened for Gang of Four on a few tours. Singer Michael Stipe has confessed to stealing several ideas from the band, including elements of their image, vocal phrasing and certain instrumental tricks.[22] An even greater debt is owed by fellow U.S. unit-shifters Red Hot Chili Peppers. According to Gill, the Chilis would freely admit to having based their entire career on Gang of Four, and Flea from the band couldn't understand why they'd never been sued.[23] Such was their devotion to Gang of Four that the Chilis hired Andy Gill to produce their 1984 debut album, although relations between hero and disciples would end up fraught. Chilis singer Anthony Kiedis was crushed – and consequently out for revenge – after glancing at Gill's notebook one day and discovering that, next to the song 'Police Helicopter', the producer had written the word 'shit'.[24] Gill had a point. The Californian funk rockers may have been fans of Gill's, but they ended up reinserting into the music several elements that Gang of Four had made it their mission to remove. Of Gang of Four's determination to eradicate the idiocy and sexism that have often blemished rock 'n' roll, Simon Reynolds has defined their approach as 'a sort of checked and inhibited hard rock: cock rock castrated, the cock lopped off'.[25] Red Hot Chili Peppers, on the other hand, are easily one of the most phallocentric bands there has ever been. They display priapic solos aplenty, stuff about a thousand old-school rock clichés into the space of a single performance, and have sung about their two principal lyrical concerns on so many occasions they even resorted to inventing their own portmanteau: Californication.

'Something can appear funky with none of the constituent elements being in and of themselves egregiously funky,' explains *Entertainment!* enthusiast Andrew Falkous. His whole house-hold, including even his pet cats, are said to be allergic to Red Hot

Chili Peppers. 'The funk element of Gang of Four is to do with a groove about the way the music all fits together as opposed to, in effect, screaming "FUNKY, AREN'T I? FUNKY, AREN'T I?" the whole fucking time like a guy who literally cannot keep his pants on.' The pursuit of this collective groove is one of many factors that has made Falkous's music with Mclusky and Future of the Left so satisfying. Aside from Red Hot Chili Peppers, other American aco-lytes of Gang of Four have included Fugazi (who the Chilis also admire but, again, fail to emulate successfully), Minutemen, Big Black, Helmet and Rage Against the Machine. As Falkous insists, 'If you play guitar in anything approaching an alternative rock band and you don't like *Entertainment!* by Gang of Four then I suggest you've probably got issues and not any of them good issues you can monetize.'[26]

Death Disco

Uglier, odder and heavier still than the post-punk endeavours mentioned above was Public Image Ltd's *Metal Box* (1979). Ironically, this album was influenced by an additional genre that was generally judged to be lighter and cheesier than funk, dub and jazz, namely disco, which even some of the other most open-minded post-punkers tended to shun because it was considered to be frivolously ephemeral and lacking in emotional depth. In an uncommon but apt observation, David Stubbs compares the relationship between Jah Wobble's rumbling basslines and Keith Levene's jagged guitar work to that of Bernard Edwards and Nile Rodgers from Chic. The difference being that PiL focused on mostly miserable subject-matter rather than celebrating the good times. Originally titled 'Death Disco', *Metal Box*'s 'Swan Lake' was about singer John Lydon's mother dying of cancer. 'Poptones' was inspired by news reports of a young girl's kidnapping. This was funk inverted, argues Stubbs. 'That's not to say that funk in PiL was merely used as an ironic counterpoint,' he adds; 'it was part of post-punk's necessary progress from monochrome to colourisation, a broadening of the palette of expression.'[27]

Despite their soft spot for all things disco, PiL were the most brazenly unlistenable post-punk band of the lot. They were also the one that earned the widest attention and therefore had the most impact, thanks to the fame and notoriety of their frontman, the ex-Sex Pistol John Lydon. The singer's next group benefited from the indulgent support of Virgin Records, who were under the impression they'd acquired a goldmine when contracting punk's brightest star. What actually transpired was that Virgin ended up bankrolling some of the most experimental mass-produced art of the era. After the Pistols' fiery split, and no doubt reeling from the mistake of having shoehorned the incompetent and self-destructive Sid Vicious into the band's line-up, Lydon wanted the bass to play a prominent and central role in his next project, formed with fellow self-confessed 'dub fanatics' Jah Wobble and Keith Levene.[28] Initially trumpeting themselves as a communications corporation rather than boring old band, PiL wanted even less to do with yester-year's punk and rock traditions than Gang of Four ever did. When asked by TV interviewer Tom Snyder why Public Image Ltd were quite so averse to the idea of rock 'n' roll, Lydon replied in a typically brusque manner and in that authoritatively flabbergasted tone of his that always suggests his own personal opinion should be patently obvious to all and sundry and he can't understand why on earth it isn't. Rock 'n' roll?

> It's dead. It's a disease. It's a plague. It's been going on for too long. It's history. It's vile. It's not achieving anything. It's just aggression. They play rock 'n' roll at airports. That's about as advanced as it can possibly get. It's too limited. It is too much like structure, a church, a religion, a farce.

If everything had gone according to plan, Lydon posited, Sex Pistols would have destroyed rock 'n' roll for good. 'Unfortunately the majority of the public, being the senile animals that they are, got that wrong. Too bad,' he sighed.[29]

By this time, Lydon had come to the conclusion that punk rock had been a false alarm. It had fallen rapidly and ignorantly into line, becoming rigid and authoritarian, with various members of its ranks dictating that punk rock had to be carried out in one strict manner and no other. In response to this stiffening of the form, Lydon now claimed that he had always believed that music should include all kinds of ideas and attitudes: 'All are tolerable. It becomes *intolerable* when one particular form takes over and obliterates the rest. That is wrong.' Lydon had decided that punk had not overthrown the old order by opening the doors for change. 'The pathetic conclusion of that movement was one load of arseholes were replaced by another load. Nothing was achieved.'[30]

Lydon was still in his early twenties when *Metal Box* came out. By that time in his life, he had experienced an unenviable and unusual amount of mental trauma, and he approached *Metal Box* as an exercise in catharsis. Lydon had survived a childhood of poverty and illness, going on to become the British tabloids' public enemy number one when barely out of his teens. To make matters worse, his virulent punk band had been exploited at the hands of their manipulative manager, Malcolm McLaren. Since that wild rollercoaster ride had derailed, the recording of *Metal Box* took place shortly after the deaths of both Lydon's beloved mother and his old pal Sid Vicious. Lydon was also recovering from the acrimony that PiL's early activities and debut album (1978's *First Issue*) had attracted from purist punks as well as the critics who seemed eager to knock the precocious Johnny down a peg a two. Although PiL were desperate to be accepted as a collective, the figurative spotlight remained squarely on their lead singer. Mentioning no other PiL members by name, *NME*'s Nick Kent bemoaned Lydon's 'flaky' words and 'plain weedy voice' while Peter Silverton of *Sounds* deemed *First Issue* to be 'arrogantly thin', with Lydon (still referred to throughout the review as 'Johnny Rotten') fulfilling his role as 'the undisputed king of Sixth Form Poetry'.[31] Granted, *First Issue* did conclude with an eight-minute repetitive mock-disco dirge called 'Fodderstompf', its lyrics appearing to non-ironically disclose the lack of thought and effort that had been put into that song in particular, and perhaps even the album as a whole. As Simon Reynolds notes, on first listen the track might seem like PiL are taking the Mickey, but Wobble's deeply trembling funk-dub bassline, the backing track's eerie electro gurgles, its loud and dominant snare sound and the sheer extremity of it all actually pointed towards the follow-up album that would turn out to be PiL's masterpiece.[32] When that second album emerged less than a year after the debut, so alien was its sound that the PiL fan and future art historian Andrew Graham-Dixon couldn't have been the only person to have had a profound experience when first listening to it, without realizing he had *Metal Box* rotating at the wrong speed on the record player.[33]

The cartoonishly belligerent Johnny Rotten persona had always been a mask, one that barely served to conceal Lydon's true personality: he was a sensitive soul who had frequently found himself backed into the corner by friends, enemies and wolves in sheep's clothing, and felt compelled to lash out and spit back. On *Metal Box*'s 'Albatross', Rotten/Lydon seeks to cast out his traumatic past, even though in his heart he knows he can never escape it. Across ten minutes of metallic guitar licks and dubby rhythms, the track's improvised lyrics channel Samuel Taylor Coleridge's *The Rime of the Ancient Mariner* as Lydon repeatedly insists that he is ridding himself of his albatross. As we all know, even when the albatross does drop from around the mariner's neck, Coleridge's character cannot truly escape his past and is compelled to wander the earth for the rest of his life, endlessly repeating his story to strangers. 'Albatross' is usually referred to as *Metal Box*'s opening number, and it's an effective, powerful and defining one at that. In fact, the album was a set comprising three 12-inch records (with a 45 rpm speed to secure a superior bass sound) that were intended to be played in any order the listener fancied. The records were concealed within a metal canister, based on a 16 mm film container. This was heavy music, musically, emotionally and even physically.

In their early interviews Public Image Ltd made bold claims that they would not resort to the tacky, old-fashioned and exhausted rock 'n' roll habit of actually touring. Instead they wanted to concentrate on beavering away in the studio and transition into film-based projects. These were noticeably Beatles-ish tactics, it has to be said, although Lydon would have baulked at such a comparison. In April 1980 PiL went back on their word by setting sail for a string of American dates. Lydon would continue, just like Coleridge's mariner, to wander the earth with his curse. A relocation to Los Angeles in the early 1980s signalled the end of PiL's vitality. Wobble had already left the group before 1981's *The Flowers of Romance*, a sparse and uncanny record on which the drums were awarded unusual prominence. Heavy despite its audacious lack of guitars, the album was derided at the time as lazily tossed off, but it has proved a much-admired reference point for later bands, such as the forward-thinking and sorely underappreciated Liars. Following Wobble's departure, Keith Levene didn't hang around much longer either, leaving Lydon to persevere with a rotating cast of proficient session musicians. A mooted title for their – or his – next studio outing was *You Are Now Entering a Commercial Zone*. This was not an ironic gesture, given the production polish and unashamed radio-baiting that was to follow.

Goth, Hardcore and More

As elder statesmen surrendered to commercial pressures and allowed themselves to be lured into profitable fads, a younger generation of musicians occupied themselves with shifting the mood from dark and jerky post-punk-funk abstraction to cleanly chart-focused pop music. They included ABC, Haircut 100 and Spandau Ballet. These acts exploited the lucrative possibilities of mixing white and black music, notes David Stubbs, 'usually by dint of having frontmen with big, epic voices and dispensing with A Certain Ratio's shroud of gloom'.[34] Mind you, ACR were not above attempting the same feat themselves. With its smooth saxophone parts, 1990's soulful 'I Won't Stop Loving You' scrambled up to number 55 in the singles chart, assisted by its big-name remixes courtesy of Bernard Sumner and Norman Cook.

Public Image Ltd had finally deteriorated into the John Lydon Fancy Pad Mortgage Repayment Show. Joy Division's ex-members regrouped as New Order and soon began trading in dancefloor-suited pop. Big-voiced ABC singer Martin Fry was busy thrusting his gold-lamé-clad thighs all over the stages of *Top of the Pops*. It's little wonder that so many misfits, outcasts and freaks shrank away from the bright lights of pop and into the welcoming shadows of the goth scene. Here could be found the atmospheric rattling of Siouxsie & the Banshees, the intense rhythms and arch melodrama of Bauhaus, the swaggering catacomb cacophonies of Sex Gang Children, the authoritative moodiness of Sisters of Mercy and the deceptively archly crafted chaos of Australian expats The Birthday Party. 'I'd hate to go down in history as the number one Goth,' The Birthday Party's singer, Nick Cave, would declare, 'the man who spawned a thousand Goth bands with stacked hairstyles, no personality, pale sick people.'[35]

If punks like Garry Mulholland, who we met in Chapter Two, felt they could enjoy Black Sabbath only clandestinely, post-punks could be more accommodating. Goth had the advantage of being an unholy marriage of all three persuasions. Siouxsie Sioux had played an active part in the punk scene. Beaten up in 1976 for sporting a provocative swastika armband, she also accompanied Sex Pistols on their infamous Bill Grundy interview for Thames Television. Other goths like Ian Astbury of Southern Death Cult (and later The Cult), considered themselves the younger siblings of the punk rock originators and hoped to fuse the energy of that movement with the elegant intensity of Joy Division or Echo & the Bunnymen. Like Nick Cave, Astbury tried to reject the term 'goth', deeming it to be 'crap'. He preferred the American alternative, 'death rock', which he considered to be more 'romantic'.[36]

Be it goth rock or death rock, this scene would also slide into the kind of regimentation that Cave, like Lydon before him, was trying to avoid. Many in its ranks would resort to style – consisting of sensational fashion statements and hammy theatrical gestures – over substance. Much goth music was dark, yes, and spooky in a Tim Burton kind of way, but it was not especially heavy, and certainly not heavy in comparison to Black Sabbath. Most commercially successful of the bunch were The Cure, who remained faithful to the black eyeliner and spidery haircuts while simultaneously transcending the limitations of the genre with which they'd been aligned. In the 1980s leader Robert Smith found motivation in his unwavering hatred of those he perceived to be the enemy, specifically the yacht-bothering New Romantics Duran Duran.[37] This helped fuel and focus Smith's unrivalled ability to craft both soporific, protracted dirges alongside three-minute love ditties of such broad appeal that his band could casually breach the Top 10 and secure invitations to headline huge festivals for the rest of his days.

Heavier forms of punk could also be found in the hardcore movements. Made up of disenchanted musicians who were often still in their teens and eager for a vessel through which they could channel their adolescent rage, energy and frustration with the world, American hardcore groups reacted to many of the musical missteps of the era, including those mentioned above, by striving to produce faster, harsher, rawer, more aggressive and shoutier punk rock material than had ever been fashioned before. Two of the most prominent exponents were California's Black Flag and Washington DC's Minor Threat. Members of each group formed their own independent labels – SST and Dischord, respectively – to spread their own music and messages as well as those of like-minded bands from the underground. Just as post-punks turned their backs on the limitations of punk, both of these bands would outgrow the formulaic and restrictive nature of the hardcore blueprint. Black Flag would dig down into painfully slow Sabbathian sludginess while adding passages of spoken word, moments of amateur jazz and lyrical investigations of solipsistic self-hatred. Minor Threat, on the other hand, split after one LP as the band grew weary of the violence that tended to break out at hardcore shows. The scene had experienced an influx of thugs who were far more interested in hitting each other and causing a ruckus than actually enjoying any of the music on offer. It has also been noted that, at this time, the other members of Minor Threat had become besotted with U2 and were keen to push their own music into similar planes, a direction that singer Ian MacKaye could not countenance.[38] MacKaye himself would move into more melodic and progressive territory with the marvellous post-hardcore band Fugazi while continuing to avoid anything remotely comparable to Dublin's finest.

In Britain a variety of terms were coined for the heavier forms of punk that were attempted to varying degrees of success: street punk, UK hardcore, D-beat, Oi!, UK82. Much of this was image-based, reliant on slogans and even more narrow-minded than the original punk scene. UK82 was derived from a song title by a mohawk-sporting Edinburgh band. The Exploited's other boneheaded tracks included 'Punks Not Dead', 'Exploited Barmy Army', 'Son of a Copper', 'I Believe in Anarchy' and 'Sid Vicious was Innocent'.

Similarly at odds with British conservatism but shrewder in their endeavours and far more articulate – and convincing – in their political and social complaints were Crass. If Sex Pistols had proselytized 'anarchy in the UK' with debatable sincerity, Crass actually lived it because they were based in an anarchist commune in Epping Forest, Essex. Formed in 1977, Crass promised to split in 1984, and sticking to this time limit fuelled their urgency and sense of purpose. The racket they made was a winning combination in that it was precise and pointed in many respects yet at the same scrappily and hectically rendered. In contest to some of the undesirables who infiltrated the hardcore scenes, at this anarcho-crusty end of punk, macho attitudes and masculine posturing were very much frowned upon. Crass were a unisex band of committed feminists and on 1981's *Penis Envy* the band's female members provided all the vocals for an album that delved deep into the themes of sexism, repression and inequality.

This anarcho-punk scene helped birth grindcore, spearheaded by bands like Napalm Death, whose own discomfort with displays of masculinity will be discussed in a later chapter. In the interim came the New Wave of British Heavy Metal. Much of this was ridiculous, not to mention noticeably lightweight on reflection, with the odd exception. Motörhead were associated with the movement, much to the irritation of their leader Ian 'Lemmy' Kilmister . . .

Motörhead

Shortly after Lemmy's death at the end of 2015, an online petition was started with the aim that one of four newly discovered elements on the periodic table be named 'Lemminium'. The elements were, as was thought to be appropriate, heavy metals. Duff McKagan from Guns N' Roses tweeted his support of the campaign, as did Earache Records, and even Professor Brian Cox from BBC2's *The Wonders of the Universe* and *The Science of Doctor Who* (and formerly

D:Ream). It was surely one of the least necessary petition campaigns in Internet history, at least until the UK's *Boaty McBoatface* debacle a few months later. Overlooking the fact that there are strict rules for naming new elements that are not likely to be amended on account of the sad demise of an important figure from the world of music, Lemmy would've hated having such an element named after him. He despised heavy metal and wanted nothing to do with it.

Lemmy had done stints in a few minor psychedelic rock bands, had roadied for Hendrix, and played a prominent role in the mighty Hawkwind before being kicked out in 1975 for preferring amphetamines and whisky over more conventional hippie drugs such as LSD and weed. Lemmy felt an affinity with punk rock, seeing it less as a fracturing moment than a much-needed, jump-starting jolt to the heart of rock 'n' roll. He saw punk as a continuation or revival of the unruly spirit of pioneers like Little Richard. Lemmy once attempted, albeit unsuccessfully, to teach Sid Vicious how to play the bass guitar. Lemmy loved rock 'n' roll and, until the day he died, his favourite band of all time remained The Beatles. Lucky enough to have seen The Fab Four in their Cavern Club days, Lemmy noted the Liverpudlians' sense of humour, the unusual guitars they wielded (Lennon's Rickenbacker, McCartney's violin-shaped bass, Harrison's Hofner Futurama), their working-class toughness and outright superiority to the 'mummy's boys' who were in The Rolling Stones. The Stones were far less original than The Beatles. They were also inferior songwriters and, in Lemmy's opinion, 'always shit on stage'.[39]

Lemmy conceived Motörhead as an English answer to MC5, and he always insisted that Motörhead were a rock 'n' roll band. It was to Lemmy's chagrin that he got lumped in with heavy metal (by casual observers and by Motörhead and metal connoisseurs alike). Lemmy felt his band shared nothing in common with NWOBHM bands like the operatic Judas Priest. Despite the longterm benefits of being associated with certain heavy metal groups, Lemmy stuck to his guns. The speed-metal musicians who held Motörhead in high regard were accused of placing too much emphasis on fast and fancy solos that were actually not all that difficult to play as they were merely reliant on classic guitar scales. The later nu-metal scene, in contrast, consisted of 'garage attendants with fucking gas masks on' who had come up with 'a riff but no song'.[40]

There are still those who refuse to accept Motörhead's lifelong refutation of heavy metal. In their history of heavy metal, Andrew O'Neill dismisses Lemmy's views as 'bullshit' and insists that the singer and bassist was wrong about his own band.[41] It's easy to understand the confusion because, on the surface, Motörhead's output shares some of the sonic characteristics of heavy metal, and the band were undeniably responsible for many of the genre's platitudes. Image-wise they dressed in biker gear or else, as on the cover of *Ace of Spades*, looked like a gang of Hell's Angels who had got a bit lost and wound up as mercenaries in the Wild West. Their name was printed in a hard, spiky font, complete with a disobediently unnecessary umlaut – an idea pilfered from Blue Öyster Cult and perpetuated afterwards by Mötley Crüe and others, not to mention Spiñal Tap. Motörhead had a very metal 'snaggletooth' mascot: a lupine skull with wild boar tusks, created by the artist Joe Petagno. The band clutched tightly to bottles of whisky and were unapologetic about their enthusiasm for accommodating women. Lemmy's lyrics often focused on subject-matter with distinctive heavy metal appeal, such as the hedonistic lifestyle of touring musicians and the more violent and bloody moments in human history. Thanks to Lemmy's growl, Phil Taylor's drumming innovations and riffs aplenty, Motörhead certainly had an influence on every metal band worth their salt.

And yet O'Neill is wrong. Motörhead were not a metal band. Despite the tendency to write songs about manly military matters, death, drugs and betrayal, Lemmy was averse to the superfluous nonsense that can blotch much that is offered by the metal world. There are few guitar solos described in Lemmy's autobiography. Those ones that are awarded a mention – the recordings of which Lemmy seemed proudest – are the most unorthodox in the discography. Eddie Clarke recorded his solo to '(We Are) The Road Crew' (1980) while supine on the studio floor, giggling his head off, with feedback flying everywhere because he was struggling to play the intended notes. That shambolic performance made the edit because it was so unusual. Clarke's solo for 'Capricorn' (1979), a song written over-night in the studio, was captured when the guitarist was tuning up his instrument and messing around with it prior (or so he thought) to properly recording his parts. When recording his improvised solo for 'Make 'Em Blind' from 1995's *Sacrifice*, Phil Campbell tripped over a couch halfway through, landing flat on his back. Lemmy loved this take so much, and again used it on the finished recording, because he thought Campbell's solo accidentally ended up sound-ing like it was running backwards. When Mikkey Dee joined the group, after prior membership of King Diamond and Don Dokken, it took him time to adjust to Motörhead's autoschediastic working methods. Dee was used to the meticulous planning and preparation of material before recording for lengthy periods in the studio in order to get everything just right. Motörhead, Dee would discover, simply hit the studio as hard, quickly and cheaply as they could before getting the hell out of there and back on the road in true biker, outlaw or pirate fashion.[42]

Originally a rhythm guitarist who had never picked up a bass before being asked to join Hawkwind, Lemmy had a healthy dis-regard for lead guitarists. He was wise to the debilitating dangers of perfectionism. As such, his band often sounded like they were about to fall off the rails in their rush to reach the end of any given song, to thrilling effect. Lemmy often played full chords on his bass, a hangover from his rhythm guitar days, but he also admired the lead guitar-style bass playing of The Who's John Entwistle. He shunned effects pedals, choosing to manipulate the settings of his

Marshall amplifiers to sound as loud as they could while hitting his bass strings as hard as possible. 'I hate it', Lemmy said, 'when I see a band and they're thumping along, the riff is great, and then the solo comes in and the riff dies because the guitar player has to play the solo.' When solos did crop up in Motörhead's work – whether they were played while falling over a sofa or not – Lemmy would up the ante on his bass, insert extra notes or chords, to keep that rumbling riff alive and maintain the thickness of sound throughout.[43] Most of all, Lemmy wanted his band to resemble an unstoppable unit, something dense and solid, not different individuals all fiddling around on solo instruments. 'I just see the wall,' he explained, 'I don't see the bricks on their own. I like it to sound like a band, like The Beatles always did.'[44]

Notwithstanding Lemmy's love of early rock 'n' roll, his insistence on the importance of 'the song', and the slightly stretched argument that his band had more in common with The Beatles than anyone in the metal canon, when it comes to Motörhead the riff is king and texture is key. As card-carrying speedfreaks, Motörhead were a lot faster than Black Sabbath but they shared much in terms of the sheer weight of their sound, the approaches they took and the criticisms they attracted, in their ability to appeal to punk rockers and metalheads alike, and to impact on many forms of heaviness beyond the narrow field of metal. Somewhat confusingly, when Ozzy Osbourne took it upon himself to rebuff his own heavy metal credentials, preferring to categorize Black Sabbath as a form of 'hard rock' that combined blues with jazz and added an extra dose of heaviness, the singer would insist that 'to me the ultimate heavy metal band, and one which has been so underrated[,] is Motörhead.'[45] There is no telling some people.

7
INDUSTRIAL ROCK

Ministry's *ΚΕΦΑΛΗΞΘ*, aka *Psalm 69: The Way to Succeed and the Way to Suck Eggs*.

I had already heard the first three Black Sabbath albums, but by the time they got to *Vol. 4* I was like, 'OK, this is the shiznit, man.' The first four or five Motörhead albums were over the top for me at the time, too. As soon as I heard that band I was like, 'Goddamn, I just wanna break into someone's apartment and steal their shit.' And that's why my pet dogs are named Ozzy and Lemmy.[1]

AL JOURGENSEN (MINISTRY)

Let's say you had discovered krautrock or other elements of the experimental European underground. You had been creatively aroused by the promises of punk and post-punk (or else you had already been knocking about and had therefore been able to manipulate punk's opportunities to your advantage). You were interested in the possibilities of mixing conventionally white and black music. You also saw the potential for broadening the palette of expression by amalgamating traditional 'organic' instrumentation with newer electronic technologies such as samplers and synthesizers. Crucially, you also wanted to maintain heaviness at all costs in order to avoid making anything that resembled 'Tears Are Not Enough' by ABC. What was a budding electric wizard to do? Industrial rock held an answer.

Very few bands have achieved the feat of erupting in popularity as their sound has become concurrently darker, odder and increasingly unsettling. Mainstream acceptance tends to demand the opposite trajectory. The hypothetical user's manual dictates that one should smooth off all the rough-and-ready edges to become a lighter, blander and more accessible affair; to fashion a product more fathomable, friendlier, more easy to market and slip into neat and tidy boxes. Achieve those objectives and before you know it your band could be on the lucrative arena circuit. But history throws up the occasional exception. Industrial rock, especially in its second phase, boasts more instances than most rival genres.

The pattern was started by none other than Depeche Mode. The group's early days involved photo shoots for which these polite suburban boys posed wearing genteel cricket whites. The band's earliest

Top of the Pops appearances saw Dave Gahan looking less like a rock star or pop singer than a sommelier trying to upsell a bottle of over-priced champers to a tableful of lunching stockbrokers. They were one of the many bands that arrived in the wake of punk but who found guitars passé and were more excited by the fresh-sounding pop music that could be made using keyboards and synthesizers. Their early single 'Just Can't Get Enough' (1981) suggested the blueprint provided by Kraftwerk had been suitably sanitized and repurposed for use as an enticing jingle in a kiddies' toy commercial.

Depeche Mode may have racked up the domestic hits early on, but globally speaking, enthusiasm was lacking. Reviewing Depeche Mode's debut album for *Rolling Stone*, David Fricke dismissed the Basildon posse as disposable riders of the ephemeral synth-pop fad. In terms of standing out, Depeche Mode possessed neither the tight hooks of The Human League nor the grandiose ambitions of Orchestral Manoeuvres in the Dark, nor the kinkier edge of Soft Cell. 'The revolution will not be synthesized,' concluded Fricke's rockist review, predicting this curiously English penchant for electronic pop music would last six months at best.[2]

At the end of 1981 founding member Vince Clarke quit Depeche Mode, to be replaced by Alan Wilder, at which point Martin Gore stepped up as chief songwriter. Already flirting with the idea of shunting the band in a darker direction and prone to dressing up in bondage gear, Gore experienced an epiphany when attending a concert by West Berlin ear terrorists Einstürzende Neubauten.

Along with acts like Cabaret Voltaire, Killing Joke and Throbbing Gristle, Einstürzende Neubauten were early pioneers of industrial rock. Although its etymology dates further back, industrial music as a term was laid claim to – or at least semi-popularized – by Throbbing Gristle and their Industrial Records imprint, founded in 1976. Pushing a greater number of literal and figurative buttons than most punk bands ever dared, Throbbing Gristle's live performances and recorded output were calculated to incite a reaction, be this more often than not a negative one. At times their actions could prove to be genuinely thought-provoking and disturbing, although their deliberately unpleasant artwork and lyrical obsessions with concentration camps, sexual abuse and serial killers hasn't aged particularly well. With deadpan vocals, found-sounds, samples and crudely played instruments all processed through a myriad of effects, the noise made by Throbbing Gristle may have been hypnotic if it wasn't so nausea-inducing. But then how else does one best treat song subjects as dark as the Moors murderers Ian Brady and Myra Hindley, as Throbbing Gristle did for eighteen unpleasant minutes on 'Very Friendly'? In fact, Throbbing Gristle's sparser and quieter songs, like the disturbingly creepy 'Persuasion', could sometimes prove more morbidly gripping than when the band were engaged in full-on aural and lyrical assaults.

For some, Throbbing Gristle were arch satirists whose fascination with humanity's worst excesses was used to expose and condemn the hypocritical mores of British conservatism. It hardly helps Throbbing Gristle's cause, however, that singer and de facto leader Genesis P-Orridge, for one, was also prone to actual horrible behaviour himself. In her account of their then romantic as well as musical partnership, Cosey Fanni Tutti has detailed P-Orridge's controlling behaviour, his cruelty and his violence.[3] Personally and creatively speaking, Throbbing Gristle was unsustainable. After their inevitable split, in 1981, Genesis P-Orridge and Peter Christopherson went on to form Psychic TV, with Christopherson subsequently leaving that project too in order to concentrate on Coil, in many circles the most highly regarded Gristle-related project of the lot. Their ex-bandmates Tutti and Chris Carter became Chris & Cosey. In 1988 Psychic TV performed at the London Astoria, billed under the rather desperate name of Throbbing Gristle Ltd. 'Take a step back, and it's just a berk with a pudding-cut farting around in a night club,' observed *Melody Maker*'s Ian Gittins. Taboos having been broken down in earlier times, P-Orridge's ability to incite shock and sensation had receded significantly.[4]

Like fellow drum machine-utilizing provocateurs Suicide, Cabaret Voltaire were knocking around before punk rock happened. Then, on account of their exploitation of electronic equipment for confrontational purposes, they were quickly labelled post-punk. Unlike Suicide, Cabaret Voltaire came not from the ever-hip avenues of New York City. They were from Sheffield, in the north of England. It was at that city's university that Cabaret Voltaire made their debut live performance on 13 May 1975, unwisely billed halfway through a disco night. Confronted by looped samples of steam hammers and aggressive clarinet parps, the crowd reacted by storming the stage and violently attacking the band.

In later years Cabaret Voltaire would complain if journalists arrived in the band's hometown when it happened to be raining because this pigeonholed and misrepresented the place as a dull and drizzly backwater. 'It's been sunny in Sheffield for days,' they informed *The Face*'s Paul Morley when he arrived to conduct an interview in 1981. It's easy to understand why Cabaret Voltaire acted so sensitively, and not just because they already had a reputation for prickly behaviour. The same writer had interviewed them a year prior, this time for an *NME* feature in which he'd noted the band's 'disconcertingly pronounced Yorkshire accents' and defined Sheffield as 'a grey place full of greyness'.[5] This was a bit rich coming from somebody who grew up in Stockport.

If the intermittently dreary weather was not an acknowledged influence on Cabaret Voltaire's sound, the racket they made was informed by Sheffield's many factories. Thinking back to his childhood, multi-instrumentalist Richard H. Kirk would recall lying in bed at night with the noises from the nearby steelworks clattering their way into a permanent position deep within in his psyche.[6] Kirk saw himself as the more 'pig-headed' member of the group, describing his bandmate Stephen Mallinder as potentially more inclined towards the idea of fame and success. (Fellow founding member Chris Watson left in 1981 for a steady job at Tyne Tees Television.) This dichotomy fostered a career that, much more so than Throbbing Gristle, would flirt with the idea of mainstream success, albeit without gaining full admittance to the glitzy green rooms. For his own part, Mallinder would boast that creating bland music was simply an infeasibility when it came to Cabaret Voltaire's agenda, and that if their performances ever became too slick it would be crucial to steer away from that by reinstating a fresh form of crudeness.[7] A little later, when promoting 1982's *2x45*, Cabaret Voltaire would speak of maintaining the same essential approach while conducting themselves with greater expertise and in a more successful way, without necessarily having to sell out. By this time, both Kirk and Mallinder fantasized about infiltrating *Top of the Pops*.[8] Together, they shrewdly navigated the leap from Rough Trade to Virgin, progressing their sound without diluting too much of the original spirit that had been dreamt up by these fans of William Burroughs, Dadaism, James Brown and the Baader-Meinhof Gang. Nevertheless, the light and cheesy funk of 1987's *CODE* for Parlophone was a step too far. By that point, the bland and slickness barriers had been breached. Even then, though, Cabaret Voltaire continued to have profound influence on a wide variety of sonic freaks, from metalheads to house DJs.

At around the same time, London's Killing Joke were also transmorphing into a funky synth-pop affair. Unlike Throbbing Gristle and Cabaret Voltaire, their punishing early work was fundamentally riff-driven, with singer Jaz Coleman's keyboards supplying creepy background atmospheres. His vocal style took the form of misanthropic chanting, with lyrics as stark as could be expected from a bloke who once addressed the audience at a Campaign for Nuclear Disarmament rally with these encouraging words: 'I hope you realize that your efforts today are all quite futile.'[9] Of all the people besotted by Killing Joke's oeuvre, one susceptible individual was

Justin Broadrick, a working-class boy growing up in multicultural Birmingham. Stoned from his passive inhalation of the weed being smoked by his reggae-loving, punk rock parents, the eleven-year-old Broadrick would wander up to his room where he would collapse on his bed and tune into the weird and wonderful world of the John Peel show. This exposed Broadrick's bleary mind to the abstract sounds of Einstürzende Neubauten and Killing Joke, among many other unusual artists. For Broadrick, the beauty of Killing Joke did not lie solely in their militant drumbeats, dirty basslines and discordant guitar serrations. The fact that Killing Joke included dub remixes on their EPs and singles was key to Broadrick's conception of Godflesh, who would become one of the quintessential industrial metal bands of all time.[10]

Two other notable acts of industrial's first wave came from even sunnier climes than Sheffield; the other side of the world, in fact. Both SPK and J. G. Thirlwell spent time living in London squats but had their origins in Australia. SPK was a project named after the German radical Marxist group the Sozialistisches Patientenkollektiv, although the band also used those same initials as shorthand for Surgical Penis Klinik, System Planning Korporation and other variations. Graeme Revell and Neil Hill conceived this act in 1978 while working together on a psychiatric ward at Callan Park Hospital in Sydney. Knowledge of this background may (or may not) have convinced listeners that SPK's shock-tactic approach possessed an air of authenticity that was lacking in less medically experienced, yet nonetheless likeminded, industrial acts. Recorded in London, SPK's debut album, 1981's *Information Overload Unit*, was an unholy mixture of hairdryer-like distortion, disturbing soundbites, primitive beats and general harsh noise. The following year's *Leichenschrei* was similarly abstract, if a touch more listenable and better produced. It was also even more potent, according to Edward Ka-Spel of Anglo-Dutch experimental rock band The Legendary Pink Dots. He felt that *Leichenschrei* was so good it could never be topped, arguing that industrial music as a whole should have ceased right there and then.[11] It didn't, of course, but perhaps SPK should have. By 1984's major label release *Machine Age Voodoo*, Revell had steered SPK into fairly cheesy synth-pop territory.

J. G. Thirlwell has recorded under a variety of aliases, the most famous being Foetus (with variations on that name including You've Got Foetus On Your Breath and Scraping Foetus Off The Wheel). In 1978 he moved to London from Melbourne, Australia. Growing up he had never felt truly at home. For one thing, Thirlwell hadn't been able to get his head around the fact that people in his native country hosted sun-drenched barbeques at Christmas time.[12] Before relocating again (to New York in 1986), it was in England where Thirlwell established his reputation. Housed in eye-grabbing sleeves that parodied totalitarian propaganda, capitalist advertisements and Pop-art posters, Foetus albums boasted a clanking and clattering mixture of layered sounds, many of which appeared to have been made through the vicious mistreatment of scrap iron. Complementing this were Thirlwell's screamed lyrics, packed with macabre humour, grotesque imagery and other angst-ridden provocations. 'Death metal groups would have sold their souls to sound this evil,' as Glenn Law put it in *The Rough Guide to Rock* when assessing 1984's *HOLE*.[13] Foetus's sound had its clownish aspects too, prone as it was to segue into circus music, noirish jazz or the *Batman* theme at amusingly unexpected moments. As well as making a name for himself (albeit as a relatively marginal figure in the grand scheme of things), Thirlwell helped Einstürzende Neubauten gain traction outside of their own country. When he negotiated a deal with Some Bizarre, Thirlwell demanded the label also release the material of Neubauten.[14]

Although Blixa Bargeld formed Einstürzende Neubauten in 1980 on little more than a whim, the group has enjoyed a long and varied career, with far-reaching resonance. As indicated by their name, which translates as 'collapsing/imploding new buildings',

Einstürzende Neubauten's iconoclastic outlook was inherited from the slightly older generation of krautrockers, who had been determined to break free from restrictive traditions and forge bold new paths in the field of loud 'rock' music. Complementing their interest in guitar drones and piercing feedback, Bargeld's band inherited Faust's enthusiasm for making music using power tools, construction materials, various other bits of metal and machinery, and similar 'found' and self-made objects. ('Found', by the way, often meant they had been criminally raided from building sites located near where the band happened to be rehearsing or were due to perform.) Over the resultant clattering, repetitive racket, lyrics were screamed and chanted. These tended to focus on decay, disease, destruction and other dismal topics beginning with 'd'. Despite such gloomy predilections, Bargeld often sounded more like a charismatic mad professor than a mass murderer, and the band's confrontational approach obscured an underlying wry wit and anarchic sense of dark humour. Even at its most aggressive and supposedly unlistenable, Einstürzende Neubauten's output always contained an elusive humane warmth. It is this aspect in particular that so many of their shoddy industrial imitators have lacked.

In January 1984 members of Einstürzende Neubauten hosted a *Concerto for Voice and Machinery* at London's ICA. The event also featured Genesis P-Orridge of Throbbing Gristle and Frank 'Fad Gadget' Tovey. Neubauten had already been banned from numerous locations for using fire in their performances and applying drills to the walls of concert venues. This particular event, it was decided, should culminate in an envisioned 'utopian' attempt to leave the stage by digging down into London's underground wartime tunnels. 'I think the ICA probably started to realise something was afoot when a cement mixer was set up on stage, alongside electric drills and jackhammers,' recalled Neubauten's Alexander Hacke. 'There was a piano, too,' he noted, 'but that would be smashed to pieces.' Hacke's job was to hurl milk bottles into the cement mixer, the shards from which flew out into the crowd. The audience soon joined in the ruckus by fighting over the drills and sledgehammers and helping to tear the building apart. After about twenty minutes, venue officials cut the power. Several attendees continued banging away with whatever they happened to be clasping. The stage now had a big hole in it, although nobody made it through to the subterranean passageways that were rumoured to lead to Buckingham Palace. Hacke remembered the performance as sounding 'like a cross between a building site and war'.[15]

Following his exposure to antics such as these, Depeche Mode's Martin Gore strove to lift the brute power and experimental tendencies of Einstürzende Neubauten and inject these into the unlikely context of pop music. Over the course of their subsequent records, Depeche Mode became a far darker and heavier affair than before, in terms of their sonics, lyrical subjects and image, with certain band members' lifestyles following suit. Overseen by Anton Corbijn, Depeche Mode's promotional videos, record sleeves and stage sets became considerably more gothic. Matching the moodiness expressed elsewhere, Gahan's voice grew steadily deeper as his haunted baritone began to personify Gore's lyrical ruminations on sin, sex, submission and sadomasochism. Having abandoned his wine-waiter outfits and woolly sports jumpers, Gahan devolved into a leather-clad gremlin-like figure with a pierced perineum and a serious heroin habit. At one point his lifestyle spiralled so low that Hollywood paramedics nicknamed him 'The Cat' on account of his regular brushes with the grim reaper.[16]

Rather than being repelled by all this, mass audiences were entranced. At the end of the 1980s, Depeche Mode were playing similar sized arenas to those of U2. Unlike Bono and Co., Basildon's finest hadn't risen to that position by polishing up their sound in order to appeal to as broad a demographic as humanly possible, or by making a Faustian pact with their manager.[17] Depeche Mode didn't even have an official manager until the belated 1994 appointment of

Jonathan Kessler, an accountant from their 1986 Black Celebration Tour who'd steadily taken on extra responsibilities, at one stage having been credited as 'spiritual adviser'. Kessler attributes Depeche Mode's success to its members' creativity, the friction between their different personalities, and the whole team's continued desire to strive towards freshness while maintaining integrity.[18]

Depeche Mode and U2's differing approaches to securing longevity can be appreciated by comparing two of their later comeback singles: 'Barrel of a Gun' and 'Discothèque' (respectively), both released on the same day in February 1997. Depeche Mode's offering had a lubricious guitar sound that blurred the lines between gothic and funky. There were icy beats, creepy scratches and weird bass throbs. Sounding somehow even deeper and more anguished than ever before, Gahan crooned about self-loathing and self-destruction amid the quietly orgasmic hum of the backing vocals. In terms of songwriting this was still classic Depeche Mode in a certain sense, yet the sonics had been refreshed and updated for the late 1990s with a respect for newfound technologies and an ear to the industrial bands Depeche Mode had influenced. 'Discothèque', on the other hand, saw U2 applying the most obvious drum loops and ham-fisted electronic effects to something that, in essence, could have been any old U2 number. If one single was a cooler older sibling with an expertise in earlier music but still deeply fascinated by the latest crazes, the other – however ironic or knowingly – was an awkward supply teacher trying to make himself look down with the kids by using inappropriate slang and references to, well, discotheques.

How to Build a Maniac Douchebag

'We're like Depeche Mode's evil twin,' boasted Ministry's Al Jourgensen in 1989.[19] This may well have been the case by that stage in his unconventional career. Back when the first Ministry album was created, Jourgensen's project was more like Depeche Mode's polite younger cousin. Jourgensen has disowned 1983's *With Sympathy* and now refuses even to utter its title. His account of the album has altered over the years in a sometimes contradictory fashion, but one version goes something like this. In his early twenties Jourgensen signed to the Arista label, who promised they would transform Ministry into the next Joy Division. The resulting Anglophilic synth-pop album was crafted mostly by producers and assistant record company goons. Jourgensen went along with this process of manipulation, relinquishing his creative control because he was young, gullible and blinkered by the enticing prospect of a career in music. He later denied having anything to do with the album besides his picture and name appearing on the sleeve, while conceding that it had in fact been his voice doing the singing. The label had given Jourgensen a fancy haircut and entirely new wardrobe, allegedly assigning him the lyrics as well (which are sung by the Cuban-American in an affected English accent). 'I was literally a product of the old-school star-making machine,' Jourgensen claimed in 2016, sounding like somebody who'd survived a stint in a boy band or had once been a child actor before going completely off the rails. 'It was revolting, disgusting and it traumatised me for years. Actually, I think without that record I wouldn't be as much of a fucking maniac douchebag as I am today. I completely rebelled against it . . . I fucking hated myself, the world, and everything around me because of that record.'[20]

Conflicting accounts suggest Arista's control was gentler and Jourgensen more consensual to the commercial sound of Ministry's debut.[21] Whether or not Jourgensen has exaggerated the story in an attempt to erase the embarrassing black sheep from his discography and to buttress the credibility of his later work, he was angry enough to sue Arista for taking advantage and, in terms of blossoming into that self-confessed maniac douchebag, never looked back. Because Ministry had sold out at the very start of their career, before knowing any better and prior to establishing a firmer identity for themselves, the incident taught Jourgensen to circumvent all compromise thereafter. With first-hand experience, he knew the grass wasn't greener on the other side and was fully aware that creative concessions led only to superficial short-term gains accompanied by a bucket load of regret and wretched self-loathing.[22]

So what did Mr Maniac Douchebag do next? Over the course of their next four albums, Ministry became a melting pot of malevolent industrial noise. Its ingredients included elements of dub, disco, Belgian hardbeat, hardcore punk, post-punk and thrash metal, often peppered with imaginative use of samples with a debt to hip-hop production teams. In kindred spirit with most of our other heavy innovators, Jourgensen was no virtuoso. Despite being a multi-talented musician who has tried his hand at guitar, violin, banjo, keyboards and saxophone, he proudly claims to have mastered none of these instruments.[23] After years of having not even touched the guitar in favour of fiddling with keyboards, he conceived thrash riffs for Ministry that consisted of simple power chords played in a jackhammer speed and fashion. 'All feel, no technique', he called it.[24] In Jourgensen's view, his true talent lay in the cutting and splicing of different elements to create an exciting new range of overwhelming sound collages. This compositional breakthrough occurred during the making of 1988's *The Land of Rape and Honey* and was inspired by the cut-up technique that Brion Gysin had introduced to William Burroughs, who then took to it with gusto for the composition of *Naked Lunch* (1959) and subsequent experimental novels. Before the ready availability of digital editing technology, this method of music-making was a painstaking as well as literally painful process in the course of which Jourgensen had to draw marks on physical reel-to-reel tapes, slice the tape into sections of equal sizes and reassemble them by hand. Fuelled by acid, heroin and cocaine, these mammoth editing sessions could last up to fourteen hours and by the end of each one Jourgensen's hands would be riddled with accidental razor cuts.[25]

Alongside counterculture icon Timothy Leary, with whom Jourgensen cohabited for two years as both a friend and a drug-research guinea pig, Burroughs was another hero and mentor to Jourgensen. Ministry were invited to Burroughs' home when seeking permission to use a spoken-word sample of the author for the 1992 single 'Just One Fix'. He and Jourgensen shot heroin together and devised new ways to murder the raccoons that were ruining Burroughs' petunia garden. The two miscreants remained in regular contact until Burroughs' death five years later.

As suggested by the company he kept, Jourgensen had a private life that matched the wild and unhinged nature of Ministry's ugly music. No strangers to destructive substance habits themselves, members of Red Hot Chili Peppers and Jane's Addiction would baulk at Jourgensen's lifestyle. As ex-Dead Kennedys rabble-rouser Jello Biafra once observed, Jourgensen defied science every time he woke up in the morning.[26] Following in the footsteps of Depeche Mode's David Gahan, Jourgensen had to be revived from clinical death on more than one occasion. In the Ministry documentary *Fix* (2011), shot on tour in 1996, Jourgensen spends an inordinate amount of time wearing a metal helmet and shouting about being a Viking with all the rowdiness of somebody who probably hasn't spent a great deal of time holed up in archaeological archives studying the vast history of the Norse peoples and the nuances of their ancient culture. At one point in the film, Jourgensen inserts his penis into a rotisserie chicken. 'The whole film is a Polaroid snapshot of a period of my life that I'm not particularly happy with,' he complained later.[27]

Like Leary and Burroughs, Jourgensen avoided the fate of his less fortunate acquaintances by surviving long into adulthood despite all of the perilous hedonism. Another thing he has in common with those two bohemian icons is that his own creative powers and cultural relevance would also gradually dim. This was in a different way to Burroughs, who remained a lifelong addict and towards the end of his days became so disengaged that he couldn't even be bothered to learn the name of his country's president.[28] By contrast, Jourgensen cleaned up in the early 2000s, whereupon his output became obsessively political. Between 2004 and 2007 Ministry released a trilogy of albums directed against the presidential regime of George W. Bush. In 2018 Jourgensen set his targets on Donald Trump with the release of *AmerikKKant*. Although some reviewers were kinder, Paul Simpson of *AllMusic* objected to the record's 'clichéd metal riffage filled with pompous squealing noises'.[29]

An Industrial Industry

In his prime, Jourgensen had been part of a wide-ranging hub of industrial artists. For someone so consistently out of his head on whatever he could get his scarred fingers on, Jourgensen was a remarkably prolific and functional addict, maintaining a prodigious work ethic through drug dependency, stints in rehab, various relapses, and all the associated mental and physical fallout. Besides his main project, Jourgensen was a founding member of the American-Belgian supergroup Revolting Cocks, who many consider to be of equal importance to Ministry, perhaps even more so. Jourgensen and several of his Ministry cohorts were involved in Lard, who were fronted by Jello Biafra. The Pigface collective was another offshoot, formed by ex-PiL drummer Martin Atkins and Bill Rieflin after their participation in the Ministry live line-up of 1989–90. Atkins was also part of Murder, Inc. alongside long-term Ministry member Chris Connelly and most of Killing Joke's personnel. Jourgensen secured production work too, overseeing albums by acts including Skinny Puppy, the Canadian industrial act with a penchant for B-movie samples and gory homemade stage props.

'My dream was to be like Al,' confessed Trent Reznor in *Fix*. 'He was the most creative guy out there at the time. And it seemed like he didn't give a shit what anyone thought about it.' Briefly a Revolting Cocks roadie until he could no longer bear having firecrackers thrown into his tour bus bunk-bed at night or waking up to find drawings of genitals doodled all over his face,[30] Reznor was involved in recording a cover of Black Sabbath's 'Supernaut' for the short-lived Ministry sideproject 1000 Homo DJs. He also contributed to Pigface. But it was with his own Nine Inch Nails project that Reznor would take industrial rock to new heights of commercial success.

Just as Depeche Mode and Ministry had before him, Reznor started out in a synth-pop vein before finding fame with a harsher style. In the 1980s he played in Option 30 (a funky outfit who were smitten with The Police), a tacky pop-rock group called The Innocent, and the OMD-ish Exotic Birds. In comparison to Reznor's subsequent output, Nine Inch Nails' 1989 debut album is a fairly lightweight affair. 'Head Like a Hole' hasn't dated too badly as a readymade floor-filler for your average alternative music club night. The gothic piano ballad 'Something I Can Never Have' possesses a timeless, haunting quality. Elsewhere, a lot of *Pretty Hate Machine*'s lyrics are blemished by an adolescent awkwardness. The rapped verses of 'Down In It' certainly have the power to induce cringes. Other forgettable tunes suffer from thin and tinny production, for which you can forgive Reznor given that he recorded the whole thing for free in quieter moments at the Cleveland studio where he was employed as dogsbody.

When other musicians were recruited to assist Reznor in performing the tracks live, Nine Inch Nails bulked up their sound with each successive tour. This was coupled with the growing influence of Ministry and Pigface. The *Broken* EP debuted this harsher and denser style on compact disc, but it was 1994's *The Downward Spiral* that caused the whole industrial scene to explode into the mainstream. Then, almost as quickly, it deteriorated into frailty and farce.

Co-produced by Depeche Mode cohort Flood, *The Downward Spiral* was industrial rock's answer to Nirvana's *Nevermind*. 'Closer' stood out as its murkily raunchy disco single, but the album remained accomplished and engaging throughout. As *Rolling Stone*'s reviewer pointed out, all the power riffs, countless layers of caustic feedback, brutal distortion and anguished vocals were plastered across tunes that were, in essence, as melodic as The Beatles' later work.[31] The album entered the U.S. *Billboard* chart at number two, and Reznor's face suddenly appeared everywhere, from the covers of specialist metal publications to the pages of broadsheet newspapers. Naturally, Reznor's fame stoked interest in like-minded industrial artists. Tracks by Germany's KMFDM cropped up the following year on the soundtracks to movies including *Bad Boys*, *Mortal Kombat* and *Street Fighter II: The Animated Movie*. It's to his credit that as the value of the industrial dollar escalated and imitators sprang up all around him, Al Jourgensen temporarily ditched his penchant for samplers and synthesizers when concocting the admirably monotonous sludge-metal aesthetic of Ministry's *Filth Pig* (1996).

White Zombie went ahead and recruited Nine Inch Nails' keyboardist Charlie Clouser to assist them on *Astro-Creep: 2000* (1995). The band's frontman, Rob Zombie, has been accused of being nothing more than a 'facsimile' version of Al Jourgensen by his ex-partner and bandmate Sean Yseult, among others.[32] Vintage acts also began chasing the industrial dollar. Gary Numan had once been at the forefront of electronic pop innovation, but by 1992's *Machine + Soul* he had taken his sound in a light funk direction and was showing a fondness for covering Prince hits rather badly. After Nine Inch Nails hit superstardom, Numan went shopping for black trenchcoats and began peddling a much darker, distinctively NIN-like sound. If not as provocatively satanic as Reznor's protégée Marilyn Manson, Numan's lyrics and album concepts also became jam-packed with religious language and atheist sentiments.

Even Numan's onetime hero, the great David Bowie, got in on the action by adopting industrial techniques for his rock-meets-drum-and-bass fusion LP *Earthling* (1997). Enlisted to remix one of the album's singles, Trent Reznor was also cast as Bowie's crazed stalker for the promotional video. The irony being that it was the once groundbreaking glam legend who was now desperately pursuing Reznor, creatively speaking. That same year, Guns N' Roses commenced work on *Chinese Democracy*, an album that aspired to jump on the same bandwagon. Because Axl Rose and his erratic, ever-changing crew of session musicians and put-upon engineers spent so long trying to perfect what they hoped would be some kind of neo-rock masterpiece, by the time the album finally hit the shelves at the end of 2008 Guns N' Roses had missed the industrial boat by a spectacular margin.

Unlike the old guard of rockers who were embracing tech to sustain relevancy, The Prodigy came from a rave background. Rock and metal influences crept increasingly into the work of the mischievous Essex outfit led by Liam Howlett, and this culminated in 1997's multi-million selling *The Fat of the Land*. A number of its tracks featured vocals from Keith Flint. Once The Prodigy's floppy-haired onstage dancer, Flint reinvented himself as a thuggish cyberpunk who snarled in close approximation of Johnny Rotten over Howlett's opaque array of ear-blistering samples. This incarnation of The Prodigy was less Ministry of Sound than just plain Ministry. The Prodigy too became more popular as their sound grew darker and more aggressive.

Kids who considered themselves too cool for The Prodigy's chart-topping blend of rave and rock music and yet still had a thirst for computer-aided tumult might have been drawn towards Atari Teenage Riot and like-minded artists on Digital Hardcore Recordings. Atari Teenage Riot took exception to The Prodigy, dismissing their rave-scene followers as vacuous pill-popping tourists.[33] Having released their debut album in 1995, ATR perhaps felt The Prodigy had stolen their thunder. Led by Alec Empire, the Berlin band weren't actually teenagers but they did dress like a futuristic motorcycle gang who'd risen from the pages of Katsuhiro Otomo's

Akira and sounded like a balaclava-muffled desktop modem throwing an anti-capitalist hissy fit on Black Friday. Despite resembling manga cartoon characters, Atari Teenage Riot came across as deadly earnest in their agenda, urging revolutionary insurrection and bemoaning the apathy of young people. 'Trouble is,' as Andy Crysell pointed out in the *NME*, 'much as Empire may hate Ecstasy and the mollifying effect he believes it's had on his generation, listening to ATR is much like munching E. First E/track: magic stuff; an exhilarating rush of madness. Thirteenth E/track: felt this before; can we do something else now?'[34] ATR borrowed a chorus from Sham 69, arguably the most vacant-minded of all the 1970s punk bands, and spoke about anarchy a lot because that's what punks used to do. The empty rhetoric of their lyrics was sloganistic without pinpointing precisely what ATR really stood for or what they wanted, other than a greater number of riots. (Where should we have these riots? Against whom should they be directed? And to serve what purposes exactly?) On the unimaginatively titled 'Riot 1995' they repeatedly yelled the word 'riot' over a looped sample of Dinosaur Jr's 'Sludgefeast', which was the easily best thing about the track. They possessed none of Einstürzende Neubauten's sly humour or underlying delicacy. Ultimately it proved impossible for anybody to take Atari Teenage Riot as seriously as they took themselves.

Returning momentarily to that breakthrough Nine Inch Nails LP, most of it had been recorded in the house where, back in 1969, the Manson Family had slaughtered Sharon Tate and her companions. Reznor had moved there in 1992. He installed a recording studio, which he named 'Le Pig' in homage to the word that had once been written on the front door in Tate's blood by her murderers, who had, you will remember, been inspired by The Beatles' 'Piggies'. Pigs crop up several times in the lyric sheet to *The Downward Spiral*, and the album title itself pays blatant homage to 'Helter Skelter'. It was as if Reznor was playing a game of one-upmanship with other artists of the industrial scene, many of whom had already contributed to the glorification of Charles Manson. Industrial rock isn't the only genre to boast its fair share of Manson obsessives – see also Henry Rollins, Guns N' Roses, System of a Down, Kasabian and others – but it does possess a greater number than most. Throbbing Gristle sported Charles Manson T-shirts, with Genesis P. Orridge taking inspiration from Manson's charismatic qualities as cult leader. Cabaret Voltaire interspersed the songs on *The Covenant, The Sword and the Arm of the Lord* (1985) with snippets from Manson's speeches and inter-views. Skinny Puppy's 'Worlock' sampled the intro to The Beatles' 'Helter Skelter' alongside soundclips of Manson's own rendition of the same tune. Rob Zombie, who narrated the 2017 documentary *Charles Manson: The Final Words*, used to perform 'Helter Skelter' in concert with White Zombie. Zombie (real name Robert Bartleh Cummings) finally recorded the song in 2018, in collaboration with Marilyn Manson to promote their second co-headlining tour.

If Nine Inch Nails could be accused of adopting Ministry's aesthetic for commercial gain, then Marilyn Manson lifted it too, but diluting the formula further. They did it while dressed as spooky-wooky Halloween baddies, taking Ministry's fashion sense to absurd levels. Marilyn Manson is the name both of the band, formed in 1989, and of their singer, who was born Brian Hugh Warner. 'A guy with a girl's name who wears makeup?' quipped the sarcastic Alice Cooper. 'I wish I would have thought of that.'[35] The band were childish enough to cover a Charles Manson song, naturally, as well as the infamously clumsy Patti Smith track from 1978 that has a racist slur in its title. Manson also threatened to record a version of the Guns N' Roses song 'One in a Million', notorious for its use of racist and homophobic epithets. The idea was eventually abandoned, although it was performed by Manson at some soundchecks.

Manson and his band of circus creeps had one half-decent album in them, 1996's *Antichrist Superstar*, on which Trent Reznor and other members of Nine Inch Nails had such crucial input that one wonders if they should have been awarded most of the credit. Manson's personal fame was boosted by an autobiography, *The Long Hard Road Out of Hell*, ghosted by the same author whose *Dirt* would rekindle unmerited interest in the wretched hair metal outfit Mötley Crüe. Providing juicy details about fellatio and self-harm in an age when not every household had access to broadband, Manson's tome appealed to those teenagers who hoped to upset their parents by drawing pentagram symbols on pencil cases.

Despite satisfying Middle America's hunger for a hate figure in the period of relative tranquillity bookended by the collapse of Soviet Communism and the terrorist attacks of 9/11, Marilyn Manson was actually a deeply conservative figure. When he rode Reznor's coat-tails to fame in the mid-1990s, the real target of Manson's animosity was not the government, religion or traditionalist parents whose buttons he liked to push. It was the then dominant grunge scene, with its politically correct, ethically minded leftist values and everyman, thrift-store anti-fashion sense. This movement, Manson believed, had robbed rock 'n' roll of its fun and theatricality. An ex-music hack himself, Manson pined for a return to what he imagined had been the golden age of the rock star, namely the 1970s and '80s, a time when heroes (Cooper, Bowie, Ozzy, Kiss) could be as outrageous, brash and entertaining as they deserved to be without attracting any sarcastic scorn from the plaid-clad cynics of Generation X.

Manson lived the American Dream. Here was a white, heterosexual, middle-class male whose hard work, unremitting self-belief and initial position of privilege elevated him to fame and fortune. To social outcasts he sold tunes berating the 'Beautiful People' before moving to Hollywood and dating a succession of them. He despised any attempts to limit his personal autonomy and had little concern for others in the pursuit of his own pleasure. An elitist who can't bear to tolerate the crudity of the masses, Manson doesn't like paying taxes, despises rap music and is offended by bad grammar.[36]

His watered-down satanism is little more than classic Republican individualism, and *The Long Hard Road Out of Hell* is Ayn Rand for people with skull encrusted thumb-rings.

Musically speaking, Marilyn Manson has relied continuously on novelty metal renditions of yesteryear synth-pop hits to secure airplay and lucrative soundtrack tie-ins: 'Sweet Dreams', 'Tainted Love', 'Personal Jesus' – the list goes on. Since the turn of the millennium, Manson's albums have plodded along the same well-trodden path with diminishing returns. *Born Villain*, released in 2012, was supposed to see Manson freed from major label restrictions and back in the driving seat after being dropped from Interscope. Inaccurately marketed as 'suicide death metal', the record featured the usual industrial shtick with Manson alternating between talky-singing on the verses and croaky-shouting on its choruses. The formula was repeated over and over again for what felt like an eternity trapped not in Hell but a very vanilla Purgatory.

Lyrically, *Born Villain* reiterated all the hackneyed themes of sex, drugs, violence, the Bible, blood, dirt, insipid profanity, scary spiders and pathological self-obsession. Three similarly tepid albums later, by early 2021 the career of this boil-in-the-bag evildoer was really starting to unravel as several women, his one-time fiancée Evan Rachel Wood among them, publicly accused Manson of various acts of physical and psychological abuse. Manson's latest record label dropped him fairly promptly, as did the manager who'd represented him since 1996. The revelations should hardly have come as a surprise, however. In the pages of *The Long Hard Road Out of Hell*, and in several interviews since its publication, Manson had bragged about his violently misogynistic urges and appetite for humiliating women. Manson had already 'told us who he was', as Jude Ellison Sady Doyle wrote so damningly. 'Yet, for Manson's millions of fans – and even many of his detractors – it was easier to see all this as social commentary, or sexual liberation, or simply stupid adolescent titillation, than it was to believe he was abusive

... Marilyn Manson is only the latest in a long line of men who were more sincere than they seemed.'[37]

Nine Inch Nails soldiered on, despite it being apparent that Reznor's heart was no longer in it. In 2005 he confounded listeners of Radio 1's *Rock Show* by guest hosting an edition of the programme during the course of which he aired a personal selection of markedly non-metal tracks. Instead Reznor concentrated on shoegaze (My Bloody Valentine, The Jesus & Mary Chain), rap (M.I.A., Saul Williams), alternative country (Wilco, Cat Power), post-punk (Wire, Pere Ubu), synth-pop (Gary Numan, Soft Cell) and indietronica (LCD Soundsystem, TV on the Radio, Autolux, Primal Scream). Four years later Reznor announced it was time for NIN to 'disappear for a while' following an obligatory 'wave goodbye' tour. He would soon resort to the lucrative reformation U-turn, of course. It's clear that Reznor would rather be dedicating himself to his award-winning film soundtrack work or performing in the less profitable How to Destroy Angels project, fronted by his wife. A lot of Reznor's interviews feel more tinged with regret than any sense of pride.

Three years after releasing *The Downward Spiral*, Reznor bumped into Sharon Tate's sister, who took him to task for exploiting her sibling's horrific death at the hands of the Manson Family. At first Reznor defended his actions by reiterating his fascination with what he called 'American folklore'. It then, finally, dawned on him that she had lost her sister in a 'senseless, ignorant situation' that he could never support: 'When she was talking to me, I realised for the first time, "What if it was my sister?" I thought, "Fuck Charlie Manson." I don't want to be looked at as a guy who supports serial-killer bullshit.' Reznor went home and burst into tears.[38] Reflecting with hindsight after each subsequent release, Reznor would go on to describe 1999's *The Fragile* as a cocaine-addled mess on which he recklessly attempted to spread what little he had to say across two CDs ('I never want to make an album like that again'), while 2005's *With Teeth* he regarded as containing several mistakes compounded by new management, too many cooks and a post-sobriety crisis of confidence.[39]

Newer Models

Later generations of industrial bands compare poorly to the early pioneers, and many of those pioneers themselves have petered out. The reasons may have something in common with one explanation for why the first *Terminator* film was artistically superior to its more commercially successful sequel, *Terminator 2: Judgment Day*, at least according to an essay by David Foster Wallace. 'There is a dense, greasy, marvellously machinelike look of *The Terminator*'s mechanized F/X;' wrote the author, 'there are the noirish lighting and Dexedrine pace that compensate ingeniously for the low budget and manage to establish a mood that is both exhilarating and claustrophobic.' The second instalment, by comparison, consists of a few spectacular set pieces strung together by 'empty and derivative, pure mimetic polycelluloid'. This movie inaugurated a genre Wallace named 'Special Effects Porn'. Bigger budgets and groundbreaking digital graphics technology resulted in cheesy, formulaic and insipid but necessarily bankable movies, less reliant on plot, characters and gripping or imaginative storytelling; almost wholly dependent on CGI baddies and huge explosions. For Wallace, the whole F/X Porn genre was defined by the paradoxical 'Inverse Cost and Quality Law': 'the larger a movie's budget is, the shittier that movie is going to be.'[40]

It is true that there was an awful lot of money sloshing around during Ministry's heyday. However accidentally, Jourgensen offset this potential quality reducer by spending significant proportions of his advances on fuelling his $1,000-a-day drug habit instead of renting the fanciest studios, acquiring state-of-the-art equipment or hiring hotshot producers. Thus, in Jourgensen's case, the pitfalls of the Inverse Cost and Quality Law, as reapplied to the field of industrial rock, were circumvented. On the other side of the coin, the tedium of Nine Inch Nails and Rammstein has swollen in tandem with their riches. Their big-budget stage show extravaganzas and expensive studio recordings are formulaic but bankable, just like the successful motion pictures condemned by Wallace as mere F/X Porn.

Since the publication of that essay in 1998, digital graphics technology has become cheaper and more widely used, and the quality of action movies has remained spectacularly dismal, with man-eating sharks flying out of the sky at any given opportunity. Lurking behind every skyscraper is some computer-generated King Kong or Godzilla rip-off waiting to stomp on a bunch of two-dimensional characters played by wooden actors who used to be wrestlers or stars of children's television shows. Superhero 'universes' are so chock-full of crossover opportunities that every Marvel or DC sequel-slash-reboot now resembles a conveyor belt of character cameos worryingly reminiscent of Andrew Lloyd Webber's plot-less *Cats*. In terms of music-making technology, long gone are the days when Al Jourgensen would cut his fingers to shreds trying to splice pieces of physical tape. The rise of software like Pro Tools or Ableton Live has allowed people to forge vast discographies from their own bedrooms and beam them straight into listener's houses via Spotify or Bandcamp. Yet most relatively well-known contemporary industrial rock acts offer few genuine thrills, while those who remain underground often struggle to accomplish much in the way of originality. Such artists tend to lack Trent Reznor's gift for writing hooks. At the same time, they cannot compete with Ministry in terms of harshness and obstreperousness.

In fact, the legacy of the genre's earlier grittiness can be found in the output of those underground musicians who swing more towards the electronic side of things by steering away from traditional guitar bases while still, somehow, maintaining an intense heaviness. Take Necro Deathmort, for example, a London-based duo whose style incorporates and often seamlessly blurs dub-infused electronics, ambient minimalism, post-techno beats, astral jazz, noirish atmospherics and doom metal. Theirs is a diverse catalogue, defiantly resistant to pigeonholing. If there is one song that can sum up Necro Deathmort, observes the duo's Matthew Rozeik, then it's the first recording they ever made together: 'Odorem Creepus' from 2007. 'I was unsuccessfully trying to work out a Melvins song on a keyboard while AJ [Cookson] manipulated the sound, and I pretty much played every note except the correct ones. It sounded fat, and we were excited by the sonic possibilities of playing heavy doomy music on electronic gear.'[41]

Another exciting post-industrial artist is Sam An, who used to record as Lana Del Rabies before changing her alias to Strega Beata. Her music has soaked up plenty of underground electronic and experimental noise influences on account of the time she spent living in Detroit, before returning to her native Tucson and then upping sticks to Phoenix. Nevertheless, compared to the output of fellow contemporary noiseniks such as Margaret Chardiet (aka Pharmakon), An's music bears scant resemblance to sheer power electronics. In fact, the underlying hooks and measured vocal techniques of her Lana Del Rabies material can be attributed to an adolescent obsession with Nine Inch Nails. At age thirteen, An was introduced to NIN via the unorthodox entry point of *Further Down the Spiral*, a companion album containing remixes of tracks from *The Downward Spiral* overseen by artists including J. G. Thirlwell, Coil and Aphex Twin.[42] A second-hand copy of *Further Down the Spiral* was the only recording An could find by the act that so many of her favourite nu-metal artists had been praising in their interviews. That album she credits with changing her life. An was so smitten with it that when she finally got her hands on the source material, hearing the original album for the first time proved to be an anticlimactic experience. *The Downward Spiral* remains one of An's favourite albums of all time anyway, but it was the 'many interesting textural, quasi-experimental things' on its remixed counterpart that really struck a chord. She wanted to hear more material like it and eventually began crafting her own unique take on that sound.[43] At the time of writing, the highlight of her discography has been the 2018 Lana Del Rabies cassette *Shadow World*, on which the blueprint of *Further Down the Spiral* has been run through a mangle and crawled out the other side as a semi-abstract and powerfully rhythmic clatter of post-NIN horror music. It's catharsis for An's own specific personal traumas as well as the more universal distress of living in a seemingly alternate-universe hellscape in which Donald Trump can be elected president of the USA.

Likewise, another artist who channels personal suffering and political exasperation into rousing post-industrial work is the multidisciplinary poet, rapper, singer, musician and playwright Camae Ayewa. She records under the alias of Moor Mother, a reference to – and reclaiming of – a pre-slavery black identity that the general public never really hears about, let alone studies as any part of their education. Ayewa grew up in a public housing project in Aberdeen, Maryland. She conceived a punk rock band when she was still in high school and later moved to Philadelphia to study photography. Her music is very visual, too, in its use of language and reference points and the way it holds a blood-smeared lens up to modern America. As a queer black woman, Ayewa's recordings are informed by her own experiences of systemic discrimination and social inequality – especially acute since the rise of right-wing Trumpian populism – as well as drawing on those of similarly downtrodden folk living under the patriarchal and racist oppression that continues to thrive in its Western incarnations and in both different and familiar forms further afield. Her output is concerned with historical wrongdoings and their legacies, too: slavery, pre-slavery, colonialism, postcolonialism, Afrofuturism. 'A lot of my ancestors are speaking through me,' Ayewa had said.[44]

'Creation Myth', the opening track on Moor Mother's record *Fetish Bones* (2016), has been called 'an 18-rated Black History Month condensed into five minutes'.[45] In addition to drawing on personal tragedies such as the death of her father, Ayewa's music, poetry and lyrics have referenced events including the Memphis race riots of 1866; more recent protests such as those following the shooting of Michael Brown in Ferguson, Missouri; the unspeakable cruelty of the Belgian Congo under the rule of Leopold II; and the global epidemic of domestic violence. Moor Mother has sampled the voices of black and queer female poets like Pat Parker and June Jordan; while *Fetish Bones* incorporates audio snippets of the police dashboard camera footage of the 2015 arrest of Sandra Bland, who was later found dead in police custody, and of Natasha McKenna, a teenager with schizophrenia who died after being tasered in prison while she was already restrained.

Moor Mother's music is researched thoroughly and is rich in specific reference points, never lazily resorting to the perfunctory sloganeering that defined the unconvincing output of Atari Teenage Riot and and later became the modus operandi of Ministry. Nor does it revel in the bourgeois-provoking shock tactics favoured by Throbbing Gristle or the *Kerrang!*-friendly equivalent that Rammstein has – and Marilyn Manson had – to offer. While filtered through Ayewa's love of language, Moor Mother's material often draws on first-hand experiences, news reports or issues that should attract media coverage but are all too often shamefully neglected. U.S. news stations tend to cover domestic violence only when it is committed by a celebrity like Chris Brown, when statistics show that every nine seconds somebody is being abused in their own home. Such widespread domestic abuse is deemed not to be newsworthy due to its commonplace occurrence, a shocking fact in itself.[46] Moor Mother avoids heavy-handedness, however, because of the chaotic and non-linear manner of her bustling electronic composition-collages, which draw from pretty much the entire gamut of humanity's musical endeavours, mashing them together in a furious maelstrom of bewildering noise and making use of in-the-moment improvisation. Although she is often seen hunched behind a table swamped with electronic musical gear, her dreadlocks flying as she bounces to the harsh soundscapes and shaking beats, every gig Ayewa plays is treated differently, with the specific performance space and audience firmly in mind, her sets altered and directed accordingly.

Even though technology has, to a certain extent, helped to democratize music-making and other disciplines such as journalism, Ayewa is concerned that there are still many voices out there that continue not to be heard. 'It costs $100 a month to have the internet in America,' she told *The Guardian* in 2017, 'it's naive to think everyone can afford it. The underground is still the folk root of everything, and that's thriving. But to get the message heard by the world . . . it's like *The Truman Show* – we can't break through the bubble.'[47] Moor Mother, at least, has made some headway. At the time of writing she remains underground – *Guardian* spotlights, festival appearances and artist endorsements notwithstanding – even though she could make a decent claim at being a one-woman Public Enemy for these uncertain times. Indeed, Moor Mother's articulately outraged industrial collages recall the speech made by one of Ayewa's collaborators, the rapper, singer, poet, writer and actor Saul Williams, back when he performed in the support slot of an extensive Nine Inch Nails world tour in 2005–6: 'This is what happens when you take off your black T-shirt and you realize you're still black.'

8
NOISE ROCK

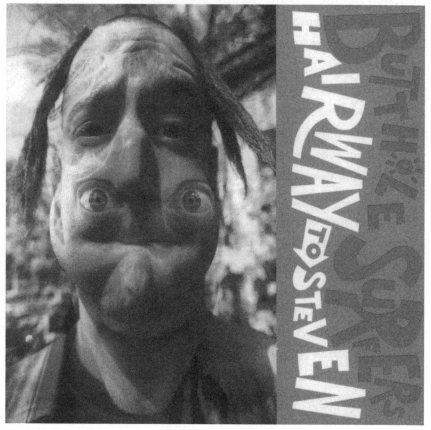

Classic rock run through a mangle: Butthole Surfer's *Hairway To Steven*.

We hate Madonna. In the same manner that we hate Henry
Rollins, and in the same manner that we hate ourselves. The
only things we really like are pot, sex, and Thai food.[1]

GIBBY HAYNES (BUTTHOLE SURFERS)

Immediately prior to their performance at Woodstock '94, the touring members of Nine Inch Nails caked themselves head-to-toe in sticky mud from the rain-soaked festival floor. Partly a gesture of solidarity with the audience, this was also a way for Trent Reznor to subvert or at least try to reconcile his mixed feelings about performing at such a 'corny', Pepsi-sponsored event (while still pocketing the fee, of course).[2] Televised on MTV as pay-per-view and defined by its muck-covered musicians and their similarly soiled instruments, the resulting performance proved to be one of the most iconic stepping stones in Nine Inch Nails' career. This brief moment of muddy camaraderie with their audience would help launch NIN into a whole new stratosphere of fame, ironically widening the distance between the band and the lives of its fans rather than bringing them closer together in filthy fraternity.

Despite the muck, Reznor and his rotating cast of collaborators could never match the sonic sludginess of their forebears and industrial rivals Ministry. Al Jourgensen's band, far more so than the highly calculated Nine Inch Nails, shared a greater affinity with the unruly agenda of the noise rock scene. Noise rock emerged and blossomed more or less in parallel with industrial rock and the two share some similarities. There are certain noise rock bands that have an industrial edge thanks to keyboard textures, say, or the use of samples. Noise rock tends to keep the emphasis on the 'rock', mind, as in the guitars, bass and drums, with the vocals sounding more human (or perhaps at times alien but at least something 'living') rather than mechanical. Ministry's kinship with noise rock was captured most obviously on tape by the 1991 single 'Jesus Built

My Hotrod', its garbled guest verses provided by Gibby Haynes of Butthole Surfers. The song was the only serviceable material that Jourgensen had ready to submit to an impatient Sire Records after Ministry had squandered most of their $75,000 album advance on hard drugs. Leglessly intoxicated, Haynes recorded his jabberings while propped up on a stool, falling off a few times and having to be hoisted back up before he passed out completely.[3] 'Jesus Built My Hotrod' went on to become one of Ministry's biggest-selling records, a feat that perhaps shouldn't have come as such a surprise to everybody involved given that it was essentially industrial-noise-rock's answer to The Trashmen's novelty classic 'Surfin' Bird'.

Butthole Surfers

It is no easy feat to summarize Butthole Surfers' music and career, if you can call it that, in the space of a few pages. A couple of writers have struggled to do it over the course of an entire book. Buttholes Surfers' history is loaded with what could inadequately be described as 'antics'. This was, for instance, a band that once relocated to Georgia with the express intention of stalking REM. The move had seemed a tremendous idea when they'd all been tripping, and the Buttholes followed through. Prior to that, the band had remained on tour for two or three years in one virtually unbroken stint, booking gigs as they went along, living like modern nomads. A whole year of this passed by before it dawned on them that it would be a sensible idea to purchase some sleeping bags. During their concerts, which might be more accurately described as 'events', a bug-eyed Haynes would fire (blank) shotgun blasts at the heads of his audience. At a festival in the Netherlands, a butt-naked Haynes attempted to invade the stage of Nick Cave & the Bad Seeds. For his insolence, Haynes was booted in the groin by Bad Seeds guitarist Blixa Bargeld. Butthole Surfers had pyromaniac tendencies too, using lighter fluid to set fire to their equipment and also themselves. There was further onstage nakedness courtesy of Kathleen Lynch, formerly known as Ta-Da the Shit Lady, whose occasional eyebrow-raising presence was noise rock's answer to Hawkwind's Stacia. At one concert in New York, urine was sprayed onto the crowd by means of the Buttholes' infamous 'piss wand': a Wiffle ball bat that had been filled up with pee. Suffice to say, there were numerous brushes with the law. A lot of weed was smoked. Gallons of beer were guzzled. Soon enough, Butthole Surfers had gained a reputation for sprinkling LSD on their cornflakes first thing in the morning, before Haynes developed a taste for even harder stuff.

Their live shows could be scenes of bacchanalian depravity, both on the part of the band onstage and the spectators below, the separation sometimes blurring in an unsavoury meeting of sex and/or violence of a verbal, visual or physical nature. 'One time in Minneapolis,' Haynes would recall, 'there was a guy who got up on stage and had his dick out and was jacking off this limp dick. Kathleen was up there with her tits way out and this guy was just up there for a long time. Then, after the show, *they arrested Kathleen*.'[4] To accompany the prurience and pyromania, the band utilized seizure-inducing strobe lighting and projections of outlandish movie footage, including stomach-churning clips of car accidents and penis reconstruction surgery. As guitarist Paul Leary always maintained, the only truly satisfying rock music is that which your mother despises and deplores: 'We made music that moms would really hate, shows included – like nudity and violence and belching flames and smoke and hideous, loud, damaging music.'[5]

Butthole Surfers were founded in 1981 by Haynes and Leary, intelligent Texan kids whose mapped-out career paths went more than a little awry. The son of a local children's television presenter known as Mr Peppermint, Haynes was a high-school baseball star who went on to study at Trinity University in San Antonio, where he was named Accounting Student of the Year. Leary, who had been raised by schoolteacher parents, was on track to become a stockbroker. Magnetized to each other's overt eccentricity, the duo began collaborating on a fanzine called *Strange V.D.* It included reproductions of the grossest medical photographs the pair could get their hands on, accompanied by fictitious explanatory captions. 'Case number 36, tacoleg. Or blackbag or pinecone butt or several others. And there'd be pictures of people with distended intestines or huge gashes in their leg or whatever, with, of course, their own descriptions. Still one of the weirdest homemade zines I've ever seen in my life,' Jello Biafra remembered fondly.[6] Haynes left his job at the prestigious accounting firm Peat, Marwick, Mitchell shortly after inadvertently leaving a picture of some mutilated genitalia in one of the company's photocopying machines. After failing to make a living at the less-than-lucrative vocation of manufacturing and flogging bootleg Lee Harvey Oswald merchandise, Haynes and Leary realized it might be easier to start a band.[7] 'Where would The Beatles be today if they had called themselves Butthole Surfers?' Leary's father once asked in a letter to his son.[8] This wasn't the first name they'd used. Earlier options had been The Dick Clark Five, The Dick Gas Five, The Ashtray Babyheads, Nine Foot Worm Makes Own Food, Vodka Family Winstons, Abe Lincoln's Bush, Ed Asner's Gay, and The Right to Eat Fred Astaire's Asshole (shortened down from The Inalienable Right to Eat Fred Astaire's Asshole).[9] Later in their career, Haynes was asked whether, if given the chance to do it all over again, he would rewind the clock and make his career trajectory somewhat smoother by giving the band a more palatable moniker. 'Yes,' he replied, 'I would name the band: I'm Going to Shit in Your Mother's Vagina.'[10]

As unpredictable as they were, and as much as their shows radiated that incredible sensation that anything could happen, there was always a performance art element to Butthole Surfers. They did not lack contrivance. Like seasoned stuntmen, the band would use sugar-glass bottles to attack one another, or to smash over the heads of friends who'd been asked to pose as belligerent stage invaders, fooling the audience into believing they'd witnessed a genuine assault. As Leary hoped to persuade the *NME*, Butthole Surfers were not particularly outrageous in the grander scheme of things, especially in comparison to some of the more outré acts the band had witnessed on their extensive travels. 'I've seen some shocking things,' he asserted. 'That pineapple coming in and out of that guy's ass at will, that was shocking. The guy shooting hard-boiled eggs out of his ass, with a drag queen standing there eating them, that was pretty shocking.'[11] In addition to downplaying their outrageousness, both Haynes and Leary were harsher critics of their own musical abilities than many of their wide-eyed reviewers. As Haynes once put it, 'I can write a melody and I can arrange songs. But I am not a musician. I have no technical proficiency at any musical instrument and a limited repertoire with any instrument.'[12] This was pretty modest considering he dabbled in the saxophone, woodblock, guitar, bass and drums, and was particularly adept when it came to altering and manipulating the sound of his own voice, be it by singing through toilet rolls or a megaphone, or assembling a rack of equipment – known as 'Gibbytronix' – with which he was able to distort, mutate and live-loop his vocals in such a loud and terrifying way that it successfully out-heavied your average guitarist's range of effects pedals. For his own part, Leary had been playing electric guitar since before the age of ten, after witnessing The Beatles' historic appearance on *The Ed Sullivan Show*.[13] Leary, too, denied that he was a good musician: 'Sometimes it's hard for me to even think of our music as music . . . It has been more of a platform to express ourselves, even though we don't know what we are trying to express. I was pretty mad at the world for a while.'[14] Drummer King Coffey was prouder of the band's achievements, albeit with firm provisos. 'When we really hit it,' he said in 1996, 'I think we're the best band on the planet. We picked up where Pink Floyd left off and added the wisdom of punk rock. We're not performance art anymore, but we are visual art in a rock mode.'[15]

As important as visuals were to the band, presence at one of their sensory-overloading live shows was not a necessary prerequisite for having one's mind warped by Butthole Surfers. Nor did one have to gaze at a freakish Buttholes record sleeve for a sustained period to experience an epiphany. Their music contained – and still possesses – that potent power all by itself, no matter how amateurish the band considered their studio performances to be. There's the ugly and lo-fi psych-punk of 1984's *Psychic . . . Powerless . . . Another Man's Sac*, with its fevered guitar tones and vocals that sound like Haynes had a groan tube lodged in his throat for much of the recording process. Then there's the trudging pace and almost gothically rendered mental fragility of *Rembrandt Pussyhorse* (1986). That was followed a year later by the denser and meatier screwed-up rock shapes of *Locust Abortion Technician*. Mind you, talking of visuals, that album's creepy clown artwork is a contender for the most apt record sleeve of all time.

'I wish I was Neil Young,' lamented Haynes in 1996, showing that Butthole Surfers' obsession with famous musicians was by no means limited to stalking REM. 'I'm not known for writing good songs. I'm known for putting my foot in my mouth and saying funny things . . . I just wish I didn't suck.'[16] A decade earlier, Butthole Surfers had used piano chords lifted from Young's 'Heart of Gold' as the basis for their cockeyed country track 'Creep in the Cellar'. Also included on *Rembrandt Pussyhorse* was a rendition of 'American Woman', accurately described by Michael Azerrad as a 'bizarre, almost cubist deconstruction' of The Guess Who's original.[17] Other Butthole covers included Donovan's 'Hurdy Gurdy Man' and 'The One I Love' by their beloved REM. The Buttholes also had a healthy habit of pinching material from Black Sabbath. The drum pattern on 'Dum Dum' was stolen from 'Children of the Grave', while 'Sweat Loaf' was an unhinged semi-cover of Sabbath's timeless weed anthem 'Sweet Leaf'. A direct reply to Sabbath was offered via the track 'No, I'm Iron Man'. Butthole Surfers' album titles took to running classic rock through the mangle too. See the *Hairway to Steven* LP or *Electric Larryland*. The former took the mock-tributes a step further by featuring no track names on its sleeve. In place of words, each song was represented by its own distinct symbol. This was a nod to Led Zeppelin's fourth LP, the difference being that where Zeppelin had come up with runes, the Buttholes used stick drawings.

Such irreverent iconoclasm did not deter John Paul Jones from producing *Independent Worm Saloon* in 1993. The legendary bassist presumed he'd been hired to give the album 'a heavy rock vibe', adding that 'it didn't work out like that.'[18] His reputation among the Buttholes can only have been enhanced by the fact that Jones had previously worked on the orchestrations for REM's *Automatic for the People*. Haynes remembered Jones as being 'like a horrible drunk when we were doing that record', adding, 'but we were loaded too . . . We basically spent a fortune to hang out with some guy from Led Zeppelin.'[19] The guy in question was not a fan of the band's 'swirly songs',[20] and this major-label debut did not turn out to be as overtly weird as the band's previous output. It still contained plenty of warped vocal and instrumental effects and other unusual forms of experimentation. 'Tongue' ends with a recording of somebody urinating, for example, while the final track incorporates a long loop of retch-inducing vomiting noises, which the band had been tempted to stretch out for forty minutes and submit to the label as their completed masterpiece.[21] The album's love songs, if that is what they are, were conceived from characteristically odd vantage points. These include 'Dog Inside Your Body', the titular lyrics being either metaphorical or denoting a Bulgakovian tale of cross-species metamorphosis, and 'Goofy's Concern', which could be mistaken for a nihilistic hardcore anthem unless full attention is paid to its tender final line. In spite of Jones's qualms, those two tracks did indeed rock hard, as did many others, in a delightfully twisted and ramshackle way.

Butthole Surfers peaked commercially in 1996 with a hit called 'Pepper'. Many compared it to Beck, although it's hard to imagine the charismatic 'Loser' star rapping about high-school rapists, amputees, car-crash victims and HIV. Earlier in their career, Butthole Surfers had recorded jingles for MTV. More recently, in 2019, their exploits were reproduced in a lavish coffee-table book, a dubiously highbrow honour for such a lairy noise rock band. Whatever they got up to, the band's members always batted off accusations of having sold out. As far as Coffey was concerned, their name alone served as a permanent badge of integrity. They could sound like Barry Manilow, for all Coffey cared. As long as they called themselves Butthole Surfers, no charge of selling out would be able to stick.[22] Haynes saw no shame in experimenting with different musical styles, from avant-garde audio collages to skewed takes on country and pop. After all, he argued, The Beatles were rightly admired for their ability to create strange psychedelic compositions as well as politer tunes like 'Rocky Racoon'.[23] Nor had the Surfers ever concealed their ambitions, no matter how unlikely their commercial prospects always seemed to be. From its outset, said Leary, the band had consistently strived to afford superior equipment, nicer accommodation, better transport and higher-quality marijuana. The guitarist had no tolerance for the pious disapproval of indie purists and felt over the moon when his band signed to the same label that had put out records by Grand Funk Railroad.[24] Besides, who can blame them after hearing about their early sleeping-bagless days of washing dishes between live dates, foraging for cans and bottles to exchange for the nickel deposit, getting attacked by redneck thugs as soon as they walked into a diner and suffering flu on the road for six months at a time?

In spite of the fact that the footage was sometimes screened in reverse, and as graphic as that footage was, there was nothing fundamentally depraved about an instructional film documenting the surgical reconstruction of the shredded penis of an Iowan farmer who'd accidentally caught his trousers in a combine harvester. 'It's a success story, actually,' as King Coffey observed.[25] The same thing might be said of Butthole Surfers. Just don't show either example to your mother.

The Jesus Lizard

I don't want to get hurt and I don't have respect for people who intentionally do it. But if you do end up bleeding on stage, it looks really cool.[26]

DAVID YOW (THE JESUS LIZARD)

Just as shockingly as Butthole Surfers, The Jesus Lizard have also been the subject of a large and glossy coffee-table book. (In line with The Jesus Lizard's compulsive use of four-lettered album titles, the name of the book is *BOOK*.) The Jesus Lizard have their own connections to Ministry, being based in Chicago and occasionally sharing stages and collaborating. There was little industrial about The Jesus Lizard, however, especially after the drum machine that was employed on their debut EP *Pure* was jettisoned in favour of powerhouse human drummer Mac McNeilly. As frontman David Yow boasted, The Jesus Lizard were also 'a lot less image conscious than someone like Nine Inch Nails. Anything you get from us comes from our music, because we don't put it across in makeup or marketing. I think that superficial stuff diminishes it anyway. People know that Trent Reznor doesn't act like that at home. Nobody buys that.'[27] Yow's bandmate Duane Denison toed the same line with a similar statement, albeit one that could be construed as more of a dig at their friends in both Butthole Surfers and Ministry: 'I'm not going to pretend that I'm some idiot who never went to school. I'm not going to go around in a top hat with a syringe sticking out of my Adam's apple. Personally, we're probably not very different from the people who come and see us.' Even many of the grunge artists, who prided themselves on their antithetical attitudes towards the ostentatious nature of the 1980s glam-metal scene, would turn out to be too 'overblown' for Denison's earthy tastes.[28]

Yow and bassist David Wm. Sims planted the seeds of The Jesus Lizard when playing together in Scratch Acid, best described as Austin's answer to The Birthday Party. 'We're not a punk band,' Yow would yell at the mohawk-sporting and skinheaded members of their audience, 'Everybody has to grow up sometime.' Then he'd hurl himself into the throng and have to punch his way out.[29] In 1987 Scratch Acid's rhythm section moved to Chicago because they had been recruited for Steve Albini's post-Big Black project Rapeman. Yow followed them, along with his guitarist friend Denison. Rapeman proved short lived but The Jesus Lizard's relationship with Albini, who was also blossoming as a recording engineer, remained intact. After that debut EP, Yow, Denison and Sims sought out McNeilly. 'You just can't beat a real drummer. It's just great. Especially live, too. It's so primal,' explained Denison,

> People love to see somebody hit things. It just adds so much energy. As well as a certain amount of swing that you just don't get from a machine. Plus I've become more and more anti-machine. I'm not anti-technology, but it just kills me to see these people come on stage and literally push buttons and not have to work at all. And yet be acclaimed as revolutionary *artistes*.[30]

In essence, then, The Jesus Lizard resembled a traditional meat-and-potatoes hard rock band, its constituent parts being guitar, bass, drums and vocals. Denison labelled these 'the four basic food groups' or 'the primary colours'.[31] His band felt no need to experiment with technology like Ministry. Nor did they possess Butthole Surfers' penchant for dazzling backdrop projections, aggressive psychedelia, stylistic eclecticism or swirly-whirly instrumental effects. It did them no harm that The Jesus Lizard had the most exciting frontman since

Iggy Pop. Taking cues from the crazier bands he'd witnessed in his Texas days – The Dicks, Sharon Tate's Baby, The Big Boys – Yow prowled the stage like a furious, flailing pterodactyl that had just woken up to find its wings had been clipped and was out to seek revenge. Contorting his body and thrusting his limbs, Yow would regularly hurl himself off the stage with complete disregard for his own personal safety and, for that matter, scant regard for anybody else's. Footage can be found on YouTube from a 1994 concert in Dallas when one audience member hurled a beer bottle straight into the back of Yow's head. The projectile succeeded in flooring the singer mid-song.[32] After a short pause, Yow rises to his feet and cracks on with the show. Yow wasn't hospitalized on that particular evening, but he was after other concerts: 'I used to get a kick out of that, thinking, "Jeez, I'm just a singer in a dumb rock band and I get put in the hospital for it?" That always impressed me. It's better than not getting hospitalized, I guess.' He sustained a different head injury when stage-diving in Zurich only to have the crowd part before him. Another time, in Albuquerque, an audience member grabbed Yow's hand at the worst possible moment, accidentally causing the singer to flip awkwardly from the stage and land on his tailbone. Yow was delighted to discover that an X-ray he was shown in hospital had been obscured by a blurry cloud, as this evidence vindicated the classic Butthole Surfers number 'I Saw an X-Ray of a Girl Passing Gas.'[33]

Asked to identify the craziest thing he ever did onstage, Yow replied that it was smoking a cigarette. 'That shit will kill you,' he warned. 'I may as well have just shot myself in the head.'[34] In person, Yow has a reputation for being a down-to-earth and chilled-out Scrabble enthusiast. Fronting The Jesus Lizard, he managed to channel a kind of primal semi-lunacy, or at least do a credible imper-sonation of what that might look like. It is perhaps significant that in middle age Yow has become interested in acting. So convincing was Yow's role as singer-lunatic that he is one of the few vocalists who has been able to get away with performing shirtless without looking like a poser. (Other members of this tiny club include Iggy Pop, Joe Cardamone from The Icarus Line and Matt Baty from Pigs Pigs Pigs Pigs Pigs Pigs Pigs.) Yow didn't draw the line at toplessness, mind. Finding himself with nothing to do during performances of a Motörhead-inspired instrumental originally titled 'Metropolis', Yow would smoke a cigarette and hold the microphone up to his exposed testicles. The song was renamed 'Tight N' Shiny' at the behest of Steve Albini, who considered it the most amusing sight he'd ever witnessed.[35] Yow's nakedness on the Cincinnati leg of the 1995 Lollapalooza festival, which he explained was done in protest to the state's obscenity trial against an exhibition of Robert Mapplethorpe's photography, landed the singer in jail for a few hours and found him banned from Hamilton County for a year. The policemen who asked for his autograph received the scrawled message, 'You suck shit. David Yow.'[36]

'The times where that had happened with David onstage, it wasn't like some leering, obscene act he was doing. If anything, it was clownish,' reasoned Denison.[37] In another interview the guitarist hoped that, for most fans at least, the spectacle of Yow came second to the incredible music made by The Jesus Lizard. Such listeners may well have been attracted initially by the singer's unruly behaviour, but they stuck around because the art stood up to scrutiny.[38] With no formal training, Yow compared his vocal skills to shooting in the dark: 'I do the best with what I have. It's kind of like making soup when you don't have anything to make soup with.'[39] It's an apt metaphor given that Yow also has a reputation as an accomplished cook. The ingredients of Yow's vocal soup included howls, yelps, screams, grunts, snarls and strange mutterings. This range of techniques has eluded the small number of Jesus Lizard cover bands that Yow has been unfortunate enough to stumble across. Their vocalists often make the fatal mistake of screaming all the lyrics at full pelt because they haven't paid close enough attention to all the whispering, crooning, mumbling and other quieter variations that Yow was always at pains to incorporate.[40]

Under the supervision of Albini, who recorded The Jesus Lizard's first four albums, Yow's parts were positioned fairly low in the mix. While Yow proved to be the focal point at live performances, these albums' mixes helped place the frontman on an equal footing with the musicians. At times it almost sounded as though Yow was drowning in the turbulent sound that was rattling around him, not least on 'Seasick' from the band's second album, *Goat* (1991), where his voice can be heard rising to the surface to bawl panicked words about his inability to swim. Fittingly, live performances of this track would often find Yow attempting to 'swim' over the heads of the audience.

Complementing his feral vocal work was Yow's talent for lyric writing, which was darkly poetic in nature and earned comparisons to experimental horror fiction. Occasionally, Yow would draw from real-life experiences by writing about people he knew. Two songs on 1996's *Shot* were about a landlord with whom he'd fallen out. 'Puss', from 1992's *Liar*, concerned a member of fellow Chicago act Urge Overkill who had pushed a female zine writer down some stairs.[41] 'If we wrote about our own lives, our songs would be boring,' Yow had explained when he was still in Scratch Acid. That band's song subjects had included its fair share of violence and murder, from the story of the man who douses his wife in gasoline and sets her on fire to descriptions of rednecks mowing down hippies in their pickup trucks. Inedible foodstuffs cropped up, too – mouldy bread, insect-laden fish – as well as cannibalistic themes, 'probably because I'm frustrated about not eating enough', reasoned the singer.[42]

Yow's penchant for drawing material from scary movies, grisly news stories, classic literature and the sinister recesses of his own imagination continued in The Jesus Lizard. On 'American BB' he wails about cutting gill-like slits into the side of somebody's neck and then blowing into them with a straw. 'The Art of Self

Defense' concerns a weeping pygmy who sneaks into people's homes to carve open the chests of his victims. The idea for 'Rope' came from a non-fiction book, borrowed from a friend, called *Autoerotic Fatalities*. The real-life anecdotes contained within its pages included one about a man who was visiting his girlfriend at her parents' house. The girl and her folks popped out to do some shopping. On return, they discovered the man's body in the backyard. 'He had dug a hole, sprayed a bunch of water in it, got himself all naked and muddy, and hung himself from a tree. And I think he had put a carrot up his ass, but I changed it to a trowel because I thought that would be funnier,' said Yow of his writing process and artistic licence.[43]

Yow certainly matched Denison's definition of the ideal rock singer: 'He's almost like the court jester, the propaganda disseminator, the visual focus, all of that. The antagonizer . . . The other guys are playing instruments and sort of have to, occasionally, concentrate. Whereas the singer, all they have to do is remember the words. And even then, not even half the time.'[44] For the record, the only time Yow forgot his lyrics completely was at a show in Milwaukee. When it came to playing 'Then Comes Dudley', Yow's mind went completely blank so he resorted to shouting the name 'Dudley' for the song's duration. On the occasions when he failed to recall smaller sections of lyrics, Yow happily spouted a load of other nonsense instead:

> That was one of the great things about being in a band like that. The other three guys were so precise in what they were doing that I didn't have to worry. I knew no matter where I landed, they'd have it covered. It's funny, I've seen reviews where they say, 'Yow was crowd-surfing most of the show and didn't miss a beat.' But really I missed quite a few beats. It just didn't matter because it worked anyway.[45]

The reason for this was that the musicians were so incredibly tight. This became especially apparent once the members, who for a long time cohabited, were earning just enough money to avoid day jobs and were thus free to write and rehearse on most days of the week. Together, they developed a squalid-sounding blues rock style as mutated and deformed via punk, post-punk and no wave. Benefiting from Albini's recording methods, which focused on capturing a raw and live feel, The Jesus Lizard's material tended to attract adjectives like 'visceral', 'primordial', 'cacophonous' and 'demented'. Indeed, matching the tone of its bleak subject-matter, the opening to 'Slave Ship' boasts one of the most genuinely evil-sounding riffs in rock history. As with Yow's vocals, there was a comparable underlying sophistication to the music itself. Despite his penchant for incredibly dirty, primitive riffs, Denison had a background in classical guitar, having studied the instrument at Eastern Michigan University. His other interests included flamenco and jazz. The jazziness can be heard at its most overt in the side project known as The Denison/Kimball Trio (who were actually a duo), although it did sometimes filter into The Jesus Lizard. The creepy and high-pitched riff that forms the basis of 'Then Comes Dudley' was lifted from the atmospheric horn notes on Miles Davis's 'Great Expectations'. Likewise, the quartet's grooving rhythm section could rumble along like a bulldozer at times, but, oh boy, could it swing when required. The Jesus Lizard had the technical chops all right, but Denison was determined for all the songs to be fundamentally riff-driven. 'Finding a melodic phrase that bears repetition isn't easy,' he explained in BOOK,

and a good riff should be repeated. Repetition creates motoric power, and a great riff should pick up momentum as it's played. That's what rock is – energy, power, dynamics, excitement . . . I always felt that focusing more on riffs and songs would better serve me than working on guitar solos and fancy licks. I think I was right.[46]

That's not to say the music Denison created with Sims and McNeilly was dumb, either. Stare deeply enough into its murky palette and you'll find the band eschewed time-honoured verse-chorus-verse-bridge-verse patterns, choosing instead to build their songs around more complex and atypical 'structural themes'. They jerked around too with time signatures, without falling into the trap of many an overly cerebral math rock group.

The juxtaposition between the precision of the music and the looser and more liberated approach of their singer made the band stand out, McNeilly would later reflect, while Denison likened Yow's voice to a 'free-jazz saxophone' with the instruments being far more 'machine-like'.[47] If they'd all attempted the abstract expressionist sax part, the band would have been a complete mess. Denison, McNeilly and Sims would even ask for Yow's voice to be completely muted from their stage monitors so the erratic nature of his vocals wouldn't break their concentration on nailing their own parts.[48] Yow's vocals and physical movements, the heavily distorted guitar tones and pummelling rhythms pushed the band's sound to the edge of chaos. In reality, The Jesus Lizard remained very much in control of their sonic tirade.

In 1995 The Jesus Lizard signed to Capitol, much to the disgust of Steve Albini. The Jesus Lizard's final two albums, 1996's *Shot* and 1998's *Blue*, were produced by Garth 'GGGarth' Richardson (Red Hot Chili Peppers, Rage Against the Machine, Ugly Kid Joe) and Gang of Four's Andy Gill, respectively. McNeilly left the band following *Shot* for family reasons, and it appears the rest of the band would've called it a day right then if they hadn't been under contract. *Shot* and *Blue* were more eclectic but also poppier than The Jesus Lizard's previous output. The instruments sounded cleaner and tinnier. Yow's voice rose in the mix in accordance with how conventional rock bands are 'supposed' to sound. As a result of such decisions, the heaviness suffered. One Amazon.com reviewer reflected the thoughts of many long-term followers when writing that several of *Blue*'s tracks resembled a Van Halen version of Scratch Acid, 'And what the hell, you can actually understand what David Yow is saying . . . something is really, really wrong here. Buy their older stuff because they used to be incredible.'[49]

There were still moments of ferocity, especially on *Shot*, and both records maintained plenty of inventive lyrical, vocal and compositional choices. Yet when emancipated from Albini's studio nous, the formula was diluted. Recording the final album, Gill added drum loops, vocal effects and other audio embroidery, techniques that might have been appropriate if working with Butthole Surfers but which were less suited to enhancing The Jesus Lizard. The results had that distant and disjointed feel that you get when a band's sound is assembled from parts that are laid down by the musicians at different times in separate rooms and later spliced and embellished with studio trickery – that is, the complete antithesis of Albini's live-in-the-studio approach, which had served the group so well before. Gill also pushed the musicians to compose in a more accessible way. It was the producer's idea, remembers Yow, to work harder on the choruses: 'We'd say, "Jeez, Andy, don't you think repeating this chorus twice is enough? Do we really need to do it three times?" And he'd say, "Well, you know, I like that pop music! Come on, David, do it again!"'[50] It now sounded, as the *Washington Post* observed, like everything had landed 'in exactly the right place', but correctness and conformity could not be further removed from what made The Jesus Lizard so special.[51] Elsewhere, *Spin* magazine dismissed *Blue*'s confused 'grunge-funk' aesthetic and compared it to, of all acts, the Spice Girls. 'Both appeal to an adolescent idea of what music is about', reads Jane Dark's withering critique, 'without appealing to actual adolescents, who know better.'[52] *Blue*'s penultimate track, 'Needles for Teeth (Version)', was assisted by hot-property remixers Danny Saber and John X. By Yow's own admission, the result sounded like a Trent Reznor out-take.[53] The push towards commerciality failed to secure the intended profitable outcomes, so Capitol dropped the band after disappointing sales figures.

Listening to *Blue* today, there are still echoes of that original ferocious spirit. The attempts to properly progress and develop fresh approaches should be admired. It's hard to deny, however, given the four or five records that preceded it, that *Blue* lacks the delectable menace of yore. The Lizard had been tamed and, from its newly encaged perspective, found few reasons to carry on breathing. The band split in 1999.

Other 'Pigfuckers'

I hate punk rock. I'm sick of having to pretend that I like it. If you took every single punk song recorded between 1976 and 1978 and added them all together, the resultant pusillanimous, piss weak mess wouldn't even equal one twentieth of the power and fury of '22 Going on 23' by the Butthole Surfers. Noise rock was my punk. And it still is.[54]

JOHN DORAN IN *THE QUIETUS*

As should have been gauged from the two preceding case studies, noise rock is difficult to define. On the one hand, we have Butthole Surfers with their live shows designed to overwhelm the senses via blinding strobes, preposterous quantities of dry ice, gross-out film footage and an outlandish dress sense. While undoubtedly anchored in 'rock', their music was similarly embellished with warped effects, vocal distortions, stylistic digressions, psychedelia and a general 'anything goes' philosophy. On the other hand we have The Jesus Lizard, a far more grounded affair, without bells and whistles and with few gimmicks besides a reckless and restless singer with a tendency for exposing his nutsack. Butthole Surfers were known for their liberal attitude towards drug consumption and enthusiasm for altered mental states. The Jesus Lizard were more partial to Budweiser and bourbon, a mixture known as a 'boilermaker', after which one of their songs was named. Apart from the odd overboard incident, David Yow developed a preference for performing when 'lubricated', meaning hitting that fine line between tipsiness and being so wasted that he couldn't be proud of the show after it had ended.[55]

So where exactly is the common ground betwixt these two groups? Let's try formulating a definition of noise rock, if that's even possible. Noise rock is much weirder than standard hard rock or the louder end of indie music, but it refrains from straying into identifiable heavy metal territory. In a punishing kind of way, it is arty, experimental and largely uncompromising, yet it is not as purely avant-garde as the straight-up 'noise music' of Merzbow, say, or Lou Reed's *Metal Machine Music*. Its bands tend to have a DIY approach inherited from the punk and/or hardcore movements. They usually value creative expression over commercial achievements (notwithstanding, as we've seen, the occasional unhappy alliance with the industry's bigger players). Noise rock sometimes has a darkly psychedelic tinge or industrial edge, although the latter tends to be cultivated through organic means rather than relying on electronics. The genre blossomed roughly in tandem with industrial rock and shares some of the same elements and outlooks, albeit with less dependence on technological innovation. Lyrically, noise rock tends to be satirical, sardonic, provocative, irreverent or off-kilter, even when the words are incomprehensively slurred, garbled, distorted or buried beneath the murkiest of riffs.

In America they called it 'Pigfuck'. The *Village Voice* writer Robert Christgau came up with this term when lumping in Sonic Youth with other 1980s 'pigfucker' bands such as Swans and Big Black.[56] Sonic Youth responded by re-releasing their song 'Kill Yr Idols' under the alternative title 'I Killed Christgau With My Big Fuckin' Dick'. Pigfucker doesn't really work as an appropriate category, though. When Christgau coined it, the expression would have implied a rural redneck backwardness thanks to the famous 'squeal like a pig' scene from *Deliverance*. That film had been released back in 1972. Later that same year, *Last Tango in Paris* included the charming dialogue, 'I'm gonna get a pig and I'm gonna have the pig fuck you. I want the pig to vomit in your face and I want you to swallow the vomit.' Unlike *Deliverance*'s hillbillies or *Last Tango*'s bitter, middle-aged misogynist protagonist, most so-called pigfuck musicians were intelligent and articulate youngsters with liberal outlooks who were based in bohemian, if downtrodden, metropolitan locales like Lower Manhattan (in the case of Sonic Youth and Swans). In spite of their defective sound and no matter what kind of high jinks they got up to in private, as their record for getting picked on by truckers in diners attests, Butthole Surfers were more likely to be targeted as prospective pigfuckees than embark on a whole lotta pigfuckin' themselves. More recently, in the UK at least, pigfucking has acquired loftier connotations thanks to a 2011 episode of *Black Mirror* and a subsequent accusation made by the businessman and ex-Conservative Party peer Michael Ashcroft concerning a bizarre university initiation ceremony involving a then future and now ex-prime minister. So to spare any innocent musicians that humiliating connotation, let's stick to calling it noise rock.

With novel ways of tuning and playing their guitars (with drumsticks wedged beneath the strings, for example), a cut-up approach to song structure and long passages of instrumental scrawl or else sheer feedback, Sonic Youth could get as noisy and atonal as the best of them. It's debatable whether their sound was ever aggressive or dense enough to be categorized as outright noise rock. In reality, Sonic Youth were alternative rock music's great straddlers. For thirty years from 1981 they nonchalantly blurred the lines between low art and high, between punk and prog, between the major labels and the DIY underground, between disposable pop culture and highbrow pretension, between melodies sung and beat poetry spoken, between musical proficiency and moments of intentional primitivism, between activist angst and slacker apathy, between selling out and staying true, between sincerity and irony, between melody and noise, between the past, the present and the future, between being just another band and being a serious contender for the band that matters most of all. Even with all that in mind, as true heirs of The Velvet Underground, Sonic Youth lie more towards the art rock end of things.

Having spawned from the same New York no wave scene as Sonic Youth, Swans positioned themselves nearer the other extreme of the noise rock barometer. Led by the obsessively driven Michael Gira, Swans grinded away with such bleakness, at such volume, and with so much withering contempt for tunes or hooks or warmth or fun or anything in the traditional rock, punk or metal canon that they were, in essence, a transcendentally repetitive and nihilistic mental demolition site. After gaining this reputation, Swans reacted against the 'really stupid' hallmark of 'loudest band in the world' by searching for alternative ways to say 'fuck you'.[57] They found the only option was to quieten down, introduce acoustic instruments and expand the role of the mononymous Jarboe, a classically trained singer and pianist. After this, Swans' output became more goth-country in nature.

The year 1986 was a pivotal one for noise rock. Sonic Youth released their third album, *EVOL*, a decisive stepping stone between their no wave origins and their art rock breakthrough moment *Daydream Nation* two years later. Ending on a locked groove with its running time listed on the sleeve as an infinity symbol, *EVOL*'s final track, 'Expressway to Yr Skull', was once described by Neil Young as 'the best guitar song ever written'.[58] Swans, meanwhile, released two studio albums, *Greed* and *Holy Money*, plus the live album *Public Castration Is a Good Idea*. The earliest official Melvins recordings were released. Butthole Surfers issued their second LP, *Rembrandt Pussyhorse*, played some of their most notorious live shows ever, and began working on their next and arguably greatest album, *Locust*

Abortion Technician. Tom Hazelmyer of Halo of Flies founded Amphetamine Reptile Records in Washington state. Alongside Chicago's Touch and Go Records, AmRep was one of the key labels for noise rock. In Japan the first album emerged from J. G. Ballard fans High Rise (originally known as Psychedelic Speed Freaks), as did the chaotic debut EP by Ruins. From the ashes of Yamantaka Eye's group Hanatarash emerged Boredoms, whose first EP, *Anal By Anal*, released the same year, featured the tracks 'Anal Eat', 'God from Anal' and 'Born to Anal'. Their sound was confrontationally messy yet colourful and playful, like an avant-garde punk band fronted by the Tasmanian Devil from *Looney Tunes*. In time, Boredoms would evolve into a warmer and more psychedelic affair with a penchant for ambitious performances backed by upwards of seventy drummers.

The following year witnessed further developments, such as the self-titled debut LP by the St Louis trio Blind Idiot God. It offered an instrumental take on noise rock with aspects of jazz, thrash, classical and dub informing its crowded cacophony. Following a few early EPs with offensive song titles like 'Cunt Tease' and 'You Look Like a Jew', plus a peculiar cassette release on which they covered The Rolling Stones' *Exile on Main Street* in its entirety, Washington DC's Pussy Galore managed three albums before disintegrating. They specialized in disjointedly rendered garage rock rackets with Delta blues leanings and were lumped in with noise rock despite the often trebly nature of their recordings. Pussy Galore splintered into Boss Hog and Jon Spencer Blues Explosion, who were more substantial, and Royal Trux, who weren't. The latter liked to flutter between sardonic sloppiness and outright cliché, their lack of substance overlooked by music journalists eager to lap up, regurgitate and glamorize the juicy details of the duo's drug-chic lives.

If you'll forgive the pun, Cows offered a lot more beef. Singer Shannon Selberg was like an unholy combination of Gibby Haynes, David Yow and Nick Cave, with maybe a little GG Allin thrown in for good measure. He'd wander onstage wearing outrageous outfits made out of fake fur, the flayed skin of a sex doll, or nothing but shaving cream. Sometimes he'd have mouse traps hanging from his ears. His arms looked skew-whiff because he'd once broken them both by falling through a skylight. Recalling the habits of the most misbehaved kid in primary school, Selberg would draw all over himself in marker pen. He was partial to a wide-brimmed cowboy hat even though he lacked bona fide redneck credentials. When not bawling lyrics about humanity's intrinsic and unending stupidity he'd occasionally add some jazzy bugle parps over the band's barrage of guitar distortion. The horn had originally been a stage prop. When Selberg found himself running out of lyrics to sing over one of the band's jams, he thought he might as well give the bugle a toot to relieve the boredom. Thereafter he gradually found himself improving at the instrument.[59] Cows retained their integrity by remaining on Amphetamine Reptile, even though this loyalty wasn't entirely down to choice. Lots of strange bands ended up on major labels in the 1990s: Melvins, Butthole Surfers, The Jesus Lizard, Babes in Toyland, Boredoms, Mercury Rev, Napalm Death, Ween, Butt Trumpet . . . not Cows, though. They were just *too* strange. 'No, we wanted to get signed by a bigger label,' admitted Selberg,

> Because no one wants to starve to death. And an underground band has a certain shelf life, you know . . . And after *Cunning Stunts* [1992] got some attention, people thought that we would streamline our sound, but we just got weirder. We never got any offers. We never even got taken out to dinner by a label. Minneapolis was actually a hotbed for talent scouts at that time, and we were bigger than most of the bands. We were playing in front of 2,000 people and they're signing bands that have only played live a few times . . . We had record labels saying stuff to us like, 'Sure, this guy's a crazy frontman, but not in a way that we can really market to anybody.'[60]

As John Dougan notes, when 1987's debut LP *Taint Pluribus Taint Unum* emerged, Cows were 'roundly derided as a talentless, tasteless joke'.[61] They didn't exactly charm most listeners thereafter. For the dedicated few, they meant a great deal more than that. The writer Michael H. Little considers himself blessed that after getting clean in 1988 he found a new addiction that was even better than drugs: Cows. 'There's no point in looking in the mirror on days when you're not yourself,' wrote Little, 'and there's certainly no point in staying clean if you don't have big noise in your life. Shannon Selberg's bugle may well have saved me from rehab, or worse.'[62]

That year also saw the disbandment of Big Black. In the time since its conception in 1981, this band had occupied a unique place in the U.S. underground. It began as a solo project on which Steve Albini aimed to emulate post-punk heroes like Killing Joke, Wire and Public Image Ltd. When Naked Raygun members Santiago Durango and bassist Jeff Pezzati (later replaced by Dave Riley) joined the fold, the project became its own beast. The drum parts were programmed onto a machine, which was credited as if it were a real person: 'Roland' (the name of its manufacturer). Albini used metal plectrums that he customized by clipping notches into them. This made for a more clattering sound when the guitar strings were struck. Durango said Big Black's approach was not to play their guitars per se, but rather to assemble noises created by guitars.[63] This, coupled with Roland's cold and inhuman beats, lent Big Black a bitingly metallic and near-industrial sound. Matching the causticity of the music were Albini's withering lyrics. Albini always insisted his words came second to the importance of Big Black's music, that they were 'largely an afterthought'.[64] It's immediately discernible they had greater deliberation behind them than that. They hit a level of literary merit that surpassed that of the impulsively taboo-prodding Throbbing Gristle, for example. Taking an unflinching look at humanity's basest instincts and impulses, Albini's vignettes were sometimes completely fictional but at other times inspired by real-life events he'd heard about or read in the news. This anthology of murder, violent sex, paedophilia, sadism and more had a cast of characters including the small-town arsonist, exploited army veteran, self-hating brothel frequenter and stinking drunk. At times this lyrical content fuelled confusion over whether Albini harboured the same unsavoury views as the miscreants whose stories he told, as if he were Chicago's answer to the Marquis de Sade. For others, Albini was a sneering moralist in the tradition of William Hogarth (to continue the eighteenth-century allusions). Rather, Albini was eager to explore the idea that no matter how civil we consider ourselves to be, we are all capable – and conceivably culpable – of utter barbarity. Unlike many of their contemporaries, Big Black never countenanced the thought of signing to a major label. Having reached the point of popularity when most bands would at least flirt with the idea of surrendering to corporate assistance in order to reach the next step on the ladder of fame, Big Black promptly split up. They'd never been entirely comfortable with the fact that when they played shows, people turned up who the band didn't know personally.[65] One such stranger approached Albini after Big Black's last ever show and asked if he could take home a chunk of the guitar that the frontman had smashed into pieces as a symbol of the finality of the occasion. The concert took place in Seattle. That kid was Kurt Cobain. He still owned that broken bit of guitar when Nirvana made *In Utero* with Albini as its recording engineer.[66]

In 1992 Albini would form his 'minimalist rock trio' Shellac, whose material arguably surpasses that of Big Black. They too would remain fiercely independent. Wanting nothing to do with the 'creeping professionalism' in which fellow underground bands had partaken, Shellac just wanted to put out music when it felt right and play the odd tour between their day jobs. No manager was required. They could organize and control everything themselves. 'I didn't want to trick anybody into buying our records,' explained

Albini in 2017. 'If you weren't interested, we weren't going to try to convince you. We've conducted ourselves that way ever since. I feel like it was the right decision then and I've been very happy with the way things have transpired in that we've never done anything embarrassing for attention and I don't feel like anybody would have ever gotten into this band under false pretences.'[67]

Lesser known '90s noise rock bands operated in a similar under-the-radar manner. Others hitched on the underground-to-mainstream trajectory to varying degrees of limited success. As great as they were, such bands never penetrated very deeply into the metal sphere and nor did they possess the radio-friendliness of the frontrunning grunge artists. Originally active for approximately a decade from the end of the 1980s, fellow New Yorkers Unsane and Helmet made a string of exemplary noise rock records but were each derailed by running out steam, luck and support. An alternative route was taken by Austin's Cherubs. Following a fistfight between drummer Owen McMahon and bassist Brent Prager outside The Casbah in San Diego, the trio broke up. This occurred before their second album had even hit the stores. Released in 1994 on King Coffey's Trance Syndicate label, *Heroin Man* gained cult status over time, partly thanks to Cherubs' alluring absence. The album was dedicated to the band's friend Dave Deluna, who had died from an overdose. The spate of other drug-related deaths that had hit Austin's creative scene around that time also informed the record's lyrics and artwork. The album cover depicts a man's body, face-down in a dirty bathtub. Heroin Man? Worst superhero ever. The record has some underlying melodic traits if you squint your ears tightly enough during songs such as 'Dave of the Moon'. With its claustrophobic wall of sound, musicianship that grows looser and more extemporaneous in the album's later stages, and Kevin Whitley's relatively high-pitched vocals operating somewhere between a growl and sheer shriek of emotional pain, the raw sound of *Heroin Man* could well be what Nirvana had envisaged when they hired

Albini to record *In Utero*, before Kurt Cobain's irrepressible pop nous kicked in and prior to the label and management bogeymen's inevitable meddling.

'Cherubs is ugly noise music and, as an adult, it kinda doesn't make sense to do that,' said an overly apologetic Kevin Whitley when his band reunited in 2014.[68] The guitarist and shrieksmith had recently turned fifty. On the contrary, as similar reformations have shown – The Jesus Lizard's triumphant comeback at the 2009 festival All Tomorrow's Parties: ATP vs The Fans 2: The Fans Strike Back! being a case in point – noise rock undertaken in middle age has the potential to make more sense than it ever did before. There are many bands that manage to age in a clumsy and embarrassing fashion, stretching their bodies and voices a few decades too far, jiggling their bespoke hip replacements while continuing to yelp about street fighting men as they did in their vibrant formative years. Others grow into their sound rather aptly. Noise rock was slower and more morose than the adolescent punk rock template from which it evolved. Bands like Unsane responded to, and reflected that feeling of, being wearily worn down by the cruelty and indifference of the world. Unsane were a thrillingly heavy prospect even when they were fresher-faced dudes who dressed like they could equally have been trading in chirpy ska punk. By 2017's *Sterilize* their battered bodies and brains were in (im)perfect sync with their surly sound. Dave Curran and Vincent Signorelli succeeded in steamrolling any rival noise rock rhythm section into surrender. Chris Spencer's virulent riffs added to the flattening. His snarled lyrics covered a gamut of hopelessness: misery, delusion, corporate greed, history's sick habit of repeating itself, running out of time, running out of breath, running ever towards oblivion . . . Consistent with most Unsane artwork, the picture on the front of *Sterilize* is splattered with blood. In the old days, this was representative of how life could end in a violent and sudden way. It was a symptom of Unsane's environment: the mean streets of New York City, which in its pre-gentrified days was a far more dangerous place to inhabit. Perhaps it's time for Unsane to find a visual way of expressing, as Spencer conveys on *Sterilize*'s 'Inclusion', that death creeps up on most people slowly.

The words above are not intended to discourage the efforts of any younger and sprightlier noise rock bands, of which there are many and yet still too few. Most of them operate in a similar manner to Big Black or Shellac, if only due to the same circumstances suffered by Cows, a situation compounded by the decreasing riches of the music industry. Long gone are the days when major labels would stumble over themselves to sign a band as bonkers as Butthole Surfers. All power to such bands. Originally expounded in the 1950s by Theodore Sturgeon as a means of offsetting science fiction's derision at the hands of literary critics, 'Sturgeon's Revelation' (otherwise known as 'Sturgeon's Law') states that '90 percent of everything is crud'.[69] This adage applies to the crappiness of most 'cars, books, cheeses, hairstyles, people and pins' just as much as it can be used to condemn sci-fi. It also applies to most bands, musicians, albums, songs, scenes and subgenres too. Noise rock is one of the few exceptions to Sturgeon's rule. That's not to say *all* noise rock bands are worth one's time. There are those whose output is consistently strong and satisfying. Others waver in quality. Some do underwhelm. Few of them, certainly less than 90 per cent, are terrible, even the ones you've never heard of beforehand and just happen to encounter in a support slot in a grotty pub and it's only their third gig and they have a name like Sex Tooth, Deep Lunge or Flaggers. The reason that less than 90 per cent of them are rubbish and why so many of them are worth watching as they fling themselves around the stage churning out a din that your parents would describe as 'just a load of horrible noise' is that, according to the attempted definition offered above, noise rock can never really be all that rubbish. If it is bad, it's usually because it has slipped into something altogether less ambitious, obstinate and rewarding than noise rock, be that ropey grunge, feeble indie rock, traditional hard rock, codified heavy metal or something a little too commercially inclined. If that has become the case, then it has ceased to be noise rock at all.

Had Cows really wanted to reach a wider audience than that offered by the 2,000-capacity venue in their hometown, it's extremely likely they'd have had to make some serious creative compromises in order to appeal to that popular demographic. It's hard to imagine they'd have pulled that trick off without having to abandon their noise-rockiness. It's more than likely they'd have sunk into Sturgeon's 90 per cent of crud and turned from Cows into cowpat. Their final album, *Sorry in Pig Minor*, came out in 1998. The person who produced it expressed sorrow that Cows subsequently disbanded, particularly at the exact point when he considered them to be better than they had ever been before.[70] He even tried to persuade them to continue going by offering his own services as the replacement guitarist for Thor Eisentrager, whose departure instigated Cows' split. As producer, he was described as having the tendency to 'throw in off-kilter effects and fiddle with the volumes of the separate components for no reason whatsoever'.[71]

That man was Buzz Osborne of Melvins.

9

SABBATH PHASE II: MELVINS' *GLUEY PORCH TREATMENTS*

Not a man to be messed with: Buzz Osborne of Melvins.

I love heavy metal, and I love the fact that it's rebel music and all that, and at least they're pissed off, but you could never convince them to shave their heads and wear pink tutus . . . That would really up the ante in my book.[1]

BUZZ OSBORNE

Leeds University Students' Union, 26 October 2018. Thirty-five years after forming, Melvins are in town to promote their latest album, 'Pinkus Abortion Technician'. It's something like their 26th full-length, but at this stage in the game who's counting that closely anymore? For this stint on the road, core Melvins duo Buzz Osborne (guitar/vocals) and Dale Crover (drums/occasional vocals) are accompanied by two bassists, Steven McDonald of Redd Kross and Butthole Surfers' Jeff Pinkus. Needless to say the sound is not lacking in terms of the low end. Towards the end of a set that has included cuts cherry-picked from throughout the band's career and even a cover of the obscure David Bowie album track 'Saviour Machine' (with McDonald taking lead vocal), Melvins lurch into 'Eye Flys'. In this rendition, the mercilessly slow and rumbling number that opened Melvins' 1987 debut LP, 'Gluey Porch Treatments', proves even slower and extra rumbly.

As the bass duo begins playing the chest-rattling opening notes, a small and slight woman politely nudges her way to the front of the crowd. While the remaining band members kick in with the drum wallops and guitar scrawl, this little woman, for lack of a more eloquent term, completely loses her shit. Her arms flail around her torso like unsecured helicopter blades. At regular intervals, her knees buckle suddenly as if in involuntary collapse before straightening back up again. With her all-angles headbanging, she is in danger of knocking herself out on the cold metal barrier serving to separate the audience from the stage. As a dance form, this sits somewhere between myoclonic seizure and a demon being exorcized from the body of Regan MacNeil. Other members of the crowd part around the woman to give her the room she requires in order to shake, convulse and windmill on the spot without injuring anybody else. Onlookers' faces display a mixture of amusement and concern. These people are poised slightly, should she require any urgent medical assistance.

After ten minutes or more, Melvins draw their vintage epic to its eventual conclusion. As the final notes peter out, the enraptured woman ceases her paroxysmal freestyle boogie, takes a deep breath and casually ambles towards the back of the room whence she originally emerged as if nothing untoward had happened at all. She is not the only Melvins fan to have expressed her enthusiasm in such an unusual, carefree and slightly precarious manner. It's befitting of a band who haven't exactly operated in an especially normal way.

Munk Petal?

In terms of the noise rock artists discussed in the previous chapter, Melvins stand out from the crowd both for their idiosyncratic sound and in terms of their wide-reaching influence. While Melvins certainly tick many of the boxes to qualify them for noise rock status, some aficionados would deny this unique band a place on the noise rock shelf, or any other shelf for that matter. Forget the shelf, in fact, as Melvins deserve an entire temple all to themselves. Besides noise rock, alternative attempts to categorize Melvins have included the labels punk metal, hard rock, stoner, doom, alt-metal and more. Their sound has been compared to a 'two-ton iron chest of blackened sludge' and summarized elsewhere as a 'combination of sudden, herky-jerky thrash (but not thrash metal) and epic stomp and sprawl'.[2] They've stuck at it longer than most, and because of their own musical heroes, as well as the bands who have in turn worshipped Melvins, their sound has been categorized both as proto-metal and post-metal (never straight-up metal). At the time of writing, there exists a three-page thread on the Melvins.net discussion boards with its topic headline asking, 'Are the Melvins Closer to Punk or Metal?' The thread offers little consensus beyond the answer of 'both and neither' and the handy proposal of an entirely new term: 'munk petal'. One person on there insists, sarcastically, 'They are grunge. Bottom line. Period.'[3]

Hailing from Aberdeen, Washington, the same city as Nirvana, Melvins pre-dated grunge and helped spur it on, and were accordingly associated with the late 1980s and early '90s Seattle scene. As if aware of the need to steer clear of the mixed blessings of being linked to Seattle, in the late 1980s Melvins relocated to San Francisco. Among the many things Buzz Osborne is eager to avoid, it's buzz. As such, Melvins succeeded in outliving grunge, unlike many bands associated with that scene, and they did it all without ever sounding particularly 'grunge' in the first place.

Roger 'Buzz' Osborne first fell in love with music at about the same age many of us do, on the cusp of teenagehood. His early crushes included Aerosmith and Ted Nugent, after which he was struck by the enigmatic spell of David Bowie. Then came the all-important revelations offered by punk rock. In their earliest incarnation, Melvins' repertoire teemed with bratty hardcore punk songs. When the *Mangled Demos from 1983* collection surfaced in 2005, reviewers tended to categorize the roughly recorded cuts as derivatively indebted to TSOL, MDC and DRI. Capturing the band in its most primitive form, even this early document contains pungent hints that Melvins were always going to do things differently, and not only in terms of avoiding an acronymic band name in favour of christening their group after an unpopular supervisor at the grocery store where Osborne worked. Included in those demos is 'Set Me Straight'. One of the first songs Osborne ever wrote, it would be pulled out of the bag in a decade's time to be recorded properly for Melvins' major-label debut *Houdini* (1993). It's doubtful Melvins were forced to revisit a track penned when they were teenagers due to any shortage of fresher material. Behind his furious work ethic lies Osborne's view that to become even vaguely successful in any walk of life, commitment must exceed the minimal efforts of a forty-hour week with weekends off.[4] It is therefore more likely that the resurrection of 'Set Me Straight' was a multi-symbolic gesture implying that Melvins had always had the goods in their repertoire; it had just taken the clueless majors a long while to catch up with them. At the same time, the track's inclusion indicated that Melvins were not about to begin altering their modus operandi, adapting their style or buckling to commercial pressures and hip radio trends just because they had found (temporary) corporate assistance.

Another precognitive number is 'Matt-Alec', a track so strong it appears in two different renditions on *Mangled Demos*. Its lyrics read as fairly typical teenage punk fare, the disillusioned protagonist being sick of trying, sick of crying and prone to banging his head against the wall in frustration. Over three minutes in length, it is the longest and slowest of Melvins' early punk numbers, its chunky riffs harking back to pre-punk hard rock while simultaneously hinting at Melvins work to come.

This evolutionary regression of sorts became more pronounced after the departure of drummer Mike Dillard, who was replaced in 1984 by Dale Crover. Although not all Melvins songs are slow – Osborne has complained that he has written plenty of fast songs too – slowness is crucial to Melvins' aesthetic and also their impact on the wider music scene. It is derived, for the most part, from Black Sabbath. While Osborne has described Sabbath as but one in around a thousand musical heroes, Sabbath remain the most manifest.[5] Alice Cooper was another key influence. So too were Kiss (or at least Kiss's initial run of albums, until around 1979's dodgy *Dynasty*). Crucially, Melvins also committed countless actions over the years that the dollar-focused Kiss would never have dreamt of in a million years. A collaboration with the experimental industrial artist Lustmord, for instance. Tracks with weird sections of musique concrète. Long periods of near silence. Long periods of *actual* silence. The sleeve to *Lysol* (1992) provided no track titles even though it contained three covers (one Flipper song plus two classic Alice Cooper numbers). The CD edition was mastered as one single unbroken track because Melvins didn't like the idea of listeners skipping forward to the next song. As well they might do, given that the album begins with two songs titled 'Hung Bunny' and 'Roman Dog Bird' (as white-label test pressings and setlists would reveal). 'Hung Bunny' is particularly fearsome, being a ten-minute sludge marathon of bowel-rattling bass, snail-paced chords played with a drop-C tuning, layers of guitar distortion as thick and dark as Rothko's paint strokes and wordless chanting of a quasi-spiritual variety. According to Crover, Melvins were trying to combine the sound of 'We Will Fall' from the debut Stooges album with the trance-inducing chanting made by the Gyuto monks of Tibet.[6] In the process, Melvins inadvertently wrote the blueprint for drone metal.

But all these tricks had their roots in *Gluey Porch Treatments*. Indeed, it is that album's 'Eye Flys' that Melvins stumble into playing at the climax of the 'live album' *Colossus of Destiny* from 2001. Here, 'Eye Flys' follows almost an hour of Melvins at their most avant-garde as they dabble in controlled ambient noise music and electronic soundscapes, utilizing vocal samples from sources including pornographic movies and incorporating other methods of audience-alienating audio turmoil. As one eye-and-ear-witness attests, when the band did finally kick in to 'Eye Flys' the rendition was so loud it caused people to clutch at their ears and writhe on the ground in agony.[7] Other fans felt ripped off after purchasing the 'difficult' recording as a full-price CD. In typically defiant manner, Osborne believes *Colossus of Destiny* is up there with the best albums that Melvins have ever done. It's one of the three records he would give to someone who was trying to understand his band. 'It always amazes me when people go, "This is bullshit, it's just noise" because it's not just noise; there's a meter and a flow to it that makes a lot of sense,' he insists.[8] It is worth noting that among the 'thousand' musical influences on

Melvins that complement that of Sabbath, Kiss and Alice Cooper are industrial provocateurs Throbbing Gristle, the extreme metal of Celtic Frost and irreverent counterculture pranksters like The Fugs and The Residents.

Just like 'Black Sabbath' from *Black Sabbath* some seventeen years beforehand, 'Eye Flys' was an audacious track with which to open a debut album. Many – perhaps the majority of – rock, metal and punk acts choose to begin an LP with all guns blazing, capturing listeners' attention from the off with one of their most immediately satisfying and lapel-grabbing compositions. Think 'Whole Lotta Love'. 'Search and Destroy'. 'Welcome to the Jungle'. 'Smells Like Teen Spirit'. The list goes on and on. Those are the kind of opening numbers that make the average listener sit up and take notice, and the kind that make superstars out of their creators. Setting the pattern for Melvins' entire career, 'Eye Flys' acts as a patience-testing challenge for anyone but the most open-minded lover of slowness, strangeness, weight and noise. In structural terms it's a sort of reverse 'Helter Skelter', with over half its opening run-ning time consisting of slow-motion bass notes, minimalist drum echoes (interspersed with the occasional spurt of jazzy hyperactiv-ity) and suspenseful abstract guitar moans and scratching sounds complete with white-noise feedback. Something vaguely resem-bling a rock song kicks in to occupy the final two minutes with slow chords, no chorus and Osborne's meticulously garbled bellowing acting as a near-parodic amalgamation of Ozzy, Cooper, Kiss and Venom. By this point, Osborne's lyrics had already progressed from expressing teenage frustration to embracing the more intangible process of declaring an identification with, erm, eye flies. Whatever they are.

The album's remaining sixteen tracks are shorter, some of them faster, but with their deep post-Sabbath riffs, muggy distortion, tumbling beats and vocal gurning, the collection does a fine job of picking punk rock up by the scruff of its tattooed neck and force-feeding it a healthy dose of heaviness. Its power reverberated across the American underground and beyond. When Dylan Carlson of Earth first heard *Gluey Porch Treatments*, he was so impressed that it threw him into the pits of despair. He decided that there was no reason for any other bands to exist because they'd never make anything as good as Melvins.[9]

Bullheads and Bulging Eggs

Like many of the most important guitarists in our history of heaviness, Osborne has little interest in sitting around practising intricate lead guitar scales. He feels this would be an intolerable and ridiculous waste of his time. There are some guitar solos on Melvins' records, and plenty of difficult music to boot – both in terms of performing it and, for some, to endure listening to it – but solos are never the focal point. Instead, Osborne prefers to work on shaping riffs, crafting songs, entertaining himself and confounding his listeners.[10] A rare talent, Dale Crover is one of a small number of musicians who could pull off a John Bonham-style extended drum solo without it seeming pointlessly indulgent. But then again, showboating is not the point. In a classic example of Melvins' contrariness, the ten-minute drum solo that concludes the *Houdini* album does not remotely resemble Led Zeppelin in 'Moby Dick' mode. 'Spread Eagle Beagle' is more like an art gallery sound-installation piece for ketamine-addled BDSM enthusiasts.

Osborne is reluctant to provide explanations for his lyrics. It's a similar attitude to that of film director David Lynch, another one of Osborne's idols, who feels no obligation to clear up the 'true' meaning of his surrealist movies. Lynch prefers to leave his pictures open to viewers' wildly different interpretations. Perhaps this is one rare example of Osborne showing concern – rather than contempt or indifference – towards his own admirers. They say 'never meet your heroes', to which might be added 'but if you do meet them, don't ask them to explain their song lyrics.' This lesson was learned by Tool guitarist Adam Jones when grilling Osborne over the song 'Boris':

> It's from *Bullhead* [1991], which is a very innovative and phenomenal record. I remember listening to the lyrics and being like, 'This is the purest, most meaningful and heaviest shit I've heard in a long time.' Later on, after I befriended Buzz, I said, 'That song really means a lot to me.' And he says, 'Oh, that song's about my cat.' So it's good to not get too analytical about this stuff.[11]

Over the decades Melvins have rattled through as many bassists as Spıñal Tap have seen out drummers, all of whom have contributed to heaviness via other activities, with the exception of Lori Black – the punk-rocking daughter of Shirley Temple – who became a photographer. Matt Lukin joined Mudhoney. Joe Preston played in Earth, Sunn O))), Harvey Milk and other acts, including his solo project Thrones. Mark Deutrom has also toured with Sunn O))) and recorded several solo albums. Ex-Cows member Kevin Rutmanis's stint for Melvins overlapped with his involvement in Tomahawk, and he's since been heard in Hepa-Titus. When Rutmanis left Melvins in 2005, he was replaced by Jared Warren from sludge-rocking power duo Big Business. As if Crover's drumming wasn't beastly enough already, he and Osborne also invited into the fold Big Business' drummer Coady Willis for that era, the double drum kits pounding listeners into submission and leaving them reeling in tinnitus.

Albeit graced with jazzy subtleties, the so-called 'Melvins Lite' incarnation with double bassist Trevor Dunn (Mr Bungle, Fantômas) was still a forceful prospect. Their 2012 LP *Freak Puke* included further testament to Paul McCartney's role as godfather of heaviness by including a Wings cover. In fact, Melvins managed to make 'Let Me Roll It' sound so convincingly their own that at least one reviewer assumed this 'stupidly beautiful' number was an original composition, having completely overlooked the fact that its 'dunt-headed lyricism' can be attributed to the same polymathic genius who gave us 'Blackbird' and 'Yesterday'.[12]

While releases like *Colossus of Destiny* proved too perverse for sensitive listeners, and despite the odd mid-LP wobble such as 2013's screwball cover of '99 Bottles of Beer', Melvins have recorded some of the most rewarding rock music of the last three and a half decades. With dazzling downtuned riffs spilling from Osborne's fingers like sparks from an angle grinder, Dale Crover's Bonham-like beats and a thundering low-end provided by whichever misfit happens to be playing bass for them at that given moment, most Melvins albums flaunt a supreme balance of crushing strength, rowdy melodies, bizarre lyrics and general sonic weirdness. It's a distinctive sound that the 2003 edition of *The Rough Guide to Rock* fittingly described as 'decidedly unsafe . . . what Sabbath would sound like with Captain Beefheart as chief songwriter'.[13] As such, Melvins have influenced everybody from cult grindcore groups like Pig Destroyer to drone metal pioneers Earth, Sunn O))) and Japan's Boris, the latter being named after the opening track from *Bullhead*, plus just about every grunge, alt-rock and noise rock band that ever formed.

Alongside the dadaist lyrics about equine gods and bulging egg tourniquets, Melvins' love for the surreal extends to their record sleeves, many of which exhibit disarmingly cutesy illustrations. Often designed by Osborne's wife Mackie, the pictures are somehow both appropriate and antithetic to the music contained within. Such eccentricity and bloody-mindedness were never likely to secure mainstream glory. The 'Jacksonville/Dallas' 7-inch features live recordings of the band berating hostile audiences, captured during two of the many miserable slots they played in the mid-1990s supporting the likes of Nine Inch Nails.

This was Melvins' brief major-label period. They signed to Atlantic after the grunge explosion, but unlike many of their contemporaries' efforts, Melvins' three major-label albums are notable for their apparent lack of record company interference. Scattered between its vaguely more 'normal' rock tracks, the so-called 'Atlantic Trilogy' includes that aforementioned stubborn ten-minute drum solo, a Kiss cover about intergenerational sex (at a time when Kiss couldn't have been less cool), several ambient noisescapes and one particularly strange outro resembling the death rattle of an unfortunate chipmunk. Needless to say, the band was cast back into the independent ocean and at the turn of the millennium began a long and fruitful partnership with Mike Patton and Greg Werckman's Ipecac Recordings, a suitable home for perennial outsiders too heavy for mainstream rock fans and simply too peculiar for outright metalheads.

Melvins clearly didn't enter the music business to make friends, and they've never been afraid of slaughtering sacred cows. Osborne's relationship with Kurt Cobain is a case in point. Cobain idolized Melvins, hung out with them in his youth, and was so blatantly enamoured with them that Nirvana's 'Milk It' (1993) is startlingly similar to Melvins' lesser-known 'It's Shoved', released two years earlier. The Cobain association helped bring Melvins to the attention of a broader audience. Cobain has a producer's credit on *Houdini*, even though he was fired from the project for being strung out on drugs. Unlike Cobain's other old pals, Osborne took to speaking about his dead friend in outrageously derogatory terms soon after his suicide. An album provisionally titled *Kurt Kobain* was changed to *Prick*, Kurt being 'a prick' for dying and ruining Melvins' plans. Their cartoonist friend Brian Walsby has created Melvins posters inscribed 'We Killed Kurt' and a T-shirt bearing a caricature of Cobain with the slogan 'The only good junkie is a dead junkie'. As then bassist Mark Deutrom put it in a fanzine interview shortly after Cobain's death: 'He died, that didn't make any difference to us. We are still making fun of him!'[14] Far from engaging in shock-tactic attention-seeking, Melvins made it their mission to prevent the tragic story of their friend from becoming a romanticized death cult of self-martyrdom. Most other voices became complicit in the reverse.

Cobain is not the only one to have been on the receiving end of Osborne's wrath. He appears to hate most fellow musicians, repeatedly asserting that 'rock people are whore-mongering drug addicts, who can't even make good music.' Specific targets of Melvins' ire have included Mötley Crüe, Courtney Love, Dave Grohl, Rob Zombie, Red Hot Chili Peppers, Weezer, Miley Cyrus and 'that little weasel in Green Day'.[15] Osborne reserves particular bile for those in showbiz who weigh into political debate. 'Any political leader that would spend time talking to Bono is fucking out of their mind,' he told the *LA Record*, a sentiment he extends to Noam Chomsky: 'Chomsky is a linguist. That's what he does best. Why anybody listens to him on politics is beyond me.'[16]

Osborne has confessed to harbouring 'classic liberal' views, which might explain his formidable work ethic and disdain for adolescent rock-star behaviour. He provocatively mocked critics of George W. Bush during the Iraq War, has ranted against the American Teamsters Union, and called the economist and columnist Thomas Sowell 'the greatest philosopher of all time'.[17] What could be more punk rock, in the context of a scene populated by lefty bohemians, than paddling against the political tide? Mind you, Osborne's contrary conservatism should be taken with a pinch of salt. Melvins have released collaborative albums with the fiercely left-wing Jello Biafra, and video evidence shows that the majority of Osborne's interview statements, which in print might appear haughtily sincere, are accompanied by an infectious, chesty cackle.

Besides, who's complaining when the guy continues to churn out such an astonishing, distinctly nonconformist discography? Like the novelist J. G. Ballard, Osborne appears to be following that famous maxim of Gustave Flaubert: 'Be regular and orderly in your life, like a bourgeois, so that you may be violent and original in your work.' As Osborne put it in an interview with *oc Weekly*, 'I live a very conservative life; any wildness comes out in the music.'[18]

John Peel famously explained his love of The Fall by saying, 'They are always different, they are always the same.' The same thing could be said of Melvins. Had they released *Gluey Porch Treatments* and then split up, died or disappeared off the face of the Earth, the seeds of the second phase of Sabbath had already been sown.

10

THE GLOBAL IMPACT OF
NAPALM DEATH'S *SCUM*

Scum by Napalm Death.

Napalm Death, whose LP *Scum* boasts twenty-eight tracks
of quite exceptionally rapid music, described on the sleeve as
'savagely brutal hardcore thrash', sounded as though they were
playing soundtracks of the end of civilisation. I liked them a
lot.[1]

JOHN PEEL

Napalm Death's first album was released in 1987, the same year as Melvins' debut, and they would go on to become good friends, even touring together at times. The two groups didn't share the same political outlook. Napalm Death espoused socialist and humanist causes with some anarchism and animal rights activism thrown in for good measure; Melvins' Buzz Osborne has long been more concerned with the inalienable freedom of the individual. It's easy to see how each extreme can develop from being immersed in punk rock at a formative age, what with punk's emphasis both on the strength of community and the importance of doing things for yourself no matter what anybody thinks of it and without anybody getting in your way. As for their differences, says Osborne when discussing the friendship, 'They're a bunch of sweethearts . . . we don't come to loggerheads in any way. That's their trip. Let them do their thing and I'll do mine.'[2]

Whereas the bands covered in the previous two chapters made punk rock heavier by slowing it down, Napalm Death's *Scum* was more concerned with making it faster and denser than anybody could have imagined. (Not bad for a bunch of sweethearts.) Napalm Death basically invented grindcore in the process, although they did do this in tandem with like-minded groups such as Ipswich's Extreme Noise Terror and Lancashire's misleadingly named Electro Hippies. Napalm Death formed earlier, mind, and the term 'grindcore' itself was invented by Napalm Death drummer Mick Harris. He can also be credited for coming up with the enduring term 'blast beat' to describe the manic drumming technique employed in grindcore and other heavy genres.

Whereas punk had come out of London, claimed *NME*'s Steven Wells, before spreading out elsewhere and then diminishing under 'the dark days of glue and anarcho-piety', grindcore was 'a totally provincial phenomenon' wherein punk was reborn with 'evangelical zeal', 'total fear of commerciality' and 'an almost anal obsession with "honesty"'. Wells didn't use the word 'grindcore' himself, instead offering terms like 'Oikcore' and 'Yokelpunk'.[3] Alas these didn't catch on. Napalm Death in particular, Wells wrote when reporting on a Moscow tour date in 1991, were 'the band that stretched the very meaning of rock until it tore'. He did add that 'If you think Napalm Death are scary, you should meet the Russian cleaning ladies.'[4] This was just weeks prior to the official endpoint of the Soviet Union.

The group of young musicians from the West Midlands who created *Scum* were as surprised as anyone that the record went on to resonate so widely and loudly across borders, oceans, genres, scenes and generations. With 28 angry and politicized songs squeezed into a taut 33-minute running time, *Scum* set new standards in brevity and extremity. It came the year after three of the 'Big Four' of the American thrash scene had released career-defining albums: Metallica's *Master of Puppets*, Megadeth's *Peace Sells . . . but Who's Buying?* and Slayer's *Reign in Blood*. The fourth act in the gang, Anthrax, had released *Spreading the Disease* in 1985 and returned with *Among the Living* in early '87. *Scum* would not prove as popular as those albums. Nor would it feature any cheesy extended guitar solos or songs about black magic. And it would outdo the heaviness of the American thrashers by a significant margin.

There is little need to reiterate *Scum*'s enduring influence on the world of heavy metal. You'll find its appearance in a thousand articles purporting to count down the ALL-TIME HEAVIEST ALBUMS EVER MADE, and nobody would dispute the impact it had on Pig Destroyer, for instance, or Full of Hell. To be perfectly honest, if you're a musician who plays – or a fan who dabbles – in any of the countless metal subgenres and you haven't already familiarized yourself with both sides of *Scum*, then, quite frankly, you haven't completed your homework.

John Peel was one of the earliest and most crucial promoters of grindcore. Peel regularly went to see Napalm Death and Extreme Noise Terror when they played in Ipswich, often accompanied by his wife Sheila and their first child, William. 'These were grimy, chaotic affairs attended largely by crusties wearing layers of shredded denim and dreadlocks thick as rope,' Sheila would write. 'The moshpit was like an initiation ritual – if you could make it out of there in one piece, you knew you could survive anything life had to lob at you. People would stagger out with nosebleeds, clutching their heads, complaining of double vision, drenched in sweat. And yet a good-natured atmosphere prevailed somehow.'[5] Peel frequently played their records on his Radio 1 show, thrilling and bamboozling listeners in equal measure, and gleefully invited the bands to record exclusive sessions for his programme. For Peel it was that initial burst of grindcore activity that was so appealing. His interest waned in the early 1990s as he noticed the 'wide-eyed exuberance' of the genre was beginning to fade and was broken down into a less immediately enthralling and perhaps even somewhat unfathomable plethora of subgenre after post-grindcore subgenre. As an alternative, Peel began looking for a similar buzz in different forms of music, and found it in his discovery of rave offshoots with superfast BPMs like happy hardcore and gabber, drawing further complaints from the less open-minded subset of his listeners.[6]

Peel's graduation from grindcore to happy hardcore is not that unlikely. The ever spiralling instances of grindcore-derived subgenres are all well and good, yet *Scum*'s impact stretches far beyond metal or even rock. Famously, the two sides of Napalm Death's debut LP were recorded by almost entirely different line-ups. The personnel from the first side of the record soon spread their sonic wings into industrial and electronic ventures. Guitarist Justin Broadrick went on to form the industrial metal band Godflesh followed by the shoegaze-influenced post-metal project Jesu. Broadrick was also part of the beat-oriented 'illbient' duo Techno Animal with Kevin Martin (aka The Bug) and has released other electronic material under the aliases Pale Sketcher and JK Flesh. The only member of the A-side trio who also performed on *Scum*'s second side was drummer Mick Harris. He, in turn, would leave Napalm Death in 1991 to form the trip-hoppy proto-dubstep outfit Scorn as well as his ambient side project Lull. Nicholas Bullen, who founded Napalm Death when he was still a teenager and performed bass and vocals on *Scum*'s first twelve songs, also contributed to the first three Scorn albums. Since then, Bullen's variety of audio experiments have included abstract soundscapes, arty sound installations, performance works for voice, acousmatic pieces and other esoteric pursuits.

Those endeavours' associations to electronica is plain to see, but the actual output of Napalm Death, and that first album in particular, has had a profound effect on countless 'non-rock' musicians. Recording as Broken English Club, the prolific DJ/producer Oliver Ho paid homage to Napalm Death in 2015 by titling one of his tracks 'Scum'. Ho discovered Napalm Death's music in his mid-teens. He was impressed by the sheer density of the sound and, when played live 'at a horrendously loud volume', its ability to physically vibrate one's body. Grindcore, Ho found, had an alien-like quality comparable to the techno music in which he would come to specialize.[7] The late Mika Vainio of Finnish electro pioneers Pan Sonic was another Napalm Death aficionado. Discussing his favourite albums with *The Quietus* in 2014, Vainio spoke of his enthusiasm for the first albums of Napalm Death and Carcass (the Liverpudlian 'goregrind' project whose guitarist Bill Steer played on *Scum*'s second side).[8] Wakefield-born Björk collaborator and Hollywood soundtrack composer Bobby Krlic (aka The Haxan Cloak) has said that his own approach towards sound itself was formulated when his older brother introduced him to records by Napalm Death and related extreme bands.[9] The multidisciplinary artist, curator and avant-techno noise-maker

Russell Haswell attributes some of his own cross-genre outlook to the experience of going to see the legendary Detroit DJ Jeff Mills on one night and attending a Napalm Death concert the following evening.[10] In 2014 the French producer and DJ Mondkopf released an album under the Extreme Precautions alias with the accompanying caveat: 'I was thinking of doing a techno EP. But I was mostly listening to Brutal Truth, Assuck, Napalm Death and Pig Destroyer at that time, so grindcore got me carried away and I went blast beat. This was a blast indeed – I did this record in a week total, a big release for me.'[11]

A Continuum of Cacophony

Nicholas Bullen left Napalm Death shortly after the completion of *Scum*'s first side and his subsequent work has demonstrated that he is not one to dwell on the past. Nevertheless, at 2017's Supersonic Festival in Digbeth, Birmingham, Bullen was commissioned to put together a special performance to celebrate *Scum*'s 30th anniversary. Dressed in a colourful shirt and regularly mopping the sweat from his furrowed brow, Bullen used a mixing desk, several microphones, various effects units and samples from the first side of *Scum* – along with an archive cassette recording of Napalm Death's first ever band rehearsal in 1981 – to create a looped and layered tornado of harsh sound. So fierce was it that Bullen's initial mixing desk gave up the ghost after less than thirty seconds and had to be hastily replaced. The second mixing desk did endure, although it might subsequently have required some urgent therapy.

Bullen named this performance *Universal Detention Centre*. Like *Scum*, it had a clear left-wing political agenda in the face of a shift to the right in UK politics (in tandem with that occurring elsewhere around the globe), as Bullen explained when we spoke a few days before Supersonic:

It does follow through on the continuum of Napalm Death from its beginnings in that I felt it was appropriate to try to address the way people's freedoms are being increasingly limited. By that, I don't mean the alt-right desire to say whatever they want! I'm thinking more about actual physical limitations on people, in terms of where they live, where they can go, and how they exist.[12]

All types of boundaries and barriers seem anathema to Bullen, and *Scum*'s influence on electronic artists is less incongruous when you consider that Napalm Death's own music was itself inspired, in part, by electronic music. By listening to John Peel, hanging around in record shops and trading cassettes in his youth, Bullen discovered the mechanical rackets of post-punk and industrial acts Cabaret Voltaire, Throbbing Gristle and The Normal. Two years before Justin Broadrick joined the band, he and Bullen bonded over a mutual love of power electronics, including the output of the Broken Flag and Come Organisation labels. 'That harshness was a big influence for me because it chimed with the harsher ends of hardcore and thrash,' Bullen recalled. 'There are passages on the first side of *Scum* that explicitly reference harsh electronics, or what would be called "noise" now. There's a passage in the song "Sacrificed", there's the beginning of the album ["Multinational Corporations"], and they were written to include what Throbbing Gristle termed the "walls of noise" as break points.'

Though it sat among a broad range of other reference points, electronic music also had an impact on Bullen's development of the distinctive grindcore vocal style.

I was really excited by the use of ring modulation in Cabaret Voltaire and Throbbing Gristle. As you discover later, the ring modulator was often used on voice in modern composition electronic works. I liked the alien-like cold and distant feeling that sound gave. In part, that was an influence of my youth and the television programmes I would watch, which often included distorted and mutated voices. I'm thinking particularly of *Dr Who*'s Cybermen and the Sea Devils. Before I was into music, when I was six or seven, I was obsessed with horror and science fiction. We definitely tried to mutate the voice as much as possible.

It has been noted that playing Napalm Death's records at an exceptionally low volume makes for a similar listening experience to the kind of peaceful ambient music pioneered by Brian Eno. I have a vague and possibly false memory of John Peel once explaining this on the radio, but others have said it was Brian Eno himself who pointed it out.[13] It can also come as a surprise when music that is considered to be 'ambient', and which might usually be played at a low and relaxing volume in the home, is performed live at an incredible volume. There was something so intense, repetitive and asphyxiating about composer William Basinski's set at the All Tomorrow's Parties festival in June 2013 that several people, myself included, had to leave the room as it felt far more likely to induce a sudden panic attack or mental breakdown than any rock or metal band I've seen. Others said they nearly fainted, likened the experience to whiteying on cannabis, or feared they might be going deaf and/or blind. The comparison between grindcore and ambient is something Bullen can appreciate and also help to explain:

> At twin points towards the ends of the spectrum, i.e. very low and very high volume, detail begins to merge into sound patterns and I can understand how you would listen to grindcore as ambient music because it would roll off the edges. What you're left with is tone, shape and sensation. The same occurs with extremes of volume. Often, people view high volume through the simple viewpoint that it's in

some way an expression of maleness; that it's designed to express in a macho way. But I don't really see it like that. I see it as another way to alter consciousness and listening, and to alter the space within a room and its architecture.

It has to be said that, whereas much aggressive and extreme music can risk coming across as decidedly laddish, this isn't the case with Napalm Death. That's true both of the formula set by *Scum* and the recorded output and live performances of Napalm Death's subsequent line-ups. Despite the music's intensity and that primal, guttural vocal style, I've never felt that theirs was an exercise in the assertion of masculinity, something that surely adds to Napalm Death's universal appeal. Bullen attributes this to the fact that Napalm Death emerged from a different 'milieu' than other heavy music.

Napalm Death comes very much out of politicized punk, which by its very nature includes a range of ideas, influences and spaces in a way that perhaps other loud, heavy rock doesn't. With Napalm Death, everything's focused on ideas in a way that you wouldn't find perhaps in the extremes of, say, modern power electronics or goregrind, which come from a different place really. Musically, they come from a similar area but the import behind it is different. It's [also] to do with the technical aspects of it. When you hit high levels of speed, there's less opportunity to replicate the more traditional tropes of rock music, the focus on overt displays of musicianship which could be seen as self-aggrandizing, because there just isn't the room to do that within the sound. When I was in Napalm Death, when we played the slower parts they acted as blocking points between the extremes of speed rather than the more clichéd approach to heavy music. Rock music's never interested me particularly. I like areas of it. But my record collection doesn't contain a lot of 'rock' music.

Scum's global reach is noteworthy too. The dance producers mentioned above come from an array of locations, and these days it's possible to find grindcore acts in virtually every corner of the planet. Also on the line-up to Supersonic 2017 were Japan's Melt-Banana, whose berserk, effects-laden cyber-grind aesthetic is greatly indebted to Napalm Death without sounding very similar to their precursors. Indeed, Yasuko Onuki's high-pitched vocal style is practically the opposite of the deep grindcore 'cookie monster' growl of Napalm Death's vocals, although as Bullen has already identified, such extremes can go full circle.

Before recording *Scum*, Bullen and his collaborators had soaked up the intense displays of sound made by vintage Japanese punk groups such as GISM, Kuro and Crow.

> One thing we loved about Japanese hardcore bands was that they were enamoured of early '80s hardcore from the UK, which was very noisy and focused on feedback and distortion. So it almost acted as a bounce-back between the two. They took that influence, made their own version and then when we heard it, it escalated what we liked in those earlier records, and moved forward. There was a level of intensity that the Japanese groups were reaching towards that wasn't necessarily replicated in England. So, within a continuum, [Napalm Death] sits as a further development, but it perhaps took that development close to its logical end, where it stops being a song and goes into pure sound.

The global influence of *Scum* wasn't restricted to Japan. The Finnish hardcore punk groups Kaaos, Cadgers and Rattus were also significant, among other international bands. 'We traded them on cassettes around the world in 1982 and 1983,' remembers Bullen. 'We couldn't afford the records. For one thing, they were imports with limited runs and we just didn't have the money. We were all schoolkids. But we could afford a pack of ten tapes and some stamps. We would regularly get compilations from Finland, Italy, Holland, Sweden, all over the world. It was very exciting.' No doubt it was equally stimulating for foreign listeners when, in return, Napalm Death fired *Scum* right back at them. Yasuko Onuki would have been fifteen years old at the time of *Scum*'s release. Four years later she would form Mizu, which would mutate into Melt-Banana.

Bullen may have long since moved on from Napalm Death but, as *Universal Detention Centre* showed, *Scum* remains an essential part of his DNA and was the launching pad to a long and varied presence in the arts. He hasn't kept up with much of Napalm Death's output since his own tenure in the band, although that's no reflection on its quality because there is no band that his 'mercurial' tastes would allow him to follow for thirty years. Napalm Death continue to perform tracks from *Scum* despite none of the current members having actually played on that debut album – not that the barrier-averse Bullen is bothered by such a thing: 'My perspective is that the members of Napalm Death now are Napalm Death,' he says,

and they have the right to go back and play that material, should they wish to. They were there at the time, Shane [Embury] and Barney [Greenway], they were all listening, and I don't see a problem with them playing that material at all. I'm certainly not precious about the songs I wrote. I'm not going to play them and why shouldn't they? As a group, they perhaps also have a desire to let their appreciative audience hear all aspects of their career. It's within that continuum of Napalm Death so it sits well.

It is doubtful there is any feasible limit at all to the extraordinary continuum of Napalm Death.

11

THE LATE 1980S AND EARLY 1990S PRE-GRUNGE UNDERGROUND

*Bad Brain*s by Bad Brains.

Rock! The lumbering warthog of music remains ugly in the navvy hands of WASP, inflexible in the throats of nearly every speed metal crew bar Metallica, and ludicrous in the leather crotches of The Cult. But Bad Brains … ahhhh … Michelangelos of moshing, theirs is the rock of ages: a slipstreaming titanium teeming firestorm dreaming rollercoaster of sound that makes one want to buffet forever in a celestial slamdance.[1]

JACK BARRON IN *SOUNDS*

Mark 'Barney' Greenway has served as lead vocalist of Napalm Death since 1990 (interrupted only by a brief period when he defected to Extreme Noise Terror for one album). As recently as 2015 Greenway was pointing out the enduring influence of Public Image Ltd on his band's ferocious music. He described his performance on the Swans-ish title track to *Apex Predator – Easy Meat* (2015) in the following terms: 'Vocally what I wanted to do with that was take Public Image Ltd-era John Lydon and multiply it by ten. He always had a really good way of spitting his vocals out, and that's what I wanted to do. And I did it. That's the first take in the studio, no pissing about.'[2] Public Image Ltd, as well as Lydon's earlier Sex Pistols activities, have remained a touchstone for people the world over who have wanted to make adventurous music since the 'bright flash' of punk. PiL didn't help galvanize a vibrant post-punk music scene solely by releasing groundbreaking records of dub-infused, emotionally raw experimentation like *Metal Box*. They also did it by acting like tossers. This was particularly true when it came to America, where PiL concentrated much of their live activities after backtracking on their original promise not to tour.

Back when he was still known as Johnny Rotten, Lydon had been a key figure in the imaginations of Minutemen, who had made the leap to break free from the covers band scene of San Pedro, California, and forge their own path as funky punks with a knack for packing heaps of musical and lyrical ideas into the brief running times of their songs. When the enthusiastic trio were given the opportunity to open for Public Image Ltd, their erstwhile hero stood at the side of the stage tapping his watch to hurry them up, even though Minutemen were only on their second song. On the sleeve of the 1987 compilation *Ballot Result*, Minutemen gave the backhanded compliment of thanking Johnny Rotten, 'or our idea of him'. They were by no means the only band to suffer a 'never meet your heroes' moment when having the misfortune of running into PiL. At another event, Public Image's management team forbade the support band, this time Boston's Mission of Burma, to use the concert hall's PA system. As Mission of Burma's vocals were being broadcast feebly out of their onstage monitors, one of the main act's roadies stalked the front row of the audience, threatening to crack with a bullwhip any punter who got too close. The Washington DC hardcore outfit Minor Threat were already sceptical about supporting PiL, having discovered they weren't going to be paid by the promoters because the headlining act had demanded such an astronomical fee. Hoping to impress nonetheless, Minor Threat bit their tongues and agreed to open the show. Adrenaline coursing through their veins from the rush of having played a blinder of a set, Minor Threat departed the stage eager to know what PiL had made of it, only to see Lydon pull up to the back of the venue in a limousine. He hadn't even been in the building. Virtually the same scenario was experienced by Scratch Acid, who also supported PiL for free only to be rudely snubbed. 'I think he just wants to make money,' reflected guitarist Brett Bradford on Lydon's behaviour. 'He's the ultimate hypocrite.'[3]

Some vengeance was had in 1986 when Green River played with PiL at the Paramount Theatre in Seattle. The local band and their friends ended up trashing the headliners' dressing room, stealing the rider, hurling luncheon meat onto the roof of PiL's tour bus and yelling their heads off in faux-British accents. During Green River's set, singer Mark Arm made the following announcement: 'Hey, if you ever want to know what it's like to become what you hated, ask the next band.' This wasn't done on behalf of other underground groups who had already been slighted by PiL, for Green River were unaware of any earlier incidents. Rather, it was a reaction against PiL's (typically, it turned out) entitled behaviour on that particular night. When he'd arrived to discover there was no La-Z-Boy recliner in his dressing room, Lydon had thrown a wobbly and threatened to cancel the show.[4] This punk rock linchpin, it transpired, had turned into a pampered prima donna. It is rumoured that in retaliation for Green River's irreverent antics, Lydon wrote the lyrics to PiL's 'Seattle'. If he did, the track hardly disproved the notion that Lydon had sunk into creative decline and commercial conformity.

Looking at it another way, Lydon certainly trailblazed the hearty punk rock tradition of annoying fellow punk rockers. Whether something is 'punk rock' or not depends largely on context. In terms of punk rock as an attitude, it is supposed to be about rebellion. It's also about confounding expectations and challenging convention. For the more imaginative and progressively minded punks, this applied as much to confronting and offending the values of their own audience as it did to railing against some abstract notion of 'The Man'. Examples of such behaviour run riot in Michael Azerrad's account of the pre-grunge U.S. rock scene *Our Band Could Be Your Life*. The author provides a telling story of one show by the boozy Minneapolis band The Replacements, recounted to him by their roadie Bill Sullivan. The anecdote could even be a contender for one of the most punk rock things that has ever happened. The Replacements were performing in Nashville at a venue bustling with VIP country music executives. Faced with that lucrative prospect, the band decided to play all their outright punk rock songs as hard, fast and loudly as they possibly could, until they had almost cleared the whole room. The only remaining audience members were a few lingering punk rockers. At this point, the band performed straight-up country numbers for the rest of the evening.[5] It's an extreme example but one that epitomizes the contrary nature of a generation of bands whose professional and creative decisions often seemed designed to intentionally annoy dyed-in-the-wool punk purists (among other perceived enemies) and which also had the consequence of resealing the link between their punk-inspired music and an older pre-punk heaviness.

When Black Flag became disillusioned with the restrictions of the hardcore scene from which they'd emerged, they exchanged skinhead buzzcuts and mohawks for longer, scraggly hair. They also made the decision to load side two of their 1984 LP *My War* with three painfully slow sludge metal numbers indebted to Black Sabbath. At that point in the band's career, with all the hardcore groups they saw around them trying to play faster and faster, this risky and sincere move was one of the most punk rock things they could have done. There was something in the water that year because Black Flag weren't the only band striving to transcend the musical and emotional limitations of hardcore. Both Minutemen and Hüsker Dü committed the supposedly heinous crime of recording experimental double albums, each one released by SST, the label founded by Black Flag guitarist Greg Ginn.

The Way of the Dinosaur

It was also in 1984 that Massachusetts hardcore upstarts Deep Wound disbanded. Done and dusted with playing snotty punk rock at breakneck speed, two members of the group forged a different path with their next outing. Back when young punks were still castigating the 'dinosaur' rock stars of yore, you couldn't get much more purposefully retrograde than literally naming your band Dinosaur. This potentially alienating act was softened a little by having to add a 'junior' for legal reasons. Nevertheless, it was a bold move to abandon playing with the pace that could have slotted Deep Wound somewhere between Millions of Dead Cops and Extreme Noise Terror and to embrace in its place, as singer and guitarist J Mascis would deem it, 'ear-bleeding country'.

Dinosaur Jr's songs tend to follow a formula. Many of them are pop songs, essentially, in terms of their verse-chorus-verse structures, with the vocals kicking in near the start of most tracks. Having said that, they are pop songs played at extreme volume and buttressed by inventively intertwining riffs, using a vast array of effects pedals and interspersed with frequent guitar solos. The 'ear-bleeding country' tag could have been used to describe the older band that Dinosaur Jr most resembled: Neil Young & Crazy Horse at their loudest, fiercest and untidiest. Young and his on–off backing band were already dinosaurs themselves by this time, their professional relationship dating back to 1969. The group managed to retain and regain respected status even after Young – ever the contrarian himself – had spoken in favour of the bête noire of the hardcore scene, Ronald Reagan. In spite of that misdemeanour, it helped Young's cause that he was one of the few rockers of the older generation who approved of punk rock and new wave. He fondly name-checked Johnny Rotten in 'Hey Hey, My My (Into the Black)' and enlisted Devo to star in his 1982 movie *Human Highway*. Later, Young would earn the nickname 'godfather of grunge'. It wasn't just for his fondness for flannel shirts.

As with Black Sabbath and Motörhead, Crazy Horse may have felt such an affinity with punk because of the criticisms they received from fans, critics and fellow professional musicians alike. David Crosby, who played with Young in Crosby, Stills, Nash & Young, seemed genuinely offended by Crazy Horse's flagrant ineptitude. 'They should've never been allowed to be musicians at all. They should've been shot at birth,' he once ranted. 'They can't play. I've heard the bass player muff a change in a song seventeen times in a row. "Cinnamon Girl" – he still doesn't know it!'[6] Crosby is oblivious to the primordial power and ramshackle charm of Crazy Horse, much of which derives precisely from their inability to play their instruments as capably as folk like Crosby would desire. For Neil Young, the rickety nature of Crazy Horse is exactly where the soul, the funk and the all-important groove comes from. 'It's not that they fuck up that makes them great,' Young explained. 'That's a by-product of the abandon they play with.'[7] As Young biographer Jimmy McDonough writes, 'At any given moment, they're capable of flubbing notes, speeding up, slowing down and generally stumbling through songs they've been playing for twenty years . . . Will the song take off like a rocket or collapse before it starts? Anything's possible with the Horse. That's the thrill.'[8] It's an approach that Young picked up, in part, from the blues musician Jimmy Reed. Listening to Reed, Young learned that the feeling of the music is more important than which notes are being played. 'Cause he played the same thing almost every fuckin' song – the changes were a little different, but always *that riff* . . . Where the fuck did *that* come from? Did he make it up or did he get it from someone else, and why is it that he plays it in every song and yet it sounds okay?'[9]

From Young, the feeling trickled down into the hands of J Mascis. Having been the drummer for Deep Wound, Mascis shifted over to guitar when Dinosaur formed. It was an instrument Mascis believed to be fundamentally weaker than the drums. He resigned himself to learning it anyway because he couldn't find any guitarists who were playing what he wanted to hear. He was encouraged by studying players like The Stooges' Ron Asheton, Greg Sage from Wipers, and The Rolling Stones: 'Things that seemed within reach, that I could try and grab stuff from and form my own style. You know, someone like Hendrix seemed like way too good to even understand what he was doing.'[10] The title track from Wipers' second album, 1981's *Youth of America*, had particular significance in the development of American post-punk, and is yet another example of punk rockers being punk rock by doing exactly what punk rockers were not supposed to do. Abandoning the poppy bursts of energy from Wipers' debut LP that had taken cues from Buzzcocks and Ramones, 'Youth of America' is like a punk rock answer to Iron Butterfly's 'In-A-Gadda-Da-Vida'. Years before Black Flag stretched out their tracks' running times, this Wipers song rumbled on for ten and a half minutes. Over the motorik propulsion of the rhythm section, Greg Sage ekes out of his guitar an incredible range of unusual textures that vaguely evoke acid rock, krautrock, dub reggae and garage rock without ever really resembling or mimicking any of those things. As lengthy as this piece of music is, and no matter how many times it is spun, it always seems to be a shame when 'Youth of America' finally fades to an end. Sage has claimed that he had held little interest in what fellow punk groups were doing at that time, although it seems obviously that he did observe what rival bands were up to before deciding to do the complete opposite. 'No one liked our LPs till years later,' he said of Wipers, whose influence would take a little time to sink in. 'I tried to write in a futuristic way, writing about what I felt the future would bring.'[11]

J Mascis's reputation as a guitar hero would steadily swell. When *Spin* put him on their cover in June 1993, his photograph appeared with the caption 'J Mascis Is God', a reference to the graffiti slogan that had deified Eric Clapton in a variety of urban locations back in the 1960s. Mascis remains, at heart, a drummer. He continues to credit that rhythmic background for the guitar style he later developed. Dinosaur Jr's actual drummer, Murph, was instructed to play the rhythm parts exactly as Mascis had written them for him. Lou Barlow, who had played guitar in Deep Wound and switched over to bass for Dinosaur, realized he was going to have to 'hammer the shit' out of his instrument if he was ever going to hear himself over Mascis's guitar playing, and this forced Barlow to develop his own novel way of playing, which often meant strumming chords on his bass or hitting the strings as hard as he possibly could.[12] Dinosaur ignored the pleas of friends like Ira Kaplan from Yo La Tengo to dial down the volume in order to unveil the impressive songwriting that lurked beneath the maelstrom. If anything, such suggestions only encouraged the bloody-minded trio to increase their volume.[13] From the outset, said Barlow, 'J wanted it to be an almost physical thing. He wanted the music to register physically as much as hearing it.'[14]

'This guitar, it's so wimpy. How can I get the same feeling from playing drums?' Mascis would ask himself. 'I just found, by playing a guitar louder, you can get some air moving and it hits your body and impacts you somehow.'[15] To achieve this, he strung one riff to another, layered on effects, and played lots and lots of searing solos. 'He was playing new wave guitar next to heavy metal guitar next to crazy Hendrix leads next to weird PiL single note things,' Barlow observed. 'He threw all that stuff together. That was probably the most punk rock thing about it.'[16] Unusually, Mascis found lead guitar easier to play than chords and once said that 'Songs are just excuses for solos.'[17] However, here we have yet another musician who subscribes to the notion that even though a guitarist gets better at playing over the years, 'you're not as inventive as when you didn't know how to play.'[18] Furthermore, Mascis sees solos not as endlessly replicable patterns or an opportunity to exhibit his dexterous abilities but as a conduit for self-expression. 'I've always thought it was really strange when people would play the same solo that's on the record. When I play a solo I'm just expressing that moment. It can go horribly wrong easily enough. Some nights you can pull stuff off, other nights you can't . . . but you don't know until you try.'[19] The fact that Mascis is one of the few guitarists on the planet who can play solo after extended solo without it coming across like pointless onanism might have something to do with his lack of ability to communicate effectively through the usual human means of speech. His interviews are notoriously punctuated by erms, uhhs, don't knows, and lengthy pauses at the end of which there might be an answer to the journalist's question or, perhaps more commonly, there might not. Dinosaur Jr were a notoriously dysfunctional group, with Barlow observing that the most common way they communicated with one another was by shrugging.[20] It is as if, whether consciously or otherwise, Mascis bottles everything up until the time comes when he is finally able to unleash his pent-up thoughts and feelings by firing off multiple shards of glorious guitar noise. This may be tenuous, but is there a correlation between certain players' verbal inarticulacy and their ability to play genuinely soulful guitar? Keith Richards has a reputation for bizarre, slurring, rambling sentences. Fairport Convention's Richard Thompson suffered from a stutter since his childhood, the guitar providing Thompson with a much-needed outlet. David Gilmour of Pink Floyd, on the other hand, speaks rather eloquently, and yet – in this writer's opinion – his comparatively inane and largely pointless guitar solos rarely seem to be saying anything much more than 'Look at me! Look at what I can do! Here's one for the readers of *Interminable Licks* magazine!'

Bad Brains

Punk also made it possible to do all this the other way round, so to speak. Rather than forming as a hardcore band, the members of Bad Brains had started out by specializing in jazz fusion under the name Mind Power. They had been raised on James Brown and admired the likes of Frank Zappa and Yes. On bearing witness to the punk boom, Mind Power renamed themselves after the Ramones' song 'Bad Brain' and repurposed their musical chops for altogether different purposes. While their friends from their neighbourhood in Washington DC were attending shows by Trouble Funk, the members of Bad Brains would be the only black people over at a different venue, watching a gig by Dead Boys. Back at home they would listen to the Ramones, The Dickies and The Clash, but they'd speed the records up to 78 rpm, and this helped Bad Brains to develop a faster and more original style of their own.[21] They also discovered reggae and Rastafarianism, and after their initial hardcore outings would use their skills to straddle punk, funk, metal, rap, reggae, dub and other styles. Put off by the violent nihilism they heard in *Never Mind the Bollocks, Here's the Sex Pistols*, Bad Brains also strove to forge a more positive take on punk. Paul 'H.R.' Hudson sang about 'PMA', the initials standing for 'Positive Mental Attitude', an idea taken from a self-improvement book that H.R.'s father had recommended: Napoleon Hill's *Think and Grow Rich* (1937).

Self-help books don't hold all the answers. Bad Brains had to watch certain rivals grow rich while they themselves were left floundering behind as highly respected forerunners who would never make the grade of superstar status. In an interview promoting 1986's *I Against I*, bassist Darryl Jenifer credited his band with basically inventing the speed/thrash metal sound, while also having the foresight to keep developing beyond that narrow style. Jenifer found it hard to understand why so few metal bands who had adopted that sound themselves and subsequently risen up to the arena circuit level wished to associate or ally themselves with his own pioneering crew. 'I mean, Metallica have said they dig us, which is cool,' he told *Sounds* magazine, 'but most of those bands don't want anything to do with us. When people like Megadeth and Slayer were no doubt listening to Boston and shit, we were playing the sort of music they still can only dream of. Now what has happened? They're all signed to major labels and doing big deal tours and we're still on the fringes.'[22] Where were the support slots that should have been offered to Bad Brains in reciprocation for their part in originating the form of music that had propelled to fame the likes of Slayer et al.? 'Maybe they're all just scared of getting blown away,' Jenifer laughed. He posited that Bad Brains also got overlooked by conservative metal fans, journalists and magazines because his band didn't have the right hair styles, didn't wear earrings, weren't white-skinned and didn't engage in 'stupid heavy metal poses'. Thus he had zero confidence that any cover features courtesy of *Kerrang!* or *Circus* (its American monthly equivalent) would be coming their way.[23] Jenifer raised some sensible points, although there were additional reasons for Bad Brain's failure to become world-conquering rock gods.

For one thing, Bad Brains had the self-sabotaging habit of splitting up (before reuniting, and then splitting again, and so on) more often than most people put the bins out. H.R. and his drumming brother Earl Hudson were lured away by other projects. Furthermore, H.R. appeared to be fiercely allergic to record deals. His sudden disappearances tended to coincide with moments when contracts were being drafted. Guitarist Dr Know speculated that, in H.R.'s imagination, such business arrangements would stifle his freedom.[24] There were plenty of other disagreements, bust-ups (sometimes violent) and further ailments. H.R. has suffered from SUNCT syndrome (a debilitating headache disorder) and schizophrenia, and back in 1987 he spent four months in jail on a charge of marijuana possession. He claimed to be as anti-drug as the authorities, 'But herb isn't a drug and that's where they make their mistake.'[25] His vocal contribution to 'Sacred Love' on *I Against I* was literally phoned in from prison. It's an eerily muffled yet spine-tinglingly soulful performance; one that Deftones' vocalist Chino Moreno seems to have been chasing for his entire career.

Motörhead is one example of a band that had the pleasure of being embraced by punks and metalheads alike. Bad Brains had this too, along with the unfortunate habit of also alienating segments of both scenes. It hardly helped their cause that they were long dogged by persistent accusations of homophobia, a prejudice that irked elements of the left-leaning hardcore contingency, among others, and rightly so. All this may have impeded Bad Brains' prospects of crossing over, but there are those – in metal, punk, in between and elsewhere besides – who cannot shake the potent effect that Bad Brains' fusion of different musical styles has had on their lives. To this day, says thrash legend Scott Ian, whenever Anthrax are working on new material, he and bandmate Charlie Benante will look over to one another and ask themselves what Bad Brains would do next and where Bad Brains might go to take the song a step further. With *I Against I*, says Ian, Bad Brains received a backlash from the so-called 'true' punk rock brigade, who viewed the band's expanded palette with suspicion. 'Ten perfect songs', was Ian's more generous assessment. All these decades later, he still listens to that 'classic album' at least twice a week.[26]

Lose the Testosterone

Ian MacKaye formed his first band, Teen Idles, after witnessing a show by Bad Brains, who he'd first met when they were handing out flyers at a Cramps concert. MacKaye remembers them being 'the coolest-looking, most heavy-looking dudes in the joint'.[27] Teen Idles and MacKaye's next band, Minor Threat, operated in the hardcore punk vein, specializing in short, fast, frantic, polemical songs that railed against political conservatism and castigated the apathetic hedonism that MacKaye saw in his generational contemporaries. After another couple of short-lived bands and an unlikely collaboration with Ministry's Al Jourgensen (Pailhead), it was as a member of Fugazi that MacKaye championed the post-hardcore sound, in alliance with similar bands on his Dischord label. In Fugazi, MacKaye was joined by Guy Picciotto and Brendan Canty from Rites of Spring, and Joe Lally, a metalhead who worshipped Sabbath-smitten doomsters The Obsessed. MacKaye conceived this project as 'The Stooges with reggae'.[28] Fugazi would go beyond that simple equation. Bad Brains' spirit of experimentation had been soaked up by superfan MacKaye. Unlike Bad Brains' habit of alternating between contrasting genres and occasionally kneading them together, which could sometimes look like they were trying on different hats for size, Fugazi's myriad of musical reference points – reggae, dub, funk, metal, punk, pre-punk, post-punk, hip-hop, jazz, Captain Beefheart and more – stewed away in the pot before emerging as a nouveau dish altogether.

They formed in Washington DC in 1987, and while their six-album run is impressive enough in itself, the live setting is where many aficionados believe that Fugazi truly shone. A militant rehearsal regime fostered a seemingly psychic connection between the individual band members. Certain live favourites would be double the length of the recorded versions when Fugazi found themselves locked in a communal groove and able to improvise around it, less like a modern-day Grateful Dead than some kind of stripped-back post-hardcore answer to Parliament-Funkadelic. While MacKaye and Picciotto were the focal point of their concerts, sharing guitar and vocal duties and leaping around with boundless energy, it was the pile-driving rhythm section of bassist Lally and drummer Canty that did much of the legwork in supplying the heaviness. Fugazi were sometimes accused of po-faced earnestness, probably by the same kind of people who like to complain about political correctness going too far. The band maintained their fierce and uninterrupted independence, supported progressive causes, and insisted on keeping their overheads low to ensure cheap – and therefore inclusive – concert ticket and record prices. They didn't want any age restrictions for their shows and were happy to circumnavigate traditional venues to ensure this. When performing, they condemned and forbade crowd-surfing and other antisocial, meatheaded behaviour. Such actions were viewed as self-righteous by some commentators, but Fugazi always had a sense of humour and had no problem laughing at themselves. As political as it often was, much of the band's output retained a lyrical and musical ambiguity that broke away from Minor Threat's earlier polemical mode of hardcore.

Keeping themselves soberly uncorrupted from intoxicating temptations like money and drugs, Fugazi were one of the few bands of their era – or perhaps any era – to actually grow better and better throughout their run. This culminated in 2001 with their career-topping final statement *The Argument*. Here, Fugazi's intense quiet–loud dynamics, their vocal howls and severe rhythms were embellished with cello, piano and percussion parts. The more punk-rock elements contrasted sublimely with the calmer passages. On its release, *The Argument* sounded like something The Beatles might have produced had they been born a couple of decades later, in the American capital, and smitten by Bad Brains. Fugazi never ran out of steam or fell out with one another. They simply went on hiatus due to commitments like parenthood. Since that time, it sometimes feels like the Western world has gone to pot in the absence of Fugazi's guiding hand.

In Fugazi, Ian MacKaye maintained a no-thrills approach to his equipment. He avoided effects pedals altogether, preferring to shake the most that he could out of the stripped-back set-up of an amplifier, a guitar and a cord connecting the two. This was a decidedly different process to that of Dinosaur Jr's J Mascis, who, as we have seen, was no stranger to stomping on a variety of boxes to achieve that literally body-shaking racket he so craved. Though he was partial to unleashing righteous extended guitar solos, the pedal-derived textures Mascis applied to his instrument exhibited his affinity with the shoegaze genre. The scene in question was championed in the British music weeklies for a brief moment before being cast out in favour of Britpop, whereupon the shoegazers suddenly found themselves mocked by journalists and unfairly caricatured as snooty elitists. In 1991 *Melody Maker* praised the immaculate serenity of Slowdive's sound. Two years later the same publication decided that it would be preferable to 'drown choking in a bath full of porridge' than ever listen to them again. Rival musicians joined in the kicking too. Richey Edwards of Manic Street Preachers childishly proclaimed to hate Slowdive more than he hated Hitler.[29] Britpop offered a more laddish alternative to shoegaze that was also less challenging. As with the American no wave scene before it, shoegaze had a strong female presence, with many of the key bands featuring women in their ranks. Unlike the female singers of the Britpop era who were pressured into posing as swaggering, lager-consuming, patriarchy-approved 'laddettes', women like Th' Faith Healers' vocalist Roxanne Stephen and Lesley Rankine of the fierce noise rockers Silverfish let loose and rocked out on their own inimitable terms.

Such bands had much to offer in terms of tinnitus-inducing, consciousness-warping noise, even if it was hard for any of them to compete with the sheer volume of shoegaze pioneers My Bloody Valentine. Perhaps because they are perceived as melodically and texturally adventurous, never conformed visually thanks to their casual shirts and librarian spectacles, and have a 50:50 male-to-female line-up ratio, My Bloody Valentine tend to remain absent from most discussions of Heavy. As countless witnesses will attest, MBV's concerts have been among the loudest ever performed, hitting particularly thunderous levels during the infamous 'holocaust section' that defines live renditions of 'You Made Me Realise'.

Incidentally, it is a little strange that so few female musicians were mentioned in Azerrad's *Our Band Could Be Your Life*, given the vital contributions they made to the rock music of the era that it covers. The all-female L7 are mentioned only in passing despite their association with Sub Pop records. Their style sat on that sublime line between ragtag metal and the denser end of punk, their choruses snarled with an angry attitude that was also irresistibly cool in its aloofness. Take it or leave it, L7 seemed to be saying through their gnashed teeth, we simply don't care one way or the other. As well as rocking harder than many of their Sub Pop compadres, L7 had a reputation for debauchery that could rival and surpass their male peers. As Cat Butt guitarist Danny Bland recalled, 'They fuckin' smelled as bad as we did.'[30]

She may always be defined by her husband and his tragic fate, but, however much she winds people up, it's a shame that Courtney Love is rarely assessed in her own right and that her music with Hole has not been taken seriously enough. Produced by Kim Gordon of Sonic Youth, Hole's debut album *Pretty on the Inside* (1991) is ferocious, scuzzy and both emotionally and sonically raw. When Love had advertised for musicians to join her band, the influences she cited had been Big Black, Sonic Youth and Fleetwood Mac. After *Pretty on the Inside*, the Mac elements floated further to the fore. Second album *Live Through This* got the balance just right. Its tunes are catchier than the debut's, without sacrificing the necessity to rock out on the regular. In that respect it is similar to Nirvana's *Nevermind*. It is also superior to that record but, because *Live*

Through This was released afterwards and in the immediate aftermath of Kurt Cobain's suicide in April 1994, it has been forever
overshadowed. The wise John Peel saw its value, listing *Live Through
This* in his top 20 albums of all time. Of Hole's defiant appearance
at the 1994 Reading Festival, Peel wrote that Hole 'teetered on the
edge of chaos, generating a tension which I cannot remember having
felt before from any stage'.[31]

Love was accused of pinching musical ideas and (anti-)fashion
tips from other acts who would either self-identify or be labelled
against their will as 'riot grrrl'. It was a scene that was mocked on
Live Through This's final track for its apparent unoriginality and
homogeneous thinking. That was unfairly dismissive given riot
grrrl's political and social significance, the different bands' diversity
of styles, and the wide and long-lasting impact it has secured. Love
was singing specifically about the scene in Olympia, Washington,
from which Bikini Kill, Bratmobile, Excuse 17, Heavens to Betsy
and Sleater-Kinney all surfaced. She will also have been thinking
about Kat Bjelland from Babes in Toyland, whose dense, menacing
and hostile sound would have been labelled noise rock if only the
Minneapolis trio had been born with penises. They had the honour,
according to Sub Pop employee and Dickless singer Megan Jasper,
of smelling even worse than L7.[32]

On the other side of the Atlantic, bands like Huggy Bear, the
aforementioned Silverfish and Daisy Chainsaw showed that women
could make just as nasty a racket as male bands. This was nothing
new, of course. At the time, however, it seemed to need reiterating. 'I
feel like people in the '90s should be a little bit smarter – or evolved,'
said Bjelland. 'Girls have been doing things for quite a long time.'[33]
Bjelland had taught herself to play the guitar, and when she formed
Babes in Toyland in 1987 she deliberately recruited women who had
never been in bands before and didn't really know how to use their
instruments. Her logic was thus: 'Hopefully, from being technically
inexperienced, you can use your imagination, and play the drums

like an instrument instead of just being a beat-keeper. And play the bass like you feel it, from your gut, instead of saying, "Here's my scales."[34] Babes in Toyland's aggressively amateurish and deliciously sloppy style sounded a lot uglier than a lot of the bona fide heavy metal that was around at the time. It felt genuinely harsh, abrasive, grinding and grimacing. To those who were enamoured by the steely precision of Metallica's self-titled 'Black Album' or the elaborate material on Iron Maiden's *Fear of the Dark*, Babes in Toyland's messier output may well have sounded like incomprehensible noise. They weren't the only group who seemed to be out-heavying what the heavy metal world had to offer at that time. When Sonic Youth's Thurston Moore came across Dinosaur Jr, he was delighted to discover their loudest moments were 'like Motörhead times ten'.[35]

Like every countercultural movement, riot grrrl would be appropriated by the mainstream. A radio-friendly and heavily marketed interpretation was created in the form of London duo Shampoo, whose song title 'Girl Power' was a phrase that had been used earlier by Bikini Kill and was then later repurposed as the catchphrase of the manufactured post-feminist pop group the Spice Girls. As Kate Hutchinson notes, nowadays the phrase 'riot grrrl' has almost lost all meaning, as it tends to crop up 'as soon as someone with a vagina starts a band'.[36]

Speaking of corporate appropriation, by 1993 Fugazi had become the band that all members of the new rock royalty were desperate to meet, to be seen with and to endorse. Nirvana, Hole, REM, Pearl Jam, Red Hot Chili Peppers – everyone wanted a piece of Fugazi. It was as if by associating themselves with the band that everybody knew would never sell out, these bigger acts might be absolved of their own sins and sicknesses. The guilt of having signed to a major label. The shame of hiring the hippest producers and mixing engineers to buff up their sound for radio play. The indignity of having written a catchy single with airplay and chart positions firmly in mind. The clichéd alcohol and drug use of the typical rock star, habits to which they had embarrassingly succumbed. The self-suspicion of slowly turning into a prima donna who had lost touch with reality and was prone to throwing a whoopsie over some minor dressing-room oversight. It would take more than singing the praises of Fugazi and writing that band name on your clothes to escape the indignity.

12

TAD:

THE HEAVIEST AND LEAST CELEBRATED GRUNGE BAND

In more ways than one, the heaviest grunge band: TAD.

Nevermind was just starting to take off and I was talking about this whole 'Grunge thing' with a friend in LA, when 'Helter Skelter' came on some jukebox. I said: 'Here's the first Grunge song; listen to it!' It sounded just awesome. You know, the guitar and McCartney's voice. So it wasn't really anything new ... I didn't invent Grunge. And Seattle didn't invent it, either.[1]

BUTCH VIG

I n 1991 Sonic Youth invited Dave Markey to film their European tour and summer festival dates for a documentary film. Their support band was Nirvana, and Markey's footage would also include Babes in Toyland, Dinosaur Jr, Mudhoney and Gumball. After the tour had ended and before Markey had put the finishing touches to the documentary for its 1992 release, Nirvana became one of the biggest bands in the world. *Nevermind*, Nirvana's second album and their first since graduating from Sub Pop to Geffen, initially entered the Billboard charts at the end of September 1991 at number 144. It wasn't a bad result for a scruffy trio from Seattle, a city then best known for its rainy weather and the emigration of Jimi Hendrix. The executives at Geffen hoped Nirvana's album might eventually match the sales of Sonic Youth's *Goo* (around 250,000). By January 1992 *Nevermind* had surprised everybody by knocking Michael Jackson's *Dangerous* from the top of the charts. It was shifting over 300,000 units a week.[2]

Two years and another studio album later, disillusioned with fame, plagued by depression, fearing divorce and blighted by heroin, Kurt Cobain killed himself. Quoting Neil Young's lyric about it being better to burn out than fade away (actually an ironic line, when you think about it, given Young's pugnacious, never-fading career), the suicide note spoke of Cobain's guilt at betraying the ethics of punk rock and his incapability to get excited by music anymore. 'Then don't be a rock star, you asshole,' replied his grieving widow, Hole's Courtney Love, when reciting her husband's note on a recording for a memorial service in Seattle. If only Cobain's career had followed in the footsteps of his old heroes Melvins it could have been a different story, says David Hepworth. Melvins navigate their lack of chart positions and foster their modest fanbase through 'careful housekeeping'. They make a living without the need to be huge rock stars. 'The Melvins make another album in the hope that they can make another one after that. They play tonight's show in the hope that there will be another one tomorrow. When the time comes, they won't burn out. They will fade away. By refusing to play the game they may win in the end.'[3]

Markey's Sonic Youth documentary was titled *1991: The Year Punk Broke*. This had a double meaning. This was the year that American 'punk' (or what it had turned into) supposedly broke through into the mainstream. It was also the moment when punk became damaged beyond repair. Nirvana were not the only ones to rise from the underground scene described in the previous chapter. More and more groups signed major label deals as soon as *Nevermind*'s success prompted an industry-wide fever for bagging 'the next Nirvana'. In the course of this process, heavier music made it onto the airwaves, into the racks of CD shops and across the pages of the music press. The rise of these so-called 'grunge' bands also meant that music previously thought to be 'heavy' had to be reassessed.

To audiences, critics and the musicians concerned alike, grunge exposed the lack of substance in the work of certain artists who had always been pegged as 'heavy metal'. Singer Biff Byford of Saxon, who had made their name as part of the New Wave of British Heavy Metal, credits *Nevermind* with giving his own band a much-needed kick up the backside. 'Lots of metal bands had all got a little bit in a rut by the time this [album] came out,' he told *The Quietus* in 2020. 'People were quite bothered about how they looked. And Nirvana smashed it to pieces. They said music should be raw and powerful – great guitar riffs, good lyrics, great melodies . . . There's a lot of menace and darkness in [*Nevermind*] and it was heavier than what other people were doing at the time.'[4]

Others were less robust in the face of this alternative rock boom. After hearing Nirvana's 'Smells Like Teen Spirit' and realizing his guitar-shredding skills had become passé overnight, Vito Bratta couldn't bear to pick up his instrument, spelling the end of his band White Lion. Hearing the same Nirvana single on the radio while driving along the Los Angeles freeway, Jani Lane of Warrant is said to have pulled over immediately in the realization that his career was over. Looking back on it, Twisted Sister guitarist Jay Jay French said the turning point came prior to *Nevermind* when MTV had decided to pass on the latest video by Thunder, who had an older-school sound, in favour of Alice in Chains' grittier 'Man in a Box': 'And that was a road less travelled, and it wiped out the dinosaurs, which were the hair metal bands.'[5]

Soundgarden guitarist Kim Thayil credits a single conversation with Melvins' Buzz Osborne as a crucial moment in the birth of grunge. Thayil and Osborne were at Mudhoney singer Mark Arm's house listening to records together when Osborne pointed out Black Sabbath's drop-D method of tuning guitars. Soundgarden adopted the technique and never looked back. 'I remember that the Alice in Chains guys at the time were more like a glam-metal boogie band,' said Thayil, 'and one day I ran into Jerry [Cantrell, Alice in Chains' guitarist] at a DOA concert, and he says to me, "Man, I love that song 'Nothing to Say.' What are you doing there?" And I told him, "Well, it's in drop-D tuning." And Alice in Chains became a different band almost overnight!'[6]

In terms of their lyrics and values, these Seattle bands were also keen to move the conversation beyond the neanderthal attitudes found in songs like Mötley Crüe's repugnant 'Girls, Girls, Girls'. 'I don't care if I never hear another person write a song about a stripper or a motorcycle again,' as Soundgarden's Chris Cornell put it. The reason Nirvana appealed to so many, Cornell decided, was that people were no longer interested in seeing 'a video of a band like Whitesnake where you have the singer's model wife doing a strip-tease act on the

hood of a Jaguar'. Whitesnake and bands like them had been pro-
jecting a lifestyle that looked exclusive, shallow and unobtainable.
Offering something different were bands like Nirvana, 'where the
band essentially look like everyone and their friends at high school
. . . And it was proof that anyone can do it. You don't have to look a
particular way. You can just be who you are, make great music, and
it will appeal to people.'[7]

With mass appeal comes fame, wealth, temptations and trappings. Mudhoney's Mark Arm would stop taking heroin in 1993 after
several overdoses and an ultimatum from his girlfriend (now wife).
He looks back on his druggy days with complete embarrassment,
having briefly resembled the kind of banal celebrity that grunge had
promised to wash away: 'I was a total cliché. I was a rock guy strung
out on heroin and, actually, for a while in there was going out with
a stripper. How did this happen to me? Of course I walked through
all those doors myself.'[8] Nowadays Arm manages the Sub Pop warehouse and Mudhoney continue to put out records on a regular basis.
Others, Kurt Cobain and Alice in Chains' Layne Staley among them,
checked out long before their time. 'Success is survival,' Leonard
Cohen once said.[9]

Nirvana may have been 'the ones', as Biff Byford saw it. Alice
in Chains may have ploughed the way for *Nevermind*. They and
Soundgarden may have exposed the inanity of hair metal. Mudhoney
may have offered scuzzy licks and provided some much-needed gonzo
humour to a scene with a reputation for existential, soul-bearing
angst. Pearl Jam may have had the Springsteenian bombast and staying power. Hole may have had a nifty three-album run anchored by a
stone-cold classic of the genre. None of these acts were the heaviest
grunge band.

Mad, TAD and Dangerous to Know

In some ways, TAD were the quintessential grunge band. They were one of the first Seattle rock groups of that generation to be written about in hyperbolic terms by the British journalists who helped publicize the American scene. They followed the typical grunge trajectory of putting out records on the local Sub Pop imprint, taking the leap from that independent label into the clutches of the majors, developing debilitating drug habits and splitting up before the end of the millennium. At the same time, TAD didn't exactly follow Soundgarden, Alice in Chains, Nirvana, Pearl Jam and Hole into becoming one of the household names that momentarily infiltrated the charts.

If TAD's career could be summed up by the title of one of their own songs, that song would have to be 'Jinx'. The opening track from 1991's *8-Way Santa* boasts bruising riffs and lurching rhythms as frontman Tad Doyle snarls a fate-tempting chorus, identifying himself as a jinx who is followed everywhere he goes by bad luck. Initially considered by critics to be the most exciting frontrunners of the grunge scene and drawing more limelight than Nirvana, Soundgarden, Mudhoney and their other touring partners, TAD would end up watching many of their fellow Seattle residents soar to fame and fortune. For their own part, TAD tended to attract misfortune. Over the course of their career, which lasted from 1988 to their split in 1999, the band suffered from a string of unusual mishaps.

After its release, *8-Way Santa* had to be removed from the shelves of record stores and reissued with blander alternative artwork. Its original cover had featured a photograph, found in a thrift store, of a trashy and inebriated couple, the male party of the pair cupping the woman's breasts, which were wrapped in a bandana. In the years since the photograph was taken, the woman in question had become a born-again Christian. When she discovered the image of her pre-conversion self on the front of TAD's album sleeve, she decided to sue. Another lawsuit was filed against Sub Pop when a disgruntled former employee informed a certain fizzy drinks manufacturer that their logo had been modified for the cover of TAD's 'Jack Pepsi' single.

TAD's luck fared little better after the band left Sub Pop, whose coffers had taken a strain under these legal issues. The band signed to the Warner subsidiary Giant for 1993's *Inhaler*, but, while out touring with Soundgarden, they were unceremoniously dropped after a promotional poster emerged that featured a photograph of Bill Clinton with a marijuana joint superimposed between his fingers. 'It's heavy shit,' read the caption. TAD were subsequently dumped by East West just a week after releasing their fourth and final studio album in 1995: *Infrared Riding Hood* received no promotion and sold poorly.

'My psyche was saying, "Shit is falling apart all the time around me",' reflected Doyle on those original 'Jinx' lyrics in 2018. He'd jotted them down quickly in the studio when everybody else was on a lunch break. 'I wasn't the healthiest person in the world. I was having trouble with a relationship. It seemed like I was only comfortable being with the guys. Even that could be tiring and you'd want a break. I admire people like [self-help guru] Anthony Robbins who can see the positive in everything. I'm not that guy most of the time. I'm cynical. I'm kind to others but at the same time I'm dark. I think that's basically what that song was about.'[10]

Suitably enough, 'Jinx' would remain on TAD's setlists for years to come, with Doyle wondering if he'd inadvertently tempted fate or cast some kind of hex on himself:

Singing those lyrics, you might actually be attracting further misfortune. I'm aware that the word is powerful and I don't go there with that shit anymore. I don't want to pollute the universe. That's something I learned. I've got grey hair. I'm an old dude. I think there's some wisdom in learning from what works and what doesn't work in your life, and that's one of the things that didn't work. But I'm still glad that song happened.

As for the Pepsi debacle, Doyle can laugh about it these days. 'At the time, we felt cursed with getting sued by a cola company. But how many bands can say that? In retrospect, it's like, hell yeah! Somebody got mad. We moved somebody.'

As setback followed setback, drug habits and correlating behaviour worsened. The 2018 Record Store Day release *Quick and Dirty* included previously unreleased studio sessions from 1999. It revealed the band still had the chops to write strong material. However, by that late stage in proceedings, certain band members were regularly showing up late to practice and it was clear that hearts were no longer in it. 'It was time to move on, more than anything. We were all at different places in our lives and it wasn't as fun as it used to be, towards the end. I don't know why. People grow apart sometimes,' sighed Doyle.

Heavy Is as Heavy Does

Happier times were had in TAD's early days. The project was conceived by Doyle alone. Like J Mascis of Dinosaur Jr, Doyle had been a drummer in bands at first, before deciding to move over to guitar and vocals. He played every instrument himself on the debut TAD single. Other musicians were enrolled to perform Doyle's material in concert and from that point onwards the project became more of a typical band. Doyle's partners-in-grunge were bassist Kurt Danielson, guitarist Gary Thorstensen (until his departure in 1994) and, by their frontman's own admission, 'more drummers than Spıñal Tap'.

Doyle had been drawn to the drums as a child because they helped vent his youthful frustrations. His elder brother, who he adored, was also a drummer. The young Tad used to sit on the floor in front of his brother's kit, imitating the beats on a collection of coffee cans and tinker toys. The older Doyle sibling was also responsible for another of Tad's early musical loves. Tad would've been about ten years old when he received a life-changing Christmas present from his brother: the first Black Sabbath album. His parents weren't impressed by the sight of this apparently satanic gift on that day of all days. But Doyle was hooked, and his mother and father's disapproval only helped solidify his allegiance to Sabbath.

Later, Doyle drummed for the band H-Hour. He steadily grew sick of hauling his kit around and finding he was always the final person left packing equipment away while everybody else in the group was having a great time drinking booze and chatting to girls. 'At that point I was really into Butthole Surfers, Big Black and a lot of the Touch and Go label's stuff. I had a drum machine and decided, at 26 years old, to teach myself guitar,' he remembered,

> Why not? So I did. I don't consider myself a guitar player. I'm a guy who plays guitar in the way that I do it. Eric Clapton is a guitar player. Jimi Hendrix is a guitar player, although he said he didn't consider himself a guitar player either and certainly not a singer, which is amazing to me ... I hadn't mastered the craft of playing drums but I wanted something different. I loved guitar feedback and the modulation of it. Steve Albini's feedback on the Big Black records puts chills down my spine. Frank Zappa's lead on 'Inca Roads' makes the hair on my neck stand up. The guitar is a unique instrument in that way. You can't get feedback out of a synthesizer or piano, unless you mic it up wrong or something.

When TAD played at the London Astoria in 1989 with Mudhoney headlining and a barely known trio named Nirvana as their opening act, the *NME* called Doyle a 'gone-to-pot Pavarotti'.[11] It was one of the more respectful descriptions of the full-figured frontperson to be printed by a grunge-hyping English press prone to portraying TAD as an exotic bunch of primitive rednecks. This image was also fed by the marketing nous of Sub Pop. The label decorated TAD's debut 7-inch, 'Daisy/Ritual Device', with a message beginning with the words 'Hi my name is Tad...' printed in scrawled handwriting that made the artist in question look like he was mentally challenged. For promotional videos, TAD were encouraged to behave like forest-dwelling psychopaths who wielded chainsaws and thirstily licked the blades of their pocketknives.

It is true that Doyle had done a stint as a butcher, and his Idaho upbringing had taught him a thing or two about how to chop wood proficiently. But these supposed wild lumberjacks were educated fellows. Danielson had an English degree and aspired to become a professional poet. Doyle had studied music at Boise State University. As if taking cues from the Soviet propaganda machine, Sub Pop were desperate to suppress knowledge that the young Doyle had once performed jazz drums in the presence of Richard Nixon.

The band themselves were complicit in playing up to the sociopathic hillbilly image. It suited their untamed sound and lyrical concerns. 'Nipple Belt', for example, is sung from the perspective of the serial killer Ed Gein. A few years later came 'Pansy', which was about another man on a murder spree, this one luring young girls into his truck with promises of candy. TAD's debut album, 1989's *God's Balls*, was named after a phrase uttered by an orgasmic priest in a porno film ('God's balls, that feels good!'). 'We were having fun exploring this redneck thing and we grew up around those people, so it was more like a jab at them than anything,' explained Doyle. 'A lot of people took it seriously and ran with it. They thought that was who we were. And that delighted us even more.' Having said that, TAD did grow weary of the white-trash albatross hanging around their necks: 'We were certainly more multidimensional than people gave us credit for. It became tired to keep hearing us lumped into that small, restraining box when we knew there was so much more to us. People pigeonhole you from the first thing [you do], and that's human nature.'

While those who knew this self-confessed 'big teddy bear' in person considered him to be a gentle, quiet and considerate character, Doyle's onstage persona tapped into his more fearsome and feral side. He would roar, sweat and headbang while, to his side, Danielson would thrash about with such abandon that over the course of TAD's career the bassist managed to crush two of his own vertebrae.[12] Between songs, Doyle would engage in fierce patter and attack hecklers with the withering force of a seasoned comedian. Like those honed by many a professional stand-up comic, this exaggerated alter ego had roots in an unhappy childhood, when he learnt to use humour as a survival skill:

> I was a fat kid in school. I got a lot of grief for that. I had to find ways to get through the day and not want to put a gun to my head from the bludgeoning and all the horrible things that kids do to each other . . . If I could make the jocks laugh, they wouldn't beat me up that day. I was a nerd, to boot. I had horrible communication skills. I stuttered. I had asthma. I was a mess. Making people laugh was really important to me. That's how I found common ground with humanity.

Those skills were transferred from the playground to the stage, where they could be used to win over audiences, or at least intimidate crowds into submission. Failing that, Doyle sometimes employed alternative techniques such as 'jumping off the stage, flying at people, and scaring the living shit out of them'.

To capture their brutal sound in the studio, TAD enlisted key producers of the alt-rock boom. Their first and final albums were overseen by Jack Endino. Prior to *God's Balls*, Endino had recorded early work by Skin Yard, Green River and Soundgarden. Afterwards, he'd produce the debut albums by Nirvana, Mudhoney and many more records besides. TAD also worked with both Butch Vig and Steve Albini before each one weaved his respective magic for Nirvana. Now working as an audio engineer, mixer, producer and mastering engineer himself, Doyle wishes he'd followed those experts' tricks a little closer. He considers Albini an 'audio scientist', completely immersed in the profession. It sounds as though Endino worked in a more freewheeling fashion: 'He was really good at going, "Okay, let's mic up that gas can, put a hacksaw to it, and see what happens".'

'You can't sing so don't even try', Albini told Doyle when working on 1990's *Salt Lick* EP. Butch Vig had a different approach for the following year's *8-Way Santa*. He helped to coax out the 'singer' that was hiding within Doyle and accentuate the melodic aspects of the group's still heavy material. 'I love Albini's honesty', said Doyle,

> but he was wrong. Butch had great ideas on how to achieve a vocal that went from just sitting there to being something that came out of the speakers and into your face, in a way that was very musical . . . I had no idea I was going to become an audio engineer otherwise I would have asked a hell of a lot more questions [with all those guys], probably to the point of being obnoxious.

Less proactive than Butch Vig was the man behind the recording desk for TAD's major label debut, *Inhaler*. This was the notoriously lethargic J Mascis. Mascis brought in some decent equipment and apparently taught Doyle to be less hard on his drummers by cutting them some slack. 'I love J and he was helpful', recalled Doyle. 'But I swear to God the guy was asleep ninety percent of the time! He got a credit for that, got paid, and got a rental car on our dime. It says "Produced by J Mascis" but I think J produced more zees than he produced any results.'

Over the years, certain friends of the band as well as their fans and reviewers have expressed surprise that TAD never broke through to the mainstream alongside the other Seattle big-hitters. It wasn't just the lawsuits, unwise decisions and lack of conventional good looks that denied TAD the keys to the castle. Occasional melodic inroads aside, TAD were harder, scarier, grittier and less fathomable than their plaid-sporting peers. TAD's slow and cumbersome riffs make even the most 'metal' grungers such as Soundgarden and Alice in Chains look poppy and polished by comparison. In 1993, Metallica, Anthrax or Megadeth would probably have killed to have written riffs as merciless as those offered by Doyle on *Inhaler*'s 'Grease Box', 'Throat Locust' and 'Pansy'.

While it has remained a relatively cult concern, TAD's output feels less dated than other key grunge records. This might be because TAD had drawn on a stranger and more eclectic breadth of sources. 'TAD are incredible,' says the journalist and author Harry Sword. 'I know they are tied in with *that word* but I see them more like Melvins or The Jesus Lizard or Eyehategod, [in the] lineage of demented genius rock 'n' roll. Dark grotesque Americana. I dislike the word grunge because it makes me think "earnest" instead of "whhoah bam ba lam."'[13] Whereas certain grunge acts were influenced in equal parts by The Beatles and Black Sabbath and, let's face it, not an awful lot besides, TAD were obsessed with the industrial metal band Head of David and the malevolent and darkly humorous Wisconsin trio Killdozer, whose records Doyle believed to be on a par with Led Zeppelin's. 'Nobody sounded like us, and we weren't jumping on anything to be noticed or comply with what was a popular norm in underground music,' explained Doyle. 'Our initial goal was to be loud, bombastic, obnoxious, and certainly throw in some rhythmic things. We'd always been rhythm-oriented. I would say, hopefully without sounding too racist, that we were not as "white" as a lot of our contemporaries. We had more soul and feel, in my mind at least. That's what gave us the legs.'

Although such influences are not immediately apparent among all the riffs and roaring, TAD were huge fans of Marvin Gaye, Sly & the Family Stone, Screamin' Jay Hawkins, Parliament-Funkadelic and Earth, Wind & Fire.

That's what we listened to a lot of the time when we were in the van going from place to place. We would pick up on those elements that didn't necessarily translate to song structure but certainly influenced us to a point where we had a heavy bass element. Our first drummer [Steve Wied] would play behind the beat like a jazz guy, like Miles Davis's drummers . . . so it's got a weird feel to it. I don't know if your normal layman would pick up on that. I grew up around a lot of jazz snobs so I can speak that lingo and actually play that shit. 'Behemoth' [the opening track on *God's Balls*] was definitely influenced by Sly & the Family Stone: the heavy beats, the huge backbeats, and the joy in that music. To us, 'Behemoth' was a joyful song. Although it sounded aggressive, it was fun as shit to play.

Still Heavy after All These Years

Nowadays Doyle doesn't seem very jinxed at all. Given the tragic fates of some of his wealthier and more famous Seattle contemporaries, Doyle turned out to be one of the lucky ones. 'We had an amazing career and I would not trade any of it for the popular conception of success,' he said. 'To me, we destroyed every night. The bands we played with, we gave them a run for their money. I wouldn't want to follow us, Jesus Christ! That band was insane. There's my own horn toot.'

After a spell in the wilderness working as a tax and mortgage consultant, Doyle now records other artists at his Witch Ape Studio, oversees the Incineration Ceremony label, and makes music both in a solo capacity and with Brothers of the Sonic Cloth, who are if anything even bloody heavier than TAD ever were. Formed about ten years before they even got around to releasing an album, Brothers of the Sonic Cloth released their 2015 debut on Neurot Recordings, the indie label founded by members of the post-metal band Neurosis. It was as if, having once out-heavied the 1990s metal and grunge scenes, Doyle returned once more to do the same thing to the newer post-metal genre. What inspired Doyle's comeback? Once again, he received a calling from the gods:

> One day, when I was driving down Interstate 805 in San Diego, I just happened to turn on the radio and 'War Pigs' by Black Sabbath comes on and it brought me to tears. I remembered as soon as that started playing that when I was a kid, the energy and the power of that song just consumed me and I go 'Wham!' This is what I always wanted to do. I've got to play music again. So that became the start of Brothers of the Sonic Cloth.[14]

13

STEVE ALBINI:
HEAVY-DUTY ENGINEER

Steve Albini performing with his 'minimalist rock trio' Shellac in 2008.

Steve worked quickly and cheaply . . . He lived in Chicago so we didn't have to pay any travel costs to record with him. He was inclined to offer more input than we were looking for, but didn't seem to mind that we generally ignored him.[1]

DAVID WM. SIMS (THE JESUS LIZARD)

Steve Albini has already made a few brief appearances in our sonic tapestry. His name has cropped up as an admirer of Kraftwerk's lack of ego and an evangelist for punk's spirit of invention. He was guitarist and vocalist for noise rock *enfants terribles* Big Black, the bloke who recorded The Jesus Lizard's best records and who told the leader of TAD not to bother singing properly. Given Albini's contributions to music – which kicked off in the 1980s and have continued unabated – and particularly the way in which his studio methods have become a benchmark for how to lay down heavy sounds on tape, it seems only right to look at his pivotal role in more detail. Albini would probably baulk at such attention. He's never been in it for the kudos, and even less so for the filthy lucre.

If he had been a greedier and less scrupulous individual, Steve Albini could have been an extremely wealthy man indeed. If not quite as rich as Croesus himself, Albini could have amassed a fortune comparable to that of whoever produced the quadruple-platinum fifth album by the ancient king's bestselling popular beat combo The Croesus Clearwater Revival in circa 550 BC. Steve Albini's coffers have never been nearly as full as those of Bob Rock, Rick Rubin, Nigel Godrich, Butch Vig or that bald ambient bloke who's complicit in much of Coldplay's and U2's chart-topping output. Why so? Well, for one thing, Albini refuses to accept points for any of the recordings in which he is involved. 'Points' is record industry slang for percentage points, meaning royalties. Rather than hoovering up those percentage points, Albini always requests a flat-fee payment as a matter of principle. If this does few favours for Albini's personal finances, which he has been known to supplement by triumphing in poker tournaments, the arrangement is to the great benefit of the musicians he records. If any band or solo artist actually manages to make any money out of their recording, they will not then have to shell out any of those profits to the guy who happened to lay it down. Not that Albini sees this as a benevolent act of generosity on his part. For Albini, it's a plain matter of ethics. 'I have to look at myself in the mirror when I shave in the morning,' he explained to Stewart Lee for the *Sunday Times*, 'I'd rather not look at a coward or someone who was exploiting people.'[2]

Another advantage of the flat-fee arrangement is it means Albini has no stake in whether the end result sells one single copy or several thousand units. There is no incentive on Albini's part, as there might well be for your average points-hungry producer, to manipulate whichever musicians he happens to be recording with the intent of prising a more commercial sound out of them. Steve Albini will not be adding a 'millennial whoop' to any given song because that's what happens to be trendy. He will not be inviting Keith Urban into the studio to provide a guest verse with an eye on the lucrative country market. Albini does not have a direct cellphone number for Snoop Dogg. He will not be jumping out of his seat and pointing through the glass window of the recording booth with a Cuban cigar clamped between his sausage fingers and hollering, 'That's the single, fellas! By the time I'm finished with you guys, I'm gonna make you bigger than Maroon fuckin' 5!' As long as the band he's recording doesn't yearn to become the next Maroon 5, the results will be exactly as the band had hoped when entering the studio. As Albini sees it, his duty is to help make the record the band envisions to the best standard that he possibly can.

In order to facilitate this, Albini's ideal situation is for the band he is recording to have their 'shit together' before they arrive at the studio. The songs should have already been completed, composition-ally speaking. Ideally, each number will already have been rehearsed thoroughly. The band should know what they want their record to sound like before they begin recording it.[3] 'Be prepared', as it is put in the title and chorus to a song by Albini's own band Shellac, a number on which Albini also claims to have been born wearing pants.

Albini avoids the common technique of recording individual players' tracks separately before building up the songs bit by bit. He prefers to capture the band performing live in the studio, and in unison. His reasoning is that there are certain natural performance elements that occur only when a band is playing together as a full unit. This could take the fairly obvious form of the other musicians softening or adapting their accompaniment when it is somebody else's turn to perform a solo. It also exists in subtler forms, and this process of give-and-take between the musicians, and the accommodations they make for one another in the spur of the moment, often occurs unconsciously and instinctively. It is not possible, as Albini sees it, to capture these crucial aspects of a band's sound by recording individual tracks on a piece-by-piece basis over a prolonged period of time: 'From my perspective the best way to get to an accurate or familiar and comfortable representation of something, is to have everybody behave normally. And that means to play the song the same way they would if they were rehearsing or playing it onstage.'[4] Bands are, as a rule, heavier live than on record, and Albini's approach to recording is conceived to lose as little of this heaviness as possible.

He is committed to analogue recording methods, avoids using popular mixing tricks like audio compression, despises Auto-Tune, won't allow Pro Tools to be used in his studio, and believes that digital recording methods have had a degrading impact on the standard of music's quality in general and that they threaten recordings' longevity. That's not to say he's opposed to innovation. His Shellac bandmate Bob Weston, who is also a recording and mastering engineer, makes sure that he does at least one thing during every single recording session that he has never done before, an approach that Albini has now adopted himself. Within the analogue para-meters, this could be an act as simple as configuring a new type of microphone, but it helps to broaden his knowledge and skill set one session at a time.[5]

Albini's flat fee remains at the same rate for most of the bands he records. It's an affordably low one, too, given the man's reputa-tion. For precise details, you'll have to consult the 'Session Booking Calculator' on the website of his Chicago studio, Electrical Audio, where fees can be estimated according to which room will be used, whether Albini is being booked or one of the other in-house engineers, and how many days are required. The studio also offers overnight lodgings thanks to its on-site dormitories.

Albini has been known to charge a larger fee for albums backed by major label funding, those with bigger budgets at their disposal and money to burn. This may seem at odds with the vocal hatred of major labels that Albini has sustained throughout his life. In 1994 he contributed an essay to a special issue, themed around major labels, of the punk fanzine *Maximumrocknroll*. Its cover featured somebody holding a pistol to their mouth, finger on the trigger, with the tagline 'some of your friends are already this fucked'. Titled 'The Problem with Music', Albini's piece bluntly condemns the naive cul-pability of A&R personnel who probably believe their own promises that nobody will meddle with the creative process of the band they are trying to woo with typically exploitative major-label contracts that tend to seduce bands with their guarantees of large-looking advance figures and other short-term luxuries. To illustrate 'just how fucked' most bands that sign such contacts wind up in the end, Albini ends his essay with a mathematical breakdown. After everybody else in the record company has been paid, legal fees and other expenses have been settled, recording, equipment and promo-tional costs sorted out along with various related overheads, each band member will have earned a third as much as they would do working in a corner shop. And this piece was written in 1994, when the industry was still booming. But, hell, 'they got to ride in a tour bus for a month.'[6]

Albini sees it as only fair to lend his services to anybody who wants to pay for them, whether they are on a major label, an independent imprint or even unsigned, whether he enjoys the act's music personally or finds it repellent. Albini is there to do the best job he can for whoever hires him. According to his buddy David Yow from The Jesus Lizard, the only band Albini ever turned down was U2.[7] For Nirvana's *In Utero*, Albini accepted a fee of $100,000 because that's what they offered him to record it. On paper that may look like a lot of money for less than two weeks' work. Had he taken royalties, Albini would continue to rake in much more profit to this very day. Albini says Geffen would have preferred Nirvana to have spent 'six months and a million dollars' on their follow-up to the global smash of *Nevermind*.[8] That's what 'the next Guns N' Roses' were supposed to do. By that point in their career, Nirvana were yearning to return to the rougher and more punk rock sound of their origins. In the process, they were hoping to repel some of the more unsavoury elements they had found to be infiltrating their audiences since that big break moment: the jocks, the GNR fans, the misogynists, the homophobes, the conservatives, the Republicans, the bullies. Albini was the perfect candidate. *In Utero*'s speedily recorded tracks proved so disturbing to the band's label and management team that they were deemed 'unreleaseable' or, to their ears at least, 'unfinished'.[9] Albini was asked to 'remix' the session or even repeat it entirely. Sticking to his guns, and unable to see how the recording of that particular set of songs could be bettered, Albini refused.[10] Known for his work with REM, Scott Litt was drafted in to tidy up the potential singles before the album was sent to Bob Ludwig for mastering. This meddling, judged Albini, resulted in a narrowing of the original dynamic range and stereo width, the unwelcome addition of a mid-range frequency boost, a compromised bass response and an overall softening of the sound – 'But the way I would describe it in non-technical terms is that they fucked it up.'[11] Albini's favourite Nirvana songs were, perhaps predictably, 'Scentless Apprentice' and 'Milk It' (original title: 'PiL').[12] These were the two most aggressive and structurally loose tracks on *In Utero*. Both feature an awful lot of screaming, and they showcase Nirvana at their instrumentally harshest, threatening to do serious damage to their equipment and in Kurt Cobain's case his own throat.

From Pixies to PJ

Albini made his name as a recording engineer locally at first. He made recordings of his own bands, picked up the rudimentary skills bit by bit, kept on learning, and made his services available to other musicians in the Chicago area because he felt they ought to be able to hear themselves back as well. From his earliest home recordings, it took about eight years before Albini could concentrate on recording full-time as his profession.

A session conducted at the end of 1987 was the first time Steve Albini recorded musicians who he had never previously met. His prior sessions had been for friends, acquaintances and friends of friends. This one was arranged by Ivo Watts-Russell of the British label 4AD, who was a fan of Big Black, admired the sound of Albini's recordings and thought it would make a good match for 4AD's latest findings. That band were Pixies, and it is no exaggeration to say that the album they made with Albini was a watershed moment in the history of alternative rock, its songs broadening the scope of the many weird and wonderful things that could be achieved within the confines of three minutes or so. With imagery lifted from the spicier passages of the Bible, *Surfer Rosa*'s tales of seedy intercourse and bloody injuries were backed by a raw and ragged sound with an astute understanding of the emotive power of dynamics. Backed by bassist Kim Deal's otherworldly harmonies, Black Francis's vocals veered between singing, speaking, shouting, screaming and a melodious manner of hollering. Sometimes this range could occur within the space of a single verse or two. The Bostonian bawler would occasionally break into Spanish and Puerto Rican slang, which he'd picked up from the six months he'd spent on the Caribbean island as an exchange student. With its shrieked lyrics about offbeat subjects, dense basslines, peculiar riffs, spiky lead guitar parts and the group's skew-whiff pop sensibilities battling against plenty of ferocious noise, the LP astounded most of those who heard it, from obscure underground artists to mainstream royalty like David Bowie (who would later cover 'Cactus').

Despite the session's important outcome, one crucial lesson that Albini learned from recording *Surfer Rosa* came from the guilt he felt afterwards. He is now ashamed that he had been 'guinea-pigging' Pixies to a certain extent. A few months earlier, when Albini had recorded *Tweez* for his friends Slint, that band felt it would be a neat idea to have no breaks between the songs. It was decided that any gaps that were present should be filled by strange effects, ambient noises or snippets of conversation. Albini then imposed that idea on the Pixies' record as well. That's why there are those tantalizing bits of casual in-studio nattering interspersed between some of the songs on *Surfer Rosa*: Black Francis's 'You fuckin die' speech; Kim Deal discussing the discreet dismissal of a high-school teacher who'd shown sleazy interest in field hockey players. This wasn't an idea cooked up by the group themselves, nor would they have necessarily wanted to include this on their record if they'd been asked. 'I feel like I externally added that to their band and now they have to answer for it,' Albini has said. 'All that little chitchat shit – they aren't really chatty people. Now it strikes me as slightly false and they have to live up to it. They've had people ask them about that in several interviews and I feel like I'm at fault.'[13] His duty as recording engineer, he has since determined, is to make the record the band wants to make and to capture the band as faithfully as he possibly can. It's a process Albini likens to getting a haircut: 'Your barber might have an opinion, your barber might show you some other options out of a book or whatever, but in the end, if you want him to give you a zig-zag mohawk with a swastika in the side, that's what he's paid for.'[14] To be fair, though, a lot of the people queuing up to pay for his services are eager for that signature heavy cut that can be offered only by this particular audio coiffeur.

Released in 1988, *Surfer Rosa* initially made a bigger splash in the UK than on Pixies' home turf, and British artists were soon eager to exploit Albini's recording nous. David Gedge of The Wedding Present had been amazed by the 'colossal' sound of Big Black when he'd attended the Leeds date of their final tour. When he got his hands on *Surfer Rosa*, 'It sounded weird and interesting but still very natural. It was big and yet intimate and there was light and shade.' Gedge felt his own music possessed those elements too, yet his band had always struggled to capture such textures on record. They hired Albini to record a couple of EPs, followed by The Wedding Present's third full-length, *Seamonsters* (1991). When arranging how much studio time was required, Gedge mentioned his group's previous album, *Bizarro*, had taken six weeks. That was way too long for Albini. 'The Beatles recorded albums in a weekend and they sounded great,' was his philosophy. 'And it's not rocket science either,' adds Gedge. 'It's just all about recording a well-rehearsed band in an acoustically suitable room with appropriate equipment.'[15] The resulting album marked the next step away from the frantic and somewhat frail indie-punk sound of The Wedding Present's earlier output, capturing a warmer, denser and slower style that boasted greater sophistication and intent.

When PJ Harvey heard *Surfer Rosa* she couldn't believe how the recording managed to make it seem like the band themselves were in the exact same room as her.[16] 'He's the only person that I know who can record a drum kit and it sounds like you're stood in front of a drum kit,' she said. 'It doesn't sound like it's gone through a recording process or that it's coming out of speakers . . . And that is why I wanted to work with him, because all I've ever wanted is for us to be recorded and to sound like we do when we're playing together in a room. And that's never happened before.'[17] It may not have been rocket science, as Gedge put it, but Harvey was astonished by Albini's unusual and meticulous approach to setting up and positioning the studio's microphones. 'He'd have them on the floor, on the walls, on the windows, on the ceiling, twenty feet away from where you were singing. He just sets it up and he's very good at getting the right atmosphere to get the best take.'[18] Recorded with Albini, Harvey's *Rid of Me* was released in 1993, the same year as Overkill's *I Hear Black*, Aerosmith's *Get a Grip* and Annihilator's *Set the World on Fire*. It managed to out-heavy them all, with their compressed drum sounds, dramatic sneers and laughably wide stances. What *Rid of Me* offered instead sat somewhere between noise rock, crushing blues rock and the meatier end of post-rock. Most takes for the album were completed in just three days.

Harvey was a huge fan of of Slint's 1991 album *Spiderland*. The follow-up to the noisier Albini-helmed *Tweez*, *Spiderland* was recorded in a similar manner, this time by Brian Paulson. By then Slint's music had matured into atmospheric post-rock territory. Harvey was so enamoured by this music that she wrote to the Louisville band offering her services as lead singer.[19] Her admiration of quiet–loud dynamics also derived from Pixies, whose mixture of dark humour and seriousness also appealed. Harvey respected the literary merits of lyricists like Patti Smith and Nick Cave and hoped to harness the same mixture of 'passion and violence' that she heard in the voice of Howlin' Wolf.[20]

As with *Surfer Rosa*, blood and other bodily fluids abound in *Rid of Me*'s lyric sheet. Following the requests of Led Zeppelin's Robert Plant and the blues precursors from whom he stole many ideas wholesale, those who demanded to have their 'lemons' squeezed until the juice ran down their legs, Harvey offered the more disconcerting proposal to rub 'it' better until it bled. Her own legs she demanded to have licked, along with her 'injuries'. In reciprocation, she would twist off somebody's 'head'. Elsewhere on the record, the lower limbs of a lover who has spurned her are amputated violently. A partner on another track cannot fulfil Harvey in either sexual or romantic terms, leaving her physically and emotionally 'dry'. Seduction is likened to a fish hook through the face. Love is something that will make a person wretch. On 'Man-Size', Harvey inhabits a masculine persona in a withering mockery of phallocentric male power. For '50ft Queenie' Harvey erases gender roles again by embodying a giant goddess who, by the end of the song, has become a king of the world, and one who is twenty inches long.

According to drummer Rob Ellis, the album's music needed to match the level of visceral aggression that Harvey was expressing in her lyrics.[21] Harvey sometimes saw it the other way round. 'For me, music is something that is very sexual,' she said. 'It's a turn-on. It's not something to do with your head, it's to do with your body, which is a very sexual instrument. To bring sexual elements into the lyrics to go with the music just makes perfect sense to me. It just happens.'[22]

Harvey had been raised surrounded by rock – quite literally, as her parents owned a quarry business, but they were also friends with people like Ian Stewart and Charlie Watts of The Rolling Stones, and the Harveys would house and feed musicians when they toured near the family's Dorset home. Having access to that kind of rock – the interesting characters who stopped by and the fascinating instruments they carried – had a deep impact on Polly, who by her early teens was busy writing her own songs.[23] By the time of *Rid of Me*, she had grown into a hollering, riffing rock god in her own right.

Harvey was occasionally lumped in with other artists, 'rock's psycho babes from hell', as Barney Hoskyns put it in *Vogue*.[24] Really, Harvey always seemed to exist in her own universe. She was too independently minded to align herself with riot grrrls, too English to be labelled grunge; her powerful lyrics and blistering vocals were too prominent for post-rock; and she would have nothing to do with the simpering lads and ladettes of Britpop. At the 1994 Brit Awards, Harvey performed a duet with the Icelandic singer Björk: a stripped-back but completely defiant and fearsome cover of The Rolling Stones' '(I Can't Get No) Satisfaction'. The following year's Brits ceremony would see the wide-kneed geezers of Blur triumph in four categories, with Oasis winning Best Breakthrough Act and the rebranded 'Modfather' Paul Weller voted Best British Male Solo Artist. However many times it is viewed, the previous year's duet between Harvey and Björk doesn't lose any of its ability to raise goosebumps. It is so self-assured and inspiring, yet, watching it with hindsight, it feels almost tragic. This was an international display of female creative power showcasing the capacity to rock out without relying on clichés, despite being a cover of one of the most imitative English bands of all time. It was everything that Britpop wasn't: two women in their twenties, each already having conveyed their own singular vision, on the cusp of long and fruitful careers, rocking out together with no need for any backing band accompaniment, in front of a huge room packed with personnel from the male-dominated music industry, fearlessly expressing their – not Mick or Keef's – dissatisfaction with the world and the way it is ordered. Although Harvey and Björk proved wise, talented and imaginative enough to secure long-lasting careers for themselves, their performance did not hold back or divert the approaching cultural tide. Instead of the Oasis versus Blur battle that would soon be played out in the tabloid and music presses, and instead of the fawned-over Union Jack dress worn at the 1997 Brits by one member – her personality reduced to 'Ginger' – of a manufactured pop group conceived by men to rob young girls of their pocket money while appropriating feminism under the slogan of 'girl power' (the term itself also stolen), if Harvey and Björk's duet had been rightly championed as the defining cultural moment of the era then history would have been very different indeed.

Don't Mention the P-word

Steve Albini, incidentally, was touring in England with Shellac when the first Oasis album came out and has described the contrast between the hype that he heard about them (including the Gallagher brothers' own self-aggrandizing interviews) and the experience of finally listening to their music: 'It was like a guy talking about how impressive this bodybuilder was and then out trots a toddler infant.' The reason Oasis didn't break America, reasons Albini, was that their success at home had been built around celebrity culture: 'Oasis didn't resonate in the U.S. because all we were exposed to was their music, which was trivial. We didn't have the luxury of the gossip, scandals and all that sort of stuff.'[25]

On the subject of celebrities, Albini is so far removed from the Mark Ronsons, Paul Epworths and Timbalands of this world that he cannot even countenance being called 'a producer'. It's a label Albini once described as 'an offensive term that does not describe me in any way.'[26] He's not even wholly comfortably being called a recording engineer, on the basis that, unlike certain other professionals he admires, he never completed a degree or equivalent formal apprenticeship in electrical engineering.

As well as objecting to the term 'producer', Albini prefers not to see his name on the sleeves of the items he has recorded because it detracts from the accomplishments of the actual musicians. He believes that, as with royalties, all attention and credit should be paid to them. Some artists have complied with Albini's wishes to remain uncredited over his three decades and counting of laying down music. This can make it tricky to trace all the records in which Albini has been involved. There have been pseudonyms, too, including The Little Weed or The Li'l Weed, Ding Rollski, Don Moist, King Barbeque, Mr Billiards, Lenard Johns, Reggie Stiggs, Robert Earl Hughes, The Proprietor, Whodini and Terry Fuckwit. On the sleeve to Slint's *Tweez*, Albini's contribution is credited to 'some fuckin derd niffer'. For those who are curious, a derd niffer is 'somebody who bats turds out of somebody else's asshole with his nose'. The young band thought this was highly amusing. Albini considered it preferable to being credited by name.[27]

Others have used his real name more craftily. As Albini's reputation as a recording engineer grew, his role in a record's creation became a handy promotional tool for musicians who harboured certain ambitions. Albini's presence implied a level of quality (in recording terms at least, if not always in songwriting) and proved useful to those hoping to make a bid for precious indie rock credibility, even when signed to a major label. This author can't be the only cardigan-wearing, beard-sporting hipster out there who has come across an unfamiliar LP in an independent record store and purchased it immediately because the artwork looked fairly promising and the words 'Recorded by Steve Albini' appeared somewhere on its sleeve or promotional sticker.[28] Such a calculated move can backfire, of course, as Albini recording alumnus Will Oldham points out: some acts trick themselves into believing that Albini's involvement will automatically result in an impressive outcome, whereas all he really does is 'turn on the tape recorder and show them what their music sounds like'.[29] This big reveal does not always come as a pleasant surprise.

To proudly display Albini's name on your album credits can bring other unintended consequences, in particular the unending curse of having to answer the following question – and countless variations on it – in every single interview you will ever have to undertake for the rest of your musical career until the blessed relief of retirement or death finally arrives to set you free: 'So . . . what was it like to work with Steve Albini?' Some musicians have had to answer this question so many times that it has started to drive them a little bit mad. One such fellow is Andrew Falkous, the guitarist, vocalist and occasional keyboard prodder in the criminally underappreciated alt-rock group Future of the Left. His earlier band, the Cardiff-based trio Mclusky, recorded their second and third albums with Steve Albini: *Mclusky Do Dallas* (2002) and *The Difference between Me and You Is that I'm Not On Fire* (2004). With their crunching noise punk riffs and irreverent lyrical observations, Mclusky were an ideal match for Albini. Unlike some bands with whom Albini has worked, in this instance the admiration was reciprocated. Albini was quoted as saying that Mclusky were the only British band worth listening to. If you pay close attention you'll spot a brief lyrical homage to Mclusky's 'The World Loves Us and Is Our Bitch' in the Shellac song 'Spoke'.

Albini and Falkous are also kindred spirits in terms of upfront honesty and general impertinence, unafraid as they are to mouth off about the artistically inferior musicians who are more successful than them in purely commercial terms. Both parties have been known to mock Billy Corgan and his Smashing Pumpkins on a routine basis. 'Smashing Pumpkins don't have anything to do with me or the way I live,' Albini said in 1994.[30] For his own part, Falkous rarely misses an opportunity to mock Corgan and Co., be it from the stage, in his interviews or in the lyrics to Future of the Left's 'Robocop 4 – Fuck Off Robocop', in which the physical appearance of the Pumpkins' frontman is compared to Lord Voldemort from the *Harry Potter* franchise.

Similar personalities Albini and Falkous may well be, but by the time Future of the Left were performing at All Tomorrow's Parties in 2009, Falkous had grown weary of having to discuss the subject of Albini with fans, casual listeners, passing joggers and journalists alike. From the festival stage, Falkous literally begged his audience not to approach him afterwards to ask him anything about the revered recording engineer. While his more incognito and perhaps less easily irritable bandmates were happy to remain at the festival for the duration of the weekend, Falkous could only muster a few hours before making his departure. 'I hate repeating myself and there's so much information out there about the man on Google,' Falkous explains.

It's a sad fact that you could do a Venn diagram of the people who go to All Tomorrow's Parties and people who are fans of Steve Albini, and it would just be a fucking circle. I love all of his musical enterprises. He's a very nice man, although apparently I'm meant to stop saying that because it spoils his hard-won reputation. Having met some proper Albini fanboys-stroke-fangirls, they think you should be honoured to have basked in the light of his drum-mic-ing. I would say I have spent 25 percent of every interview I've ever given talking about Steve Albini. Sorry, Steven Albini. That's his name. That's his full name. If he wants to abbreviate it, that's his business but I'm guessing that's not what his birth certificate says.[31]

Instead of asking the exact same question to the countless musicians who have worked with Albini, if the uninspired music journalists who keep on asking it had the foresight to conduct the prerequisite research required of a quasi-thorough professional, then they'd soon discover that it is very rarely met with anything approaching the kind of juicy answer that's anticipated. (This expectation is presumably based on Albini's slightly misleading reputation for being spiky.) More likely, they'll discover that Albini's working methods are relatively quick, that he has a great deal of experience in the art of recording, is particularly good at capturing a strong drum sound, has an unrivalled ability for putting microphones in the right places and, above all, that he is a consummate professional. 'What do people think it's like to work with Steve Albini?' retorts the exasperated Falkous. 'He's a guy, with a body and a head. He presses record when you start playing. You need to say whether or not you like the take or not, and then you get to keep it or you do another take.'[32]

In recent years the 'What's it like to work with Steve Albini?' epidemic has spiralled so far out of control that it has been asked of bands who haven't even worked with Albini in the first place.

When the instrumental rock band Russian Circles were promoting their 2016 album *Guidance*, produced by Converge's Kurt Ballou, they were asked how Ballou's approach differed from their previous experiences of working on two records with 'the legendary Steve Albini'. Bassist Brian Cook had to politely explain that Russian Circles did not record those albums with Albini. The band *had* recorded at Albini's Electrical Audio studios but the engineer for those sessions was Greg Norman.[33] Anticipating the same embarrassment, noise-rock-meets-thrash-metal band Oozing Wound sent out a warning to their Twitter followers ahead of their fourth album's release in 2019: 'Just as a lil pre-empter [*sic*] as I've already seen this a couple of times, STEVE ALBINI did not RECORD THE ALBUM. Gregoire Yeche did at Electrical Audio, which Steve runs. Looking forward to seeing all the coming misinformation. It's gonna be fun!'[34]

One insight into Albini's working methods came courtesy of a feature on the Canadian noise rock trio METZ, whose 2017 album *Strange Peace* was recorded by Albini (rather unnecessarily, it has to be said, seeing as the self-production on that band's two prior albums had been so proficient at replicating Albini's signature traits in the first place). Apparently, Albini does not eat anything all day long. He has breakfast in the morning and then doesn't consume any solids for the entire time he spends in the studio because he feels it will make him 'lazy and sluggish', which can be detrimental to productivity. Then at the end of the day he goes home and cooks a big meal to share with his wife Heather.[35] Sometimes, according to The Breeders' Kelley Deal, in the middle of an otherwise serious conversation, Albini will 'lean over a cheek and fart without blinking an eye. And it's not like he's doing it to get a reaction, and it's not like this huge stinky thing. [He'll say] something about, "It's a natural bodily function."'[36] He also enjoys setting his farts on fire, and his shoes, among other things. Albini's scientist father, in the final third of his life, worked in the field of forest fires and how to control them, so make of that what you will.

Albini was so eager for his name to be kept off record sleeves that in 1991 he wrote an article for *Forced Exposure* that comprised 'eyewitness record reviews' of albums by artists who'd had the gall to credit his involvement. Offering a simple and sincere 'bless you' to the artists who had respected his requests for anonymity, Albini went on to assess the works of Pixies, The Breeders, The Wedding Present, Bitch Magnet, TAD and others without holding back. *Surfer Rosa* may have done much to put his name on the map as a so-called 'producer', but to Albini this record was nothing more than 'a patchwork pinch loaf from a band who at their top dollar best are blandly entertaining college rock'. The first album by Kim Deal of Pixies' side project The Breeders was deemed 'nothing special' by the man who recorded it. The Wedding Present, he wrote, were such swell guys you'd let them date your sister. 'But Jesus, are they vulnerable,' he added. The post-hardcore group Bitch Magnet drew ire for listing Albini as 'producer' on their *Star Booty* EP when all he really did was 'help three college bozos remix some sorry class-project recordings'. Rather than placing it on the turntable, Bitch Magnet's 'poor wittle wecord', advises Albini, would be best used as a dinner plate. Having learned their lesson, the next time Bitch Magnet worked with Albini he was credited under the alias Arden Geist. For Membranes' *Kiss Ass . . . Godhead!* Albini was credited as a producer despite having worked on only a couple of songs in Chicago before helping the band mix some extra songs in Leeds, duties for which Albini said he had never been paid. 'I no more "produced" it than did I reach into my butt crack and discover it,' he wrote.[37]

Record Things as They Are

Snubbing royalties. Preferring his name to be left off the sleeves of the albums he's recorded. Reeling at the term 'producer'. Recording the band as accurately as possible, as they themselves hope to be heard and as their fans have experienced in concert. Loath to mould artists into a more commercially appealing prospect. Openly and publicly insulting the artists he's worked with and deriding the records he's had a hand in birthing. All this is the complete antithesis to how many professionals, particularly the big-name ones, have conducted the business of 'producing' musical artists. Take Mike Chapman, for example. His role as producer of *Parallel Lines* involved not just recording Blondie but coercing and manipulating them into playing 'properly' in a tighter and more professional sense, altering the lyrics to be less trashy and humorous and more 'emotional', persuading Debbie Harry that she should sing 'in tune', foregrounding melody at all costs, and making the band do take after take after take until they reached the high standards that Chapman believed, correctly, would get Blondie's music aired on all the pop radio stations.[38] *Parallel Lines* was one of the records that helped usher in a new era of studio gloss.

In turn, Albini and his disciples reacted against mainstream 1980s production, characterized by its emphasis on synthesized accompaniment, gated reverb plastered all over the drums, similar effects on the vocals and a general glossiness comparable to that found in the pages of *Cosmopolitan*. This was heard on records by everybody from Madonna to Def Leppard; production which at the time suggested something boldly futuristic but soon enough made every record sound dated. In this sense, Albini's ethos was less a radical new approach to the recording process than a return to an older professional philosophy. After all, what had John and Alan Lomax been doing when they traipsed across America to record its native folk music? They used a cylinder machine, an invention created by Thomas Edison and his team, the first people in human history to record and reproduce an intelligible sound. Lead Belly was one musician recorded by the Lomaxes. His later studio recordings were conducted by Moses Asch, whose raison d'être was to record music as accurately and truthfully as possible with the interfering effects of production kept to the barest minimum. As Asch put it himself, his mission was 'to record things *as they are*'.[39]

Albini's approach has also been compared to that of Harry Vanda and George Young. Unlike the duo's more meticulous work for the pop artists they also produced, Vanda and Young's production on AC/DC's initial run of albums was based around quick, mostly live takes, with overdubs used only for lead guitar breaks and vocal tracks. Ambient microphone positioning was key to capturing the 'sweet spots' and a whole spectrum of sound, and avoiding the tighter, stiffer and overly interfered results of rival recordings. Vanda and Young used psychological approaches too, purposely winding up musicians before a take to coax out the most aggressive performance possible. It was anathema to the tastes of Atlantic Records, who were banking on AC/DC breaking out into the global marketplace. George Young noted that 'The American market likes to think that being heavy has to be very nice to the ear. Whereas our approach was more of a rough and ready attitude where any extra noises, like a snare drum rattling, all adds to the atmosphere . . . We wanted to try to get the energy and the danger that you got in a pub.'[40] Rowdy pubs are all well and good. Atlantic had their sights on U.S. sports stadiums. Vanda and Young politely stepped back and a new producer, Robert Lange, was installed for the band's sixth record, *Highway to Hell*. Lange would later spend literally years working on Def Leppard's *Hysteria*, recording everything separately and meticulously piecing it all together in steady stages, with a further five months taken up on mixing, so that in the end no hair was out of place.[41]

Along with Crazy Horse and Willie Nelson, AC/DC are one of the 'dream' artists that Albini often says he would love to have the chance to record. As for Albini's band Shellac, one of the few cover versions the trio has ever attempted was a lumbering version, verging on a postmodern deconstruction, of AC/DC's 'Jailbreak'. Their influence has had an impact not just on his engineering philosophies but also his musicianship, which, as Albini freely admits, is limited by his own lack of time and inclination to develop his skill set further in terms of sophisticated technique. Malcolm Young is one of

Albini's all-time guitar heroes because he 'played partial bar-chords for forty years and always sounded fantastic', maximizing the impact of the music by using limited or restricted methods. An example Albini gives of Young's brilliance is that, although AC/DC's songs are essentially defined by the guitarist's authoritative riffs, Young was shrewdly unafraid to *stop playing*. This would seem counter-intuitive. The egos of most rhythm guitarists wouldn't allow it. On songs that Malcolm Young arranged for AC/DC, there are points when Angus Young stops playing rhythm guitar in order to break into a solo. Most bands, at that moment, would overdub a second rhythm guitar track to compensate for Angus's momentary rhythmic absence. It seems the obvious thing to do in order to fill the gap. Not only does Malcolm Young avoid doing that, he goes one step further, and in the opposite direction. There is an instrumental passage with no vocal required. Angus Young shifts from rhythm to perform the lead. And Malcolm Young stops playing his rhythm part too. It's supposed to be, in theory, the song's biggest moment, yet at this point AC/DC make everything sparser, focusing attention on the lead, bass and drums. Then, at the end of this ostensible high point, when Angus shifts back to rhythm and Malcolm begins playing again, the intensity blows the roof off. It's simple. It's effective. In Albini's words, 'it's also very easy, because it means that you just have to do nothing for a little while, but most rock musicians are afraid or ashamed to do nothing.' Guitar magazines, he adds, are always banging on at length about how to the play the guitar. 'It's never about the part where nobody plays.'[42]

Bob Rock had once been Metallica's very own version of Mike Chapman or Robert Lange, duly polishing up the thrashers, ironing out their creases and convincing them to dabble in sensitive ballads in order to reach the dizzy heights of mainstream success. They achieved this feat with 1991's self-titled record, also known as *The Black Album*. Producer Rock was still working with Metallica when the divisive *St Anger* was completed in 2003. That album was, to a significant extent, overshadowed by its accompanying documentary, *Some Kind of Monster*, which cannot be viewed without the movie evoking unfortunate echoes of Spinal Tap (and Metallica deserve respect for even releasing it). As perceptive critics noted, *St Anger*'s rough-and-ready production, its clanking drum sound and obstinate lack of guitar solos resulted in a record that was noticeably similar to the minimalist noise rock style of Albini's Shellac. Metallica could have saved themselves a lot of their hard-earned dollars if they'd forgotten about Bob Rock altogether and gone straight to the real thing.

Albini's engineering talents have added heaviness not just to rock music but to other genres as well. She seems to have withdrawn from the industry of late but, between 1999 and 2010, the singer-songwriter Nina Nastasia recorded all her albums with Steve Albini. The singer and harpist Joanna Newsom acquired his services for 2006's critically acclaimed *Ys* and called him (whether he liked it or not) 'pretty much the best producer in the world'.[43] Albini has recorded folk and country artists, post-rockers, metal bands, noise acts, slowcore, math rock, jazz rock, post-hardcore, everything in between and a lot more besides. He's worked with household names like Jimmy Page and Robert Plant, all the way down to the obscure Belgian noise rock bands Raketkanon and Cocaine Piss. Even getting in on the action now are artists far removed from the rock music that is traditionally seen as Albini's area of expertise. See *The Centre Cannot Hold* by the principally electronic composer Ben Frost.

Some artists have been so satisfied with Albini's results that they have requested the opportunity to re-record their old material with him at the helm in order to finally be able to experience it how they had always wanted it to be heard. Around the time they were celebrating the twentieth anniversary of 1987's *George Best*, The Wedding Present decided to re-record the album in its entirety. On releasing the new version in 2017, the band said they'd had difficulty convincing Albini to do it but in the end had managed to twist his arm. 'Everything is bigger,' The Wedding Present boasted. 'The combination of Albini's recording and the ultra-talented Graeme Ramsay on "real" drums brings these frantic songs to life. However, the real difference comes out in the way those super-fast, ever-jangly guitars sound . . . they're warmer, they're rockier, they're more modern. More . . . Albini!'[44] U.S. rockers Cheap Trick did the same thing with the songs from *In Color*, originally made in 1977. In Cheap Trick's case the Albini version has not been given a commercial release and, as such, seems to have been completed purely for the band's own satisfaction and sense of closure. The songs themselves were good enough on the original version, explained guitarist Rick Nielsen, 'but sonically it's wimpy and we're not wimpy.'[45]

Albini's anti-corporate views may have come across as puritan in the 1990s when money was still sloshing around the music industry, certain independent labels like SST had gained a reputation for improper remuneration of their artists, and records as wonderfully bizarre as Boredoms' *Chocolate Synthesizer* were released by majors as big as Warner Bros. As the bottom has fallen out of the music industry thanks to the rise of the Internet (of which Albini is a fan because it has rendered record labels 'irrelevant' and anybody can upload their music for it to be heard virtually anywhere in the world[46]), Albini's punk rock spirit has become more pertinent than ever. It isn't just strange underground bands who sound like an armoured bison headbutting an iron girder who are having to do-it-themselves anymore. To most musicians besides your Ed Sheerans and The 1975, DIY is the way of the world. It's a situation that might seem unjust as musicians with no label support slog up and down motorways in between shifts at their exhausting day jobs, travelling in rickety vans to perform a few songs and hopefully flog a few T-shirts. But there's another way to look at it. 'Shellac is a hobby for all of us,' says Albini.

In saying that, we take it very seriously. It's the single most important thing that all of three of us do. We don't rely on Shellac as a means of earning a living, so we have a lot of freedom. We can do literally whatever we want with this band. It's extremely liberating to know that you don't have any obligations, responsibilities or pressure on you. We can treat the band as pure pleasure and as something to be enjoyed.[47]

14

SABBATH PHASE III: EARTH, SLEEP, ELECTRIC WIZARD AND OTHER ASSORTED STONERS

Dave Harwell and Dylan Carlson of Earth, the latter wearing
his Morbid Angel shirt with pride.

Monotony, either in its sensation or its infliction, is simply
the quality of a person. There are no dreary sights; there are
only dreary sightseers.[1]

G. K. CHESTERTON

orilla, Manchester, 15 August 2014. Twenty-five years after forming, Earth are in town to promote their eighth studio album. The support band for tonight is GNOD, an avant-garde, genre-shifting unit who are based nearby at Islington Mill in Salford. At times GNOD have been known to play sets of rollicking space rock in the Hawkwind tradition. When they feel in danger of being pigeonholed or happen to find themselves booked by too many psych-rock festivals on the trot, they're likely to turn up with a bunch of electronic equipment and no guitars to perform one long 'horrible, weird techno thing' (as they would describe it themselves), even if that causes the rock purists to flee in disgust. 'It's this natural way that we've fallen into working,' the band's Paddy Shine has explained. 'It also depends which members are around, who wants to play. It is nice to get a steady line-up together, but we do get bored pretty fast.'[2] On this particular evening, GNOD opt for a forty-minute, slowly unfurling, single-song set of hypnotic jazzy abstraction. A recording of this will be included as a bonus disc at the end of their forthcoming studio marathon 'Infinity Machines', 'just to send those last bits of brain scuttling for shelter', as one critic will write.[3]

As for the headliners, 'Primitive and Deadly' is the fifth Earth LP since Dylan Carlson reactivated his main musical project after several years in the wilderness. In a less jarring or provocative manner than GNOD, this is another band that has offered its fair share of surprises. The latest being that, after a few albums of honing songs with a cleaner guitar tone, 'Primitive and Deadly' is slathered in the thick kind of distortion in which Earth specialized back in the early 1990s, when few people were interested. There are also some vocals *on the new record, the first time that's happened since 1996. With the album's guest singers absent from the tour, Earth perform the songs in their instrumental form, drawing no complaints from the reverential audience. A significant proportion of them are wearing black hoodies. Carlson introduces the next song: 'There Is a Serpent Coming'. Perhaps 'snail' would have been a more appropriate choice of limbless slitherer. Even though the latest Earth album has swapped clean tones and cello accompaniments in favour of re-embracing fuzz and feedback, the compositions remain in Carlson's preferred tempo: verryyy, verrryyyyyyyy slooooooooooow. He casts a calm and commanding presence at the front of the stage, his grizzled features flanked by wispy grey mutton chops. Betwixt the crow's feet, those grey-blue eyes of his have seen some things. Carlson raises his guitar with pride as he gradually moves his fingers (tattooed, like much of his wrinkling skin) from one prolonged note to the next. It's hard not to fixate on the mesmeric sight behind him, however. Earth's drummer, Adrienne Davies, gradually extends her arms high into the air before each measured whack of the kit. It's funny how she literally resembles slow-motion footage of a classic rock drummer, and it makes you wonder why all those other drummers out there are always in such a hurry. Slowness is so often linked to dullness or boredom in the popular imagination, be it in film, music, TV, literature or life in general. Most people would probably get bored of Earth's music pretty quickly. But right now, as Carlson weaves his deliberately sluggish guitar licks along to Davies's stately beats, the effect is somehow soothing and thrilling at the same time. Time? Time itself no longer feels like such a substantial concept anyhow. If we need to sprint to the railway station to catch the train home it no longer seems so important. We'll catch it or we won't . . . Another one will be along at some point in the middle of the night or early hours of the morning. What are we supposed to be doing tomorrow? It doesn't matter anymore . . . I could float here forever . . .*

Earth 2: Special Low Frequency Version

Way back in 1969, Black Sabbath changed their name from Earth because there existed another band called Earth who were already operating on the UK gig circuit. Twenty years later in Olympia, Washington, Dylan Carlson founded a new band that he christened Earth, presumably because 'Black Sabbath' was already taken. Carlson's Earth did not pay tribute to the mighty Sabbath in name alone.

As it happens, the original British Earth disbanded after their second single, 'Resurrection City / Comical Man', released at the tail end of 1969. Two decades on, when Dylan Carlson formed his own Earth, Black Sabbath had made it to their fourteenth studio album. Featuring only one original member in the form of tenacious guitarist Tony Iommi, *Headless Cross*'s accompanying personnel were Cozy Powell (drums/percussion), Laurence Cottle (bass), Tony Martin (vocals) and Geoff Nicholls (keyboards). Queen's Brian May provided a guitar solo on 'When Death Calls'. *Headless Cross*'s appraisal by some as the best Sabbath album in years only goes to show how low standards and expectations had sunk. Lyrical platitudes about Satan, spirits, blood and witches did little to anchor Sabbath back to their radical origins. Musically speaking, *Headless Cross* was defined by its glossy 1980s-era production, overly compressed drum sound, arena-rock keyboard tones and Martin's vocal histrionics. Trailblazers no longer, Sabbath were caught hanging shamelessly on the coattails of the New Wave of British Heavy Metal while floundering in pale imitation of Iron Maiden, Judas Priest, Van Halen, Def Leppard, Scorpions and Europe's 'The Final Countdown'. To make matters worse, that style itself was already old hat by this late stage in the decade. Much like punk's displacement of prog, the excess, extravagance and inherent ridiculousness of the 1980s metal scene was exposed and supplanted by the rise of the harder, faster and more extreme thrash genre, the thrillingly trashy sound of Guns N' Roses' debut LP, the uglier sound of modern noise rock and the emerging grunge scene. When bands like Nirvana waged their cultural war against hair metal while singing the praises of Black Sabbath, it wasn't *Headless Cross* they had in mind.

The second concert ever attended by young army brat Dylan Carlson was by Black Sabbath, who were at that time fronted by Ronnie James Dio. Aged fifteen, Carlson lapped up *Born Again*, Sabbath's 1983 album with Deep Purple's Ian Gillan installed as temporary lead singer. (It's the one with the awesome devil baby on the cover.) Along with many others, Carlson quickly lost interest in the diminishing returns of Sabbath's ongoing activities. 'I didn't pay that much attention to Sabbath when it was like the Tony Iommi show,' he would later reflect. 'I mean, I love Tony Iommi and all, but it seemed like those records had a different singer every time. They lost a lot.'[4] Searching for an alternative, it's as if Carlson worked backwards, digging further and further into Black Sabbath's history, and then, when all to be found there had been thoroughly exhumed and examined, he managed to burrow even deeper when making his own music with Earth. As much as it ushers in the next phase of the Sabbathian mode, *Earth 2* also represents a kind of drastic regression. Covering Black Sabbath for *Sounds* magazine, Peter Silverton had noted that 'Heavy metal is, after all, rock reduced to its narrowest base – volume, emphatic rhythm and incantations to boogie.' Writing those words in 1978, Silverton hadn't imagined that such a style could be reduced and distilled even more thoroughly. Yet that is exactly what Carlson would eventually manage to do. 'What Sabbath play is the root of just about everybody's style,' continued Silverton. 'Only where Sabbath stop is where most people start.'[5] It was inconceivable that where Sabbath stopped, it was possible to put the heavy metal wagon into reverse, to look backwards, to delve deeper, to reduce the formula even further, to strip it even of its rhythm and boogie.

Cast your mind back to *Lysol* by Melvins. It begins with that audacious ten-minute opening number, eventually segueing into the

LP's seven-minute second track of similarly sludgy malice. Only later does it reward patient fans of more conventional rock with its recognizable Alice Cooper covers. *Earth 2* exhibited the same manner of audaciousness. Only in this instance, it lasted for the duration of the entire album. It was not a short album either, eventually clocking in at 73 minutes and 13 seconds. *Earth 2* was recorded in August 1992 at Avast Studios in Seattle. It was around this time that Carlson was given one of the most valuable pieces of wisdom he's ever received. It will come as little surprise to learn that this advice came from none other than Buzz Osborne of Melvins. 'Doing music,' Carlson was warned, 'you can go two ways: jump on the hot thing or do your thing and keep doing it well. If you choose the latter you won't have to compromise and eventually people will begin to notice.'[6]

Much of the music discussed in the present volume would take a while to catch on. This includes Earth and most of the other stoner, doom and desert rockers described below, whose music would find its audience very slowly, which is perhaps befitting of a style that is not concerned with fast tempos. They would toil in the shadows while others jumped on various bandwagons in a usually regrettable way. But all the time Earth, their brethren and their offbeat output were keeping the true Sabbathian spirit alive and making its essence ever more potent. Their music would be discovered by those seeking alternatives to the mediocre heaviness offered by the mainstream, and as the 2000s rolled on, many of them would eventually be spoken of in heroic terms.

For a long time, Dylan Carlson's principal role in popular culture was as the shady best friend who had purchased the rifle that Kurt Cobain used to commit suicide. The Nirvana star had convinced Carlson the gun was for self-protection. The year before Cobain's death, in February 1993, *Earth 2* had been released by Sub Pop. At that time, the Seattle imprint was the hippest record label in the world, having issued records by Nirvana, Mudhoney, Soundgarden, Afghan Whigs, Screaming Trees, TAD, L7 and others. Bemused were those who purchased *Earth 2* on the basis of its label logo alone, expecting to hear the next superstar grunge band. Its content may even have surprised the small number of folk who were already familiar with Carlson's project. Earth's previous release, the thirty-minute *Extra-Capsular Extraction* EP, had used a drum machine and occasional vocals (provided by guests Kurt Cobain and Kelly Canary). *Earth 2* stripped away those fancy embellishments. Filling a whole CD, *Earth 2* (subtitled *Special Low Frequency Version*) essentially consisted of vastly distorted and low-tuned guitar riffs, played at an agonizingly slow pace.

Although most grunge acts were prone to name-checking Black Sabbath as a major touchstone, Carlson was more of an outright metalhead than his Sub Pop contemporaries. Such grungers wouldn't be caught dead in a Morbid Angel T-shirt, as worn by Carlson on the back cover of *Earth 2*. Carlson remembers being mocked by a certain member of a certain fellow Sub Pop band for buying records by UFO and Diamond Head.[7] Not that Earth appealed to many heavy metal fans any more than they did to grunge enthusiasts. Carlson remembers the late '80s thrash craze when countless bands were competing against one another to be the fastest act on the planet. Contrarian Carlson took the opposite route. Observing the breakneck pace of Slayer, of whom he counted himself a fan, he asked himself what would happen if the riff from 'Raining Blood' were to be played at the slowest pace possible.[8] 'My musical origins come from growing up listening to Black Sabbath records, seeing the Melvins perform and reading about musicians like La Monte Young and Terry Riley,' as Carlson neatly summed up Earth. The influence of Young and Riley meant that there was more to Earth's strange relationship with timings than mere slow Slayer riffs. 'La Monte Young wrote some technical articles that I read about the false harmonic that's generated from the vibration of the ear,' Carlson explained later. 'Before I started playing with anybody I took a guitar and tuned it to open strings. I was training myself to hear the overtone series and combining that with a rock or metal aesthetic.' When his fingers hit a dissonant note, rather than thinking in terms of traditional rhythms or beats, Carlson would count the number of vibrations that resonated before he moved on to the next part of the composition. 'It was like listening to that and hearing what was going on in the upper registers of that kind of music. A lot of people think that the drone in music is just making a noise but there's actually a structure to it that evolves out of the overtone series.'[9]

Back among the lower-brow references informing Carlson's work were the guitar techniques of Ted Nugent, particularly in the way that songs like 'Hibernation' and 'Stranglehold' made such powerful use of repetitive riffs and amplifier feedback. Only for Carlson, Nugent's material never went far enough.[10] Earth's work ended up sharing more in common with minimalist composers than anything in the traditional rock or metal canon, and in doing so *Earth 2* took the Sabbathian blueprint to one of its claustrophobic logical conclusions. Carlson had found Young and Riley through The Velvet Underground, who he'd discovered in his mother's record collection. Carlson's grandmother was Scottish, and he has speculated that this ancestral line caused him to be atavistically drawn to drones because of its importance in traditional Celtic music, most notably in the form of the bagpipes.[11] As for digging back beyond Sabbath, it was as if Carlson and then bassist Dave Harwell had the revelation that the best part of The Beatles' 'I Feel Fine' is its opening few seconds of intentional feedback. Likewise, it could be said that the juiciest sections of any given Hendrix track are its intro riff and the prolonged ringing out of its final sensual chord. The busy blues-based frivolities of the verses and choruses merely get in the way of those glorious bookends. All-too-brief magical moments such as those, Earth realized, were so satisfying that they were worth capturing, repeating and exploring – ad nauseam and in a raga-like fashion – for far longer than anybody had bothered attempting before. This idea may not have been a widely valued endeavour when *Earth 2* first emerged. Over time, the record has revealed itself as a vital document in the history of drone rock and drone metal.

Earth 2's impact is most obvious in its influence on Sunn O))), the robe-wearing drone metal superstars who have headlined large festivals and performed at numerous prestigious locations including London's Royal Festival Hall and the world's largest labyrinth, Labirinto della Masone in Parma. The core duo – Stephen O'Malley and Greg Anderson – have readily confessed that the concept behind Sunn O))), and the project's early works in particular, were made in direct homage to Earth. Their name was inspired by the Earth live album *Sunn Amps and Smashed Guitars*. The first Sunn O))) release, *The Grimmrobe Demos* (1999), climaxed with a 21-minute track named 'Dylan Carlson'. When *Earth 2* first appeared, as O'Malley informed *The Wire* in 2004, most people who heard it were so baffled they refused to take it seriously. In 1990 he saw Earth perform live, as a bass and guitar duo, in a support slot for the pop-punk group Seaweed. The mosh-hungry audience were less than impressed by the sight and sound of two blokes sitting in chairs and 'playing super fucking slow', remembered O'Malley. 'I think they were trying to be the antithesis of what was going down at the time in the hardcore scene. Dylan told me that they were just slowing down Slayer riffs as slow as they could play them – while they still had some form. I think that's a great way to make a song.'[12]

As O'Malley's bandmate Greg Anderson recalled, when Sunn O))) first started 'it was just Stephen and I getting as high as possible, hooking up as many amplifiers as we could, and emulating the riffs on *Earth 2*. For the band to grow into something that was its own beast was a big accomplishment.'[13] Later Sunn O))) recordings have remained rooted in that Earth-derived philosophy while exploring how it can be shifted down different avenues. This artistic journey has involved collaborations with various metal and rock vocalists, taken inspiration from jazz greats like Alice Coltrane and Miles Davis, and incorporated a wide range of contributors including orchestral instrumentalists and choirs. Sunn O))) have grown steadily in popularity since the turn of the millennium. Their grand status and widely documented activities, which have included the establishment of the esteemed independent label Southern Lord, have introduced a far broader audience to the sound originally pioneered by Earth. Credit where credit is due, O'Malley and Anderson have never missed an opportunity to acknowledge Carlson as their muse.

For a while, Sunn O))) were also filling the hole left by Carlson's departure from the music scene. Cobain's death had badly shaken Carlson. Under the circumstances, Carlson's own drug habits worsened. Following *Earth 2* he made two more studio albums. The material on 1995's *Phase 3: Thrones and Dominions* was recorded in two separate sessions, each one a year apart. Reluctant and frustrated, Sub Pop had to be persuaded to even bother releasing it. Carlson's least favourite Earth album, *Phase 3* was later judged 'unfinished' by its principal creator, who said he'd made it at his lowest physical and mental ebb.[14] However, *Phase 3* did at least prove that Carlson was no one-trick pony. Its material ranges from concise tracks with a curiously warm glow of distortion ('Harvey' and 'Song 4') to sprawling efforts such as 'Thrones and Dominions' and the disorientating bluster-like tape loop of 'Phase 3: Agni Detonating over the Thar Desert . . .' Next came an even bigger surprise. While 1996's *Pentastar: In the Style of Demons* still contains moments of minimalism and ambience, it's the closest Carlson has ever come to recording ordinary rock songs. It includes a cover of Hendrix's 'Peace in Mississippi'. This came in at a snappy six minutes, unlike an earlier rendition at a gig in New York, filmed by MTV and attended by a plethora of A&R people, where Earth launched into the Hendrix song but ended up just repeating the same glorious riff for 45 minutes.[15] Carlson even sang on a couple of *Pentastar*'s more conventional tracks, suggesting there might have been a parallel universe in which Earth were a lucrative desert rock band. Carlson couldn't keep it together, though, and *Pentastar* was followed by his lengthy absence from the music scene. This involved years of addiction, a stint in jail for residential burglary, more than one spell in rehab and a period of steady employment at a picture-framing firm.

Pioneered by Earth and later adopted by Sunn O))) under the mission of performing it at volumes intended to 'massage the listeners' intestines into an act of defecation',[16] the drone metal sound is not for everyone. When *The Guardian* sent Mark Beaumont to review a Sunn O))) concert in 2015, the long-time *NME* scribe and author of the biography *Muse: Out of This World* was unmoved, emotionally speaking if not also in terms of his bowels. For Beaumont,

> once you attune to the volume, Sunn O))) are largely a dull indulgence . . . where other nosebleed acts such as My Bloody Valentine and Swans bury melodies in their sonic sunbursts, Sunn O))) merely worship decibels and endurance, the musical representation of a slow death from an aggressive disease.[17]

Sunn O))) cannot compete with My Bloody Valentine for the affections of indie fans. Much MBV material is, at its core, indie rock that happens to be played at ear-shattering volume through lots of amplifiers, drenched in reverse reverb, with copious use of the tremolo arm. Swans have more in common with Sunn O))), particularly where the former's earliest and most confrontational approaches are concerned. But again, Swans arguably have more in common with blues and perhaps even pop traditions than Earth and Sunn O))). While buried deeper than in the work of MBV or Swans, there is melody and there are delicate details hidden within the decibel worship enacted by these drone metal practitioners. To discover these, you just have to look (or hear) a little harder.

Writer and musician Alan Licht has pointed out that *Earth 2* is actually a lot more complex and far less fathomable than has been appreciated by both its naysayers and many of its imitators: 'Unlike a lot of more recent noise underground stuff, which (to me) is relatively factorable, this is technically boggling drone music – the sustain is achieved not just with distortion but through overdubbing, and there's clean guitars in there too – even on headphones it's hard to tell what the fuck they're really doing.'[18] Music journalist Tom Scanlon, meanwhile, commends the subtleties of Carlson's guitar technique:

> To characterize Carlson's Earth music as merely sloweddown rock is a gross underestimation. His are sophisticated, complex compositions, deeply digging into individual note vibrations before moving on to the next . . . like a rock climber searching for the right grip.[19]

There is something uniquely thrilling about a work of art that should, in theory, be pretty boring but that in actual fact proves not to be a tedious experience at all, that threat of potential dullness contributing only further to the overall frisson of encountering and enjoying the supposedly tiresome artwork as a sensory and cerebral experience. Just try reading the exquisitely detailed and beautifully composed passages in Herman Melville's *Moby-Dick* when Ishmael is banging on about whale anatomy for page after page. Sneak up to the Rothko room in the Tate Modern and sit there for a week or two. Immerse yourself in the monotonous comedy of Steve Coogan and Rob Brydon in *The Trip*, or else *Stewart Lee's Comedy Vehicle*: the humour contained therein might momentarily cease to be funny because it is quite so repetitive, and yet that bloody-minded repetition and resistance to the variation and pace of standard comedy techniques is paradoxically pleasing. Surrender oneself to the monotony and this unconventional style of meta-comedy becomes extra funny. Discover the forty-minute rumination on purchasing yoghurt from a supermarket that Stewart Lee's ex-comedy partner Richard Herring detailed in his divisive stand-up show *Someone Likes Yoghurt*. Deemed 'worst comedy experience of 2005' by the *Daily Telegraph*, it was actually one of the most finely written and pointlessly pedantic comedy routines of all time. It elicits reoccurring belly laughs, in part, because it really shouldn't be all that funny in the first place. It is satisfying because the rules of mainstream comedy dictate that it should not be.

When you've finally reached the end of *Moby-Dick*, why not crack open the spine of *The Pale King*, David Foster Wallace's unfinished masterpiece about the beauty, power and untapped potential of boredom? 'Sometimes what's important is dull,' writes Wallace in a chapter of dialogue between three (or four?) colleagues who, it seems, are probably trapped in an elevator together. 'Sometimes it's work. Sometimes the important things aren't works of art for your entertainment.'[20] Set in the offices of the Internal Revenue Service, the novel reads as though Wallace was trying his damndest to write something that was objectively boring. He failed to do so because his brilliant brain couldn't manage it. It's easy to imagine why boredom offered potential solace for Wallace, a writer whose intellect sparkled like several Catherine wheels going off at the same time and who couldn't allow himself to own a television set because he was drawn to its glow like a drug addict to the cooking spoon. He was an author who craved respite from both the 'total noise' of the media culture on which he often commented as well as the irrepressible busyness of his own whirring intellect.

On a parenthetical note, Wallace is said to have enjoyed REM's *Monster* (1994). A record designed for the hugely popular group's return to the live circuit after an absence from the stage of over half a decade, *Monster* shocked listeners by rocking so hard in comparison to its hushed and reflective predecessor *Automatic for the People*. The oft-discussed grunge influence on *Monster* is apparent. Yet with its dense layers of distortion, manipulation of amplifier feedback, fuzzy riff cycles and underlying drones, *Monster* also represents REM at their Earth-iest. On it, Peter Buck repressed his usual intricate way of playing the guitar and eschewed the signature jangly sound of previous recordings. Dominating the mix, Buck's emphasis shifted to big, powerful chords, overwhelming distortion and liberal use of tremolo and delay. Maximalist in terms of volume and texture, yet minimalist in terms of its technical chops, this approach both complemented and further complicated the horniness of Michael Stipe's lyrics. 'A lot of records are from the heart. This one's from the crotch. It's a dick record,' bragged the singer in a 1994 documentary.[21] Back then, Stipe was only beginning to make vague public pronouncements about his bisexuality. For an apparently phallic record that has been defined as 'brash, sexual and disgusting', there is little macho about *Monster*. Instead, Stipe becomes what Claire Biddles calls 'an embodiment of queer excess'.[22] At the same time, there is something bewilderingly flaccid or even impotent about the sound of this loud 'dick' record. The elements that would have made for a conventional arena rock album are offset by all sorts of contesting creative decisions: the muted sound of the rhythm section, for example (despite it being drummer Bill Berry who had insisted the band needed to rock out this time around). Lower in the mix than usual, Stipe veers from drowned-out baritone to androgynous falsetto. In the view of one critic, Buck failed to supply any identifiably 'good riffs' because the guitarist had supposedly 'discovered all the unused knobs and switches on his guitar' and decided to 'abuse' every distortion pedal he'd found lying around.[23] In comparison to *Automatic for the People*'s immaculate multitracked compositions, *Monster* had a more casual and spontaneous feel, which was interpreted as 'offhand' and 'indifferent'.[24] The compact disc has such an omnipresence in charity shops across the land precisely because REM had dabbled in an unusual and unnerving type of ambiguous heaviness, one very different to that being hawked by the younger grungers and other populist rock acts like U2. Fleeing with their fingers in their ears, mainstream listeners found *Monster* to be oppressively loud ... and tedious. Among Stipe's less carnal *Monster* lyrics are those to 'Let Me In', REM's tribute to their (and Dylan Carlson's) late friend Kurt Cobain. Just try taking the music from this virtually percussion-free tune. Then mute Stipe's vocal track for a moment. Slow down the warped riffs a touch further and stretch the results out for an additional fifteen minutes. Loop them if you like. Add an extra splash of bass. The result would sound rather like *Earth 2*.

After completing *The Pale King* and revisiting *Monster*, join the select club of people who have read and relished *Something Happened* (1974), Joseph Heller's underappreciated follow-up to *Catch-22*. Published thirteen years after his debut, Heller's second novel does not concern the plight of American soldiers in the closing years of the Second World War. Rather, it takes the form of a long stream-of-consciousness monologue from the mind of an affluent advertising executive in the post-war period. So rambling and digressive is this book, it almost merits the alternative title *Nothing Happens*. Its protagonist, Bob Slocum, passes on to other workers in his office all the boring and routine work that lands on his desk. This makes his own boredom even less sufferable, because then he has nothing to do at all.[25]

Writing in defence of so-called boring films, Erick Neher tells us that 'A work that appropriates the viewer's control over the flow of time, especially one that that moves at a deliberate pace, can cause feelings of frustration that correlate with boredom.'[26] This has become increasingly apparent as the public's attention spans are being altered and, let's face it, considerably reduced by smart TVs, mobile phones (which are actually pocket computers), omnipresent Wi-Fi and mobile data access, streaming media platforms and a techno-capitalist culture that encourages instant gratification on the part of the customer. As Neher argues, one of the crucial agendas of modernism, be it in literary, visual, operatic or cinematic form, was to challenge the audience by rejecting linear narrative and classical forms.[27] Boredom is a subjective notion, as Neher emphasizes. What one person finds 'boring', another person can find 'hypnotic', and another person might find it to be 'riveting'.[28]

The cinema of 'austerity', 'mystification' and 'alienation' is too often dismissed as 'boring' where a more appropriate and less pejorative term would be suitable, says Neher. 'Some films require a slow and deliberate approach in order to convey their meaning and intention,' he concludes. 'In an ideal world, a good "boring" movie encourages the spectator to accept, even revel in, the lack of traditional stimulation or coherence and to use the resultant clear space to observe and meditate on the deeper meanings contained therein.'[29] The same could be said about austere and mystifying music that some critics would dismiss as an exercise in dull indulgence.

Journalists like Beaumont find drone metal to be tedious, and yes, *Earth 2* should be boring as on the surface so little seems to be happening. Its lack of action differs greatly from what is expected of rock music. It teeters on the edge of being a boring experience, it flirts with tedium. And yet, somehow, it isn't boring at all. This is one of the many beautiful aspects of *Earth 2*. See Licht's defence offered above or the way that some quiet drums rise to the surface of the thirty-minute final track 'Like Gold and Faceted' before disappearing again. That's not boring. It's hilarious. It teases the listener with a brief whiff of the classic form of rock music. I also believe that Earth's glacial tempos are capable of slowing down time, or at least seeming to do so. Forget aiming to inspire headbanging; it's as if Carlson seeks to stop the clocks from ticking, the tides from lapping in and out and the globe itself from spinning. As the Internet has made the 'total noise' of culture and society even less ignorable, and virtually inescapable, music that provides relief from this commotion becomes all the more valuable.

Carlson modestly insists that he earned his reputation as a pioneer because, back in the day, he came up with 'one good idea'.[30]

That idea – the slow repetition of a riff – innovatively conjoined two elements that did not previously belong together (La Monte Young and Slayer), thus fitting Mark Fisher's definition of the most common way in which we experience weirdness: surreal montage.[31] In truth, though, Carlson has had loads of great ideas. Much to his credit, when he returned from his picture-framing duties in the mid-2000s Carlson resisted the temptation to merely rehash the sound on which Sunn O))) had since capitalized. With slow drummer extraordinaire Adrienne Davies in tow, Earth Mk II remained downbeat in tempo yet now freshly clean-sounding, with a largely undistorted guitar tone and an eerie spaghetti-western vibe. Influenced by the novels of Cormac McCarthy, Neil Young's *Dead Man* soundtrack and the vintage guitar twangs of Duane Eddy, comeback album *Hex; or, Printing in the Infernal Method* (2005) opened the gateway to Earth's subsequent progressions. Later albums have drawn on Fairport Convention and Pentangle rather than Black Sabbath and Diamond Head, although Carlson's goal has always been to transcend his influences rather than imitate them.[32] Earth in its second incarnation has also incorporated a diverse rotating cast of collaborators, including jazz guitarist Bill Frisell, multi-instrumentalist Steve Moore and cellist Lori Goldston. With *Hex*, then, Carlson radically remoulded Sabbathian traits for a second time. He has continued to do this over and over since then, while simultaneously staying true to his original principle of basing his music around slow-paced riff repetitions. *Primitive and Deadly*, released in 2014, reintroduced guest vocalists (Mark Lanegan and Rabia Shaheen Qazi) and upped the density of the distortion once again, without neglecting the compositional processes that Carlson had developed since Earth's return. Its follow-up, 2019's *Full upon Her Burning Lips*, stripped Earth back to the core duo of Carlson and Davies, with the guitarist limiting his layers of effects in aiming to hone a more 'sensual' style.[33] One of the most effective and simplest cures for boredom, writes Professor Peter Toohey, is variety in experience.[34]

In one of *The Pale King*'s key chapters, the character Meredith Rand has a 'tête-à-tête' with Shane Drinion, a colleague about whom she is irresistibly curious, partly because he is so fascinatingly boring and also 'kind of tiring'. By his other co-workers, Drinion is dubbed 'Mr Excitement'. 'The nickname is obviously sarcastic,' he observes dryly. As Rand puts it to Drinion at one point in their long conversation, 'It's like you're both interesting and really boring at the same time.'[35] When he is completely immersed in a particularly boring task, Drinion is known to levitate out of his chair. In the notes he left behind, which indicated where the plot of *The Pale King* was supposed to be heading, David Foster Wallace wrote of Drinion:

> It turns out that bliss – a second-by-second joy and gratitude at the gift of being alive, conscious – lies on the other side of crushing, crushing boredom. Pay close attention to the most tedious thing you can find (tax returns, televised golf), and, in waves, a boredom like you've never known will wash over you and just about kill you. Ride these out, and it's like stepping from black and white into colour. Like water after days in the desert. Constant bliss in every atom.[36]

Such are the sentences that comprise *The Pale King*. Such are the resounding vibrations of *Earth 2: Special Low Frequency Version*.

Sleep's *Dopesmoker*

INTERVIEWER: What made you guys decide you were gonna play songs about weed?
MATT PIKE: I think it was the weed.[37]

Formed in San Jose, California, Sleep were a mutation of the crusty metal band Asbestosdeath. Guitarist Matt Pike and bassist Al

Cisneros spent much of their spare time smoking pot and dropping acid. At one such session, the pair had a path-altering revelation while listening to Black Sabbath. There and then Cisneros decided they should rename the band Sleep and reinvent themselves in the image of the first four Sabbath albums, which they now considered to be gospel. From this point, Sleep's 'entire universe' would revolve around Black Sabbath. 'We couldn't understand why the bands that we didn't like were playing so fast,' noted Cisneros.[38]

Released shortly before co-guitarist Justin Marler quit the group to become an orthodox monk on a remote Alaskan island, Sleep's *Volume One* showed promise but contained scant indication that they would blossom into something truly special. Once they had pared down to a trio, the band soldiered on with *Sleep's Holy Mountain*, released in 1992 on Earache Records. Albeit still scrappy in places, this record was even more Sabbath-smitten than the first. Replacing the Orc-like communal bellows that had dominated *Volume One*, Cisneros's lead vocals exhibited a softer singing style, a sort of tuneful chanting and a better ear for melody than before, both of which were clearly indebted to (you guessed it) Ozzy Osbourne. With Marler out of the picture, there was also more instrumental responsibility on Cisneros's bass-bearing shoulders, so *Holy Mountain* also sounded groovier, more spacious and less stiff. With the band demonstrating increasing rock-god potential, offers started rolling in from bigger labels seeking to tempt Sleep out of their Earache deal for LP number three.

In the end, the band decided to sign with London Recordings. This was a label that did not exactly specialize in the heaviest of artists. Its roster included Bananarama, East 17 and Jimmy Somerville. If signing to London seems counterintuitive, Sleep figured that it meant they wouldn't be lumped in with a bunch of other, less ambitious heavy bands, as well they might were they to belong to a more metal-centric label. Crucially, the trio were also promised full creative control. They attempted to take complete advantage of this when conceiving their next album. It would consist of just one enormously long song.

For a while, rumours circulated that Sleep had blown their entire six-figure album advance on marijuana. This was a complete exaggeration. Each member merely owned 30 ounces, at all times, of various potent cannabis strains. 'I don't know if you've ever smoked out of a coconut chalice with a hose,' Matt Pike would later strive to recall, 'but, dude, it's the highest you can possibly get. You forget your name, your address, you talk to the dog and the dog talks back. It gets fucking weird.'[39] Other portions of Sleep's advance were spent on clearing debts, hiring studio time, replacing broken equipment, avoiding day jobs and ordering custom-built amplifiers (green ones, naturally). As well as coming over a little bit Dr Dolittle on hallucinogens, another thing that got weirder was Sleep's music.

There was a four-year gap between the release of *Holy Mountain* and the recording of their next album, largely owing to legal tussles between London and Earache, whose contract with Sleep needed to be bought out. For the band, much of this limbo was spent writing, developing, altering, expanding and road-testing a new composition they had christened 'Dopesmoker'. Guiding them in this mission was the weed, the universal hand of Sabbath and the song itself. Asked about the writing process, Shane MacGowan once cited Irish folk musician Christy Moore with having imparted the following words of wisdom: 'Songs are floating around in the air all the time, melodies, phrases. And you've got to pluck them down out of the air – otherwise they'll drift by and Paul Simon or some other bastard will get them.'[40] Similarly, Cisneros feels that riffs are always drifting around in the atmosphere: 'They are constantly playing; I never feel like I create a riff, rather, the musician calls it into the open. The mind and the outer external instruments (nervous system, limbs, bass guitar, drums, etc.) are just the bridges over which the thoughts and vibrations are carried.'[41] Sleep are merely a vessel for the mysterious and omnipresent riff. Sleep are not its architects.

If such wisdom is to be believed, 'Dopesmoker' guided the band as much as the band guided the song, and before they knew it the song had swelled to album-length proportions.

It had also begun to dawn on Sleep that there could be a potential audience for such an outrageous pursuit. Tour dates supporting Nik Turner's version of Hawkwind had exposed Sleep to a particular breed of music fan who likes to drop the needle on a record and then do nothing else but sit and listen intently to that record in a meditative and perhaps inebriated state for the complete duration of its running time.[42] The singer-songwriter, raconteur, acidhead and Faber-published author Julian Cope is one such individual. He rightly recommends purchasing a CD version of *Dopesmoker* rather than the alternative option of a double-vinyl pressing for the explicit reason that it means 'you can get utterly narnered once you've put it on and not have to get up for almost an hour and ten minutes.'[43] By the time of Sleep's Hawkwind tour, the song hadn't quite reached its eventual length, although even in its embryonic stages it was substantial enough for Sleep to walk onstage and introduce their set with the line 'Hi, we're Sleep and this is our last song.'[44]

The album, all one song of it, was recorded in two month-long sessions with Billy Anderson at Record Two Studio in Comptche, California. Even when broken down into shorter sections because the reel-to-reel tapes could only hold twenty-odd minutes apiece, this drawn-out composition still required a lot of memorization on the part of its weed-addled musicians. According to Pike, he and his bandmates started to go mad from learning, rehearsing and performing the song over and over again.[45] It got even slower. It grew even weirder.

By the end they had two or three different recorded renditions of the unfeasibly long song, none of which filled London Recordings with confidence. Sleep probably should have heeded the advice of Steve Albini and his article 'The Problem with Music', published the year after *Holy Mountain* was released. They should at least have taken into account the warnings of all the people in bands they already knew who had signed to majors before wholeheartedly regretting it, and who had been advising Sleep to avoid falling into the same trap.[46] If London Recordings had no heavy metal bands on its roster at the time of Sleep's signing, the label used to have one in the form of Bristolian thrash outfit Onslaught. It would've been worth Sleep's time to have had a word with them. Onslaught had delivered two underground thrash classics, 1985's *Power from Hell* and 1986's *The Force*, after which London signed Onslaught with the intention of polishing them up in order to break the lucrative American market that had been revealed by the success stories of Metallica, Megadeth, Anthrax and Slayer. The label demanded Onslaught's third album be re-recorded with a completely different vocalist, instigating the unceremonious ejection of Sy Keeler, who was replaced with Steve Grimmett from Grim Reaper.[47] With 1989's *In Search of Sanity* Onslaught achieved their highest ever UK chart position, but in the process they had lost a singer as well as their edge, not to mention the adoration of hardcore thrash fans and an important part of themselves. It would be Onslaught's final album until the mandatory middle-aged reunion, which occurred in 2005 with Keeler back in his rightful role.

'Being on a major label is not something that everybody can do,' reflected Sleep drummer Chris Hakius in 2006. 'It really depends on how much ass-kissing and giving in and changing things for other people you wanna do, because those are the things that kind of determine your success. That's why there's a lot of shitty music on the radio and TV.'[48] However naively, Sleep never anticipated having to navigate their way through the music industry via compromise and bottom-kissing. A change in company structure and the shake-up of its personnel meant the A&R person who had been looking after Sleep suddenly vanished. The trio found themselves working for a company that was not particularly thrilled with the prospect of a sixty-plus-minute doom album that consisted of only one track.

Faced with such an unmarketable prospect, the label hired Dave Sardy to remix the record. His credits included *One Hot Minute* by Red Hot Chili Peppers and Slayer's dodgy punk covers album, *Undisputed Attitude*. At this point, Cisneros seriously considered stealing *Dopesmoker*'s master reels in order to destroy them. Pike was equally appalled when he heard talk of 'radio edits', a proposal he deemed an outright impossibility given that a single Sleep riff could last as long as other bands' whole songs.[49]

Ten months of toing and froing ensued as the corporate bods parachuted in various engineers tasked with having to edit and remix the record in the face of an increasingly irritable and disillusioned band who eventually became sick of having to listen repeatedly to their song and various disrespectful splices of it. Compounding that, Cisneros and Hakius were becoming steadily sick of each other's company. Eventually all parties simply walked away. London refused to release the album and Sleep disbanded.

In Sleep's absence the record gained mythical status, especially as various botched or bootlegged versions began to dribble out into the marketplace years after its recording, casting their spell over those open-minded fans of heavy music who were lucky enough to hear it. These editions included a press promo CD printed by London Recordings then quickly withdrawn because the release had been cancelled. That version was a mere 52 minutes long and was retitled *Jerusalem*. The album became available to the public via a bootleg version without any label behind it, followed by pressings from Rise Above Records and The Music Cartel. These, again, carried the 52-minute version, this time divided into six separate tracks (with no gaps in between). In 2003 Tee Pee Records issued *Dopesmoker* in its 63-minute form with a sleevenote message reading, '*Dopesmoker* is an alternate version of *Jerusalem* that we felt our fans might enjoy. This early version, as yet unheard, contains a more dynamic recording and a heavier mix. So get high, crank it up and listen with open ears and mind.' This release also boasted a second track, a live recording of an unreleased number called 'Sonic Titan'. Cisneros said this version of *Dopesmoker* wasn't exactly what the band had submitted although it was the closest yet to what they had originally envisaged. He also said he wished it had never been released at all, likening the experience to being a dead writer rolling in their grave because of an unfinished novel that had been completed by a substitute author who'd had no knowledge of the intended plot. Pike, on the other hand, was happy to see it released, seeing as they had all put so much time and effort into its creation. Hakius has issues with the various editions' sleeves: 'I meet people at shows who get all kinds of messages out of that album. Some are completely Satanic and evil, some are completely spiritual, and some are like they were sniffing glue at home. And that's what happens when other people decide what your album art is gonna be.'[50]

Because of the haphazard nature of its release, album reviews were sporadic and brief. *Kerrang!* editor Phil Alexander gave top marks to one limited pressing of *Jerusalem* in 1998. 'Listen to it in "normal" surroundings and you won't understand the five-K rating,' he warned. 'On headphones, in the context of a darkened room, "Jerusalem" is a gut-wrenching, blissful experience. It doesn't get heavier than this. Ever.'[51] Because the band was inactive at the time, there was no capitalizing on the praise, leaving *Kerrang!* to run features on Dez Fafara from Coal Chamber, to take that same week's cover star as an example.

In 2012 another version, remastered and housed in yet more new artwork, came out on Southern Lord, the label run by Sunn O)))'s Greg Anderson. He describes it as one of his 'bucket list' records for the label; an album he'd listened to repeatedly since getting his hands on a copy in the late 1990s:

> It was a perfect storm when that record came out, because I was getting super deep into Black Sabbath. I'd always been a fan, but at that time it had reached the point of ridiculous

obsession. So when *Dopesmoker* came out it felt like the most amazing tribute to Black Sabbath that was possible. And by a band from the underground! Black Sabbath, Led Zeppelin, or The Who are like these massive rock gods who you'll never ever meet in your life. Sleep were these three dudes who were exactly like me, smoking as much pot as I was, and just playing Black Sabbath riffs. It was very cool to see.[52]

Following Sleep's disbandment, Pike dusted himself off and immediately set to work with the faster and more technically minded thrash outfit High On Fire. This project makes greater use of Pike's community college training in jazz improvisation and music theory, the presence of which lingered only in some of Sleep's occasional guitar solos. Sleep, he says, was not about attempting to execute anything too fancy or trying to show off: 'It was more about feelings and religion and spirituality. We were all trying to find God.'[53] One of the greatest lessons Pike took from Sleep was an appreciation of musical space:

> You don't have to fill up every single moment with noise. I'd rather wait and drop the bomb at the perfect moment than barrage you into submission – Sleep proves that one well-placed note can say more than 150 perfectly played notes.[54]

'There's more space for the groove and breathing and the flow,' Cisneros has elaborated. 'Really fast doesn't make any sense to me. It's gotta have that groove or it's kind of a pointless exercise.'[55] Deflated in the wake of the *Dopesmoker* debacle, Cisneros couldn't muster the courage to make music again for a number of years. He re-emerged in the mid-2000s with the drums/bass duo Om, with Hakius in tow for their first three albums. Unlike High On Fire, Om continued down the *Dopesmoker* route by pursuing an almost raga-like form of spiritual drone metal. In December 2007 Om played a gig that went on for five hours. The event took place, naturally, in Jerusalem. 'Nothing like it will probably ever happen again,' Cisneros said afterwards. 'It was really beautiful. It was overwhelming . . . It didn't feel like it went on that long. It was a personal experience of relativity.'[56]

In 2018 the reformed Sleep, now with Neurosis's Jason Roeder on drums, released their fourth album on 20 April, otherwise known as 'Weed Day'. The interior section of *The Sciences'* gate-fold sleeve features a photograph of a breakfast table. An image of Tony Iommi's face appears – much like that of Jesus, according to tabloid news stories – burnt into a piece of toast. Bill Ward (absent from various Black Sabbath reunion events) is represented as a missing person on the side of a milk carton. The butter is labelled 'Butler', after Geezer, who is also paid homage in the title of the fourth track, 'Giza Butler', the lyrics for which cite the 'Sabbath day' and 'Iommic Pentacost'. Ozzy Osbourne is represented in a slightly subtler manner, in the spilt glass of orange juice. This refers to the singer's appearance in Penelope Spheeris's 1988 documentary *The Decline of Western Civilization Part II: The Metal Years*, where Osbourne talks about the hard work required to be a successful rock band, the trappings of fame and the dangers of drug addiction. Ozzy then attempts to pour some orange juice into a glass but misses the vessel and splashes the liquid all over the table.[57]

For some, *The Sciences'* fine collection of phat doom numbers is Sleep's best record. Others still hold a flame for *Holy Mountain*. *Dopesmoker* is, undeniably, the record that secured Sleep's place in history. It was here that the Californian stoners took Sabbath's 'Sweet Leaf' to its logical conclusion by recording their hour-long epic preaching the sacred benefits of weed. The lyrics begin, almost ten minutes in, with words about dropping out of life with a bong in one's hand and following the direction of the smoke to a magical land that is filled with riffs. It has time signatures that shift around without the listener's full realization. Mysterious multiple tones float in and out of earshot and vary each time you hear it. There are elongated guitar solos that occasionally rise up out of the din to complement the riffs that ebb and flow and just keep building and rolling like the tides of the ocean.

Cannabis has different effects on different people in different ways. Even in small doses it can have wildly different results on an individual each time he or she uses it. As far as dope-smoking musicians are concerned, from the paranoid to the elated, one word that crops up regularly is 'space'. For jazz musicians, smoking pot opened up the possibilities of alternative types of spaces and new pathways, helping to make the genre more improvisatory and expressionist. Jamaican dub artists insisted they heard music differently thanks to cannabis inhalation. Lee 'Scratch' Perry spoke of hearing space in the tracks. RZA of Wu-Tang Clan rapped of how weed opened his mind, his distinctive production on *Enter The Wu-Tang (36 Chambers)* being particularly notable for its savvy use of space.[58] It hardly needs reiterating that, much more so than LSD, pills, powder or any other substance, weed was the drug of choice and preferred creative aid of Paul McCartney, writer and instigator of the spacious proto-doom landmark that was 'Helter Skelter'. The Beatles were introduced to the herb by Bob Dylan, and McCartney didn't stop partaking in the puff until he was aged about seventy. His ode to pot, 'Got to Get You into My Life', talks of rides and roads and finding an alternative kind of mindset at the end of the journey. Interviewed, McCartney has described the effects of marihuana as 'literally mind-expanding'.[59] As we have already seen, the members of Sleep spoke of the importance of space. The journey described in *Dopesmoker*'s lyrics incorporates caravans migrating across a sand-shrouded landscape, weed priests traversing the vast space of the desert accompanied by magnificent beasts with huge balls of herb bound to their backs, the unremitting flow of the Jordan River, a 'marijuanaut' who flees Earth to cultivate cannabis on distant planets . . . Well, you can't find more space than away in outer space itself. How did Lee 'Scratch' Perry describe his Black Ark recording studio again? That's right, he called it his space craft . . .

Dopesmoker's audio power is so potent that writer Dan Franklin can't be the only individual to have considered it along these lines: 'I stopped smoking marijuana thirteen years ago. I don't need to anymore: I listen to Sleep.'[60] You don't have to be on board with Sleep's weed worship to appreciate *Dopesmoker*. What you must subscribe to is the beauty, strength and capacity of The Riff. As Joseph Stannard has argued in *The Wire*, in Black Sabbath the lyrics penned by Geezer Butler and brought to life by Ozzy Osbourne were communicating directly with the invigorating sound emanating from Tony Iommi's thunderous guitar patterns. Whether having been given the strength to climb via the mountains up to the moon on 'Supernaut' or in the more primitive expressions of 'All right now!' and 'I love you!' that Ozzy yelps on 'Sweet Leaf', Osbourne is expressing a love for the music, for The Riff, itself. The same goes for the lyrics to Sleep's *Dopesmoker*. As red-eyed as the musicians may have been, *Dopesmoker* is no mere cannabis psalm. It is in thrall to The Way of the Riff. As Stannard puts it, '[Sleep's] Jerusalem is a "riff-filled land" and their exhortation to "arise, arise, arise" cannot be fulfilled by monolithic bong alone.'[61]

Electric Wizard's *Dopethrone*

INTERVIEWER: And what would you like Electric Wizard's
   eventual epitaph to be?
JUS OBORN: 'They recorded other LPs apart from crappy
   Dopethrone.'[62]

Nominative determinism is the hypothesis that individuals tend to gravitate towards professions that best suit their names. Hence history has thrown up the sterling work of Bruno Fromage, former managing director of the Danone dairy company. And let us not forget the Belgian defensive midfielder Mark De Man, or the career of East Midlands TV weather presenter Sara Blizzard. Can it be pure coincidence, then, that the second phase of the Sabbathian mode was ushered in by Melvins, who are fronted by a man called Buzz Osborne? Phase III of the Sabbathian mode, meanwhile, was boosted by another person whose family name is noticeably similar: Justin Oborn of Electric Wizard.

According to the writer, editor and broadcaster John Doran, Electric Wizard are the heaviest band in the world. And he should know what he's talking about because until fairly recently he resembled someone disinterred from a Bronze Age burial mound. Doran says he once dropped the Electric Wizard track 'The Satanic Rites of Drugula' while DJing under 'the oppressive weight of bad drugs'. As he glanced up from the record decks, Doran – who is a recovering chronic alcoholic and now mostly drug-abstinent – suffered a hallucination that the pub's landlord had grown a pair of bright red horns and was breathing fire. Electric Wizard leader Jus Oborn has experienced similarly disturbing sights while performing. Certain visions have been so ghastly that Oborn cannot even bring himself to describe them. As well as freaking out onstage, Oborn writes about the hallucinations he's experienced while under acid's unpredictable spell. He wants his band's music to convey the LSD experience better than words ever could and hopes for his songs to be as mind-altering as the drugs themselves.[63] 'If you've only heard Elvis, I guess something like the cartoon psychedelia of *Sgt Pepper's Lonely Hearts Club Band* is going to sound pretty fucked up but to our ears it sounds like playground music,' says Oborn. 'To be truly psychedelic the music has to be able to alter your mind so you lose touch with your body.'[64]

Oborn grew up in the market town of Wimborne in Dorset. King Crimson's Robert Fripp was born there. So too was Montague Druitt, one of the suspects in the Jack the Ripper case. Thomas

Hardy wrote one of his many miserable novels while living in Wimborne. King Aethelred of Wessex is buried in its minster. According to census figures, 60 per cent of Wimborne's adult population are married and the town has the highest life expectancy for both men and women in the whole of the UK. It's little wonder that so many of Oborn's lyrics are fixated with death and depravity.

Before discovering heavy metal, the young Oborn's obsessions included horror comics and scary movies, H. P. Lovecraft, Edgar Allan Poe and the occult. His earliest memory involves watching a horror film with his mother when he was four years old.[65] In his teens Oborn became fascinated by death metal and black metal. Having taken his fashion tips from the Brazilian extreme metal band Sarcófago, Oborn was bullied, spat on and beaten by trendier locals as punishment for the social crime of looking different. His feelings of alienation were compounded by the small town's authority figures, including the police who visited the family home to warn Oborn's parents that their son was involved in blasphemous activities. This only encouraged Oborn to embrace his persona more steadfastly. Soon he was identifying as a devil-worshipper who shouldn't be messed with lest his evil stare burst his enemies into flames. He remembers that at one point, pushed to the brink, he had assembled a 'small arsenal' of weaponry stolen from his granddad's shed, including a sawn-off shotgun, a pistol, a long-barrelled rat gun and a range of poorly homemade incendiary devices.[66] Fantasies of inflicting harm on others were coupled with suicidal thoughts, but Oborn couldn't go through with killing himself because he didn't want to impose a painful loss on his mother.[67] Instead he found solace, belonging and a sense of purpose by connecting with like-minded outcasts across the world. Oborn was highly active in the close-knit international tape-trading community and swapped cassettes with all sorts of people, including Max Cavalera (Sepultura), Fenriz (Darkthrone) and Euronymous (Mayhem).[68]

Prior to forming Electric Wizard in 1993, Oborn played in the death metal outfit Lord of Putrefaction. His creative path was permanently altered when, high on mushrooms, he had an epiphany while listening to Black Sabbath, just as the members of Sleep had experienced on the other side of the Atlantic.[69] That moment sealed Oborn's commitment to doom. Black Sabbath's imprint is all over Electric Wizard. There are the enormous slow riffs played on downtuned and hideously distorted guitars, plus lyrical subject-matter that often concerns the uncanny and macabre. Their very name is an amalgamation of two Sabbath tracks: 'Electric Funeral' and 'The Wizard'. The font on the cover of Electric Wizard's first album matches that of Black Sabbath's self-titled debut. The title of their ninth album, *Wizard Bloody Wizard*, was adapted from Sabbath's fifth.

That might all sound worryingly like tribute band territory, and there have been moments when Electric Wizard have slithered into burlesque. Conceived as a 'funeral boogie' record, 2017's *Wizard Bloody Wizard* was lighter and more playful than many of the group's older recordings. Cynical listeners might find that the lyrics to its six relatively snappy tracks read like a fairly tacky index of Sabbath/Wizard platitudes: drugs, death, violence, Satan, sex, more drugs, Satan again, coffins, candles, sinful caresses . . .

No matter. For this is Electric Wizard we are talking about. They have long earned the right to do whatever they please. Plus anybody who dares question the group's dark majesty too harshly could wind up with a demonic curse placed on their sorry head. Electric Wizard's claim to critical immunity comes on account of the many times they've hit the perfect sweet, dark spot. A case in point is their spectacular third album *Dopethrone*, from the year 2000, which far exceeds the realm of mere Sabbath parody. Electric Wizard have recorded many fine records over the years. Even so, *Dopethrone* stands out as a widely recognized milestone in doom and is considered by most to be the band's outright masterpiece.

Before *Dopethrone* came Electric Wizard's 1995 self-titled debut – a record Oborn felt had failed to be as heavy as he'd envisaged – and their second effort, *Come My Fanatics* (1997), which did a grander job of sowing the seeds for the heaviness that was to follow. *Come My Fanatics* did not spring out of nowhere. Back in the 1980s, the blueprint set by the slowest and gloomiest numbers from Black Sabbath's early run of albums had been developed into a distinct underground subgenre thanks to the work undertaken by disciples like England's Witchfinder General, Sweden's Candlemass and, in America, the unholy trinity of Saint Vitus, Trouble and Pentagram.

Following the tradition of Napalm Death members leaving the group in order to embark on wholly different musical missions, vocalist Lee Dorrian quit after 1989's *Mentally Murdered* EP to form the far doomier Cathedral. He had never been quite the same since, at aged fourteen, he was introduced by a friend to Black Sabbath's *Master of Reality* album. 'It changed the way I looked at music,' he said. The two hash cakes he'd consumed that day may have assisted the epiphany.[70] As label boss of Rise Above Records, Dorrian would also act as linchpin of the wider scene by releasing the music of fellow doomsters such as those featured on the 1991 compilation *Dark Passages*.

Some of the aforementioned doom acts would wind up veering into the territory that blemished later Sabbath releases, or else they failed to insert much freshness into the patterns laid down beforehand. Certain acts leant too lazily on genre clichés or well-worn formulas. The production choices used on some of the doom records of the 1980s have not aged handsomely. Paradise Lost, My Dying Bride and Anathema made waves in the 1990s as part of the Peaceville Records roster. Hailing from different locations in the north of England, this trio of bands became known as 'The Peaceville Three'. Each of them started out producing heavy music and then all, as Andrew O'Neill aptly puts it, 'went a bit flouncy'.[71]

Dorrian himself has freely admitted that Electric Wizard's second album was a pivotal moment for doom, raising the bar and setting the standard for all that would follow. Sabbath may have been their ultimate idols, but Electric Wizard were also smitten with space rock, classic Detroit garage bands and British shoegaze. One of Sabbath's earliest revelations had been to corrupt rock 'n' roll with traits lifted from the horror movies, such as those produced by Hammer studios, that had gripped the youth of the 1960s. Electric Wizard were fans of those films too, as well as the more extreme horror movies, slasher flicks and video nasties that had followed in their wake. Add to that a fixation with esoteric science fiction novels, biker movies, trashy pulp magazines, vintage European pornography and plenty of bad acid trips and you have all the ingredients for a new phase in doom. The production on Electric Wizard's records may sound superficially grotty yet it is rich in depth, flavour and stodge, like the most delicious service station pork pie. The warped instrumental effects and massive doses of distortion owe less to Geezer Butler than to Butthole Surfers. Matching the agenda of Hawkwind, Motörhead, Melvins and many of our other heavy magi, Electric Wizard are concerned not so much with fancy guitar licks as creating an all-engulfing atmosphere with which to pound listeners into a twisted state of consciousness. If you're not on drugs when you listen to Electric Wizard, you will feel like you are. If you do happen to be on drugs, well then God help your sorry soul.

As Dorrian put it, '*Come My Fanatics* blew everything apart and sent everything off the scale because it was a completely fuck-off sounding record. No frills but done with such fucking venom but also otherworldliness.' He remembers being disturbed, at first, that the drums were buried so deep in the mix. Dorrian soon came round to the mugginess and, when listening to it stoned on his bed, decided it was the most amazing thing he'd ever heard.[72]

Electric Wizard's next record was even bigger and nastier. Although it didn't trouble him so much at the time of *Dopethrone*'s recording (perhaps because of his drug intake), Oborn has since realized that Electric Wizard were suffering from bitter intra-band tensions. Oborn even alleges that his fellow band members, bassist Tim Bagshaw and drummer Mark Greening, were pushing to incorporate hip-hop and grunge influences into Electric Wizard's doom template; suggestions that were shrewdly disregarded.[73] The Britpop scene, meanwhile, infused *Dopethrone*'s gestation less in the musical sense than in terms of having-it-large hedonism. Oborn recalls Bagshaw's admiration for Oasis's 'you've got to live it' attitude as a reminder that we're only on this planet for a brief amount of time and you have to make the most of it (that is, by getting completely off your face).[74]

Under pressure from label boss Dorrian to deliver fresh material, the trio hit the Chuckalumba recording studios in Dorset and surrounded themselves with bongs. They had originally intended to placate Dorrian by recording an EP. Instead, Electric Wizard ended up churning out so much high-quality material they felt compelled to release the whole lot. The weed, beer and acid that had informed the band's earlier records was now compounded by the introduction of harder drugs and the trio's graduation to full-bore 'paranoid speed freaks' who cohabited with their drug dealers. During the recording, band members kept threatening to murder each other. At one point, Oborn ended up holding a baseball bat to the head of a producer in order to convince him to turn the guitars up even further.[75]

Recently surfaced camcorder footage depicts lots of joints being smoked and the perpetual guzzling of Stella Artois taking place in a dimly lit, rural studio.[76] It looks not entirely dissimilar from the rickety house that acts as the location to the terrifying climactic scene of *The Blair Witch Project*. In one clip, Oborn demonstrates how to load up, light and smoke a bong. He seems jovial. The final shot shows Oborn leaning on one arm in front of a lyric sheet with his eyes closed. He appears to have fallen asleep standing up. Too much herbal consumption, perhaps? Or, rather, has he been possessed by the malevolent spirit of a seventeenth-century forest-dwelling sorceress?

As well as its obvious debts to Sabbath, *Dopethrone* was influenced by early Alice Cooper, the sludgy second side of Black Flag's *My War*, extreme metal pioneers Venom, a million obscure horror movies along with their unsettling soundtracks, and the less *Kerrang!*-friendly sources of loudly psychedelic experimental bands such as Loop and My Bloody Valentine. All this was filtered through Electric Wizard's warped, troubled and possibly haunted psyches. Out of the narcotic fog emerged a stone-cold classic.

Harbouring a terrifying swagger and infectious air of malevolence, one of *Dopethrone*'s most brutal tracks is 'We Hate You'. The song's title was partly a reaction against Ozzy Osbourne. Despite being one of Electric Wizard's all-time heroes, Ozzy had begun to irritate Oborn by 'always going on about how much he fucking loved everyone' (although as recordings of Ozzy-era Sabbath concerts demonstrate, this was hardly a new habit of his).[77] 'We Hate You' was also written after news had broken of the Columbine High School massacre of 20 April 1999, in which two teenagers murdered twelve of their fellow students and one teacher. In the wake of the incident, media attention was fixated on the killers' favourite music and the band T-shirts they wore. Fingers were pointed at Marilyn Manson, who back in those innocent pre-9/11 times was disproportionately credited (by himself, among others) with posing some kind of credible threat to the good ol' wholesome American way of life. Before Manson could cobble together his own patchy reaction to Columbine with his band's fourth album, *Holy Wood*, Jus Oborn channelled into 'We Hate You' his own schoolboy experiences of being goaded by small-town locals and labelled a freak.

Buried in an engine-rev of distortion, 'We Hate You' begins with a sample of dialogue lifted from the 1970 screen adaptation of H. P. Lovecraft's *The Dunwich Horror*:

'You see man as a rather dismal creature.'

'Yes. Why not? Look around, you'll see what's there. Fear and frightened people who kill what they can't understand.'

Executively produced by Roger Corman after American International Pictures' string of Edgar Allan Poe adaptations, the movie spins a tale of madness, murder and satanic ritual. Filmed in California shortly after the Manson Family had run rampage, *The Dunwich Horror* injects into Lovecraft's 1920s source material that feeling of hippie free-love ideals being bent to more sinister purposes. Thirty years on from the Manson murders, the Columbine massacre played a similar role in the wider cultural consciousness. Occurring on the cusp of a new decade, dominating the media and even romanticized to a certain extent in some quarters, each event evoked the dawn of a darker era after a happier period of relative optimism.

Contrary to reports circulated widely in the press shortly after the killings and which have continued to thrive in the popular imagination, the research conducted by Dave Cullen suggests the Columbine massacre was not caused by bullying, the school's 'jocks' were not in fact singled out for attack, and the killers were not social pariahs or members of the high school gang of goths known as The Trench Coat Mafia.[78] Nevertheless, the events and the way they were reported reminded Oborn of the torment he had suffered in his own teenage years. 'I couldn't believe someone actually did it,' was his initial reaction to the news. These kids had gone through with the kind of violence Oborn had once planned or at least daydreamed about committing himself.[79] Oborn's equivalent of The Trench Coat Mafia had been The Evil Gang, united by their denim jackets with the same Hawkwind patch sewn on the back. Columbine encouraged Oborn to look back on his years as a 'teenage suicide freak' and dwell on his vivid memories of what it was like to feel 'hopeless', to want to kill himself and everybody else. 'We could have gone that far at one point,' he believes.[80]

Dopethrone is bookended by samples from the American television news programme *20/20*, which has run on the ABC network since 1978. The two clips used by Electric Wizard come from an episode originally broadcast on 16 May 1985. It concerned an alleged rise in devil worship and satanic ritual. Hugh Downs's report included interviews with experts like Sandi Gallant ('a San Francisco policewoman and now a leading authority on satanic crime, a speciality other cops often scoff at'). It made a point of highlighting the satanic nature of heavy metal and the genre's nefarious influence on impressionable young minds. As Downs narrated,

> According to most groups it's all done in fun but according to police it's having an effect on many children; a growing subculture that mixes heavy metal music with drugs and the occult. In addition to groups that are blatantly satanic, there are also many recordings which some believe may contain satanic references in the form of backward messages.

As the Detroit DJ Chris Edmonds demonstrates in the footage, if you play Led Zeppelin's 'Stairway to Heaven' in reverse, you can clearly hear Robert Plant sing the words 'My sweet Satan'.[81]

Far from satirizing or trivializing conservative paranoia, at their most nihilistic Electric Wizard give the impression that they rather hope the fears of anti-metal reactionaries are founded in truth. Oborn and company would like to believe that their music does possess such malevolent, intoxicating and indoctrinating powers. As if to stoke the fire, *Dopethrone*'s CD booklet includes a slogan advocating the legalization of not only drugs but 'MURDER'.

Dopethrone isn't all about mass shootings, however. Another track is a tribute to cult fantasy character Conan the Barbarian. Exceptionally sludgy with a certain elusive catchiness to it, 'Barbarian' boasts a fierce low end and, like other tracks on the album, is decorated by Hawkwind-esque spacey swirls. As Oborn has pointed out, there is more intricacy, detail and subtlety to the album's makeup than is usually acknowledged. The sound incorporates a number of 'sonic layers' that had to be built up in a meticulous manner and which are only detectable under careful and repeated listening.[82] This it shares with other landmark moments in the history of heaviness, *Earth 2* being a good example.

Elsewhere, 'Funeralopolis' is led by a creaking Geezer Butler-indebted bass groove that soon becomes swamped in fuzz. With Oborn's snarled vocals buried deep in the audio smog, the lyrics might have remained a mystery were it not for their reproduction in the accompanying booklet. They forecast an imminent nuclear apocalypse, expressing rage at the political leaders and 'corporate maggots' who are complicit in its instigation. At the same time, Oborn bids a firm good riddance to this hopeless planet. As if conjuring the fallout to fruition, in the second half of the track's near-nine-minute running time Electric Wizard become possessed by that loose Motörhead spirit of barely being able to hold it together (albeit in slower fashion than Lemmy's breakneck crew).

A fifteen-minute track consisting of three subsections, 'Weird Tales' is almost punky at first until it decelerates into a crunchily lo-fi take on space rock, eventually drawing to a close with about three minutes of amplifier gurgles. If the aforementioned forbidden grunge direction did manage to sneak its way into the album at any point, it is in the grooves of 'I, The Witchfinder', especially in the way the quieter passages spotlighting the rhythm section are juxtaposed with loud explosions whenever Oborn's riffs re-penetrate. In its lyrics, Oborn inhabits the character of Albino, the disfigured witch hunter from the 1970 West German horror flick *Mark of the Devil*. The film's original-language title is the more upfront: *Hexen bis aufs Blut gequält*, literally translating as 'witches tortured until they bleed'. In 1984 VHS copies of the movie were seized, confiscated and destroyed in the UK under Section 3 of the Obscene Publications Act 1959. Oborn-as-Albino growls about determining his victims' guilt before he even captures these women to put them on trial, acknowledging the misogyny that lay at the heart of the early modern witch hunts. 'I . . . love how these films really present the whole episode in history as basically an abuse of power and exploitation of the superstitious peasants,' Oborn has said, adding that he doesn't believe the situation has changed much since.[83]

While many metal publications have gleefully bought into the supposed wickedness of Electric Wizard, this should all be taken with a pinch of salt. As subsequent releases have made increasingly apparent, there has always been an element of English high campness buried in the band's aesthetic, serving to exonerate Electric Wizard from the 'tru-kvlt' attitudes of a minority of po-faced metalheads. Slow, hostile, substance-addled and not lacking humour, *Dopethrone* has rightly, if only steadily, earned its podium position as a masterpiece of doom.

In describing the thinking behind *Dopethrone*'s title track at the time of the album's release, Oborn explained that its concept was thus: 'we're the kings of the fucking dope scene, and hopefully we'll control all the dope in the world one day.'[84] It has also been suggested that 'Dopethrone' was written in response to Sleep's similarly titled *Dopesmoker*. Where Oborn's lyrics for 'Dopethrone' open with talk of receiving a prophecy from a dope priest, Sleep's Al Cisneros sang of a procession of weed priests. Sleep offered repeated instructions to pursue the smoke towards a land that is filled with riffs. In turn, Electric Wizard described an altar fashioned from weed and smoke. There are differences too. Sleep's lyrics contain greater religious imagery, both biblical and Rastafarian. Electric Wizard's own paean to the power of the herb is more concerned with references to Lovecraftian sorcery and sky-tearing feedback emanating from amplifiers wielded by three weed wizards, by which they must surely mean themselves.

Like *Dopesmoker*, Electric Wizard's dope-opus took some time to catch on beyond the dedicated doom dungeons where Dorrian and his ilk reside. These days there can barely be found a 'Heaviest Albums of All Time' listicle that fails to mention *Dopethrone*.[85] Any that do are deeply suspect. It certainly got under the skin of its listeners. As for Electric Wizard's wider career, their longevity recalls Buzz Osborne's advice to Earth's Dylan Carlson. Do your own thing and keep doing it well. Resist any momentarily hip bandwagons. Loyal followers will latch on eventually. As Oborn puts it,

> sticking to the music you really love is the key. Not swaying too much. I mean, I've never been one for jumping on all these lame trends, but then again some other bands do and maybe they're pretty genuine with it. I would stick to tradition, what I've always liked[,] and I think that carries its own rewards in the end. You stick with something and it becomes a craft.[86]

Oh, and be sure to follow the Tao of The Riff: 'It is a way of life that I'm espousing to people. I feel that this is the way. For us it is a cult. The cult of the riff. The mindless worship of the riff.'[87] Amen.

Other Stoners

> Kyuss got noticed because it didn't give a shit if anyone noticed it. It's like huddling around something and pretty soon everyone crowds around because they wanna look at it. And it could be a piece of dog shit, but you've got a crowd of 500 people trying to look at it. Bands miss that, they scratch and they crawl.[88]

JOSH HOMME

Stoner rock fans tend to discover albums like *Dopesmoker* and *Dopethrone* by working backwards from poppier equivalents. One of the most common gateway stoner bands is Queens of the Stone

Age. For a while they came across as a 'band' in a fairly loose sense, more like an unruly pirate ship with a rotating crew of talented rapscallions led by the impulsive captain Joshua Homme, their hits occurring pretty much as happy accidents. It has since become an increasingly slick, stable and professional operation, allowing Queens to become so popular that their audience demographic includes those whose only other rock-based interests are Foo Fighters, Royal Blood, Arctic Monkeys and Muse. For the more curious, QOTSA opened the door to a whole new world of riff-centric guitar music that encompasses everything from the doomy sound of Sleep to the kind of desert rock now being heard in the least likely of places. See the instrumental quartet Causa Sui, for instance, and its members' El Paraiso label, based in the sand-covered and cacti-laden land of Denmark.

Unlike Electric Wizard and Sleep, Josh Homme claims never to have harboured even a passing interest in Black Sabbath. When his pre-QOTSA group Kyuss kept drawing comparisons to Sabbath, Homme's reaction was a frankly blasphemous 'Fuck you – I never heard 'em.' Echoing Budgie's approach in the early 1970s, Homme's idea of Kyuss was 'to not let yourself be influenced by any music'. In order to adhere to that self-imposed rule, Homme claimed to draw inspiration from novels and movies instead.[89] This is absolute nonsense. Brant Bjork was a founding member of Kyuss, drummer on all but the fourth and final album, and composer of many of the band's tunes. He has happily admitted to being raised on Black Sabbath among other classic rock acts. So too has Nick Oliveri, bassist on the first two Kyuss LPs and a key QOTSA member during the latter's halcyon period of 1998 to 2004. Crediting Sabbath as his first musical love, Oliveri was introduced to *Paranoid* under the guidance of his uncle.[90] Kyuss's low-tuned riffs and basslines can clearly be traced back to Sabbath. Towards the end of their career, Kyuss even covered Sabbath's 'Into the Void'. This would have been hard for Homme to pull off if he'd never actually heard it.

The idea that Kyuss drew solely from non-musical sources is even more absurd. Granted, they were never as obsessively smitten with Sabbath as were Sleep or Electric Wizard: also infused in their sound was material by The Cult, Deep Purple, Blue Cheer, AC/DC, ZZ Top and Kiss. Like many post-hardcore, noise rock and grunge musicians, the members of Kyuss had grown up with punk before finding themselves playing slower and chunkier music than the hardcore blueprint dictated. As Brant Bjork explained in 1992, the key to Kyuss's sound was that they came from a punk rock background and were impeded from being an outright metal band. 'We're not good enough to play metal,' he admitted.

> I could not do a drum solo to save my life . . . I couldn't imagine Josh breaking out into some amazing Eddie Van Halen guitar lead. With the exception of Scott [Reeder] over here, Mr Bass Master, we couldn't be a metal band if we wanted to be . . . We're a bunch of punks playing rock.

Coming from this background, there was a certain amount of shame in being associated with Sabbath. As Homme mentioned in the same interview, 'in my day if you were into punk and listened to Sabbath, someone's gonna beat your ass.'[91] Furthermore, the rejection of Sabbath was an attempt to avoid that same fate that most bands strive hardest to evade: being pigeonholed. This is unavoidable, however, and the term used to bundle up Kyuss with similar artists would be 'desert rock'.

Kyuss were part of the Palm Desert Scene, cutting their teeth at generator parties in the sands around Joshua Tree. These casual shindigs were organized by Mario Lalli of Across the River and Yawning Man, both bands having significant impact on the younger Homme's musical endeavours. Out in the desert where the local police force rarely bothered to roam, beer could be drunk, marijuana could be smoked, hallucinogens could be imbibed and barbeques fired up.

Escaping the constraints of the average suburban house party, here bands could play deafeningly loud sets all the way through to the morning. A world apart from LA's glitzy and glamorous Sunset Strip scene just two hours' drive away, the desert scene had more in common with the DIY agenda of punk. Nevertheless, its location never suited the frantic pace and urban politics of punk. This meant that a lot of the Palm Desert crew ended up playing material that was more spacious and jam-derived; a style that ended up being reminiscent of the pre-punk hard rock of the 1960s and '70s. Even if Homme genuinely wanted to avoid Sabbathian traits in favour of sticking to hardcore punk, the environment wouldn't allow it. In contrast to Homme, Kyuss producer Chris Goss was an unashamed Sabbath-head, his own band, Masters of Reality, being named after the third Sabbath album. As an expert in such matters, he was able to pinpoint the difference between Black Sabbath and Kyuss (with a little help from the latter's singer): 'It's an open horizon, and nothing sounds closed in. John [Garcia] said it best – "Black Sabbath was heavy, but it sounded indoors. Kyuss sounds like it's outdoors."'[92] Goss had been to see Kyuss when they played in LA, in front of small and hostile audiences who were used to the cock rock of the Sunset Strip. 'I was blown away and immediately feared some schlock, '80s metal producer would ruin them,' he told *Kerrang!*

> Metal was thin and bassless at the time; hockey stick guitars and anal staccato stylisms. Metallica and Megadeth records sounded like grasshoppers beating on tin thimbles to me. Kyuss was the antithesis of all of that. Low and loose, like a big fat ass. Even bigger than my fat ass.[93]

Fellow outdoor types to emerge from the same scene included Fu Manchu, through whose ranks Brant Bjork also passed. They were a hardcore band at first before the desert imposed itself fully on their group mindset. A contender for the most joyful and Tiggerish of all the desert rockers, Fu Manchu's vocalist Scott Hill prefers to focus on good-time zz Top-style subject-matter such as weird beards and outer space. He seems determined to do for various forms of American transportation what Kraftwerk did for the Autobahn, be it the skateboard, Chevrolet, custom van or dune buggy. The band have an infectious energy carried over from their punk origins, arrive bearing planet-sized riffs and are a dab hand with a catchy yell-along chorus.

Eddie Glass and Ruben Romano left the ranks of Fu Manchu in 1996 and went on to form the power trio Nebula. Musical differences were partly behind the fracture, yet Nebula's sound doesn't depart massively from the parent group. Double the bands; double the music. Who's complaining? At times, Nebula's output can be a little sloppier or looser than Fu Manchu's and it is also open to the occasional use of softer textures and instrumental embellishments, be it acoustic guitar patterns or Doors-ish organ chords. Having said that, the emphasis tends to remain on the groove and the fuzz.

Needless to say, none of this stuff is remotely doomy. Mind you, neither were all of Sabbath's songs. See the love song 'Sabbra Cadabra', complete with its boogie-woogie piano parts provided by guest musician Rick Wakeman of Yes fame, who was paid for his contribution in beer.[94] There's also the McCartney-esque piano ballad 'It's Alright', written and sung by drummer Bill Ward. You could also look at most of the material on 1978's messily eclectic *Never Say Die!* Nevertheless, rich in sand and bathed in sunshine, this wasn't post-war Birmingham. Palm Desert shared little with the creepy English landscape of rural Dorset where Electric Wizard's Jus Oborn was raised. Nor did it resemble the rain-swept streets of Seattle where various stars of the grunge scene became hampered by dangerous drug use. It's telling that on Queens of the Stone Age's semi-satirical anthem 'Feel Good Hit of the Summer', the list of drugs that comprise its only lyrics does not include heroin or any of its synonyms.

'We weren't from Seattle; we were too lowbrow for that,' said Bjork. 'We were dope-smokers – I was listening to a lot of Cypress Hill back then. Other than Monster Magnet, rock bands weren't talking about weed when we were around.'[95] Hailing not from California but New Jersey, Monster Magnet had an affinity with desert rock but their style also incorporated elements of space rock, garage rock, heavy metal and sounds derived from similar leather-jacketed ne'er-do-wells. Monster Magnet became bona fide rock stars (albeit fairly briefly) with 1998's *Powertrip*. The stoner equivalent of *The Rise and Fall of Ziggy Stardust*, the album was a self-fulfilling prophecy written by frontman Dave Wyndorf when he was holed up in a Las Vegas hotel room. Already in his forties, Wyndorf reacted to record company complaints that Monster Magnet weren't selling enough records by writing his most accessible collection of songs, with lyrics based on his Sin City surroundings. This last-ditch attempt to stay signed could be used as evidence of cosmic ordering: the album sleeve featured buxom scantily-clad models and raining banknotes, and that's exactly what *Powertrip* attracted, allowing Wyndorf to finally live out his lifelong rock star fantasies of debauchery, at least until the wheels fell off in a spiral of (prescription) drug addiction and his band slinked back into the realm of cult concern.

'I wrote [*Powertrip*] really bitter and fuckin' snide,' Wyndorf explained, 'and I was like, "do I have to put tits and money on something to make it sell?" and I did and it did! It was funny. I put big tits on it and money and sure enough it sold a fuckload. I really don't think it was the music, I think it was because of the way it was marketed.'[96] The videos for the album's singles also had a part to play. These were affectionate pastiches of the promo style favoured by hip-hop superstars, particularly those directed by Hype Williams, complete with twerking ladies, shiny suits and fisheye camera shots. By appropriating this Monster Magnet were acknowledging not only that they were playing an old-fashioned form of rock music but that rock music as a whole felt outmoded. Rap stars were the modern-day rock stars, and guitar bands who in turn aped hip-hop stylings looked absolutely ridiculous, whether visually (and knowingly) as in Monster Magnet's case, or musically, as with nu-metal. *Powertrip* sold over 500,000 copies and was awarded Album of the Year by both *Kerrang!* and *Metal Hammer*.

Although he would never be as brazen as Josh Homme in denying the impact of Sabbath, Wyndorf doesn't have time for bands who are incapable of looking beyond that single paragon. 'Nothing against stoner rock,' he says, 'but a Sabbath riff is a Sabbath riff . . . You've got to add something else to it. You've got to own that shit, or who the fuck cares?'[97] Wyndorf's list of his most formative records includes Lenny Kaye's *Nuggets* compilation and albums by The Groundhogs, Grand Funk Railroad, Jethro Tull, Atomic Rooster, Blue Cheer and Blue Öyster Cult, alongside obscurer records by Dust, Captain Beyond and Sir Lord Baltimore.[98] Tellingly, he did not select any Sabbath albums. Mind you, there's no Hawkwind on the list either, even though they are clearly as precious to Wyndorf as Black Sabbath are to Sleep and Electric Wizard.

Delve further back into the catalogue and you'll uncover Monster Magnet's superior and more influential (albeit lower-selling) work. Debut album *Spine of God* (1991) was a scuzzy, sleazy and swirlsome concoction of punk, metal, garage rock and space rock. The riffs come thick and fast while the blasts of lead guitar, Hawkwind-ish effects, discordant noise and piercing feedback feel like they have emerged both spontaneously and perfectly. Wyndorf's lyrics are almost parodic – a checklist of druggy, sexual and satanic matters – yet free of cliché nonetheless thanks to his use of idiosyncratic wordplay and references to Wyndorf's imaginary deity The Bull God. Even wilder is *Tab*, which was recorded beforehand but released after *Spine of God*. 'This ain't a followup,' announced *Tab*'s sleeve. 'It is what it is.' Purportedly an EP because it only contains a handful of songs, *Tab* boasts a fifty-minute running time, 32 of which are taken up by the eccentric title track. One of the first (and best) things Monster Magnet ever recorded, and a staple of their early live sets, this half-hour epic was influenced by Hawkwind, Amon Düül II, Alice Cooper and Skullflower. Built upon a short chord sequence that is repeated for the duration, the hastily and roughly recorded track is plastered in cosmic guitar effects, screeching feedback and unearthly lead guitar work. Over this ambling space rock din, Wyndorf moans, chants and yelps his wordless vocals. About eleven minutes in, he begins a sweary but largely indecipherable spoken-word section that close listening suggests might have something to do with stealing something.

Basically, if Sleep's *Dopesmoker* is too metal for you, try easing yourself into the world of expansive and abstract stoner rock with *Tab*'s title track. Half the length of *Dopesmoker*, it is not as doom-ridden or Sabbath-smitten as Sleep, yet no less of a mind-bending journey into the outer limits of heaviness. Wyndorf's material thereafter would remain fundamentally 'song-based', but if the sheer trippiness of *Tab* is your bag, it's worth investigating the weird world of John McBain, the guitarist who was sacked from Monster Magnet after those sparkling early releases. Pre-dating Monster Magnet, his Evil Acidhead project with Greg Chapman makes *Tab* look like Coldplay. Compiling their original late '80s cassette releases, *In the Name of All That Is Unholy* is an exhaustive 78-minute slab of malevolent avant-acid mayhem constructed from psychosis-inducing lo-fi loops, creepy organ, deranged off-road noodling, all manner of antisocial guitar fuzz and lots of ugly feedback. Forget garbled vocals. Here there are none at all, apart from the brief appearance of a demonically distorted speaking voice, doubtlessly designed to freak out the listener even further. Nor are there any drums, percussion or rhythm to speak of. It is vaguely reminiscent of some lost Ween demos that Gene and Dean decided not to release because they sounded too upsettingly mushroomed even for their indiscriminate tastes. A more recent and digestible example is 2016's *Lost Chants/Last Chance*, which McBain recorded over the course of one weekend in collaboration with Kandodo, who feature members of Bristol's answer to Monster Magnet, The Heads. The vinyl edition is cut at 45 rpm, enabling the listener to slow it down to 33 rpm if they prefer, while a recording of the latter warped-down version comes as a bonus disc with the CD pressing. Just like when John Peel used to accidentally play something at the incorrect speed, the slower disc matches the quality of the 'normal' 45 original, if not surpassing it, making this phat wodge of wordless space rock doubly good value.

Speaking of CDs, the format itself had played its own important part in the development of the stoned goings on mentioned above. The compact disc had allowed more music to be stored on a physical format than ever before. Where once a listener had to haul themselves to their feet after about twenty minutes to turn an LP over to its next side, a CD could accommodate eighty minutes of music, if the artist desired. A downside of the format, for those musicians who believed their work merited complete attention on the part of the listener, was that consumers could now skip tracks at the push of a button. This was much easier than lifting the needle of a turntable and placing it back down again at a different position on the grooves of a record. While Sleep's *Dopesmoker* was not recorded digitally, it did exploit the available space on compact disc and, in its complete form, was meant to be listened to in its entirety whether or not the listener was, like Julian Cope, 'utterly narnered'. Electric Wizard's *Dopethrone* likewise made deft use of the format. Its lengthy multipart songs blending seamlessly from one track to the next, it merited listening to as one complete whole rather than in bits, and was initially only available to buy on CD. In Kyuss's case, although 1994's *Welcome to Sky Valley* contains a series of clearly separate compositions, the band seriously considered issuing the record as an unbroken piece of music with no track indexes at all. This attempt to defy the skip button would have made the CD similar if not to Sleep's one-song *Dopesmoker* then at least to Melvins' earlier *Lysol* album. In the end, Kyuss decided that one single track would be a little severe. They compromised by having *Welcome to Sky Valley*'s ten songs divided into three long movements (plus a goofy hidden track known as 'Lick Doo'). The sleeve notes included the instruction: 'LISTEN WITHOUT DISTRACTION'.

15

THE NADIR:
THE LATE 1990S AND
EARLY 2000S

Fred Durst bags Noel Gallagher's autograph at Reading Festival, 2000.

Oasis – heavyweight champions of British rock – are being challenged by the new giants of metal, Limp Bizkit. In a confrontation that makes the Liam Gallagher vs Robbie Williams skirmish pale into insignificance, Limp Bizkit have thrown down the gauntlet by accusing Oasis of cheating them out of their rightful place on the Reading & Leeds festival bill. Limp Bizkit say they expected to be third on the bill, appearing before Primal Scream and Oasis. They claim Oasis demoted them to fourth place, taking the stage after The Bluetones and before Foo Fighters, because Liam and co. were scared to follow them too closely.[1]

MELODY MAKER

In his book *Perfecting Sound Forever* (2009), Greg Milner cites Shellac's 'Wingwalker', a song about a woman who performs acrobatic stunts on the wings of aeroplanes, as the model example of a record that sounds three-dimensional, perhaps even four-dimensional, 'so that the music not only existed as an object, it also moved in the world, imprinting itself by the way that its shape – the peaks and valleys that defined the wingwalker's physical and psychological journey – seemed to make the air molecules dance as the shape unravelled'.[2] Other people higher up in the music industry had different ideas of what made a good-sounding (or, rather, a *successful* sounding) record. From the mid-1990s onwards Steve Albini kept on making music with Shellac and recording that of others in ways that challenged the mainstream's methods of composing, producing, mixing, mastering, releasing and packaging its wares. Albini continued to sway his many disciples and his methods have had a lasting impact, not least in the way his recording techniques offered a viable alternative to the tyranny of compression, an unfortunate trend that really took hold as the new millennium approached.

As Milner explains in detail, a 'Loudness War' was taking place. Striving to make their music jump out of the speakers by making it louder than everybody else's, record companies would decrease or 'compress' the dynamic range of a song so that its average levels were almost as high as the peaks, the competition between labels leading to an unprecedented widespread lack of dynamic range. The result was that many songs released at this time sounded very loud but not especially good, and were often strangely repulsive to experience, as the music had not been allowed to breathe as it should. This wasn't a genre-specific phenomenon. Major culprits cited by Milner include records by Red Hot Chili Peppers, Black Eyed Peas, Rush, Flaming Lips and Oasis.[3]

The Loudness War coincides with the sorriest period in our tapestry. It is entirely possible that heavy music at this time took a hit because *everything* had become so loud, making it hard for heaviness to compete. Loud is not the same as heavy, however, as anyone will tell you if they've listened to Red Hot Chili Peppers' ridiculously compressed 'Scar Tissue' next to the jagged 4D stomp of Shellac's 'Wingwalker'. There were other problems contributing to the nadir.

Slight Return

In order for the movement to be successful, and as soon as it was conceived, Britpop had to be marketed as a break from what had gone before. It didn't have to represent a severance from the more distant past, however. The revival of mod scooters and Small Faces tropes would prove most useful in bolstering this unashamedly regressive form of British indie rock. The immediate past (or, rather, what was actually still the present in the early days of Britpop) needed to be defined as the enemy. In doing so, it was as if the 1960s-smitten Britpoppers were winding the clock back to a time before grunge, before metal, before punk, before acid rock, before The Beatles had recorded 'Helter Skelter': a return to the era before heaviness.

'If punk was about getting rid of hippies, then I'm getting rid of grunge,' declared Damon Albarn of Blur in 1992. 'It's the same sort of feeling: people should smarten up, be a bit more energetic. They're walking around like hippies again – they're stooped, they've got greasy hair, there's no difference. Whether they like it or not, they're listening to Black Sabbath again. It irritates me.'[4] A year earlier, Blur had participated in a co-headlining tour with Dinosaur Jr,

My Bloody Valentine and The Jesus & Mary Chain. In order to wrestle the spotlight away from those older acts, Blur were on a mission to make rocky weirdness seem old hat. Naturally shoegaze came under attack as well as grunge. These sonically adventurous bands were recast by the media as haughty and pretentious. Swervedriver were doubly criminal, given their admiration for American culture. The Oxford group were smitten with Dinosaur Jr, toured the United States in support of bands like Monster Magnet and Soundgarden, and had lyrics inspired by Hunter S. Thompson's *Rolling Stone* shenanigans. By the time Swervedriver's third album arrived in 1995, most of the UK had already gone Britpop loony. The band thought a bass-driven but catchy number called 'The Other Jesus' was the obvious choice of lead single. Creation Records' head honcho Alan McGee ignored them, opting for the string-laden ballad 'Last Day on Earth'. It failed to capitalize on the success of Oasis's overblown 'Whatever' and the label dropped Swervedriver a week after the album was released. Swervedriver's fellow shoegazers either fizzled out, disappeared for years or diluted their sound in line with the charting Britpop bands of the era. Shoegaze's reputation didn't recover for decades. Most notably of all, My Bloody Valentine withdrew from live performances and struggled to complete the ideal third album that their perfectionist leader, Kevin Shields, had in his head. Shields became a hermit-like creature, occasionally working with Primal Scream and constantly failing on his promises to deliver new material. When MBV eventually returned in 2013, long after the dust had settled, Shields declared that Britpop had been a government conspiracy. When the MI5 files are finally released, that will prove it.[5]

Everything went wrong on this planet in the absence of My Bloody Valentine, argued John Doran. MBV's disappearance left a void into which flooded a plethora of inferior guitar bands. This paved the way for Britpop, which in turn begat Cool Britannia, off the back of which Tony Blair was elected prime minster. In its support of America's 'war on terror', Blair's New Labour government joined the attacks on Afghanistan and Iraq, the seismic global impact of which is still being felt. My Bloody Valentine's hiatus is, therefore, indirectly responsible for the current dire state of the world (at least according to Doran).[6]

It was not just grunge and shoegaze that were demonized by Britpop. Anything even vaguely connected, be it older or current, was dismissed alongside. When reviewing Pixies' posthumous *Death to the Pixies* compilation in 1997, David Stubbs of *Uncut* magazine defined the mood of the UK music scene when he asked, 'Were they [Pixies] really to blame for all those smelly American longhairs with Black Sabbath fixations (Black Sabbath, I ask you) and nothing but nothing to say?'[7]

Along with noise rock, the idea of riot grrrl also came under attack in the new era of Cool Britannia, where lads could be lads and women had to be banter-loving 'laddettes' or risk banishment from the blokes in charge. 'How many riot grrrls does it take to change a lightbulb?' joked Blur bassist Alex James in *Melody Maker*. 'None, because they're never gonna change anything!'[8]

Bemused American rock stars reacted to Britpop in a variety of ways. The capricious Evan Dando of Lemonheads fame was among the more accommodating parties. He became Noel Gallagher's drug buddy for a little while. Evan and Noel co-wrote a song together, and Lemonheads covered Oasis's 'Live Forever'. In 1996 The Brian Jonestown Massacre of San Francisco tried to jump on the bandwagon by taking the frankly desperate step of releasing an album with a Union Jack on its cover. Others were less favourable. Melvins recorded a jaunty Britpop parody called 'In the Rain' for which they adopted comedy English accents. J Mascis was not impressed by his label's suggestion that the bankable Liam Gallagher might like to sing for Dinosaur Jr.[9] Sonic Youth's ever-amiable Thurston Moore agreed to remix a Blur track, although he later admitted that he had never been a fan of the band. Metallica did become interested in Britpop, however. Unlike the cynical Steve Albini (and most of America), drummer Lars Ulrich was obsessed with Oasis. His bandmate James Hetfield said that metal needed to 'go away' sometimes. In its place, he was enjoying the 'moody' sound of Radiohead's *OK Computer*.[10] In 1999 Metallica recorded a live album with the San Francisco Symphony Orchestra, the result being less Richard Wagner and more McAlmont & Butler. But you can't blame Metallica for wanting to distance themselves from the American metal scene, given what that had to offer at the time.

Big Shorts and Baseball Caps

Besides the Britpop distraction, American rock and metal music had its own problems to deal with. As early as 1993, in an interview with Matthew Smith-Lahrman, The Jesus Lizard's Duane Denison predicted the rise of what would become known as 'nu-metal':

> DENISON: A lot of white kids are into rap, metal and rap. That's where it's at for a lot of white kids.
> SMITH-LAHRMAN: Northwestern college kids. The upper-crust of financial kids are way into rap. The white males are way into real hardcore rap.
> DENISON: Yeah. It's a chance to feel naughty. Singing about things that they have no understanding of.[11]

Out of this new batch of shorts-sporting nu-metallers, Deftones were an exception. Chino Moreno's vocal dexterity was a firm step above his contemporaries. He was a fan of post-rock as well as smooth and moody 1980s pop music. Guitarist Stephen Carpenter, on the other hand, always pined to be in an extreme metal band like Meshuggah. As such, no Deftones album is ever heavy enough for Carpenter. This artistic tension, and its push-and-pull dynamic, helped place Deftones in an ambiguous middle ground. Like other nu-metal bands, they employed a turntablist, although Frank Delgado did not trade in hip-hop-influenced scratching. Delgado used his record decks in a much subtler manner, providing background textures and eerie, gothic ambience. The effect was almost as if Deftones had appointed Philip Jeck, the English avant-garde composer who manipulates old vinyl to create original atmospheric sounds.

Most of the other nu-metal bands acted as though they had decided to base their entire repertoire around the Faith No More single 'Epic', ignoring the fact that Faith No More were a genre-straddling bunch of tempestuous weirdos with decidedly catholic tastes who openly despised their imitators. If there was another reference point for nu-metal, it was 'Killing in the Name' by Rage Against the Machine, whose debut album no critic has ever been able to describe without using the word 'incendiary'. Nu-metallers adopted all of the swearing but none of the Marxist sentiment of RATM. Faith No More were less concerned with direct political radicalism, while Mike Patton's lyrics also tended to resist pursuing anything particularly heartfelt or personal. He had a greater interest in singing from different characters' points of view: that of a small child, for instance, or the various extremities of middle-aged men. Another was sung from the perspective of a distressed surgical patient. Other songs contained obscured references to Blondie and Madonna. Keyboardist Roddy Bottum, one of the first openly gay rock stars, wrote the fellatio-celebrating 'Be Aggressive' for Patton to sing with characteristic gusto.

Nu-metallers tended to be neither as politically active as RATM nor as creative as FNM. Their lyrics were characterized by boil-in-the-bag angst that appropriated the rapping style from African American culture and repurposed it to express their own privileged pain and false sense of victimhood, a process satirized in a politely savage manner on Ben Folds's 2001 single 'Rockin' the Suburbs'. As for nu-metallers' attitudes towards sex and gender, they made the words sung by Anthony Kiedis of Red Hot Chili Peppers look like the carefully considered analysis of a highly qualified psychosexual therapist. One of the many low points of the entire genre is 'All in the Family' by Korn. It features Jonathan Davis and guest vocalist Fred Durst of Limp Bizkit rapping about the length of their penises and calling each other 'faggot'. Back on Korn's first album, Davis had screamed that word as a reclamation of the insult with which the school bullies had once taunted him. Korn also had a song called 'Kunt', which is essentially a long and sweary tirade of misogynistic abuse. Dez Fafara of Coal Chamber has claimed that his band were frontrunners in a scene that helped rescue Los Angeles from all the hair metal bands.[12] This doesn't quite stack up when grunge had already made hair metal look old-fashioned. Besides, many nu-metal bands seemed eager for a return to pre-grunge showbiz neander-thalism. Durst clearly idolized Mötley Crüe, becoming friends with their drummer, Tommy Lee. In 1999 Lee would form his own nu-metal project, Methods of Mayhem (featuring guest spots from Durst, Kid Rock and others) as an excuse to rap about his suppos-edly enviable yet emotionally empty sex life. Limp Bizkit, Korn and other nu-metal celebs would appear in the charming *Backstage Sluts* series of adult DVDs. Even the more tasteful Deftones had lyrics about bitches and whores, plus a young bikini-clad woman on one of their album sleeves.

The all-female Canadian band Kittie, who were only teenagers when their first album came out, were ostracized by male members of the nu-metal scene. Kittie could barely play their instruments, claimed Coal Chamber's Mike Cox. He alleged that Kittie's songs were written for them by the Lander sisters' father (also their man-ager) and that Lander Senior had paid for both radio play and prominent support slots. Other men asked Kittie's guitar tech if he had been hiding offstage somewhere during their gigs where he was able to play their guitar parts for them. Others assumed there were male musicians hiding behind Kittie's amplifiers who were surrepti-tiously performing this material that young women were apparently incapable of nailing themselves.[13] After their debut album, Kittie doubled down on the fierceness with material influenced by death metal bands like Cannibal Corpse, thereby out-heavying the laughably formulaic Coal Chamber by a significant margin.

Nirvana had once sought to repel the jocks in their audience by kissing each other on television. They also promoted equal rights and feminist causes. Once the ex-adolescent outcasts of the nu-metal scene struck gold, they seemed far more content with satisfying alpha males. They welcomed the bullies, whose behaviour they ended up replicating. With the jocks aligned, 'sports metal' was another term that emerged and was applied to Fred Durst's testosterone-fuelled Limp Bizkit. Shortly after arriving on the scene, they were deemed a 'half-baked Korn clone' by *Kerrang!* 'There's too many of these little bands running around right now, and the Bizkit represent the bottom of the barrel, all superficial posturing and nothing underneath,' observed Don Kaye after he saw the band supporting Faith No More in New York. Even Faith No More seemed curiously pallid that night, Kaye noticed.[14] FNM would disband the following year, so perhaps they already felt they were going through the motions. Witnessing the monster they had helped birth at first hand, in the form of Limp Bizkit, couldn't have helped. The Bizkit would, despite Kaye's warnings, rise to the status of *Kerrang!* cover stars. Indicative of just how far sports metal grew, in 2001 Durst would appear on the front page of monthly dad rock bible *Q* magazine.

With questionable intent and varying degrees of success, older metal bands like Machine Head and Slayer began dabbling in rapping and other momentarily fashionable nu-metal tropes. It would have seemed more sincere had it felt like the rap verses had emerged from a genuine love of hip-hop instead of having been inherited second-hand from fellow metal acts. Disillusioned by what he saw as the infiltration of 'frat boys' into the metal scene, guitarist Kerry King was disengaged from the writing process of Slayer's 1998 effort

Diabolus in Musica (though, weirdly, he did pen the rapidly sung lyrics to 'Stain of Mind', which is easily the most nu-metal song on the record).[15] Having dipped his toe into nu-metal waters with some of the material on Sepultura's *Roots*, Max Cavalera formed Soulfly and packed its songs with nu-metal guest spots. New York's Anthrax, the only one of the Big Four thrash bands to hail from the East Coast, had long championed the joys of hip-hop. They'd rapped on the Beastie Boys pastiche/homage 'I'm the Man' back in 1987. That same year, Chuck D gave Anthrax a shout-out on 'Bring the Noise' because he'd seen the band sporting Public Enemy T-shirts. In 1991 Public Enemy would appear on Anthrax's thrashed-up cover version of the same song. Along with Rage Against the Machine's first album and Faith No More's 'Epic', Anthrax's take on 'Bring the Noise' can be considered a nu-metal blueprint. Yet when nu-metal took over the airwaves, Anthrax resisted pleas from their label to properly cash in. This didn't do much for their sales at the time but left them with dignity intact. There were some riffs on 1998's *Volume 8: The Threat is Real* that could be identified as vaguely nu-metal in nature. Schizophrenically, its most nu-metal song, 'Inside Out', also features an acoustic guitar part and passages where Anthrax threaten to go full grunge. The album includes frantic hardcore punk, old-school thrash, slower and groovier numbers, a track that resembles Soundgarden and a summery cowbell-sporting song that could have been written by the desert rock band Fu Manchu. In this melting pot of styles, *Volume 8* even boasts an Anthrax-go-country number. It's like Metallica's 1990s *Load/Reload* period only looser, wilder and more carefree. Around this time the band also recorded a fairly faithful rendition of Radiohead's 'The Bends'. They were all over the place. Anthrax have always been the least serious and least precious of the Big Four, and the ones who are taken most for granted. They often seem to be considered the least cool as well, like a nerdy sibling that the rest of the family patronisingly tolerates but neglects to mention at length in the annual Christmas round-robin. That's reason enough to suspect Anthrax may in fact be the coolest of the bunch.

Admittedly, nu-metal does share several of our recurring heavy characteristics. It's based around big riff repetitions, with the guitars down-tuned like Sabbath to make them all the more deeper and fatter. There's much emphasis on the bass, partly thanks to its appreciation of hip-hop. It doesn't rely on distracting technical prowess. It was charged with being simple and dumb, accusations that in this case stick pretty firmly. Without Deftones, nu-metal was shallow and without substance. Its main innovation was to mix metal and rap elements, which, as we've seen, had already been done. It never possessed the forward-thinking adventurousness of post-punk, say. It didn't burrow deeper into the crater to the netherworlds offered by Sabbath. It didn't wallow in its own textures or slow down time itself like the meditative drone metal kickstarted by Melvins. Many of the songs were recorded, mixed and mastered as crassly as they had been composed, and no doubt the Loudness War contributed to nu-metal's unpleasantness on the ear. Damon Albarn complained of the genre's flatness when promoting *Blur: The Best Of*. 'I can't stand them. Can't stand anything like that,' he replied when asked for his opinion of Limp Bizkit. 'I guess it's probably because I'm too old to understand it. It has a really cheap sound. I don't mean that in a derogatory way, they don't sound very sincere, the sounds. They sound very well put together in the studio but they don't seem to have a real joy in the texture of the sound.'[16] This was ironic coming from Albarn, given that his own band's rise and general gobbiness had helped to virtually obliterate shoegaze, a sound that always gloried in texture above all its elements.

Nu-metal also rose too quickly, being swiftly accepted by the mainstream before its practitioners had time to develop their ideas more sensitively and sensibly. In line with the simultaneous rise of reality television and celebrity culture, and less conflicted by the idea of success than the grunge bands who'd strived to retain their formative punk rock values to varying degrees of success, even if it just meant name-checking Fugazi, nu-metal acts seemed to want to get as famous as possible as quickly as they could, without giving much thought to honing their craft or putting any time aside to dwell on the irreversible missteps they were about to undertake. To achieve this, a lot of them relied on breakthrough kooky cover versions, again making a pig's ear of the Faith No More technique. Faith No More had removed from their repertoire a cover of 'War Pigs' by Black Sabbath after it had gone down a bit too well with the metal purists in their audience, as well as one of the people in their own band. Drummer Mike Bordin, bassist Bill Gould and keyboardist Roddy Bottum were prone to reining in guitarist Jim Martin whenever his playing became too histrionic, ensuring that his solos were kept to a minimum. Hemmed in by such restrictions, Martin spent the recording sessions for *The Real Thing* on an obsessive self-appointed quest to unearth the ultimate guitar tone.[17] When its follow-up, *Angel Dust*, was being made in 1992, Martin was mourning the death of his father and understandably disengaged from the recording process. He would record his parts at night when the rest of the band were absent. Then his colleagues would turn up in the morning to complain that Martin's parts were too metal-inclined, melodic, twiddly or Zappa-like.[18] *Angel Dust* would be Martin's final album with Faith No More. He went on to become an award-winning pumpkin farmer. 'War Pigs' would be replaced in FNM live sets with faithful renditions of Commodores and Bee Gees hits. They also took Dead Kennedys' 'Let's Lynch the Landlord' and completely de-heavied it by turning it into a crooned lounge tune. Again, Deftones showed a similar degree of intelligence. Their respectful recreation of Sade's 'No Ordinary Love' was not remotely suitable to metal club-night slamdancing. Thus Deftones avoided that particular type of albatross.

Others were not so astute, having witnessed the success that Marilyn Manson had enjoyed off the back of his rocked-up take on

Eurythmics' 'Sweet Dreams'. Limp Bizkit followed suit, breaking through with a cover of 'Faith' on which the first verse is relatively similar to George Michael's original, after which arrives all the novelty shouting, big old riffs, crude turntable scratches and the lyrical addition of 'GET THE FUCK UP!' Orgy are known solely for covering 'Blue Monday' by New Order. Coal Chamber tackled Peter Gabriel's 'Shock the Monkey', on which they were joined by Ozzy Osbourne, with whom they happened to share a manager (Ozzy's wife, Sharon). Alien Ant Farm whacked the power chords all over 'Smooth Criminal' by Michael Jackson. 'My only hit song was a cover of a child molester,' singer Dryden Mitchell lamented in 2015 while on a nostalgia tour with fellow has-beens P.O.D. and Hoobastank.[19]

Slipknot didn't have a mischievous cover version in their repertoire. They made up for this deficiency by using the classic marketing gimmick of wearing masks, and not in a cool way like the unruly Funkadelic-meets-Voivod-meets-Troma world of GWAR. As a result, Slipknot became one of the most successful metal bands in the world.

Commercial Suicide Pacts

It wasn't just the ascendancy of nu-metal that tarnished this period. Derivative post-grungers like Nickelback and Creed popped up alongside bouncy pop-punk groups, the latter even lighter than punk rock had been in the first place. Where Fugazi and their Dischord cohorts had expanded the palette of hardcore while remaining independent and socially and politically minded, much of this was lost in translation by later generations of 'emotional hardcore' or simply 'emo' bands that signed up to majors as soon as they could, tended not to associate themselves as closely with progressive causes or ethical practices, and narrowed their lyrical scope to focus almost exclusive on the subject of toxic relationships.

Written by bitter, wounded and jealous man-boys, many emo lyrics now read like the Reddit rantings of the incel community.

We can see that the rot had set in by looking at *Metal Hammer*'s top 20 albums of 1999.[20] For a start, it was topped by what is the least heavy album on its whole countdown: ex-Soundgarden singer Chris Cornell's decidedly folky *Euphoria Morning*. The chart also included the right-wing rap-rock clown Kid Rock and the most commercial Foo Fighters record so far. At number six was the second album by Britrock band Feeder. Their debut had taken its cues from Smashing Pumpkins, but *Yesterday Went Too Soon* sounded about as heavy as The Stereophonics, who, incidentally, also managed to creep into *Metal Hammer*'s top 20.

Heaviness was in a state of utter panic. There are countless examples from this era of prior practitioners of the form who, in trying to swim with the tide, suffered an identity crisis so seismic that they would never fully recover. In the first half of the 1990s Manic Street Preachers had taken their cues from The Clash, Public Enemy and Guns N' Roses' best and least bloated moments. They were an androgynous mess of eyeliner, lipstick, bravado and feather boas. Their troubled guitarist and lyricist, Richey Edwards, self-harmed in the middle of an NME interview. Their singer wore a balaclava, provocatively, on *Top of the Pops*. Bleak and grimy, 1994's *The Holy Bible* was full of references to irrepressible Western consumerism, anorexia, totalitarianism, self-abuse and serial killers. After Edwards's subsequent disappearance, the remaining trio began dressing in trendy shirts and smart trainers and surrounding themselves with orchestras.

With circulation figures in freefall, *Kerrang!* magazine didn't know what to do either. *This Is My Truth Tell Me Yours* (1998) was Manic Street Preachers' second album since their capitulation to orchestral Britpop. It would later be pinpointed as the Manics' commercial peak but creative low point in Bob Stanley's comprehensive history of pop music.[21] On the week of the album's release,

Kerrang! claimed that *This Is My Truth Tell Me Yours* was 'arguably their strongest work to date' and awarded the record full marks, albeit in an apologetic review that referenced Burt Bacharach and The Walker Brothers and made it very clear to the magazine's readers that the Manics no longer rocked to even the slightest degree.[22]

That same year, Smashing Pumpkins suffered their own artistic deflation. Half a decade earlier the ambitious Chicago band had released one of the heaviest albums of the grunge era outside the discography of TAD. Produced by man-of-the-moment Butch Vig, *Siamese Dream* had as many as a hundred guitar tracks in a single song and flaunted a 1970s rock sound so layered that your average stereo system could do it little justice. Five years on, as band members fell by the wayside and heaviness flew into turmoil, Pumpkins leader Billy Corgan couldn't decide whether to go down an industrial-electronic goth-pop route or embrace stripped-down acoustic folk. The result was a sad, grey and overlong mulch of both forms. Corgan was imbibing 'copious quantities' of ecstasy when making the record in question, *Adore*.[23] This could account for his wavering mindset and also raises the question of just how maudlin this already quiet and weepy LP would have sounded without all those happy pills.

On the plus side, the era included a few largely neglected although still fascinating near-career-suicide records. Moby couldn't have mistimed things more when, in 1996, he momentarily abandoned disco-friendly dance tunes for screaming over the top of Ministry-esque industrial thrash guitars and covering the cult art-punk band Mission of Burma. Because *Animal Rights* hardly sold any copies, Moby was subsequently forced to take a different tack by appropriating a load of old Alan Lomax recordings for 1999's *Play*, flogging the results to colossal marketing companies, buying himself a luxury penthouse apartment and spiralling into drug and alcohol dependency.

Unlike the Manics, fellow melodic Britrockers The Wildhearts did not respond to Britpop by sprucing themselves up. They did the opposite. Ginger, the band's mononymous singer and guitarist, felt that dance acts like The Chemical Brothers and The Prodigy were outstripping all the guitar bands around that time in terms of their excitement and volume. To compensate, The Wildhearts fitted drummer Ritch Battersby's kit with electronic drum triggers that discharged sampled sounds of explosions and traffic accidents whenever he played a beat. Owing to a newfound interest in sound-scapes, The Wildhearts also wrote (or rather didn't write) lengthy blank sections into their songs that had to be filled by improvised chaos. One of these sections, the middle part of the furious 'Why You Lie', contains a sample from Lucio Fulci's cult horror film *The Beyond*: a little girl shouting 'Mummy!' before a woman's face is splashed with acid. Smothered in distortion and screeching with feedback, this is the harshest track on an already savage-sounding album and has more in common with noise artists like Merzbow, Wolf Eyes or Hair Police than it does with the pop-rock mini-hits with which The Wildhearts had made their name.

Endless, Nameless's mix was so rough and full of static squeals that some punters returned their copies to the shop under the mis-taken impression that there had been a manufacturing fault. Others deemed the album unlistenable. Not that Ginger cared. 'We were just so pissed off with the whole industry,' he recalled in 2018:

> At the time, I could see them all killing themselves with the amount of money they were charging for CDs and the rise of the digital download. I was so disgusted by the whole thing, I wanted to make an artistic statement while we still had record companies willing to fund the recording ses-sions. We wanted to make something that was going to be a fuck-you, that was going to make actual waves and not just money. And we did. To this day, it stands up as a fuck-you record. People said it was too noisy. How the fuck can a rock band be too noisy? When I was a kid, Motörhead were

a lot noisier than ABBA. They were both great but weren't trying to do the same thing. I still believe that a lot of rock bands are playing it too safe . . . It was a band saying 'fuck you', sounding 'fuck you', meaning 'fuck you'.

Having unleashed his most intense and violent-sounding music to date, and with band members in the grip of addiction to some of the nastiest drugs, Ginger split the band on the eve of the album's release. He feared that if he didn't, at least one of them would end up dead.[24]

Northern Ireland's Therapy? had not managed to fully sabotage themselves with 1995's *Infernal Love*, the creepy and gothy follow-up to 1994's pop-metal masterpiece *Troublegum*. In 1998 they dabbled with a similar image to their pals in Manic Street Preachers. Having previously looked like a squat demon biker who'd stepped out of a Frank Kozik cartoon, singer and guitarist Andy Cairns could be seen clean-shaven with short hair and smarter clothing on the insert to 1998's *Semi-Detached*. That was quite enough Britpop compromise for him. After their label A&M folded and Therapy? found themselves lumped with funding a European tour through their own publishing royalties, the band retreated to Milton Keynes to record their own equivalent of *Endless, Nameless*. Their 1999 *Suicide Pact – You First* was recorded cheaply and quickly, although the band still found time to sample the beating wings of a trapped butterfly and undertake 666 seconds of field recording in a Milton Keynes shopping centre. One song was recorded in the woods at night. Having grown jaded with coupling their metal riffs with Undertones melodies, Therapy? embraced the more abrasive ideas of Captain Beefheart, Black Flag, The Stooges, The Jesus Lizard, Motörhead and Nick Cave.

The sessions were recorded by Howard 'Head' Bullivant, who admitted to having never enjoyed *Troublegum* but had been a fan of Therapy?'s mini-albums from the early 1990s when they had sounded like Killing Joke trapped in a damp basement and begging for their freedom through the floorboards. When they heard *Suicide Pact – You First*'s grubby mix, fans complained that Cairns wasn't singing properly anymore. In fact, he'd been listening to a lot of Aphex Twin at the time and was impressed by the vocal manipulations on some of his tracks.[25] No singles were released to promote the record because, well, what would be the point? Contributing to heavy's nadir, Radio One had no specialist rock show between the years of 1993 and 1999. When it was resurrected with Mary Anne Hobbs as presenter, she declared live on the airwaves her feelings that every single copy of *Suicide Pact – You First* deserved to be set on fire and thrown in the bin.[26]

Aside from the longer-established rock bands who seemed to be suffering public mental breakdowns, there were also a number of exciting younger UK acts operating at this time. Groop Dogdrill were a trio from Doncaster who released two albums of exquisitely anguished masculinity-in-crisis alternative rock cuts before splitting up when no record company would sign them. Part Chimp specialized in making a Sabbath-meets-Sonic Youth racket that is rumoured to have been louder than a jet engine crash-landing onto a scrapheap full of armour. Like My Bloody Valentine, they felt it best to hand out earplugs to their audiences. Despite receiving positive reviews in certain quarters, such acts tended to be marginalized by the press and were mostly ignored by the public.

Given that the original members of Black Sabbath finally reunited during this era, it is ironic that in many ways the Sabbathian spirit appeared to be at its lowest ebb. The ear-shattering My Bloody Valentine had gone into hiding. After his wraithlike appearance in Nick Broomfield's woolly *Kurt & Courtney* documentary, Earth's Dylan Carlson was on his own long withdrawal from the business of making music. Grunge, noise rock and riot grrrl bands were dropped in their droves from record labels eager to capitalize instead on more conservative fads. Making Sabbathian music at this time was less cool than it had been to be a fan of them (or Budgie) in the 1970s when they were considered to be Led Zeppelin for ignoramuses.

Luckily, however, the Sabbathian spirit is always bubbling away somewhere under the surface. And so it was during this nadir. It just needed to bide its time before it could froth up again.

16

THE 2000S NOISE SCENE

Burned Mind by Wolf Eyes.

Getting older, I don't feel the need to name a track 'Stabbed in the Face' anymore.[1]

AARON DILLOWAY (EX-WOLF EYES)

I t wasn't just the stoner, doom and drone epics provided by the likes of Earth, Sleep and Electric Wizard that bubbled away below the surface to keep the spirit of heavy alive once Britpop, pop-punk, emo and nu-metal made an ugly mess of festival bills. By the early 2000s an exciting renaissance in noise music was taking place. It was enabled by changes in technology and distribution, newfound critical respect for the likes of Merzbow and Lou Reed's *Metal Machine Music*, and the blanket blandness of heavy's nadir driving discontented listeners to the furthest extremities of harsh and ugly music. Some people would claim it didn't even count as real 'music' at all. It was also encouraged and patronized by an older generation of rockers who had found themselves nonplussed by much of what was occurring around them. Such folk were unmoved by the successful bands around at the time that purported to rock but actually did not. They had also seen several styles of music start out as exciting and radical, only to dilute into something safer and sanitized. 'I have a great deal of time for all of these noise terrorists – it's modern avant-meets-stoners in a basement,' Henry Rollins would enthuse. 'If you watch [Wolf Eyes or Dead Machines] gigs on YouTube, it's flannelled longhaired guys hunched over laptops playing with effects pedals as eight people watch with tallboys in their hand going, "Oooooooh!," in some freezing basement in Michigan or Ohio. It's so underground that it has to have integrity.'[2] Rollins was turned on to this noise scene by John Olson's American Tapes label, with which he would become obsessed, as was Thurston Moore of Sonic Youth. Moore was put off, initially, when he heard the misleadingly banal name of Olson's imprint. Then Moore discovered the limited runs of bizarre items that were appearing on American Tapes: 'his first tapes were crazy, because they were covered in crushed glass and bolted shut – there was no way you could listen to it unless you had a toolbox.'[3] If you managed to prise open these mini Pandora's boxes, the music that escaped was just as abrasive. The material slotted neatly alongside the early industrial cassettes that Moore had collected back in the 1980s as well as harsh Japanese tape releases he'd amassed in the years since. It had long been standard Sonic Youth practice to share their spotlight with oddballs from the underground.

People who had observed Sonic Youth's rise at first hand noticed the band's tendency to employ shamelessly hardnosed networking techniques with the aim of advancing their standing. This felt unseemly to those who were happier to remain underground. After all, it was a habit one might find flourishing in the viper's nest of 1980s yuppie culture rather than behaviour expected of a New York art rock group. Sonic Youth did not share the same Reaganite politics as many young upwardly mobile professionals, but they were guilty of schmoozing in order to make headway. Be it with fellow musicians, music promoters, record company employees, radio DJs or influential journalists, Sonic Youth knew who to rub elbows with and how to do it. Bob Bert played drums on the first couple of Sonic Youth LPs and observed how bassist Kim Gordon would make a beeline for any notable music hack who happened to be at the same party as them.[4]

As anyone could have predicted, indie purist Steve Albini took Sonic Youth to task for signing to Geffen at the start of the 1990s. In other people's eyes, once Sonic Youth were on a major label and enjoying circulation on MTV, the band acted with dignity and integrity, continuing to make many bold and experimental records. The main reason Sonic Youth had signed to a major in the first place was never to become champagne-swigging superstars. They were under no illusion of that circumstance ever transpiring, so they conducted their activities and managed their finances accordingly and in a level-headed manner. Being on a major label meant that Sonic Youth had access to health insurance, which, as Thurston Moore has often reiterated, no independent label could offer them at the time.[5] He and his bandmates also made considerable efforts to continue promoting the sounds that were emerging from the underground in the hope of helping such culturally valuable music to reach the wider audience it deserved. Thus acts like Bikini Kill, Pavement and Nirvana were taken under the wing of Sonic Youth. Albini took exception to this as well. He felt Sonic Youth's dalliance with the corporate music world gave credibility 'to some of the nonsense notions that hover around the star-making machinery', and that these actions represented a 'corruption of a perfectly valid, well-oiled music scene' that Sonic Youth had abandoned:

> I think what they did was take a lot of people who didn't have aspirations or ambitions and encouraged them to be part of the mainstream music industry. They validated the fleeting notions that these kids had that they might one day be rock stars. And then they participated in inducing a lot of them to make very stupid career moves.[6]

Sonic Youth's own music may feature lengthy passages of ear-piercing feedback and multi-guitar skronk work replete with unconventional tunings, but it is not the heaviest brand of art rock on the market. They gradually outgrew the abrasive no wave style of their origins, taking their music into more elegant directions. Even so, by the turn of the millennium Sonic Youth had become enthusiastic patrons of the noise music scene. Just as they had given a leg up to grunge and riot grrrl groups in the previous decade, they embraced the opportunity to offer support slots to acts like Wolf Eyes and Hair Police and to talk up these groups in interviews. This coincided with the most uncompromising phase of Sonic Youth's own career since the earliest days. In 1997 *Anagrama* marked the first in a series of experimental, often improvisational and mostly instrumental records released via the band's own SYR imprint. Some of these jams were shaped into more substantial pieces for 1998's 'proper' studio album *A Thousand Leaves*. Depending on the disposition of the listener, this divisive LP either ushered in a bold and even more progressive phase of Sonic Youth or resembled the point at which the group finally disappeared up their own backsides for good. The following year's *SYR4: Goodbye 20th Century* proved even more challenging. Across two discs with track lengths ranging from twelve seconds to more than thirty minutes, art rock's artiest band reinterpreted works by composers including John Cage, Steve Reich, Yoko Ono, Pauline Oliveros and Christian Wolff. 'Goodbye 20th century and good-bye career,' joked the *NME*. 'This is like listening to a gaggle of small children playing with pans,' said *Kerrang!*, concluding, 'This is shit.' Meanwhile, the compilers of *The Wire*'s end-of-year chart declared it the second best album of the last twelve months.[7]

In his scathing *Pitchfork* review, Brent DiCrescenzo gave Sonic Youth's subsequent studio effort 0.0 out of 10. A proud Chicagoan, DiCrescenzo interpreted *NYC Ghosts & Flowers*' minimalist noodling and Beat poetry vocal choices as the epitome of the vacuous pomposity that thrived among the beret-clad bohemians of Manhattan. Ironically, at least part of this sound could be attributed to the fresh perspectives offered by Sonic Youth's new (temporary) recruit and co-producer Jim O'Rourke, a veteran of Chicago's experimental music scene. 'Now, finally, my generation has its *Metal Machine Music*,' grumbled DiCrescenzo, 'an unfathomable album which will be heard in the squash courts and open mic nights of deepest hell. At least Lou Reed had the good grace to keep his mouth shut on his grinding hallmark of pretentious ejaculation.'[8] Little did DiCrescenzo realize that, far be it from remaining the touchstone for lazy and unlistenable drivel, *Metal Machine Music* was about to have an impressive resurgence.

Once considered by many to be the worst album ever made, Reed's 1975 double LP of searing discordance and formless feedback contained no vocals, no drums, no riffs, no solos, no 'songs', no 'music' (per se) and nearly ended Reed's career. While it always retained some curio status, its reissue in the year 2000 gave critics and consumers the opportunity to reassess its merits. 'There may be no album that is *more* rock 'n' roll than *Metal Machine Music*,' proposed David Fricke in his liner notes. Around the same time as Buddah Records' reissue, experimental composer Ulrich Krieger embarked on the preposterous task of transcribing *Metal Machine Music* into notation for performances by his chamber ensemble Zeitkratzer. This helped convince Reed – who in the past had veered, depending on his mood, between justifying *Metal Machine Music* from a variety of often contradictory positions to disowning it completely – that the work did have genuine artistic value. This led to Reed's re-embracement of noise in the formation of the Metal Machine Trio (Reed, Krieger and Sarth Calhoun).

When Sonic Youth took part in the *The Wire* magazine's 'Invisible Jukebox' – a regular feature in which musicians are played music, blind, and asked if they can identify the artist and track – guitarist Lee Ranaldo pinpointed the feedback screeches of *Metal Machine Music* within an instant, specifying just as quickly that they were listening to side four. It's the record's best side, he noted. 'I wouldn't want it on CD,' added Thurston Moore. 'It's way too layered.'[9]

Merzbow

From the futurist composers, found-sound artists and musique concrète of the early twentieth century through to *Metal Machine Music*, the post-industrial power electronics scene and the work of 'Japanoise' artists such as Merzbow, noise music practitioners have antagonistically challenged accepted norms of musical beauty through 'non-musical' and anti-melodic practices. It's an idea that has a long history. Even so, from the early 2000s, noise music found a new lease of life.

The Wire had been reviewing and namedropping Merzbow (the recording alias of Masami Akita) since the early 1990s, but the magazine didn't secure an interview with the elusive Japanese noise-monger until 1997. A cover feature followed in August 2000. Merzbow's earliest recordings date back to 1979 and only gradually attracted discussion outside the confines of publications dedicated to experimental music and obscure extreme music fanzines. While noise music may have remained a relatively niche prospect, and Akita's uncompromising sonic aesthetic has continued to be used as a cheap punchline in some quarters, publications who wouldn't have touched him beforehand began covering Merzbow too. His first commercial boost occurred in the mid-1990s when selected albums came out via Release Entertainment. A sub-branch of the esteemed metal label Relapse, this imprint's reputation and distribution reach meant Merzbow CDs became readily available in retailers throughout the world. In particular, the hellish artwork to 1994's *Venereology* appealed to the grisly tastes of metalheads. A sticker on the front boasted it was 'The most extreme recording you will ever own!!!'

We have seen how Earth's Dylan Carlson sought to take the final ringing chords of his favourite rock songs and stretch them to album length. Masami Akita's original plan for Merzbow was to do a similar thing with the most extreme elements of rock performance. He relished the sound of The Who's or Jimi Hendrix's guitars being smashed violently into multiple pieces. His preferred section of King Crimson's '21st Century Schizoid Man' was its final moments of disorderly chaos. The best bit of any Emerson, Lake & Palmer concert was the moment when Keith Emerson plunged a set of knives into the keys of his Hammond organ. Those were the things that Akita loved most about rock music. The problem being, he was forced to sit through all the expendable parts to get there:

the melody, the rhythm, the 'stupid vocals'. He looked for ways to recreate and sustain 'only the violent, noisy, brutal, sick' parts of rock and to do it in a more dispassionate manner, thus removing any trace of 'emotional gimmick'. Akita yearned to glory in its sound and texture instead.[10]

In the decades since the Merzbow project began, Masami Akita's output has become no easier to categorize. Though his creations are perennially pigeonholed as noise music, anti-music and even uber-music, the sheer magnitude of his output will always present an obstacle to easy classification. Consider Mike Connelly's comments in the opening episode of Merzcast, one of two entirely separate podcasts launched in 2019 that try to get to grips with Akita's gigantic discography: 'Like, what is he thinking when he's doing this?!'[11] Interviews with the man himself have often served to muddy the waters further. In Brett Woodward's *Merzbook* (1999), Akita is quoted as saying his track and album titles are 'not chosen to convey any meanings. They are merely selected to mean nothing.'[12] And yet, when this committed vegan dedicates his tracks to an endangered species and utilizes manipulated samples of the animal in question, the results are as loaded as 'Wildlife' by Wings or Linda McCartney's 'Cow' (a co-write with Carla Lane). Merzbow's methodologies have also been a slippery business. After a period of abandoning analogue techniques in favour of a supposed allegiance to digital purity, handmade or modified stringed instruments crept back into Merzbow's equipment lists, along with synths and effects pedals, used in combination with computers.

Merzbow's style is famous for its excess, sheer extremity and unapologetic harshness, but the dins he makes are more nuanced than first meets the ear. His (anti-)music makes deft use of space, flux, flow, movement and detail. These are qualities that few of his noisy imitators have managed to master. Much like narcotics, Merzbow's music affects different people in different ways and, even in small doses, can have a different impact on the individual each time they experience it. It can induce alarm or elation. Sometimes it feels overwhelmingly suffocating; at other times it can be meditative or cathartic. It is certainly not monolithic, and the idea that Merzbow releases all sound the same is mistaken, unfair and ill-informed.

Sonic Youth, as you'd expect, sang the praises of Merzbow and would go on to collaborate with him. Back when they were still a couple, Thurston Moore and Kim Gordon owned an Australian Shepherd dog which they named Merzbow. Moore came up with the idea of recording the barks of Merzbow the dog and sending them off to Masami Akita for a Merzbow-meets-Merzbow collaboration. 'I think it might be good as a seven-inch,' Moore enthused, although as far as I know the project never came to fruition.[13]

The New Weird

Another thing that Sonic Youth did around this time was to help nurture the multi-genre movement named 'New Weird America', a term coined by writer David Keenan for the cover feature of the August 2003 edition of *The Wire*. This was an umbrella term for various freak folk, psychedelic rock and free rock acts who, although spanning a disparate range of styles, did seem to share a certain abnormal, anti-mainstream and independent spirit. A number of these acts ended up releasing material on Ecstatic Peace!, the label overseen by Thurston Moore. None of them were coerced into recording with a slick production team as might have been the case had they acquired major-label funding, and their output would not exactly approach platinum status. Even so, Moore's label did a fine job of taking 'dissolute artists' from New Weird America, as Joseph Stannard put it, and encouraging them to 'tighten up their game to a point just short of conventionality'.[14]

Once known (albeit not widely) for the shambolic and clanking nature of their extemporary rock racket, Magik Markers tidied themselves up a little for 2007's *Boss*. Produced by Sonic Youth's Lee Ranaldo (who also contributed guitar and glockenspiel parts), its tracks were more structured and cleaner than Magik Markers' earlier releases without watering down the band's innate badass-ness. Most unexpected of all, *Boss* included Magik Markers' first attempt at a fragile piano ballad. (If evidence were needed of their aforementioned badass-ness, by the way, it's worth noting that axe heroes including both Thurston Moore and J Mascis have cited Magik Markers' Elisa Ambrogio as one of their favourite guitarists on account of her thrillingly primal and non-traditional approach to playing.[15]) A similar evolution occurred when Ecstatic Peace! released albums by the hazed-out psych duo MV & EE and Brooklyn's Religious Knives. It became increasingly common for the former to be compared to Neil Young (with or without Crazy Horse, depend-ing on the nature of the release and the extent of collaborating musicians). Having earned a reputation as droney krautrock fans, Religious Knives introduced a lot more melody and traditional song structure for 2008's *The Door*.

Sonic Youth continued to offer support slots to bands they considered to be interesting and exciting. Liars were one of the few genuinely progressive acts to come out of the 2000s New York rock scene. Any suspicions they might have been tempted to plough the same furrow as their contemporaries were put firmly to bed by the release of the band's second album in 2004. It was a playfully uncompromising concept album about witchcraft titled *They Were Wrong So We Drowned*. Revelling in repetitive, clanky rhythms and seemingly random washes of electronic, amplified and acoustic noise, it felt like the new millennium's answer to PiL's *Metal Box*. Angus Andrew's vocal contributions were less concerned with harmony or melody than chanting, literally like a person possessed, about bones, brooms, man's jealousy of horses and 'Blood! Blood! Blood! Blood!' Greater still was 2006's *Drum's Not Dead*, its sound centred around the percussive pummelling of, you guessed it, two drumkits. If *They Were Wrong So We Drowned* was their *Metal Box*, this was Liars' *The Flowers of Romance*. They've barely taken a misstep since.

Liars were at the superior (and less commercially triumphant) end of the NYC scene that had also birthed LCD Soundsystem, Yeah Yeah Yeahs and The Strokes. Those bands' careers were given a boost by the hyperbolic coverage they received in the pages of the *NME*. Conor McNicholas was editor of the *NME* from 2003 until 2009, when he left for a short-lived stint at *Top Gear* magazine. Proud of himself for creating 'a scene out of thin air', McNicholas had instigated a policy of reserving the pages of his weekly music paper for the exclusive appearance of musicians with 'good hair and good shoes'. The quality of a band's music was essentially immaterial. What mattered to McNicholas was appearance. 'I can't get excited about a band that doesn't look good', he has explained, citing Franz Ferdinand as a perfect example of a well-dressed band.[16] These are the kind of words that would make Steve Albini want to pick up a vintage spring-reverb unit and throw it straight through the window of the offending publication's offices. 'The New Rock Revolution', as the *NME* called it, bridged the gap between Britpop and the dreaded 'landfill indie' scene, the latter term coined by *Word* magazine writer Andrew Harrison to describe the plethora of unremarkable guitar bands that blossomed briefly in the later noughties. This feeble attempt to revive the rock genre with a handful of bands that had impressive footwear (and hence often came from privileged backgrounds – see The Strokes, The Libertines et al.) resulted in the promotion and rapid ascent of some of the weediest guitar-based acts to trouble the airwaves since the punk era, give or take the flimsier end of Britpop.

You can read further about the activities of these *NME*-endorsed bands, if you must, in Lizzy Goodman's *Meet Me in the Bathroom: Rebirth and Rock and Roll in New York City, 2001–2011*. In that same city, and a world away from The Strokes' social circle, a local antidote was provided in the form of No Fun Fest, organized by the Venezuela-born noise musician and computer games developer Carlos Giffoni. During its six-year run from 2003 to 2009, the annual festival's line-ups resembled a veritable who's who of U.S. noise musicians plus a few lucky foreign interlopers like Norway's Jazkamer and the Scottish, Brighton-based Dylan Nyoukis from Prick Decay and Blood Stereo. This included the scene's 'Most Wanted (Wolf Eyes, Hair Police, Double Leopards), Most Wasted (Nautical Almanac, Magik Markers) and Most Hated (To Live and Shave in LA, Prurient)', as Tony Herrington put it in *The Wire* when reviewing a DVD that chronicled the first two years of the festival. There were appearances from 'respected elders and progenitors' alike, including members of Sonic Youth performing in various impromptu side projects and, come the festival's final edition, a set from full-band Sonic Youth proper. Herrington's review ended with this ominous line: 'Conceived as a celebration of Noise, the No Fun fest might just turn out to be its death knell, and *Fun From None* a document of the wake.'[17] Although Herrington's diagnosis turned out to be a little premature, it certainly had prescience.

Curated by Thurston Moore, All Tomorrow's Parties' Nightmare Before Christmas event of 2006 brought artists as uncompromisingly heavy as Ashtray Navigations, Nurse with Wound, The Dead C, Hair Police, Wolf Eyes and Prurient to the carpeted bingo halls of Butlins in Minehead, Somerset, billing them alongside names more recognizable to indie rock fans: Sonic Youth, Iggy & the Stooges, Gang of Four, Flipper, Melvins, Dinosaur Jr. It's fair to say that any punter who didn't leave that weekend with ringing ears had spent far too much time on the arcade slots or snoozing in their chalet. One of the most face-melting sets came from anti-music veterans The New Blockaders, who turned up to show the younger kids of noise how it was done, standing virtually motionless behind tables laden with heaps of wired-up equipment and all wearing intimidating balaclavas. The fifty-minute single-track set was recorded and released as *Das Zerstoren, Zum Gebaren*, but you'll have to turn the volume up an awful long way on the stereo before what was captured on that CD even begins to resemble how it felt to be witnessing it on the day. Not long into The New Blockaders' performance, my own brother, the internationally respected historian of modern civil liberties Dr Chris Moores, wandered off to investigate the festival's other stages. When he returned prior to the climax, Chris observed that The New Blockaders' racket sounded exactly the same as when he had departed and enquired whether it had been like that all the way through. That philistine doesn't understand the nuances.

As well as providing adventurous listeners with respite from The New Rock Revolution, the 2000s noise scene's international reach was aided by its coinciding with that brief moment when the rise of the Internet encouraged listeners to discover and share with one another all sorts of weird and wonderful music that had previously been inaccessible to them, and which fans would then purchase directly from artists' or independent labels' webshops because there were no copies stocked in the local HMV or equivalent chain. This was before technology like Sonos encouraged people to dispose of physical record, tape, CD and CD-R collections altogether in favour of streaming algorithmic playlists at the prod of an iPhone. In the 2000s most computers still had inbuilt CD drives. The scrapping of iTunes by Apple in 2019 has discouraged people from even purchasing and collecting MP3 files, persuading the public instead to sign up to the subscription streaming service Apple Music. It appears increasingly common that the only people willing to continue with the antiquated habit of directly paying for music are vinyl fetishists and those who feel a moral obligation to support musicians financially. As a response, the cult Somerset stoner rock trio Henry Blacker have offered the following maxim: 'If you've listened to something three times or more on YouTube or Spotify or what-the-fuck-ever, you should buy it. No excuses. Go to the label or the band or a shop. And buy it. No excuses. Support the thing you dig.'[18]

Henry Blacker's commandment is unlikely to catch on beyond the demographic who already exercise such ethical consumer choices.

Noise Not Music? Music Not Noise!

One particular noise group who blossomed during the period under discussion were Wolf Eyes. The project began in Detroit, Michigan, in 1996, originally as a solo outfit of high-school dropout and skateboarding enthusiast Nate Young. Aaron Dilloway joined the fold in 1998, dividing his time between playing in Universal Indians with John Olson. Olson, in turn, was absorbed into the Wolf Eyes line-up in the year 2000 when Universal Indians ceased operations. He had impressed Young and Dilloway after being invited to accompany them onstage and choosing as his instrument a 15-foot slab of sheet metal. Olson took to this with such dedication that he ended up cutting himself in several places and had to visit the hospital afterwards.[19] The miseries of an incessant touring regime and his move to Nepal caused Dilloway to quit Wolf Eyes in 2005. His replacement was Mike Connelly of the like-minded noise band Hair Police from Lexington, Kentucky. In 2013 Connelly was substituted for Crazy Jim Baljo. At the time of writing, Wolf Eyes is operating as a duo comprising Olson and Young.

The members of Wolf Eyes have been known to tell fibs about their past and exaggerate certain details, and they have not always been the most accommodating of interview subjects. When John Doran turned up, hoping to interview the band, at Wolf Eyes' chalet during an All Tomorrow's Parties festival he found them all 'sitting in a row wearing Manowar T-shirts, watching a Manowar DVD, refusing to talk about anything other than Manowar'.[20]

Wolf Eyes were fans of metal (Manowar especially) and punk rock, but they were also fans of The Velvet Underground, The Stooges, the mayhem of Captain Beefheart's *Trout Mask Replica* and the disorientating production techniques employed by King

Tubby. However, a more accurate impression of their music can be provided by noting their admiration for the bloodcurdling soundtrack to Tobe Hooper's masterpiece of horror cinema *The Texas Chain Saw Massacre*. Originally released in 1974, the film is a (cannibalistic) feast for the senses thanks to its unforgettable visuals and deeply unpleasant set pieces. Like all the greatest horror movies, the feeling of inescapable dread that it imparts to its viewers is given immeasurable amplification by its powerful score. Far from fashioning a typical or traditional film soundtrack, Hooper and his musical aide Wayne Bell were keen to blend the boundaries between what might be thought of as conventional 'music' and that which would be considered mere 'sound'; 'That wonderful grey mushy area,' as Bell called it. Normal instruments were used, although these would often be manipulated, treated, mistreated or warped in unusual ways, alongside found instruments like the kind of rudimentary musical toys that small children are given to play with at school. Inanimate objects were battered too. In addition, the vicious whirring blades of Leatherface's chainsaw itself cut through the soundtrack at various points, causing further upset and alarm to the audience.[21]

It could be said that Wolf Eyes aimed to instil comparably discomforting feelings in their listeners, using similar techniques to Hooper and Bell, as they set out to create wilfully unpleasant music that might have been excruciating for them to play let alone to experience as an innocent punter. As it had with The Stooges several decades earlier, the destitute nature of Detroit fed into Wolf Eyes' music. In 2013 Detroit became the largest U.S. city to file for bankruptcy, and although it recovered from this status at the end of the following year, it remains 'a fucked-up place', as Baljo put it in 2017. 'You can walk a block from our studio and see a war zone, decay and mother nature taking over.'[22]

Unlikely as the union was, Wolf Eyes spent a couple of years signed to the Sub Pop label, which, since abandoning its grunge focus several years prior, had pivoted to releasing music by polite, sensitive and accessible alt-country and indie rock artists like Iron & Wine, The Shins and The Postal Service. Nestled among this cardigan-clad roster were the Wolf Eyes albums *Burned Mind* (2004; featuring the classics 'Stabbed in the Face', 'Urine Burn' and 'Black Vomit') and its official follow-up *Human Animal* (2006; its final track, which was also used as the climax to many live sets, was a cover version of a track by the punk band No Fucker that doubled as Wolf Eyes' statement of intent: 'Noise Not Music'). Between those two albums, there were at least forty lower-key releases for aficionados to attempt to keep track of. They were often recorded at home or on the road, and Young views the more limited cassette, CD-R and vinyl releases as diary-style objects. These documented the 'research and development' stages that led up to the 'proper' albums. Wolf Eyes' fecundity can also be attributed to sheer necessity. Early on especially, the band found they needed to flog handmade merchandise to make enough money to be able to afford to eat something and move on to the next low-paid gig.[23]

In an earlier chapter, Steve Albini compared punk rock to a brilliant flash that was over quickly but cast long shadows. The same could be said of the 2000s noise scene. Carlos Giffoni retired his No Fun Fest after six years. His pronouncement that 'The noise scene is dead, long live the noise scene!' suggests some semblance of continuity.[24] Truth be told, Giffoni's own solo material has embraced the plusher and more twinkling aesthetics of the acid house scene. As long as you're not easily distracted by what sounds like a serial nuisance caller whispering creepily into your ear, you could have a jolly good dance to some of the later Prurient LPs. Ex-Yellow Swans member Pete Swanson forged his own skewed take on beat-driven techno, while his former partner-in-noise Gabriel Saloman went on to compose ambient scores for contemporary dance pieces. At one time a member of both Wolf Eyes and Hair Police, Mike Connelly formed Clay Rendering with his wife Tara; its gothy darkwave sound was not a million miles away from the synth-backed angst of Nine Inch Nails. As Cut Hands, onetime provocateur William Bennett has foregrounded his polyrhythmic African influences and – while accusations of cultural appropriation bordering on outright racism have continued to dog him – he has dialled down on much of the offensive and confrontational behaviour that defined the output of his former project, Whitehouse, which was active from 1980 to 2008. Recalling earlier times, Bennett has lamented that 'Philip [Best] and I had an incredibly belligerent and arrogant attitude, which looking back makes me think we were a couple of assholes.'[25] Just when you think you've found an artist who will stick to vehemently unprogressive 'harsh wall noise' as performed with a bin-bag over his head, it transpires that Vomir has unmasked, picked up an acoustic guitar and begun dabbling in 'ultra-shit folk'.

For their own part, Wolf Eyes' recent material has become mellower and more spidery, with a greater emphasis on composition, less reliance on broad textures, and fewer instances of the band members popping drugs and making up sets on the spot. Not wanting ever to end up stuck in a rut, Olson decided to wind down his American Tapes label and in 2013 he declared that noise music was finished.[26] Despite this renunciation of noise, Wolf Eyes persisted. In doing so, the band has moved on, considerably, from Young's original intentions of 'making sounds that were painful – making unlistenable and irritating music'.[27] Their style may be slightly calmer and more considered these days, yet it is no less exciting to experience nor any less boundary-pushing in its objectives. The band call their newer trajectory 'Trip Metal', but they're more like the world's spookiest and scuzziest beatnik jazz combo.

Despite their fondness for the manipulation of electronic equipment, Wolf Eyes also pride themselves in having remained, essentially, rock-based in their agenda, unlike certain other graduates of the No Fun Fest. Wolf Eyes see these rival artists as having 'fizzled out' into introspective synth-based material, its intentions so meditative and internally (rather than externally or socially) focused that it becomes the diametric opposite of what punk rock was supposed to symbolize, at least in Olson's view anyway. In those who have shifted from the rotten basements where noise music once thrived to more sanitized dancefloor situations, Olson also suspects that appropriation, insincerity and a lack of demonstrable understanding is at play: 'A lot of these cats digging into the techno trend don't seem to be too-well versed in the history of dance music and that culture. So what they're coming out with is on the wrong side of naive and amateur. It seems like a lame attempt to get more people to gigs.'[28]

Whether they have remained grounded in rock (however convincing that claim may be) or moved on to investigating the possibilities of techno (be it in a successful or amateurish fashion), the abandonment of noise by most of the 2000s scene's stars (if we can call them that) is reminiscent of those musicians who were animated by punk rock's promises before stretching and sprawling out into less idiomatic and freer post-punk realms. Only this time, the progression has gone from the heavier end to the lighter end of the sonic spectrum rather than vice versa. This was an inevitability, really. After all, anybody open-minded enough to play noise music in the first place would never be so narrow-minded as to stick to it.

17
POST-ROCK AND POST-METAL

Favourites of Stuart 'Mogwai' Braithwaite and Lou 'Metal Machine Music' Reed:
Bardo Pond are heavier than they look.

I really believe in my heart that we're one of the punkest bands
in the world.[1]

STUART BRAITHWAITE (MOGWAI)

If you didn't want to listen to anything quite as extreme as outright noise music while Limp Bizkit and Oasis were arguing over who should be positioned where on the Reading and Leeds festival bill, there were other assortments of heaviness to be found in the fields of post-rock and post-metal. Musicians in both these varieties of 'post', like various electric wizards in previous years, were concerned with texture over text. Their song structures often looked more like ambient or classical works instead of following stiffer and more conventional formulas. Granted, they may not have been heavy all of the time. Post-rock and post-metal bands had plenty of quieter, gentler and more tranquil songs (and sections within songs). When the time came for the heaviness to explode out of the amplifiers, they did it with such a force it could feel like the rapture had finally arrived.

In 1999 the Glaswegian band Mogwai began selling a new line of T-shirts bearing the slogan 'Blur: are shite'. The colon positioned after the affronted group's name was intended to make the statement read like a dictionary definition. 'It's factual,' asserted Mogwai guitarist Stuart Braithwaite at the time, 'and if there's any legal problems about it I'll go to court as someone who has studied music so I can prove they are shite.'[2] In Blur's defence, they had just released their most experimental album. Already on 1997's self-titled album, the London-based Britpoppers had shifted away from the pseudo-Kinksian lyrical caricatures and knees-up faux-Cockneyisms of their earlier hits in favour of contriving a fuzzier and more ambiguous sound inspired by American indie rock. Its follow-up, *13*, included moments of gospel, cacophonous effects-laden alt-rock, nods to the jazz legend Sun Ra, shoddy punk rock, attempts at lo-fi, lethargic space rock, and miniature tracks slotted between the more substantial compositions.

Mogwai, who only rarely include singing on their own tunes, were particularly offended by *13*'s lyrical content, a significant proportion of which focused on Blur singer Damon Albarn's split from Justine Frischmann of Elastica. 'Using the break-up with your girlfriend as a marketing tool is one of the most disgusting things I've heard in my life,' Braithwaite complained.[3] It's possible that Blur were exploiting public fascination with Albarn and Frischmann's relationship as a means to almost trick their fans into listening to music that was more challenging than they were accustomed to.

Seeing as Albarn's band were one of the biggest-selling linchpins of the entire Britpop scene, Mogwai were already against everything that Blur represented. Mogwai had sworn that they would never perform on the defining British television show of the era *TFI Friday*, whose host Chris Evans was deemed to be 'a completely obnoxious prick'. Nor did the Scottish provocateurs have the time of day for any of the associated 'Britcool' pop culture icons such as the Young British Artists and their apparent figurehead Damien Hirst, famed for his carcasses-in-formaldehyde artworks and widely reported party trick of publicly inserting a chicken bone into the end of his penis. To Braithwaite, it all looked like a 'really cosy, west-London, jokey, cocaine-fuelled social circle. To be honest,' he said, 'I just found it really gross.'[4]

It's little wonder that Mogwai didn't feel like part of the club. They were, geographically and culturally speaking, a very long distance removed from the chumminess of the Groucho Club and the market stalls of Camden Town, where people would purchase Union Jack stickers to attach to their *Quadrophenia*-inspired mopeds. Mogwai's musical touchstones included not The Who or Small Faces but more left-of-field UK acts like My Bloody Valentine and The Cure, and fellow Scottish melodic din-makers The Jesus &

Mary Chain. What's more, Mogwai delved far deeper than the likes of Blur into the experimentation of the American underground, soaking up the work of Louisville's Slint and Rodan, two acts who graduated from playing post-hardcore to operating in a more considered and spacious vein. Slowcore groups like Codeine and Low informed Mogwai's quieter moments, while art rock veterans Sonic Youth further nourished Mogwai's love of outrageous guitar noise. 'The Diamond Sea' is the twenty-minute track that concludes Sonic Youth's *Washing Machine* album, which was released in 1995, the same year Mogwai formed. Thurston Moore's brief verses aside, most of the track's running time consists of free-form, feedback-filled instrumental guitar noise, delicate in certain places, severe and engulfing at others, with echoes of Crazy Horse, Glenn Branca and Lou Reed's *Metal Machine Music*. Braithwaite used to hang out at the home of his bandmate Dominic Aitchison, whose father owned a record player that could play vinyl in reverse as well as forwards. There the pair would listen to 'The Diamond Sea' repeatedly, first forwards and then backwards, as if Sonic Youth's track wasn't abstract enough on the first rotation.[5]

Mogwai's repertoire has had its fair share of soft and gentle songs, including the cosy winteriness of 'Burn Girl Prom Queen', featuring accompaniment from the Cowdenbeath Brass Band. Other tracks, such as 'New Paths to Helicon Pt 1' and 'Like Herod' flip between delicate note-picking and massive explosions of loud distortion. Many of the tracks on Mogwai's second LP, *Come On Die Young* (1999), remained deliberately hushed because the band were apprehensive of being caricatured as 'the Status Quo of quiet-loud'.[6] Instead Mogwai built up the suspense like crazy by cleverly sequencing the album so that the truly heavy numbers appeared only towards the end of the tracklist. This rewarded – and woke up with a jolt – any listeners who had stuck around for that long, through all the preceding autumnal moodiness, with the soul-cleansing distortion of 'Ex-Cowboy' and the apocalyptic penultimate number,

'Christmas Steps'. In concert, however, Mogwai have remained a consistent threat to the auditory nerves of those foolish enough to abstain from earplugs. Aidan Moffat, the singer of Arab Strap who contributed vocals to Mogwai's 'R U Still in 2 It' from their 1997 debut album *Young Team*, remembers he and his friends keeping a close eye on Braithwaite whenever they saw him perform. 'You can't tell when you watch Mogwai now because Stuart's a lot more subtle and they rehearse more but back then he had to tell the band when the loud bits were coming, so we would watch his foot, down the front, and when his foot started tapping…' That was the signal to take a big sniff of poppers to chemically enhance the already blissful crescendos.[7]

Despite their calmer and more introspective or melancholic passages, it was Mogwai's intention to ROCK right from the moment of their inception. As evidence, Braithwaite cites the explosion of an amplifier at the band's first ever rehearsal. 'The thing about noise is it confuses your brain,' he has said, 'so if tunes are hidden in it, that makes them more rewarding. There are a lot of bands tighter or more technically proficient than us that don't get the same kind of reaction.'[8] It should come as no surprise that Mogwai are disciples of Black Sabbath. Early on, Mogwai recorded a (slightly slapdash) cover of 'Sweet Leaf' from *Master of Reality*. The Glaswegian recording studio established by Mogwai in partnership with producer Tony Doogan in 2005 was given the revealing name Castle of Doom. Having said that, Mogwai identify themselves as being fans of Heavy, rather than being heavy metal fans. Metalheads, once claimed Braithwaite, 'will like Slayer, which is fair enough, but then they'll like Queensrÿche as well: there's no quality control.' He expressed suspicion, too, of 'people who dress heavy but don't sound heavy.'[9]

Philadelphia's Bardo Pond have an incredibly heavy sound yet they dress as casually as they come. Their long career has therefore been consistently ignored by the areas of the press that purport to specialize in covering heavy music but fail to do this when there aren't enough leather jackets and spiky jewellery on display. Bardo Pond are also fronted by a woman, Isobel Sollenberger, so there may well be an element of sexism – unconscious or otherwise – accountable for the neglect, an extra hurdle to success compounded by the fact that the band's music is arguably too heavy for fans of weird stuff and too weird for fans of heavy stuff. Perhaps it isn't quite right to say that Bardo Pond are 'fronted' by Sollenberger. Yes, she stands at the front and centre of the stage when they perform. In terms of the sonics, though, and the way that Bardo Pond records are mixed, Sollenberger's vocals and occasional flute work are part of the holistic and egalitarian whole. Its other constituent elements are Clint Takeda's rumbling basslines, the reliable backbeat of Jason Kourkounis and the thick and colourful smog of noise emanating from the guitars of brothers John and Michael Gibbons. Thanks to the crowded pedal boards at their feet, the Gibbons manipulate the sound of their instruments with a glorious gallimaufry of filter, delay, reverb and swampy distortion. Some Bardo Pond numbers contain additional layers of electronic tinkerings and supplementary organ parts, though these are mostly suffocated, it has to be said, by the band's propensity for amplifier worship. The resultant cacophony is heavy but not aggressive. There is an intangible quality to their heaviness, and the sprawling nature of many of their songs mean that, as Lucy O'Brien has put it, 'Tunes disappear down rabbit holes of distortion and delay, while Sollenberger floats like Nico over the drones.'[10] This misty shapelessness to Bardo Pond's sound has contributed to their remaining a cult concern. Other critics haven't always known how to handle the ambiguous and transcendental style in which Bardo Pond specialize. Despite having occasionally written about them in more positive terms, *Pitchfork* has also condemned the band's 'tiresome excess'.[11] Metal publications, meanwhile, on account of Bardo Pond's lack of confrontational aggression, usually opt to ignore them completely.

'Clearly, it's an acquired taste,' reasons Cory Rayborn, whose Three Lobed Recordings has been responsible for releasing a thick wedge of Bardo Pond's discography.

> Your average Top-40-orientated person is not ready to sit down for some heavy, effects-driven, 10-minute droney thing. You have a limited audience to begin with. But why it's never broken past that limited audience is kinda beyond me. Because how someone like Sigur Rós, Explosions in the Sky or Godspeed You! Black Emperor can get to their level of popularity . . . Those aren't necessarily things that are super similar, sonically, to Bardo but they've a lot more in common than not. How those can be legitimately popular crossover-type things [but not Bardo Pond], I don't know. It's weird.[12]

While Bardo Pond are great to listen to at home, in the live setting their enormous sound has the potential to induce out-of-body experiences, whether mind-altering substances are part of the equation or not. Andy Duvall of the psych bands Zen Guerrilla and Carlton Melton thinks he first heard Bardo Pond in the year 1991.

> I thought they sounded very much the way Philadelphia felt like in the summertime: hot, thick, sticky, sweaty, dizzy, sloppy, *heavy*. I remember just how *huge* they sounded compared to anything else going on at that time. I also remember feeling as though I might have fallen over from their sonic onslaught, had I not been leaning against the warehouse wall.[13]

Being literally blown to the floor by a band's sonic onslaught would also have appealed to Stuart Braithwaite. Before forming Mogwai, he was drumming in a band called Eska. Given Mogwai's capacity to inflict sporadic blasts of chest-rattling guitar noise, it's likely this multi-instrumentalist shares the ambition of drummer-turned-guitarist J Mascis to make guitar music of such force it can physically impact its audience. Around the same time that Braithwaite and Aitchison were spinning 'The Diamond Sea' in both backwards and forwards rotations, they heard Bardo Pond on John Peel's radio show, an encounter Braithwaite described as a life-changing experience. 'There's something really powerful and simultaneously fragile to it,' he said of Bardo Pond's music. 'I definitely think of Mogwai as a psychedelic rock band. Much more than a bloody post-rock band anyway!'[14]

Mogwai had a similar treatment to Bardo Pond regarding the publications that chose to ignore them in spite of the group's palpable heaviness. Mogwai quickly gained coverage in *Melody Maker* and the *NME*, not least owing to their habit of gleefully criticizing other artists promoted in the same papers' pages, such as Somerset rockers Reef and a certain mod revival group nicknamed by Braithwaite as 'Abortion Colour Scene'. Interviews promoting their debut *Young Team* saw Mogwai complaining that they were being overlooked by *Kerrang!* even though, in the band's own humble opinion, they rocked harder than '90 percent' of the acts covered by the weekly metal magazine.[15]

Perhaps *Kerrang!*'s editors were put off by the 'post-rock' label, which Mogwai have never been able to shake. When Simon Reynolds coined the term in 1994, he had in his mind artists like Bark Psychosis, Seefeel and Disco Inferno, whose work drew on arty progenitors such as Brian Eno, The Velvet Underground and Sonic Youth. Reynolds defined post-rock as music that used 'rock instrumentation for non-rock purposes, using guitars as facilitators of timbres and textures rather than riffs and powerchords'. Some of these acts, he noted, were keen to cross-breed the guitar-bass-drums set-up of the traditional rock band with computer technology.[16]

Mogwai's mission to rock hard placed them somewhat at odds with this definition. They revived the idea of using rock instrumentation with the intention to rock, albeit not in the traditional or conventional way. Too many 'art rock' bands, said Braithwaite, had forgotten about the necessity to actually rock. 'They're too busy "arting"', he complained.

> We're a rock'n'roll band that avoids clichés. We don't have choruses. If we write a good tune and we think it's going to sound good being played for five minutes, we're not going to play it for two minutes just because [Radio 1 DJ] Steve Lamacq would prefer it that way. Art forms have got to progress.[17]

Progression was a key principle for Braithwaite, who deemed the very idea of post-rock to be absurd because of its implication that rock was dead, that it was over, that its lineage had finally drawn to a close, an argument that Braithwaite would emphatically contest. 'We're as heavy as fuck!' Braithwaite declared when *Kerrang!* did get around to interviewing Mogwai. 'I can do plenty of Yngwie J Malmsteen riffs if you want, but I'd rather not because it's shite. Anyway, my room is painted black and covered with upside down crucifixes.'[18]

More elusive than the outspoken Mogwai were Godspeed You! Black Emperor, who tended to shy away from interviews because they preferred to let their music, liner notes, soundbite samples and other, sometimes cryptic, transmissions do the talking. They emerged from Montreal, then a cheap place to rent accommodation and a city with plenty of disused industrial spaces where parties and gigs could be hosted in ease, nurturing a vibrant underground arts scene. In terms of creative and economic independence, these Canadians took inspiration from hardcore progressives like Minutemen and Black Flag. Godspeed admired those bands' work ethic and contentedness to spend hours travelling ludicrous distances in a cramped transit van to perform in front of small-but-loyal audiences. Listening to their output, you could be forgiven for thinking Godspeed had been raised on Wagner. Released in 1997, their debut album *F# A#* ∞ set the tone for all that would follow. At this point the band's line-up had ten members (trimmed down from an earlier total of fifteen): two drummers, three guitarists, two bassists, a French horn player, a cellist and a violinist, and no singer. Guest musicians and other instruments also appeared on the recording. A rare moment of group singing appears quietly on the second track, but the album's most notable voices are the sampled ones that the band used alongside field recordings to embellish their atmospheres. Each long track consisted of several movements, the slow and considered music gradually building up to moments of blistering crescendo. With its nods to the work of Ennio Morricone, Godspeed's version of post-rock resembled the soundtrack to an epic dystopian thriller. In turn, this sound would go on to influence cinema. Godspeed's music was exactly what Danny Boyle had in mind when he was working on the zombie thriller *28 Days Later* (2002). An extract of the Godspeed song 'East Hastings' can be heard in Boyle's film but most of its score was composed by John Murphy, who aped the Canadians' musical ideas so closely they probably should have sued. The crime writer Ian Rankin is another post-rock fan. He has been known to name his detective novels after songs by Radiohead, Joy Division and others. One suspects he would like to bestow the same honour on one of his favourite Godspeed or Mogwai tracks, the main problem being the former tend to plump for impenetrably portentous titles that would look rather odd on the shelves of Waterstones (*Strung Like Lights at Thee Printemps Erable* by Ian Rankin, anyone?), while Mogwai are prone to assign their songs flippantly irrelevant and often silly names like 'Batcat' and 'You're Lionel Ritchie'.

Given Godspeed You! Black Emperor's populous line-up, contemporaneous projects abounded. These were often recorded in the same studio as one another, Montreal's Hotel2 Tango, and released by the associate indie label Constellation Records. Such acts included A Silver Mount Zion (a sparser take on the Godspeed style and one that permitted prominent singing, however warbling it may be), Do Make Say Think (lusher and more elegant than Godspeed, with jazzy tendencies akin to Chicago's Tortoise) and Fly Pan Am (prone to greater hyperactivity than Godspeed and with a more schizophrenic approach to genre cross-pollination, the organized chaos of their dense sound exemplifies the messier and sprightlier end of post-rock).

Such distractions, coupled with the collective's discomfort with their own success, would eventually lead to a hiatus. By the year 2000, Godspeed found that they had graduated to larger venues such as The Garage in Glasgow (capacity: seven hundred). In a rare interview conducted at that time, guitarist Efrim Menuck likened the Godspeed live experience to a group of miserably unwell monkeys imprisoned in a cage. Like Big Black's split in an earlier decade, Godspeed couldn't get their heads around the apparently alienating experience of having a few hundred people turn up to see them play before everybody simply left again, without saying anything, remaining as distant strangers. They were also wary of repeating themselves, loath to become a one-trick pony. The fear was well founded. After a three-album run culminating in 2002's *Yanqui U.X.O.*, Godspeed's unwieldy titles had become easy to parody while their music was beginning to feel less fresh than it once did, characterized as it always was by long droney passages, slowly cranking up the tension until that inevitable orgasmic crescendo. The following year they went on indefinite hiatus. In 2010 Godspeed would reassemble, showing a newfound willingness to tread the boards of theatres, festival stages and arenas in front of thousands of doting strangers, and returning to the winning formula for the purposes of composing their new material.

During Godspeed's absence, fans of the post-rock formula could enjoy the continuous presence of Texas's Explosions in the

Sky (arguably the true 'Status Quo of quiet-loud') alongside other acts on the rosters of labels like Kranky and Temporary Residence. Recently, post-rock-as-cliché has found its apogee in the form of the bow-tie-clad London outfit Public Service Broadcasting. They couple instrumental compositions with audio archive snippets to such unbearably twee effect that critic Luke Turner has fittingly described it as 'the musical equivalent of one of those dreadful Blitz-themed club nights where people who work in advertising get drunk while dressed in '40s garb before going home to clean up the gin sick with a Keep Calm & Carry On tea towel.'[19]

Post-metal

Stuart Braithwaite's view that the idea of post-rock is fundamentally absurd has not prevented music journalists from whacking the same prefix at the front of countless genre names in order to indicate some kind of emboldened progressive departure. Before post-rock there had been post-punk and post-hardcore. Soon after post-rock entered the lexicon, 'post-metal' was adopted to describe bands who were making similar leaps in a different field. While the post-metal canon is wide and diverse, the relevant acts eschewed the traditional formulas of metal songwriting, integrating ambient, psychedelic, avant-garde, neo-classical and drone elements into their gradually unwinding compositions. Drone metal forerunners Melvins and Earth had already pointed the way forward, along with industrial metal titans Godflesh.

Oakland's Neurosis had four albums under their belt before 'post-rock' was even coined, let alone 'post-metal', although it did take them a few goes until they really began to break new ground, their early material having been written fairly firmly along hardcore punk lines. However, Neurosis started extending their running times, using the extra space to investigate other textures and musical digressions and to experiment with ambience and sampling.

Instruments from outside the metal tradition were introduced too, including space rock synthesizers and even bagpipes. The vast library of samples they assembled included everything from screams or snippets of dialogue lifted from VHS tapes (often pitched downwards, played in reverse or manipulated in other ways) to recordings of vacuum cleaners.[20] Their fifth album in particular, 1996's *Through Silver in Blood*, is considered a defining moment in post-metal history. Wallowing in the darkness of their personal lives (at the time, guitarist and vocalist Scott Kelly had 'a serious meth habit' and no fixed abode[21]) and with a sadistic desire to make their audiences suffer too, when road-testing the songs prior to recording the band would say to themselves, 'Oh that part was brutal at sixteen times, let's do thirty-two instead,' and 'Oh, that was really hurting people. Let's double it.'[22] When Neurosis supported more popular metal bands, some audiences would respond by pelting projectiles, but this group of musicians was never going to pander to fashions.[23] Slowly and surely their music began to find a loyal audience, and when major labels started sniffing around the band couldn't bear it. 'The conversations we had with labels were disgusting,' recalled Neurosis's other guitarist and singer Steve Von Till. 'It was all these sports-team references or like fucking Pink Floyd, "Have a Cigar."'[24] Neurosis tested the waters by coming up with eccentric projects to pursue, 'like to make an art film and a book and a magazine, putting Neurosis at the core of some sort of fucked-up art movement'. Lo and behold, both parties heard alarm bells. 'They didn't know what the hell to do with that and we thought that they were cheesy, so it's probably good that we avoided that. We dodged a bullet,' concluded Von Till.[25] Instead they enjoyed a fruitful relationship with Relapse and also established their own DIY label, Neurot Recordings. With their independent spirit and desire to challenge listeners, it's little wonder they found an ally in Steve Albini, who has recorded several Neurosis albums, beginning with 1999's *Times of Grace*. For Albini, 'A key thing that separates them from the metal genre is their affect.

Metal is usually emotionally dry, but Neurosis at full tilt is like being hit by a gale drenching you in the blood of your enemies.'[26]

Neurot Recordings also hosted likeminded artists. It sat among other key post-metal labels like Relapse and Hydra Head, the latter established by Aaron Turner, who has played in Isis and a variety of other projects. Isis's artistic peak would be their 2002 masterpiece *Oceanic*, after which their direction went a little Tool-wards before their split in 2010. *Oceanic*'s chugging, downtuned riffs are complemented by subtle electronics, ghostlier passages of melodic ambience and vocal contributions courtesy of Maria Christopher of the Massachusetts indie band 27. Across the course of its hour-long duration, the album's lyrics weave a tragic tale of obsession, incest and suicide. Listeners might need the lyric book to keep track of the plot, mind, as Turner's growls are low enough in the mix to avoid distracting attention from the powerful music.

Hydra Head's roster encompassed those with proggier tendencies (Cave In, Kayo Dot), the sludgy noise rock duo Big Business, violently misanthropic avant-rockers Oxbow, underground metalcore heroes Botch, Justin Broadrick's shoegazey post-Godflesh project Jesu and Chicago's Pelican. The latter outfit released their entirely instrumental debut LP *Australasia* in 2003. Apart from its penultimate track, which offered a little breathing space with the bonus appearance of a singing saw, the record was virtually unrelenting. Each ten-minute track clobbering listeners around the ears with riff after riff after merciless riff; it was as if Mogwai had been completely stripped of their un-rocking quieter passages. Having had this gauntlet thrown down, and fresh from touring alongside Isis, Mogwai then decided to capture a sound that was more aggressive, abrasive and faithful to their live shows after two relatively subdued and prettier albums, *Rock Action* and *Happy Songs for Happy People*. Their 2006 *Mr Beast* featured monstrous numbers like 'Glasgow Mega-Snake' and 'We're No Here' on which the heaviness was kept to its highest setting for the entire duration of each track.

As with the artists labelled 'post-rock', many of their metal counterparts took similar exception to the genre they'd been assigned. Aaron Turner preferred to think of his particular niche as 'thinking man's metal', which, unfortunate gender bias in its phrasing aside, is understandable. Much post-metal material is more suited to meditation, deep philosophizing or intense study than it is for the purposes of headbanging (a physical act that would have to be undertaken in a comically slow-motion fashion).

It just goes to show how important punk rock has been in terms of its attitudes and multi-interpretable ideologies that despite Pelican's music possessing the barest minimum of the sonic characteristics that are associated with that genre, guitarist Trevor de Brauw insists that his band identifies chiefly as punk. Youthful involvement in the punk scene helped shape every aspect of de Brauw's life, he says, and especially his philosophy regarding music, which he defines as 'honest, direct, ethical, and intimate'.[27] Neurosis's early material owed clearer stylistic debts to hardcore punk, and despite all the sludgy tempos, eerie keyboards, bagpipe parts and metal-guy beards that have been weaved in or sported over the years, they too would like to believe they have remained faithful to their original punk rock spirit. Regarding the post-rock bands under discussion, Mogwai's punk rock attitude was symbolized in the band's outsider status during the era of Britpop hegemony, and it found an outlet in their nonconformist material and withering contempt for the many lesser bands who were among their contemporaries. The allegiance was made more apparent by the opening track on *Come On Die Young*. It samples a television interview with Iggy Pop from 1977 in which the proto-punk ex-Stooges star discussed 'punk rock', a term he believed was used to disparage the value of the passionate music being made by rebellious iconoclasts like Sex Pistols. 'I don't know Johnny Rotten,' Iggy drawls, 'but I'm sure he puts as much blood and sweat into what he does as Sigmund Freud did.'

Godspeed You! Black Emperor and their associates had similar feelings to Iggy Pop about, this time, the term 'post-rock'. To the artists involved, it felt derisive, reductive and imposed on them against their will. Constellation Records' 2001 compilation CD *Constellation Music until Now* included an essay clarifying what had been the label's mission from the outset: 'to enact a mode of cultural production that critiques the worst tendencies of the music industry'. In contrast to, say, the professed socialist activities of Rage Against the Machine, whose decision to sign to the Sony conglomerate was defended on the grounds of spreading the message as widely as possible, the back cover of Godspeed's *Yanqui U.X.O.* displayed a diagram charting the damning business links between arms manufacturers and major record labels (Sony being one of the listed culprits). 'So fuck post-rock,' Constellation's compilation essay continued, 'and the smooth untroubled consumption it enables.' Again, despite the apparent differences in musical style, Efrim Menuck insists a clear line can be drawn from the outbreak of punk rock to the more recent activities of Godspeed You! Black Emperor.[28]

A little late to the post-metal party was a certain proto-punk legend who, on what would turn out to be the final album of his long and admirably volatile career, enlisted the services of the biggest actual-metal band in the world to record a collaborative album so punk rock that some of its bewildered listeners were riled enough to send death threats to its makers.

It is a mistake to consider Lou Reed and Metallica's masterpiece *Lulu* (2011) in terms of any kind of logical continuation in the discography of either the planet's most successful metal group or the shades-sporting artist behind 1972's much-loved *Transformer*. Even when you consider Reed's history of upsetting his own fans with recordings like *Metal Machine Music* or the rock-operatic misery of *Berlin*, and even when you take into account Metallica's habit of confounding their own core audience with controversial actions such as releasing ballads, avoiding guitar solos for an entire album or cutting their hair short, *Lulu* stands out as a different beast altogether. Rather, it should be taken as a never-to-be-repeated, idiosyncratic slab of avant-garde conceptual art. If anything, think of *Lulu* as an ambitious and impressive post-metal opus. Most, if not all, of the required elements are all present and correct. There are the protracted songs based around repetitive, cyclical riffs. There is the emphasis on timbre and texture. There are passages of spoken word to help facilitate the record's perplexing narrative (this one inspired by the works of Hanover's Frank Wedekind, who lived from 1864 to 1918 and specialized in bourgeois-baiting theatre). The places where the collaborative unit are rocking out emphatically are tempered against more elegant moments that incorporate classical strings and ominous existential drones.

Before *Lulu* had been released, people were already calling it the worst album of all time. 'Even in that regard, it disappoints,' concluded one of its many negative reviews. *Pitchfork*'s summary of this 'exhaustingly tedious' project also mocked reports that Metallica had wept with pride during the recording process.[29] Listening back, you can hear why they were so moved. Reed unlocked something in the thrash-turned-arena-metal superstars. Chuck Klosterman may have used his own assessment as an excuse to go on a bizarre pro-capitalist rant about how the collapse of the record industry should not be celebrated because it results in bands like Metallica making the kind of music they want to make instead of 'good music' that is 'designed to generate revenue'.[30] But surely it is that attitude that results in the lowest-common-dominator, most easily marketable trash that fills music charts across the globe and prevents artists of Metallica's status from making any of the risky decisions that are required to actually come up with fresh and forward-thinking ideas. The creative freedom they regained from working under Reed's loose directions meant that Metallica suddenly sounded more spontaneous, lively, liberated and artistically fulfilled than they had since about 1986. As for Reed, he was widely chastised for hyping *Lulu* as 'the best thing ever done by anybody'. This is not the same thing as promising universal appeal, hardly something Reed would have either expected or craved.

As once argued in an essay by the art historian Quentin Bell, the difference between good art and bad art can be identified in the differences between sincere or artificial sentiment. 'The sentiment in a Van Gogh is in the highest degree personal,' wrote Bell, 'he is moved by a pure and uncalculating desire to make pictorial statements.' During his own lifetime the Dutch painter's work was 'almost universally condemned for its ugliness and its ineptitude'. Faced with hostility and indifference, Bell's 'good artist' strives onward nevertheless, battling against popular conceptions of beauty. In contrast, the 'bad artist' accepts these popular notions immediately (or perhaps after a brief struggle) and is then 'continually driven to a compromise, to an insincere bargain which results in falsity of sentiment, in bad art'. Lou Reed sits firmly in the former category, as somebody who never seemed too worried about offending everyone around him let alone all his listeners, while the art that Klosterman longs for Metallica to keep on churning out ad nauseam is clearly that of the 'bad artist'. As Bell says, 'These artists had completely accepted the opinion of their age as to what constituted a beautiful picture, and, having done so, addressed themselves to the beautiful with horrifying success.'[31]

The double album's later tracks are particularly rewarding, and it's telling that a number of one-star reviews quoted *Lulu*'s provocative opening lines and yet somehow failed to mention 'Junior Dad', the twenty-minute closing number that provides the album's most emotionally powerful moments. With orchestral backing, 'Junior Dad' boasts an alluring melody and sees Metallica perform with a sense of subtlety and nuance they have rarely displayed before. Given the feedback, they probably never will again. It's doubtful whether certain critics, on deadline, even made it that far into the album's ninety-minute running time before drawing their conclusions, let alone awarding *Lulu* the gratifying repeat listens it requires to unveil its gnarled beauty.

Again, it's an acquired taste. To paraphrase Cory Rayborn, *Lulu* is not something that your average Top 40-oriented listener is ready to sit down, enjoy and understand. Nor was it, it seems, something Lou Reed's fans were ready to comprehend or tolerate. It was certainly not welcomed by Metallica's more easily rattled disciples. Such folk hadn't been trained for this rumbling, grinding, semi-improvised, ninety-minute droney post-metal thing.

It must have felt a little galling for poor old Metallica when Scott Walker's 2014 collaboration with the drone-metal duo Sunn O))) was greeted with routine praise across much of the media. This is because that joint record, *Soused*, operated in a similarly 'difficult' and highbrow vein to *Lulu*. What's more, it was done in a way that, for me, felt haughtier and harder to love. By then, Reed had already departed this world. *Lulu* was both a remarkable and suitable parting gift from the old contrarian. Towards the end of his life, Reed had discovered the beauty of Bardo Pond. He and his wife Laurie Anderson had invited them to perform at the Vivid festival they jointly curated at Sydney Opera House in 2010. Almost exactly a year later, Reed had hooked up with Metallica and was busy recording the heaviest album of his career. It's entirely conceivable that the ethereal heaviness of Bardo Pond, their simultaneous body-shaking power and underlying fragility had rubbed off on Reed. While Michael Gibbons said he'd have been more interested in *Lulu* had Slayer been involved instead,[32] Bardo Pond paid tribute to Reed in 2014 by releasing a cover version of 'Ride into the Sun', a track dating back to Reed's time in The Velvet Underground. In doing so, Bardo Pond applied the rack to Reed's delicate little ditty, stretching it out to twenty minutes and transforming it into a cathartic sidelong post-rock-psych-gaze eulogy. Its lyrics about yearning to escape the ugliness of the city for a life in simpler and more scenic surroundings became a metaphor for Reed's departure from this mortal realm. The discordant noise breakdown in the middle of Bardo Pond's rendition of 'Ride into the Sun' perfectly captures the pain felt by those the dead leave behind.

18

SABBATH PHASE IV: PIGS PIGS PIGS PIGS PIGS PIGS PIGS AND THE MODERN HEAVY UNDERGROUND

Live at The Fulford Arms: Matt Baty and John-Michael Hedley
of Pigs Pigs Pigs Pigs Pigs Pigs Pigs, 2018.

We were like, 'Let's start a band called fuckin' Pigs. Actually, let's call it Pigs Pigs Pigs Pigs Pigs Pigs Pigs and it'll be really obnoxious on posters.'[1]

MATT BATY (PIGS PIGS PIGS PIGS PIGS PIGS PIGS)

The Fulford Arms, York, 29 November 2018. Pigs Pigs Pigs Pigs Pigs Pigs Pigs are in town as part of their 'King of Cowards' tour. The venue, if you don't happen to know it already, is a small and single-roomed pub. The maximum capacity is 150 people or thereabouts. The 'stage', if it can be called such a thing, is lower than the average step. Between the bar at one end of the room and the performance space at the other, the audience is packed like sardines in a tin. Perhaps that should be 'sardines in a sauna', given the stifling communal body heat at work and severe lack of ventilation. One audience member must be suffering from some kind of thermoregulatory disorder or else is wearing a particularly embarrassing T-shirt under the parka jacket that remains zipped up for the duration. The parka person aside, sweat starts to drip off everyone and everything inside the Fulford Arms as the five-man band rumble through their unceasingly hefty material. Look closely and you can even spot the sweat trickling from singer Matt Baty's eyelids. The omnipresent red lighting makes the circumstances seem all the more infernal. Baty says he can feel momentary relief coming from a slight waft of air that kisses the back of his neck every now and again. He couldn't work out what it was at first. Then he realized this intermittent breeze was emanating from bassist John-Michael Hedley's burgeoning mullet, flapping away as he headbangs in time to the music.

Baty is soon down to his shorts, as is usually the case at Pigs' gigs whether they take place in rooms that are quite this sweltering or not. He is not showing off. Although Baty is said to be a big fan of American wrestling, he's no Macho Man Randy Savage. Nor does he sport the beefy pectoral muscles of other singers famed for their toplessness, such as Black Flag's Henry Rollins, whose own hypermasculinity inspired the erotically voyeuristic lyrics to Sonic Youth's 'Hallowe'en'. Baty can bellow like the best of them but his short and (at this point) slightly tubby physique do not quite scream 'Adonis'. 'I'm absolutely incapable of growing facial hair and also chest hair,' Baty confessed to the 'Drowned in Sound' website earlier in the month, 'I'm so smooth on my chest, there's something about that I quite like.' Baty's lack of shirt is not an exercise in ape-like chest-beating. It's more subversive and light-hearted than that. It stems from Baty's insecurities and feelings of inadequacy in the face of societal machismo, including the thick, manly beards that have come back into fashion and which Baty is unable to grow himself. 'The tops off thing now feels like a middle finger to that,' he's explained. 'It worked its way into lyrics in the first album as well, there were little bits and pieces that touched on – what's the phrase that gets used a lot at the moment? – toxic masculinity . . . I do a lot of flexing on stage. It's in jest and it's to make a point about that kind of mentality.'[2] Baty believes that heavy music, in its earlier days, used to be 'for everyone'. At some point down the line, it was hijacked by the macho contingent. The singer hopes Pigs' activities can help to undermine that uber-male exclusivity, even if it's not what his band expressly set out to do.[3]

Alongside the ironic flexing, many of Baty's stage moves appear to be sacramental. In time to his band's sledgehammering music, he will make the slow and steady sign of the cross, place his hands together in prayer, take to his knees, and adopt similar gestures you'd expect more from a stained glass-surrounded priest than a mostly naked rock singer at one end of a particularly humid alehouse. After the gig, with our ears ringing, the winter night cooling our bones and cigarette smoke wafting through the air like church incense, a friend turns to me and asks, 'So . . . are they . . . a "Christian" band?' Well, less so than Black Sabbath were . . .

Porcine of the Times

In a surprising yet welcome turn of events, the self-described 'precious metal' outfit Pigs Pigs Pigs Pigs Pigs Pigs Pigs have become remarkably popular for such an unruly band. In the course of promoting their second album, 2018's *King of Cowards*, Pigs went from playing in pokey little pubs like the one described above to performing in front of sizable crowds at festivals like End of the Road and Latitude.

Granted, the Newcastle-based band has shortened its track lengths a little over the years, and this has made the pieces of music more digestible to the average listener. Released back in early 2017, Pigs' debut album *Feed the Rats* was bookended by two monolithic songs that were each over fifteen minutes long. Another track, one-third of the length, was sandwiched in between. And that was the whole album. On it, the disenchanted northerners spliced repetitive Sabbathian riffs with mucky Monster Magnet-ish space rock swirls while their singer growled like a lost Lemmy deprived of amphetamines. Woven among all the domineering riffs were psychedelic and noise rock tropes, an appreciation of the open-ended experimentation of post-metal, and the hazy legacy of *Dopesmoker*, *Dopethrone* and other assorted doped-up opuses. 'The 17 minute long "Icon" is a wonderfully nebulous porcine glot,' noted *The Monitors*' Luke O'Dwyer, 'A track that winds up then down, then up again like a fucked helter skelter.'[4] Those final words were formatted as if he meant a big slide, but perhaps The Beatles' number was not far from the back of the writer's mind.

The compositions on Pigs' subsequent records have been slimmer, length-wise, yet no less crushing. The healthy Sabbath fixation and psychedelic doom tropes remain in place, while the riffs continue to come thick and fast (and phat). Following on from the religious content of Geezer Butler's lyrics, the songs on *King of Cowards* explored the lifelong psychological impact and unshakable guilt that comes with being brought up under strict Catholicism. There is a chance Baty's words and the Trinitarian gestures that have accompanied them onstage could be interpreted as commitment to Christianity. It's something he's given some thought to:

> That has crossed my mind a couple of times, that it may come across that I'm actually promoting Christianity or Catholicism as a life choice, but, erm, I'm not. By the same token, I don't want to feel like I'm bashing it, or pointing fingers at people's beliefs and faiths, because I'm not into that either. I suppose I'm just addressing my own experiences of it. As long as you're not hurting people. You can point out the massive flaws of it, as an institution. But when it's just ordinary people going about their lives and that's one of the things they've picked to try to make sense of the world, then it feels a bit more crass to call them an idiot or whatever. Do you know what I mean? But, no! We're not a Christian band! I've heard it's quite a big market though, Christian rock. Maybe if the next album tanks, we'll evolve into a Christian rock group.[5]

Despite Baty's upbringing, the band's material is not all fire and brimstone. Evoking darkness and misery, the term 'doom metal' has never done justice to how fun and cathartic that style of music can be, no matter how sluggish its pace, how morbid its lyrics and how deeply tuned the power chords. If you want to throw them in with the doom metal scene, Pigs are arguably the most fun band of the lot. 'I feel that sometimes the kind of music that we play can be very serious and a bit dark whereas there's some levity in what we're doing,' Baty has said.[6] 'Shouting "bastards!" is undeniably aggressive,' notes guitarist Adam Sykes, 'but the idea of shouting the word "bastards!" over and over and over again is pretty daft in itself.'[7] That's not to say Pigs don't take their art seriously, mind, or that it isn't sincere. In fact, it's got to have more honesty to it than those gothier types who pretend to be unhappy 100 per cent of the time. Much of the material on *King of Cowards* may have been rooted in Baty's Catholic guilt but, as the man himself has explained from the stage while wearing Adidas shorts, a green sparkly hoodie and few other items of clothing, the song 'Cake of Light' was written about what would happen if Aleister 'wickedest man in the world' Crowley were to make an appearance on *The Great British Bake Off.*

Viscerals, released in 2020, expanded the piggy palette further, again without sacrificing the heaviness. Tracks like 'Halloween Bolson' offered plenty of phenomenally hefty riffs to keep the doomheads, erm, happy. Album opener 'Reducer' momentarily moved the spotlight away from the crushing power chords to fore-ground its blasts of dizzying space rock lead guitar. 'New Body' was Pigs' most explicitly noise rock-like song to date. A thrash influence rears its head elsewhere and there's even a strange, almost dubstep intermission with some spoken-word vocals involving some kind of extended gastronomic metaphor. With their upbeat, snarl-along choruses, the double whammy of 'World Crust' and the Beyoncé-alluding 'Crazy in Blood' were the poppiest Pigs songs yet, if you can call them that, though they still had more in common with High On Fire than Destiny's Child. The album's promotion, which had included dates booked for the band's first American tour, was scuppered by the outbreak of COVID-19. This didn't prevent the group's reputation from swelling like a corn-fed porker.

The band members have modestly claimed that Pigs' music is 'incredibly derivative' and that it doesn't do 'anything wildly different'.[8] Just as the sense of despair and disillusionment in Geezer Butler's lyrics was engaged in reciprocal nourishment with Black Sabbath's blackened music, the levity identified by Baty spills over into the sound of Pigs. This is, in part, what has made Pigs stand out and attract a broad audience. After all, another unexpected development is that despite the band's debt to the Sabbath sound, Pigs' audience does not seem to consist solely of card-carrying metal-heads. Pigs have been playlisted by BBC 6 Music, a station that traditionally hasn't offered a huge amount of daytime radio play to artists of the doom, sludge, stoner or metal persuasions. Few of the accompanying acts on the bills of the music festivals at which Pigs have performed have even approached their heaviness. On the subject of Pigs' music and its reach, Baty says,

> I don't experience it as something abrasive or dark and I think that's possibly opening our doors to a wider audience who feel like they can enjoy it as well . . . quite often music like ours gets cornered and tucked away in specialist shows or journalism which is great but I think what's great that's happening with our band is showing there's a hunger and thirst for it. People are enjoying our music that might not otherwise come across it. It goes to show, if you put this music in front of some people they might think 'wow this is great and I'm surprised that I really enjoy it' and I think that's a beautiful thing.[9]

As they've said elsewhere, Pigs hope to show people that their style of music is not the exclusive property of 'some big bulky guy covered in tattoos with long hair'.[10] It is certainly encouraging that, all these years down the line and with just the odd tweak here and there, the Sabbathian spirit lives on and continues to infect new hosts.

The band having always described themselves as a joke that got out of hand, Pigs' success seems to be more of a happy accident then any kind of contrived career push. Back in the late 1980s, John Peel wrote of his admiration for Butthole Surfers' choice of band name. He said it offered proof that they were 'not one of those bands hoping for a fun-run on the underground scene before exploding into big pop'.[11] A nightmare for word counts and subeditors every-where, the daft name Pigs Pigs Pigs Pigs Pigs Pigs Pigs implies a similarly, if not quite as rude, non-commercial and uncompromising outlook. Guitarist Sam Grant, who is also the group's producer, has described it as an 'ego inhibitor. Having a silly name stops you getting ahead of yourself or hungering for success and keeps you focused on making music you believe in.'[12]

This Is Why Radiohead Hate You

The members of Pigs Pigs Pigs Pigs Pigs Pigs Pigs cut their teeth playing in even stranger bands in Newcastle. It's a relatively small city where the handful of folk who are obsessed with esoteric and adventurous music tend to gravitate towards one another, and the musicians among them end up playing in each other's unusual projects. Before taking up singing, Baty played drums in the delightfully named Khünnt. A band definitely not aiming to explode into 'big pop', Khünnt were a ferocious-sounding arty sludge metal outfit whose bassist was fellow Pig John-Michael Hedley. Baty and Hedley also comprised the rhythm section of Blown Out, an instrumental power trio known for their spritely and lengthy space rock jams. Blown Out guitarist Mike Vest's other projects have included Bong, 11Paranoias, Drunk in Hell, Haikai No Ku, Melting Hand, Oblivion Reptilian, Dodge Meteor, Lush Worker, ozo, Lobster Priest and countless more. As a teenager, Vest taught himself to play guitar and formed a school band called Evil Mountain that performed Iron Monkey covers and material of a similar nature. When he discovered Sunn O))) – who he once saw perform in the Cumberland Arms pub to about fifty people – Vest became a convert to the magic of feedback and drone. Thereafter he formed the mighty Bong. Although their activities are less widely reported as other big names in the field of drone metal (who mostly happen to be American), Bong's output has been said to equal the quality of the greats and the godfathers of the genre, including Om and Earth.[13] Vest remains – and is likely to remain – one of the more arcane electric wizards, plodding his way through the underground. While Pigs have hardly had to quit their day jobs and clearly harbour no ambitions to become the next Def Leppard, Vest has distanced himself from his ex-Blown Out colleagues, by whom he seems to feel abandoned.[14] Vest's pursuit is a noble one nevertheless, not least on account of his ability to churn out high-quality avant-garde rock music, both collaboratively and alone, at such an inexhaustible speed that he makes even some of the prolific jazz greats look like lethargic couch potatoes.

It was in the small independent venues of Newcastle that the members of Pigs were able to hone their craft and establish their creative outlook and artistic ethics, in a place that is a long distance away from the traditional UK music industry hotspots, not just geographically speaking but also in cultural terms and in a commerce and business sense. Big labels and music managers don't tend to bother venturing up to Newcastle on a regular basis. Industry bods spend most of their time in London, occasionally travelling north only as far as Manchester, where they can scout out the latest batch of Factory Records-fixated New Order throwbacks. 'You could be the greatest band on earth playing in Newcastle,' insists Baty, 'and no-one will ever fucking know about you. Sometimes people talk about it as if you're on Mars.'[15] To put a more positive spin on this situation, this neglect means the bands living and working up there are not subject to industry pressures or the meddling nature of A&R men. Thus Pigs have been free to rock as weirdly as they want, remain as scruffy as they wish to remain and, in the case of Hedley, grow a mullet. Besides, many of the peculiar and obscure bands from Newcastle (not to mention those hailing from other locations, too) have at least had the opportunity to have their records put out by Baty's own small independent label, Box Records.

Most of Pigs' own records have been released by Rocket Recordings. It's perhaps the most widely known of a host of like-minded independent UK labels that includes Riot Season, God

Unknown and Hominid Sounds. On their rosters we can find further examples of exciting contemporary heaviness either waiting to break out, as Pigs have done, or remain bubbling under the surface – just as worthwhile and noble a pursuit – in the manner of the maverick Mike Vest.

Bands from elsewhere in Britain include long-running cult rockers Hey Colossus, whose early material sounded like Mad Max trying to grunt his way out of a giant bowl of Rice Krispies. Their bassist, Joe Thompson, has written a book about what life is like in an underground rock band. One of the mottos contained therein is this: 'bands who don't change over their years of existence are bands that are lying to you. Bands shouldn't be giving you what you want, they should be dragging you around and challenging you.'[16] Practising what they preach, Hey Colossus' material has grown catchier and more accessible of late. They have even done it without compromise, which is no easy trick to pull off. A testament to their perseverance, hard graft and good taste, Hey Colossus have been one of the few bands to keep on improving over time, probably because they haven't been ruined by that pesky creativity sapper known as success. *Dances/Curses* was released in 2020, seventeen years after the band formed, and was their strongest and most fully realized work yet. The double album's tracks range from the psych-kraut epic 'A Trembling Rose' (twenty minutes long if you include its accompanying 'Reprise') to the catchy three-minute banger 'Medal', with plenty of adventurous croon-rock elsewhere, plus a guest spot from celebrity HC fan Mark Lanegan. If material this good had been released by a band with the same marketing power behind it as Biffy Clyro, it would have been hailed throughout the world as one of the best rock albums in recent memory. Instead, it didn't even appear on a reputable indie label like Rocket Recordings (who HC have worked with before) because Thompson decided to put it out on his own small DIY imprint, Wrong Speed Records. Is Thompson shooting himself in the foot or sticking to his principles? Thompson sees it more in terms of laying down the ground rules for the future: 'It's 100% time for all bands to take control of their shit.'[17] It would be nice to see Hey Colossus become as successful as Pigs; to see all their hard work pay off. As well as being a full-time postman and a family man, Joe Thompson plays in another band, too, Henry Blacker, who are essentially Somerset's answer to Queens of the Stone Age, even though, again, they are not exactly a household name.

This is just the tip of the iceberg when it comes to those who are churning out interesting music on a regular basis even when it seems like the odds are stacked against them. 'Music is a communal action,' writes Thompson.

> It should be brought back to this, it's an art form for every-one. It should be available for everyone to play and watch at a cost that is in no way prohibitive. If you want to spend £80 to see Radiohead or whoever, then go for it but be aware that it's that price because they hate you. They hate you having money instead of them. Their record label hates you. Their record label hates you for having money for beans and tea bags.[18]

Musicians such as Thompson grew up listening to bands like Fugazi and Big Black, swotting up on Ian MacKaye's and Steve Albini's ways of working, recording, gigging and distributing their wares. There is less of a choice these days when it comes to avoiding the more sinister machinations of the music industry. Because the music business is less robust than it was in its heyday and fewer people even feel the need to pay for music anymore, no major label is ever going to gamble on turning GNOD, Teeth of the Sea or Necro Deathmort into the next Nirvana (or the next Muse or Royal Blood or whoever). Thompson subscribes to Albini's notion that 'If you're only doing it for a paycheck, you're going to be bad at it.'[19] Hey Colossus do pretty much everything off their own backs and pile any negligible profits they happen to make back into the band by purchasing new equipment and suchlike. This approach has stemmed a string of incredible records, even if they don't always get the exposure or the recognition that they deserve. Like many of our heavy innovators, it could be a while before their impact is truly appreciated.

Along with Pigs Pigs Pigs Pigs Pigs Pigs Pigs, somebody else who has broken out from the Newcastle scene is neo-folk musician Richard Dawson. In his work, we can see how the history of heaviness has inspired music that ostensibly appears to be rather far removed from the world of heavy, if we are to focus on just one example. Dawson's non-folk influences range from the cosmic jazz of Sun Ra to the saccharine electro-pop of PC Music's SOPHIE, while also navigating a host of things in between. The first music Dawson properly fell in love with was heavy metal. When rifling through his sister's collection of LPs, the young Dawson was attracted to Iron Maiden's vibrant artwork, and thereafter their music. 'Where Eagles Dare' (1983), Dawson insists, contains three of the greatest guitar riffs of all time, all within the space of a single song.[20] The first record Dawson owned himself was *Disco Volante* by Mr Bungle, the avant-garde rock band fronted by Mike Patton of Faith No More. 'I think my parents wondered what the hell was going on up there,' Dawson remembers, 'this music is really frightening, with a malevolence to it. There's a bit of daftness, but not much, and even the daftness is quite nasty.'[21] Dawson also cites as his favourite band the genre-straddling self-described 'New Wave of Finnish Heavy Metal' group Circle. Dawson compares Circle's music and eclectic discography to the work of French experimental composer Éliane Radigue and Sun Ra: 'I feel a lot of kinship with them – this music which is both very ancient and futuristic all at once.'[22] With that kind of musical education, it's little wonder Dawson was drawn to the fellow oddballs in Khünnt, to whose *Failures* LP he contributed additional guitar parts. During the recording process, Dawson disobeyed all warnings that were given to him and proceeded to turn a modified twin amplifier up so loud that when he gently touched his guitar the resultant noise physically hurt his face and caused the other band members to drop to the ground in submission.[23]

Just as the music of Pigs Pigs Pigs Pigs Pigs Pigs Pigs has reached a broad audience without compromising on heaviness or integrity and has managed to appeal to people who haven't yet discovered the wider doom scene, Richard Dawson's records have been embraced by those who don't spend an awful lot of their time deeply immersed in the neo-folk scene. Matt Baty and John-Michael Hedley have both performed stints in Dawson's backing band. The first time the pair, along with fellow future Pigs member Sam Grant, came across Dawson was in a Spanish restaurant near Newcastle United's St James' Park football stadium. On the first floor, the tables would be pushed to one side to accommodate an open mic night. 'I don't know who was organizing this,' says Baty, 'but it was so eclectic and open-minded. You'd get real mad performance art stuff. Then you'd get me, Sam and Johnny doing improv noise sets. And then you'd get people playing acoustic guitar for twenty minutes as well.' At one of those nights, Dawson turned up and played a ten-minute song detailing how each one of his pet cats had died when he was growing up. 'I was just sat there with tears running down my face,' Baty remembers. 'It was so fantastic, touching and really raw. I had kind of been in awe of him ever since that moment.'[24]

Later, when the person who was going to put out Dawson's *The Magic Bridge* album on vinyl reneged on their offer after deciding that it 'sounded like it had been recorded in a bin', Baty's Box Records imprint stepped in. 'I know we talk about Black Sabbath all the time, and we're asked about Black Sabbath all the time,' says Baty,

but for me I'm just as . . . actually, I'm *more* influenced by bands that we've gigged with or people like Richard, who you've seen develop and who you've believed in from that very first moment that you heard him. I'm influenced particularly by Richard's music in that way because it's pure and it's honest and he's always stuck to his guns about what he wants to do, and what he doesn't want to do, and that's such an important thing, so I've always admired him for that.[25]

Baty sees a similar attitude inherent in other bands he's met along the way, with whom he feels an affinity; those that are doing their own thing and doing it by themselves. He cites as examples bands like Manchester's ILL (a feminist group with a post-punky feel) and Luminous Bodies, a Butthole Surfers-worshipping noise rock band with two drummers, fronted by Gordon Watson from Terminal Cheesecake. In Pigs' early days of being booked to play small venues by fellow bands and like-minded promoters around the country, 'We started to fall down a rabbit hole and found this amazing network of incredible people, all across the UK and extended over into mainland Europe,' says Baty.

It feels mad that Pigs have gotten to where we are at the present, with just that kind of philosophy. Obviously we are driven and we're ambitious, but it's fundamentally about having a lot of fun with this and just meeting and connecting with as many good people as possible. You just keep working your way forward with that mission. There are so many bands that are overly concerned with the journey ahead and asking 'How do you get there?' There's no particular route. There's no shortcut. There's just your music and enjoying it and that's it. If you start worrying about anything else, outside of that, it just kills it and makes it stressful. So don't think about it. Concentrate on your music and enjoy the people that you meet because there are some amazing characters out there, and 'characters' is the right word! I'm just as inspired by all of that as I am by Black Sabbath and Motörhead, you know.[26]

As for Pigs Pigs Pigs Pigs Pigs Pigs Pigs' reciprocal influence on the music of Richard Dawson, Baty can pinpoint at least one way in which his band has had a direct impact on their alt-folk friend. The incident he has in mind happened at a gig in Edinburgh in 2017, after Baty and his Pigs bandmate John-Michael Hedley had been recruited as Dawson's rhythm section:

> The *Peasant* album had just come out and Richard has . . . no . . . he *had* (in the past tense) this acoustic guitar. *His* acoustic guitar. It was really battered. He'd had it for years. It was almost synonymous with him. Just after the soundcheck, he propped it up against his amp or something and wandered off. And then I just heard this massive CLANK. Johnny had knocked it over. I don't know what had happened because it made such a huge sound. It had only fallen sideways onto the floor, but it sounded like somebody had chucked it off the top of a building. It made such a horrible sound. It sounded serious. But it looked fine, so Johnny just propped it back up. When we went back because we had to soundcheck something else, Richard started trying to tune his guitar and he said, 'Erm . . . has anything happened to my guitar?' Johnny said he'd knocked it just a little bit and it tipped over. It turned out the neck had completely snapped. It was horrible because it was the first night we'd ever played as Richard's backing band. Me and Johnny were nervous anyway about doing it live. And then that happened. So Richard ended up having to go to a music shop and getting a replacement one, which he really didn't like. After doing a couple of gigs with that newer guitar that he absolutely hated, he brought this electric guitar along that he'd quite recently bought and he said he was going to try that. We did a soundcheck and it sounded *amazing*. It worked really, really well. And he's never looked back! He's been doing electric ever since.

In some small way, that's maybe how Pigs have influenced Richard. Or at least Johnny has, with his sabotaging of Richard's equipment.[27]

19

NEVER SAY DIE

I like noise. I like big-ass vicious noise that makes my head
spin. I wanna feel it whipping through me like a fucking jolt.
We're so dilapidated and crushed by our pathetic existence we
need it like a fix.[1]

STEVE ALBINI

Richard Dawson's music has been hailed as state-of-the-nation
material that 'refuses to sugar-coat a broken society' and isn't
afraid to 'wade into the barbarism of modern life'.[2] Whereas
2017's *Peasant* was a concept album set in pre-medieval times that
acted as a metaphor for the struggles of the contemporary age, *2020*
(released in 2019) directly addressed life in austerity Britain in the
aftermath of the seismic decision to leave the European Union.
(Dawson has also quipped that *2020* is in fact an elaborate metaphor
for the Middle Ages.) With its vignettes about depressed and
disillusioned council workers, anxiety-ridden joggers, racist attacks
on scapegoated minorities, disabled people having their living
allowances revoked, the fallout from insufficient flood defences,
and Amazon warehouse workers urinating into plastic bottles
through fear of missing their shift targets, *2020* held a mirror up to a
country falling apart at the seams. The resonating sound of Dawson's
electric guitar makes its presence felt throughout, especially on the
abrasively lurching sections of 'Civil Servant' and the chugging,
metal-referencing riffs of 'Jogging'.

Dawson's music is not without humour and, electronic, ambient
or rocking embellishments aside, remains rooted in the folky vein.
Nevertheless, there are thematic echoes here of the impetus that was

behind Black Sabbath's origins and their desire to produce material that was bleak enough to reflect what was really going on in the world they saw around them.

The subject-matter of Pigs Pigs Pigs Pigs Pigs Pigs Pigs' songs is not as directly political as Dawson's tuneful character studies. Though still relatable, their lyrics tend to be hinged around Matt Baty's mission to understand his own place in the world and figure out how to cope with life's challenges on an individual level. (When not concerned with Aleister Crowley's fictional turn on a popular televised baking competition, that is.) His words are usually concerned with 'the more primal aspects of being a human and also the confusion of being a human and being alive'. Having said that, he adds that 'It's impossible not to be influenced by politics or just what you see around you in your own smaller communities, I suppose, as well as a larger one, and even a global one. It's impossible not to be affected by that. At least it is for me, anyway. On an emotional level, it's really difficult.'[3] The northeast of England is one of the regions worst hit by successive Conservative governments' austerity measures. In 2019 it was reported that one death per week in Newcastle, where Pigs and Dawson are based, was a direct result of Tory austerity.[4] In February 2020 improvements in life expectancy in England were seen to have had stalled for the first sustained period in over a century following a decade of government cuts, with the largest decreases in life expectancy occurring in the most deprived 10 per cent of neighbourhoods in the northeast.[5] In June 2020 it was reported that the northeast sustained a higher number of excess deaths during the COVID-19 pandemic than anywhere else in the country. The UK as a whole had Europe's highest rate of excess deaths from COVID-19, a humiliating statistic that some experts have attributed to years of spending cuts and deepening economic inequality.[6] Prime minister Alexander Boris de Pfeffel Johnson promised a 'world-beating' response to the pandemic, and in a grim way he was right.

These are strange, uncertain and unhappy times we are a living in, with doomy music being an appropriate soundtrack to that. The purest and most forlorn form of doom has already been done many times before, and, as Baty has said, there is a differing levity to the music of Pigs Pigs Pigs Pigs Pigs Pigs Pigs, driven by his band's desire to avoid too much solemnity. For a band named after swine, they are not ones to wallow. Their music is still rooted in doom but there is a celebratory aspect to Pigs' lively and inclusive concerts and an elusive warm-hearted spirit in their compositions. This helps to distinguish Pigs from the blueprint provided by Black Sabbath and their doom metal successors, and from Sabbath's overriding mission to make music that sounded as miserable as people's lives were in places like the Blitz-wrecked Birmingham of the post-war years. In this respect, Pigs Pigs Pigs Pigs Pigs Pigs Pigs are perhaps the perfect heavy band for Britain in an age of austerity and the chaos and uncertainty created by the decision to sever itself from the European Union, neither of which are going to end any time soon. The strange and unprecedented socio-political situation that we've found ourselves in does feed into the 'surrealism and wonki-ness' of Pigs' music, says Sam Grant. 'There has never been a point in our lifetime where catharsis is more necessary than now,' adds his bandmate Adam Sykes.[7] There is every reason to sink into despair, but at the same time we cannot abandon hope, optimism, fun and our sense of community. All is not lost. That is how I feel whenever I see a performance by Pigs Pigs Pigs Pigs Pigs Pigs Pigs.

It is a similar feeling to the experience of listening to The Beatles' 'Helter Skelter'. The thrill derives from that invigorating mixture of raw emotion, expressive riffs, thick textures, general unruliness, slight preposterousness and an almost festive feeling of sonic destruction. As we saw earlier, 'Helter Skelter' was not just about Paul McCartney trying to outdo The Who by laying down an extremely heavy song about going up and down a fairground ride. McCartney also had in mind the laughable impermanence and inevitable demise of every empire in history. That idea seems very much in the air right now, in the sense that Britain's exit could inspire other EU countries to follow suit, potentially spelling the demise of the European project; but perhaps it's more feasible that we are looking at the end of an empire in a more domestic and psychological respect. Britain is likely going to have to ride out, somehow, a dismal and protracted period of instability, estrangement, incessant trade negotiations and economic strain (and much worse, to put it mildly). There is going to be a painful period that will necessarily instigate some sobering self-reflection, after which the national psyche will finally have to recognize and come to accept Britain's diminished position on the world's stage, and therefore let go of its baseless patriotic superiority. The nation will have to take a long, hard look at itself in finally grasping that it has been a very long time since it could really describe itself as 'world beating' in any area other than successive governmental cock-ups. The country and its more jingoistic subjects will be forced to come to terms with the fact that this place is no longer the mighty imperial nation of the past, a realization that is long overdue. As the Danish finance minister Kristian Jensen put it when Brexit negotiations were taking place in 2017, 'There are two kinds of European nations. There are small nations and there are countries that have not yet realised they are small nations.'[8] Both the United Kingdom and the United States, once top dogs of the world, are trapped in the 'nationalism of decline', as Jeff McMahan writes in the *New Statesman*:

Citizens in the U.S. and the UK are uneasily if not always consciously aware that their countries are plummeting from their former positions of global preeminence. Large segments of these populations are thus desperately seeking to blame scapegoats and also to be assured that renewed national glory is imminent. The Tory slogan, 'Global Britain', is not only a pitiful echo of Trump's Make – or, now, Keep

– America Great Again, but is also a scarcely veiled appeal
to nostalgia for Britain's imperial past.[9]

The lyrics to Pigs' 'Rubbernecker' express 'feelings of desperation
and eroding senses of community in a world that's seemingly
gone completely mad', explains Baty. 'The central character is the
clown, who attempts to detach himself from the world he observes
as chaotic and unruly. The more he isolates himself, the more he
yearns for kinship but the ever growing forces that reinforce his
terror of the outside keep him rooted in his confinement. It's a sad
song really.'[10] I wonder if the clown in question has spent much time
hurtling down his circus's helter skelter.

Various other 'empires' may well be on their last legs right now
in other, perhaps less foreseeable, respects. Then again, maybe every
age has had an end-of-empire feel to it. People have been pessimis-
tically preaching the imminence of the apocalypse since humanity
could first conceive of such an idea. Ruminating on the apocalyptic
nature of postmodernist literature as the year 2000 approached,
back when America's principal worries were oil prices and Marilyn
Manson, Steven Shaviro wrote that 'we must confront the fact that
the only "end of history" is that history is always ending, so that in
fact there is no end to history . . . we may say that the Apocalypse
has already happened; or better, that it is happening right now,
continually and inconclusively, even as we speak.'[11]

Talking of doomsayers, it has become a fairly common occurrence for, about every six months or so, some arts critic who is
suffering from a terrible bout of imagination block to pen an article
about the rock genre being dead or guitar music being 'over', supposedly superseded by younger and momentarily trendier genres. In
retaliation to such claims, rock musicians and their defenders will
react by defiantly declaring from the stage or in an interview with
Rolling Stone or from the rotting deck of the sinking ship that 'rock
'n' roll will never die'. What's more, according to veteran journalist

David Hepworth, the age of the rock star is well and truly finished, and it has been since the death of Kurt Cobain in 1994.[12]

Whether Hepworth is correct or not, we will never see a corresponding end to heaviness itself. While certain key elements have remained intact, heaviness has existed in many different forms, been produced using all sorts of different methods and agendas, and has been transformed, adapted, reinvented, transfigured and deformed continuously down the generations. And, much like Celine Dion's robust heart, heaviness will go on. In what kinds of ways, we can only begin to imagine. On the precise nature of any future incarnations of the Sabbathian mode, speculation is all that can suffice at this point. One thing that's for certain is that even the radically mutated survivors of the impending nuclear fallout will need heaviness to get them through the problems they will have to face. Who knows how they might create it? By running a lead pipe across a smouldering corrugated roof while chanting forsakenly at the sunless sky, perhaps? Whether performed by blurry-eyed guitarists, computer-aided whizz-kids, or a sentient robot generating its own white noise feedback concertos to soothe the existential hyper-angst of its fellow automatons, heaviness will be around as long as there is someone, or something, to hear it.

REFERENCES

Preface

1 Roy Wilkinson, 'Crouching Tiger, Hidden Depths?', *Q* (July 2001). The article included a quote taken from Marilyn Manson's official website, serving to pinpoint that particular artist's problem with Limp Bizkit: 'The illiterate apes that beat your ass in high school for being a "fag" now sell you tuneless anthems of misogyny and pretend to be outsiders.'

2 Andrew Collins, *That's Me in the Corner: Adventures of an Ordinary Boy in a Celebrity World* (London, 2008), p. 144.

3 On the subject of Pantera let me point you in the direction of Dan Franklin's book *Heavy: How Metal Changes the Way We See the World* (London, 2020), and its excellent sixth chapter, in which the author offers a persuasively Nietzschean take on Phil Anselmo, the band's troubled and controversial singer.

4 Jimmy McDonough, *Shakey: Neil Young's Biography* (London, 2002), p. 163.

5 June Harris, 'Bobby Vee: The Old Rock Has Gone for Good', *Disc* (2 December 1961).

6 Alan Smith, 'Pat Boone: Why I Became a Beatnik', *NME* (9 March 1962); June Harris, 'Thirty-minute Song Will Make Mancini a Fortune', *Disc* (9 June 1962).

7 Harris, 'Bobby Vee'.

8 Alan Smith, 'Beatles Almost Threw "Please Please Me" Away', *NME* (8 March 1963); Alan Smith, 'The "Twist and Shout" Battle Hots Up! (And How the *NME* Helped)', *NME* (19 July 1963).

9 June Harris, 'The Tremeloes: Hit Sound? It's Played Out, Says Brian Poole', *Disc* (4 January 1964).

10 Keith Altham, 'The Troggs: *From Nowhere the Troggs* (Fontana)', *NME* (1 July 1966); Keith Altham, 'The Troggs: Double-top Troggs in America and Britain!', *NME* (12 August 1966).

11 Deena Weinstein, 'Just So Stories: How Heavy Metal Got Its Name – A Cautionary Tale', *Rock Music Studies*, 1/1 (2014), p. 45.

12 Chris Welch, 'Will Nice Get Lost among the Commuters?', *Melody Maker* (22 March 1969).

13 Adrian Booth of Rotherham in *Record Collector* (July 2020).

14 Michael Hann, 'Killing It Live: The Murder Capital Interviewed', www.thequietus.com, 23 October 2019.

15 I mean, everybody's got time for the conceptual gonzo metal of GWAR, right? Seeing as the band are not of this planet, its personnel consisting of intergalactic barbarian warriors, they get a free pass. See also Parliament/Funkadelic.

16 J. J. Anselmi, *Doomed to Fail: The Incredibly Loud History of Doom, Sludge and Post-metal* (Los Angeles, CA, 2020), pp. 156, 158.

17 Tony Bacon, 'Paul McCartney – Meet The Beatle', *Bass Player* (July–August 1995).

18 Paul Du Noyer, *Conversations with McCartney* (London, 2015), pp. 79–80, 187, 216. 'It's like one note: down-to-Duke's-Place. Louis is singing and he goes "take it, Duke!" Duke's on the piano, and the cheek of him, he goes *dn-dn-dn-dn* on one finger. Next verse comes around, you expect him to go [*mimes flourish of triplets*], but it's *dn-dn-dn-dn*. It's almost embarrassing, except it's just so ballsy. That is *good*.' (p. 216.)

19 Steve Albini, liner notes to Big Black, *The Hammer Party* (Touch and Go, 1986).

Introduction

1 *The Beatles Anthology* (San Francisco, CA, 2012), p. 311.

2 Ian MacDonald, *Revolution in the Head: The Beatles' Records and the Sixties* (London, 2008), p. 298.

3 Sean Egan, ed., *The Mammoth Book of The Beatles* (London, 2009), pp. 176–7.

4 Gerald Carlin and Mark Jones, '"Helter Skelter" and Sixties Revisionism', in *Countercultures and Popular Music*, ed. Sheila Whiteley and Jedediah Sklower (Farnham, 2014), p. 96.

5 David Sheff, *All We Are Saying: The Last Major Interview with John Lennon and Yoko Ono* (New York, 2000), p. 200; Jan S. Wenner, 'Lennon Remembers, Part One', *Rolling Stone* (21 January 1971).

6 'The Beatles Album Tracks in Depth', *Record Mirror* (16 November 1968).

7 Geoffrey Cannon, 'Back to Spring: The Beatles: *The Beatles (White Album)*', *The Guardian* (26 November 1968).

8 Barry Miles, 'The Beatles: *The Beatles (White Album)*', *International Times* (29 November 1968).

9 MacDonald, *Revolution*, p. 260.

10 Jaan Uhelszki, 'Noel Gallagher Interview', *Addicted to Noise* (March 1995), archived at http://jameshakermakery2k.tripod.com, accessed 23 January 2020.

11 Carlin and Jones, '"Helter Skelter" and Sixties Revisionism', p. 96.

12 Barry Miles, *Paul McCartney: Many Years from Now* (London, 1997), p. 488.

13 Chris Butler, 'Metal's Patient Zero: Helter Skelter', www.invisibleoranges.com, 3 May 2017.

14 Bob Spitz, *The Beatles: The Biography* (New York, 2005), p. 793.

15 Mark Lewisham, *The Complete Beatles Recording Sessions: The Official Story of the Abbey Road Years, 1962–1970* (New York, 2013), p. 154.

16 'Killing Joke's Youth on His 13 Favourite Records', www.thequietus.com, 29 March 2011.

17 Jed Gottlieb, 'How Soundgarden's Fearlessness was Inspired by The Beatles', www.ultimateclassicrock.com, 13 July 2011.

18 Hank Shteamer, *Chocolate and Cheese* (London, 2011), pp. 11–12.

19 Rob Chapman, *Psychedelia and Other Colours* (London, 2015), p. 114.

20 'Mudhoney Tourbook, 1991', www.ocf.berkeley.edu, accessed 3 June 2018.

21 Lianne Steinberg, 'Mudhoney: Working Men's Club', *Plan B* (August 2006).

22 Julian Cope, *Copendium: An Expedition into the Rock 'n' Roll Underwerld* (London, 2013), p. 178.

1 The Prehistory

1 Muddy Waters in James Rooney, *Bossmen: Bill Monroe and Muddy Waters* (New York, 1971), p. 112.

2 JR Moores, 'It's Rock 'N' Roll, Jim, But Not As We Know It', liner notes to Heldon, *Interface* (Bureau B, 2020).

3 Chris Smith, *101 Albums that Changed Popular Music* (Oxford, 2009), p. 16; Greg Milner, *Perfecting Sound Forever: The Story of Recorded Music* (London, 2010), p. 95.

4 Andrew O'Neill, *A History of Heavy Metal* (London, 2018), p. 11.

5 Dave Peabody, 'Blues History', *fRoots* (August 2005); Owen Adams, 'The Demon Barber of British Blues', *Record Collector* (February 2008).

6 Richard Williams, 'Sister Rosetta Tharpe: The Godmother of Rock'n'Roll', www.theguardian.com, 18 March 2013.

7 Ray Coleman, 'Ringo [The Silent One]', *Melody Maker* (14 November 1964).

8 Rooney, *Bossmen*, p. 144.

9 Arnold Shaw, 'The Rhythm and Blues Revival: No White Gloved, Black Hits', *Billboard* (16 August 1969).

10 Rob Chapman, *Psychedelia and Other Colours* (London, 2015), p. 127.

11 Den Simms, Eric Buxton and Rob Samler, 'They're Doing the Interview of the Century – Part 1', *Society Pages* (April 1990); Paul Zollo, 'Frank Zappa (1988)', *Rock's Backpages Audio*, www.rocksbackpages.com, accessed 31 January 2020.

12 *Neil Young: Don't Be Denied* (*American Masters*, PBS, 2009).

13 Garth Cartwright, 'Obituary: Link Wray', *The Guardian* (22 November 2005).

14 'Iggy Pop Interview on *The Colbert Report* 29/4/13', www.dailymotion.com, accessed 6 June 2018.

2 Sabbath Phase I: Black Sabbath

1 Andrew Tyler, 'Black Sabbath', *Disc and Music Echo* (20 January 1972).

2 Aaron Schmidt, 'Sleep Interview', www.thrashermagazine.com, 16 October 2018.

3 www.facebook.com/ozzyosbourne/posts/10153319761462318, accessed 28 July 2020.

4 Bruce Springsteen, *Born to Run* (London, 2016), pp. 100–103.

5 Bruce Springsteen & the E Street Band, 'The River', *Live 1975–85* (Columbia, 1986).

6 Mick Wall, *Black Sabbath: Symptom of the Universe* (London, 2014), p. 68.

7 Max Nicholson, 'Geezer Butler: Rock God', https://uk.ign.com, 28 June 2010.

8 Jon Weiderhorn, 'Black Sabbath Bassist Geezer Butler Gets Paranoid', www.noisecreep.com, 30 July 2010.

9 Joel McIver, *Sabbath Bloody Sabbath* (London, 2014), pp. 10–11.

10 Mat Snow, 'Ozzy Osbourne Speaks! (1991)', www.rocksbackpages.com, accessed 15 August 2019.

11 David Gans, 'Interview with Ozzy Osbourne 1/10/82', www.medium.com, 17 April 2018.

12 Paul Gabriel, 'The Enduring Riff Rock of Black Sabbath', *DISCoveries* (June 1996).

13 Snow, 'Ozzy Osbourne Speaks!'

14 Bob Stanley, *Yeah Yeah Yeah: The Story of Modern Pop* (London, 2014), p. 567.

15 Gans, 'Interview with Ozzy Osbourne'.

16 Metal Mike Saunders, 'A Dorito and 7-Up Picnic with Black Sabbath', *Circular* (25 September 1972).

17 Pete Silverton, 'Black Sabbath: Apollo Theatre, Glasgow', *Sounds* (27 May 1978).

18 Keith Altham, 'Black Sabbath: To Knock or Not to Knock the Rock', *NME* (14 April 1973).

19 Metal Mike Saunders, 'Black Sabbath: *Master of Reality*', *The Rag* (20 September 1971).

20 Andrew L. Cope, *Black Sabbath and the Rise of Heavy Metal Music* (London, 2010), p. 28.

21 Raoul Duke (Hunter S. Thompson), 'Fear and Loathing in Las Vegas: A Savage Journey to the Heart of the American Dream', *Rolling Stone* (11 November 1971).

22 Billy Walker, 'Black Sabbath: A Band of Our Time?', *Sounds* (14 August 1971).

23 Harold Bronson, 'The Wit and Wisdom of Ozzy Osbourne; or, For the Best Coke Call Black Sabbath', *UCLA Daily Bruin* (30 June 1972).

24 Jim Esposito, 'Black Sabbath: *Volume 4*', *Zoo World* (25 November 1972).

25 Max Bell, 'Black Sabbath: *Volume 4*', *Let It Rock* (December 1972).

26 Wall, *Black Sabbath*, p. 72.

27 Cope, *Black Sabbath*, p. 19.

28 Ibid., pp. 20, 29, 33, 45.

29 Wall, *Black Sabbath*, pp. 150–51.

30 Garry Mulholland, 'Black Sabbath – Garry Mulholland's Punk Eye View of *Vol. 4* Onwards', www.thequietus.com, 23 September 2009.

31 Joel McIver, 'These Are Not Lovesongs', *Record Collector* (November 2005).

32 Nick Kent, 'Public Image Ltd.: *Public Image Ltd.*', NME (9 December 1978).

33 Andy Gill, 'Mark E. Smith's Record Collection', *Q* (October 1990).

34 Denzil Watson, 'Dickies Interview', www.pennyblackmusic.com, 29 November 2005.

35 Tony Dewhurst, 'Mark E Smith Speaks Out as The Fall Return to Clitheroe after 28 Years', www.lancashiretelegraph.co.uk, 12 April 2013.

36 Tony Stewart, 'Ozzy Osbourne: Beyond Black Sabbath', NME (3 December 1977).

37 David Hepworth, *Uncommon People: The Rise and Fall of the Rock Stars* (London, 2017), p. 154.

38 Lester Bangs, 'Black Sabbath', *Rolling Stone* (17 September 1970); Lester Bangs, 'Bring Your Mother to the Gas Chamber – Part One', *Creem* (June 1972).

3 Acid Rock and Beyond

1 Charles Bukowski, *Erections, Ejaculations, Exhibitions and General Tales of Ordinary Madness* (San Francisco, CA, 1974), p. 440.

2 Tom Sykes, 'Eric Clapton Apologizes for Racist Past: "I Sabotaged Everything"', www.thedailybeast.com, 12 January 2018.

3 Stewart Lee, 'Can Harry and Meghan Make Britain Whole Again?', *The Observer* (3 December 2017).

4 Rob Chapman, *Psychedelia and Other Colours* (London, 2015), p. 86.

5 Ibid., p. 32.

6 Timothy Leary, *Flashbacks: An Autobiography* (New York, 1990), p. 61.

7 Jack Hutton, 'Ringo on Drums, Drugs, and the Maharishi', *Melody Maker* (2 December 1967).

8 Joshua M. Greene, *Here Comes the Sun: The Spiritual and Musical Journey of George Harrison* (London, 2006), p. 16.

9 'Ringo Starr', *Melody Maker* (31 July 1971).

10 Chapman, *Psychedelia*, p. 92.

11 Roy Hollingworth, 'Hendrix Today', *Melody Maker* (5 September 1970).

12 'Frank Zappa – On Drugs 1971', www.youtube.com, accessed 23 January 2021.

13 https://twitter.com/shit_rock/status/1102930816877895680, accessed 22 January 2021.
14 Chapman, *Psychedelia*, p. 88.
15 Quoted in Alan Robinson, liner notes to Paul Kanter and Grace Slick, *Sunfighter* (Retroworld, 2018).
16 Mark Paytress, 'High Priestess', *The Guardian* (15 November 2002).
17 Chapman, *Psychedelia*, p. 321.
18 Ibid., p. 319.
19 Ibid., p. 320.
20 Ibid., p. 322.
21 'Stuart Maconie's Freak Zone', BBC 6 Music (15 December 2019).
22 'NOFX Q&A', www.nofxofficialwebsite.com, accessed 4 January 2020.
23 Richie Unterberger, 'Review: The Maze, *Armageddon*', www.allmusic.com, accessed 9 January 2020.
24 Steve Miller, *Detroit Rock City: The Uncensored History of Rock 'n' Roll in America's Loudest City* (Boston, MA, 2013), p. 61.
25 Ibid., p. 55.
26 Ibid., pp. 16, 18–20.
27 Ann Moses, 'Blue Cheer', *NME* (2 March 1968).
28 Lester Bangs, 'A Reasonable Guide to Horrible Noise', *Village Voice* (30 September–6 October 1981), reprinted in Lester Bangs, *Psychotic Reactions and Carburetor Dung* (London, 1987), p. 305.
29 Michael Heatley, 'Now Yer Squawkin': The Story of Burke Shelley and Budgie', www.loudersound.com, 10 April 2017.
30 Chris Salewicz, 'Rapping with a Burke from Budgie', *NME* (29 June 1974).
31 Simon Frith, 'Budgie: *Squawk*', *Let It Rock* (November 1972).
32 George Starostin, 'Budgie', https://starling.rinet.ru/music/budgie.htm, accessed 28 July 2020.
33 Dale Berning, 'Nothing But Heart: Alan Sparhawk of Low's Favourite Albums', www.thequietus.com, 29 March 2012.
34 Adrian Lobb, 'Just Some Modern Rock Songs: Stuart Murdoch's Favourite Albums', www.thequietus.com, 4 September 2013.
35 Thomas Hasson, 'Page 33 1/3: Sam Fox's 13 Favourite Albums', www.thequietus.com, 14 August 2012.
36 Julian Marszalek, 'AC/DC: Disco Punk Funk Glam Rock Brit Pop Superstars', www.thequietus.com, 15 April 2009.
37 Michael Hann, 'Peerless. Extreme. Experimental? AC/DC's *Powerage* Turns 40', www.thequietus.com, 30 April 2018.
38 Jesse Fink, 'The Youngs: The Brothers Who Built AC/DC: Riff Raff', www.popmatters.com, 31 July 2014.
39 Dayal Patterson, 'Joking Aside: Jaz Coleman's 13 Favourite Albums', www.thequietus.com, 26 March 2012.
40 Anthony O'Grady, 'AC/DC: Australia Has Punk Rock Bands Too, Y'know', *RAM* (19 April 1975).

41 'AC/DC on Sex Shops, Masturbation and Hating The Ramones', www.abc.net.au/doublej, 1 May 2014.

42 Michael Hann, 'AC/DC – Their 40 Greatest Songs, Ranked!', www.theguardian.com, 30 July 2020.

43 Dave Haslam, *Sonic Youth Slept on My Floor* (London, 2019), p. 37.

44 Carol Clerk, *The Saga of Hawkwind* (ebook, London, 2009), pp. 278–80.

45 *Rockfield: The Studio on the Farm* (BBC4, 2020).

46 Julian Cope, *Japrocksampler* (London, 2007), p. 15.

47 Grayson Haver Currin, 'In Search of Les Rallizes Dénudés', www.redbullmusicacademy.com, 8 December 2014.

48 Cope, *Japrocksampler*, p. 270.

4 Funk

1 Thomas Sayers Ellis, 'From the Crib to the Coliseum: An Interview with Bootsy Collins', in *The Funk Era and Beyond: New Perspectives on Black Culture*, ed. Tony Bolden (New York, 2008), p. 97.

2 Jimmy McDonough, *Shakey: Neil Young's Biography* (London, 2002), p. 140.

3 Rick James (with David Ritz), *Glow: The Autobiography of Rick James* (New York, 2014), p. 73.

4 Dave Zimmer, *Crosby, Stills & Nash, the Biography: The Definitive Inside Story of the Supergroup* (New York, 2000), p. 100.

5 McDonough, *Shakey*, p. 320.

6 Ibid., pp. 316, 320.

7 Joel Rosenman, John Roberts and Robert Pilpel, *Young Men with Unlimited Capital: The Inside Story of the Legendary Woodstock Festival Told by the Two Who Paid for It* (New York, 1974), p. 153.

8 Kris Needs, *George Clinton and the Cosmic Odyssey of the P-Funk Empire* (London, 2014), pp. 9, 15.

9 Rodney Carmichael, 'Giving up the Funk: George Clinton Says Goodbye to the Road', www.ew.com, 22 May 2019.

10 Needs, *George Clinton*, p. 63.

11 Brian Hiatt, 'The Last Word: George Clinton on Alien Encounters, Trump's Lack of Funk', www.rollingstone.com, 22 February 2018.

12 Needs, *George Clinton*, p. 65.

13 Suzie McCracken, 'Playing the (Baker's) Dozens: George Clinton's Favourite Albums', www.thequietus.com, 9 July 2015.

14 Julian Marszalek, 'Getting Hypnotised: John Robb Finds the Funk in Unusual Places', www.thequietus.com, 12 July 2017.

15 Needs, *George Clinton*, p. 184.

16 Ibid., p. 88.

17 Ibid., p. 160.

18 Candice Pires, 'Bootsy Collins: 'LSD was a Big Part of Why I Left James Brown's Band', *The Observer* (29 October 2017).

19 Fred Wesley Jr, *Hit Me, Fred: Recollections of a Sideman* (Durham, NC, 2002), p. 194.

20 Jim Carroll, 'For Fred Wesley, the Army was Easier than Playing with James Brown', www.irishtimes.com, 17 June 2014.

21 Wesley Jr, *Hit Me, Fred*, pp. 193–4.

22 Needs, *George Clinton*, p. 139.

23 McDonough, *Shakey*, p. 513.

24 Needs, *George Clinton*, p. 207.

25 Ibid., p. 105.

26 Ibid., p. 130.

27 Ibid., p. 184.

28 Joseph Stannard, 'Goat "Stonegoat/Dreambuilding" Review', *The Wire* (June 2013).

29 Gerald F. Goodwin, 'Black and White in Vietnam', *New York Times* (18 July 2017); Amy Nathan Wright, 'A Philosophy of Funk: The Politics and Pleasure of a Parliafunkadelicment Thang!', in *The Funk Era*, ed. Bolden, p. 40.

30 Needs, *George Clinton*, p. 143.

31 Ned Raggett, '40 Years On: Funkadelic's *Let's Take It to the Stage* Revisited', www.thequietus.com, 14 July 2015.

32 Lois Wilson, 'Who Says a Funk Band Can't Play Rock?', *Record Collector* (September 2018).

33 McCracken, 'Playing the (Baker's) Dozens'.

34 Stuart Cosgrove, liner notes to *Techno! The New Dance Sound of Detroit* (10 Records, 1988).

35 Laurie Tuffrey, 'Stream Bardo Pond's RSD Trilogy', www.thequietus.com, 24 June 2014.

36 Donald Adderton, 'Her Act Too Spicy for U.S. Tastes; Betty Davis Finds Success in Europe', *Jet* (15 April 1976).

37 Joshua Klein, 'Review: *Betty Davis/They Say I'm Different*', www.pitchfork.com, 22 May 2007.

38 Julian Cope, *Copendium: An Expedition into the Rock 'n' Roll Underwerld* (London, 2013), pp. 178, 186–7.

39 Albert Freeman, 'Pan Sonics: Mika Vainio's Favourite Albums', www.thequietus.com, 1 September 2014.

5 The 1970s Experimental European Underground

1 Michael Watts, 'Can: *Tago Mago*', *Melody Maker* (29 January 1972).

2 Brad Erickson, 'George Clinton and David Bowie: The Space Race in Black and White', *Popular Music and Society*, XXXIX/5 (2016), p. 569.

3 Joe Banks, 'The Strange World of . . . Hawkwind', www.thequietus.com, 17 August 2020.

4 Martin Hayman, 'Can: Communism, Anarchism, Nihilism', *Sounds* (24 February 1973).

5 David Stubbs, liner notes to Can, *Tago Mago* (Spoon, 2007).

6 Urich Adelt, *Krautrock: German Music in the Seventies* (Ann Arbor, MI, 2016), p. 11; David Stubbs, *Future Days: Krautrock and the Building of Modern Germany* (London, 2017), pp. 5–6.

7 'Motorik' refers to a repetitive beat in 4/4 time that was used by Neu! and other krautrock bands including Can. It influenced many other artists, from David Bowie to Boredoms. Others called it the 'hammerbeat' or 'Dingerbeat' (after Klaus Dinger of Neu!). Dinger himself considered it the 'Apache beat' but that term never really caught on. Biba Kopf, 'On The Road Again', *The Wire* (June 2001).

8 Stubbs, *Future Days*, pp. 147–8.

9 Ibid., pp. 194, 202.

10 Ibid., p. 6.

11 Ibid., p. 122.

12 Ibid., p. 123.

13 *Krautrock: The Rebirth of Germany* (BBC4, 2009).

14 Ian MacDonald, 'Faust: The Sound of the Eighties', *NME* (3 March 1973).

15 Andy Wilson, *Faust: Stretch Out Time, 1970–1975* (London, 2006), pp. 25, 95.

16 *Krautrock: The Rebirth of Germany*.

17 Stubbs, *Future Days*, p. 213.

18 Ibid., pp. 33–4, 50–51, 89–90, 126–7.

19 James Johnson, 'Can Can . . . and They Will', *NME* (5 February 1972).

20 Andy Gill, 'Faust: Deconstructing the Nuts, Bolts and Girders of Rock – or Simply Having a Smashing Time?', *Mojo* (April 1997).

21 Alan Hardman, 'Richard Pinhas: The Man and His Music', *Electronics and Music Maker* (September 1982).

22 Vic Garbarini, 'Rude Boys: An Interview with Joe Strummer and Robert Fripp', *Musician Magazine* (June 1981).

23 Hawklord, '*Interface* Customer Review', www.amazon.com, 31 March 2005, accessed 23 January 2021.

24 Richard Pinhas quoted in JR Moores, 'All Things Must Crash', liner notes to Heldon, *Stand By* (Bureau B, 2020).

25 Jim Allen, 'There is No Prog, Only Zeuhl: A Guide to One of Rock's Most Imaginative Subgenres', www.daily.bandcamp.com, 5 October 2020.

26 Paul Stump, 'Different Drummer', *The Wire* (July 1995).

27 Basil Francis, 'Nyl – *Nyl*', www.theprogressiveaspect.net, 16 February 2015.

28 Warren Hatter, 'Concrete Science Fiction Riot: Why do We Ignore the 70s French Underground?', www.thequietus.com, 13 August 2019.

29 David Shettler, 'The Top Five Richard Pinhas Albums', www.metrotimes.com, 5 October 2016.

30 Klemen Breznikar, 'Baby Grandmothers Interview with Kenny Håkansson', www.psychedelicbabymag.com, 17 December 2018.

31 Alf Björnberg and Thomas Bossius, 'Introduction: The Small Country that Grew Big', in *Made in Sweden: Studies in Popular Music*, ed. Alf Björnberg and Thomas Bossius (Abingdon, 2017), p. 5.

32 Jim Weir, 'Once Upon a Time in Sweden', *The Wire* (January 2008).

33 Sverker Hyltén-Cavallius, 'Progg: Utopia and Chronotope', in *Made in Sweden*, ed. Björnberg and Bossius, p. 68.

34 Ibid., p. 66.

35 'Pärson Sound – 1968 – *Pärson Sound*', www.surfingtheodyssey.blogspot.com, 12 May 2015.

36 Thomas Tidholm quoted in Mats Eriksson Dunér, 'We Never Changed Chords', liner notes to International Harvester, *Remains* (Silence, 2018).

37 Ibid.

38 Hyltén-Cavallius, 'Progg', pp. 71–2.

6 Punk Rock: The Non-Heavy Genre that was Vital for Heaviness

1 JR Moores, 'A Very Selfish Enterprise: The Strange World of . . . Shellac', www.thequietus.com, 3 August 2017.

2 *Classic Albums: The Sex Pistols – Never Mind the Bollocks, Here's the Sex Pistols* (DVD, Eagle Vision, 2002).

3 Harry Sword, 'Neanderthal Underswing', *Record Collector* (June 2014).

4 Dan Ozzi, 'Loud and Louder: Aaron from Isis Interviews Trevor from Pelican', www.vice.com, 16 October 2013.

5 Joe Thompson, *Sleevenotes* (Keighley, 2019), p. 167.

6 Steve Hanley and Olivia Piekarski, *The Big Midweek: Life Inside The Fall* (Pontefract, West Yorkshire, 2016), pp. 34–5.

7 Quoted by Steve Pringle, 'YMGTA #28 – The Marshall Suite', www.youmustgetthemall.wordpress.com, 26 August 2019.

8 *On Bass . . . Tina Weymouth!* (BBC4, 2019).

9 Simon Reynolds, *Rip It Up and Start Again: Post-Punk, 1978–1984* (London, 2019), p. 185.

10 Dave Haslam, *Sonic Youth Slept on My Floor* (London, 2019), pp. 37–8.

11 Reynolds, *Rip It Up*, p. 180.

12 Paul Sullivan, *Remixology: Tracing the Dub Diaspora* (London, 2014), pp. 47–8.

13 Chas de Whalley, 'The Slits: *Return of the Giant Slits*', *Record Mirror* (14 November 1981).

14 *Here to Be Heard: The Story of the Slits* (DVD, Head Gear Films, 2018).

15 David Stubbs, 'The Thin Boys: Post-Punk Funk', *Record Collector* (January 2019).

16 Richard Gehr, 'The Oral History of the Pop Group: The Noisy Brits Who Were Too Punk for the Punks', *Rolling Stone* (7 November 2014).

17 Peter Silverton, 'We Know There's Something Wrong Somewhere: The Pop Group', *NME* (24 March 1979).

18 Paul Rambali, 'The Pop Group: *Y*', *NME* (28 April 1979).

19 Stubbs, 'The Thin Boys'.

20 Gwen Ihnat, '"Art Meets the Devil via James Brown": The Everlasting Impact of Gang of Four's *Entertainment!*', www.avclub.com, 26 September 2019.

21 Reynolds, *Rip It Up*, p. 113.

22 Will Hodgkinson, 'New Adventures in Hi-fi', *The Guardian* (10 September 2004).

23 'Andy Gill: Major Labels will Rip You Off, Unless You're Coldplay or U2', *Metro* (24 January 2011).

24 Anthony Kiedis with Larry Sloman, *Scar Tissue* (London, 2005), pp. 142–3.

25 Reynolds, *Rip It Up*, p. 127.

26 JR Moores, 'My Dad Wrote That Better: Andrew Falkous' Baker's Dozen', www.thequietus.com, 11 April 2018; Corey Beasley, 'To Hell with Good Intentions: An Interview with Andrew Falkous', www.cokemachineglow.com, 18 February 2015.

27 Stubbs, 'The Thin Boys'.

28 Reynolds, *Rip It Up*, p. 7.

29 'Public Image Limited Interview with Keith Levene and John Lydon on The Tom Snyder Show 1980', www.youtube.com, accessed 23 January 2021.

30 'Public Image Ltd. – Countdown Interview 1979', www.youtube.com, 11 November 2017.

31 Nick Kent, 'Public Image Ltd: *Public Image Ltd.*', *NME* (9 December 1978); Peter Silverton, 'Public Image Ltd: *Public Image*', *Sounds* (9 December 1978).

32 Reynolds, *Rip It Up*, p. 13.

33 *John Lydon: A Culture Show Special* (BBC2, 2010).

34 Stubbs, 'The Thin Boys'.

35 Jack Barron, 'The Needle and the Damage Done', *NME* (13 August 1988).

36 Alex Ogg, 'Goth: Back in Black', *Record Collector* (December 2007).
37 Dorian Lynskey, 'The Cure's Robert Smith: "I was very optimistic when I was young – now I'm the opposite"', *The Guardian* (7 June 2018).
38 Michael Azerrad, *Our Band Could Be Your Life: Scenes from the American Indie Underground, 1981–1991* (New York, 2001), p. 153.
39 Lemmy with Janiss Garza, *White Line Fever* (London, 2003), pp. 28–9.
40 Ronnie Dannelley, 'Interview with Lemmy from Motörhead', www.earcandymag.com, 20 June 2000.
41 Andrew O'Neill, *A History of Heavy Metal* (London, 2018), p. 71.
42 Lemmy, *White Line Fever*, pp. 138, 125, 270, 265.
43 Fred Villano, 'Lemmy: The Final Interview', www.bassplayer.com, 23 December 2015.
44 Joe McIver, 'From the Vault: A Frank Interview with Lemmy, 2003', www.bassplayer.com, 3 May 2019.
45 Sylvie Simmons, 'Ten Questions for Ozzy Osbourne', *Mojo* (November 2000).

7 Industrial Rock

1 Jon Wiederhorn, 'The Gospel According to Al Jourgensen', www.loudersound.com, 4 October 2017.
2 David Fricke, '*Speak & Spell* Review', *Rolling Stone* (13 May 1982).
3 Cosey Fanni Tutti, *Art Sex Music* (London, 2017).
4 Ian Gittins, 'Throbbing Gristle: Astoria Theatre, London', *Melody Maker* (11 June 1988).
5 Paul Morley, 'Cabaret Voltaire', *The Face* (September 1981); Paul Morley, 'The Heart and Soul of Cabaret Voltaire', *NME* (29 November 1980).
6 Stephen Dalton, 'Cabaret Voltaire', *Uncut* (February 2000).
7 Morley, 'Cabaret Voltaire'; Morley, 'Heart and Soul'.
8 Adam Sweeting, 'Cabaret Voltaire', *Melody Maker* (26 June 1982).
9 'Killing Joke – CND Rally, Trafalgar Square, London 26/10/80 (Full Set)', www.youtube.com, accessed 23 January 2021.
10 Kate Hennessy, 'Interview: Justin Broadrick', www.thequietus.com, 3 October 2014; Kate Hennessy, 'Central to Process: Justin Broadrick's Favourite Albums', www.thequietus.com, 16 October 2014.
11 'The Legendary Pink Dots', *Snowdonia* (1987), archived at www.brainwashed.com, accessed 26 January 2021.
12 David Gordon, 'Interview with J. G. Thirlwell', www.aesop.com (February 2017).
13 Glenn Law, 'Foetus', in *The Rough Guide to Rock*, ed. Peter Buckley (London, 2003), p. 385.
14 Simon Reynolds, *Rip It Up and Start Again: Post-Punk, 1978–1984* (London, 2019), p. 483.
15 Alexander Hacke, 'How to Destroy the ICA with Drills', *The Guardian* (16 February 2007).

16 Keith Cameron, 'Dave Gahan: Dead Man Talking', *NME* (18 January 1997).

17 Lara Marlowe, 'Former U2 Manager Paul McGuinness: Cracking Crime on the Côte d'Azur', www.irishtimes.com, 7 June 2015.

18 Richard Smirke, 'Depeche Mode Manager Jonathan Kessler: "Friction is what keeps them creative"', www.billboard.com, 14 November 2017.

19 Michael Corcoran, 'The Night Chicago Died', *Spin* (April 1989).

20 Kiran Acharya, 'Revolting Lots: Al Jourgensen's Favourite Ministry Albums', www.thequietus.com, 27 April 2016.

21 'Session with Robert Roberts', www.prongs.org, accessed 13 August 2018.

22 Steven Blush, 'Ministry: Cult of Personality', *Spin* (October 1991).

23 Acharya, 'Revolting Lots'.

24 Al Jourgensen with Jon Wiederhorn, *Ministry: The Lost Gospels According to Al Jourgensen* (Boston, MA, 2013), p. 94.

25 Ibid., p. 85.

26 Ibid., pp. 135–7; ibid., p. 106.

27 Gina McIntyre, 'Ministry Frontman Al Jourgensen Sues Makers of Behind-the-Scenes Documentary "Fix"', www.latimes.com, 20 April 2011.

28 Jourgensen, *Ministry*, p. 136.

29 Paul Simpson, '*Amerikkkant* Review', www.allmusic.com, March 2018.

30 Jourgensen, *Ministry*, pp. 117–18.

31 Jonathan Gold, '*The Downward Spiral* Review', *Rolling Stone* (24 March 1994).

32 Jourgensen, *Ministry*, p. 171.

33 RJ Smith, 'Atari Teenage Riot: What's the Frequency, Alec?', *Spin* (March 1998).

34 Andy Crysell, 'Atari Teenage Riot: *60 Second Wipe Out*', *NME* (8 May 1999).

35 Samantha Anne Carrillo, 'Infinitely More Mr Nice Guy: Alice Cooper Talks Hollywood Vampires, God, Golf and Marilyn Manson', www. alibi.com, 30 May 2013.

36 Tucker Carlson, 'Marilyn Manson Has a Secret', *Talk* (November 2000).

37 Jude Ellison Sady Doyle, 'Marilyn Manson Told Us Who He Was', https://gen.medium.com (3 February 2021).

38 Mikal Gilmore, 'Trent Reznor: Death to Hootie', *Rolling Stone* (6 March 1997).

39 Stevie Chick, 'Nine Inch Nails: To Hell and Back', *Kerrang!* (2 April 2005); 'Nine Inch Nails' Trent Reznor: "I Don't Care How Many Records I Sell"', www.blabbermouth.net, 25 September 2007.

40 David Foster Wallace, 'The (as it were) Seminal Importance of Terminator 2', in Wallace, *Both Flesh and Not* (London, 2012), pp. 177–89 (originally published as 'F/X Porn' in *Waterstone's Magazine*, Winter/Spring 1998).

41 JR Moores, 'Don't Call It Synthwave: Navigating Necro Deathmort's *Overland*', www.daily.bandcamp.com, 6 October 2017.

42 Aphex Twin's 'remixes' turned out not to be remixes at all but rather original compositions submitted by the mischievous electronic musician known also as Richard James, who hadn't even bothered listening to the original NIN tracks he'd been commissioned to rework.

43 Joseph Stannard, 'Vicious Spiral: America's New Age of Anxiety is Channelled into Epic Noise in the Hands of Lana Del Rabies', *The Wire* (May 2018).

44 Andy Battaglia, 'For Moogfest, Michael Stipe, Lonnie Holley, and Transhuman Futurists Commune Down South', www.artnews.com, 29 June 2017.

45 Ben Beaumont-Thomas, 'Moor Mother: 'We Have Yet to Truly Understand What Enslavement Means', *The Guardian* (20 April 2017).

46 Jasper Willems, 'Distorting the Present: DiS Meets Moor Mother', www.drownedinsound.com, 17 January 2017.

47 Beaumont-Thomas, 'Moor Mother'.

8 Noise Rock

1 Phyllis Heller, 'This Butt's for You', *Spin* (June 1986).

2 'Trent Reznor Brings "Welcome Oblivion" to Studio Q', www.youtube. com, accessed 23 January 2021.

3 Al Jourgensen with Jon Wiederhorn, *Ministry: The Lost Gospels According to Al Jourgensen* (Boston, MA, 2013), pp. 131–2.

4 Dean Kuipers, 'Texas Crude: The Butthole Surfers – Humor and Horror on a Texan Scale', *Spin* (July 1990).

5 Michael Azerrad, *Our Band Could Be Your Life: Scenes from the American Indie Underground, 1981–1991* (New York, 2001), p. 293.

6 John Morthland and Joe Nick Patoski, 'Feeding the Fish: An Oral History of the Butthole Surfers', *Spin* (November 1996).

7 Azerrad, *Our Band*, pp. 276–7.

8 Charles M. Young, 'Butthole Surfers: America's Most Notorious Psycho-delic Rock Band', *Rolling Stone* (26 December 1996).

9 Morthland and Patoski, 'Feeding the Fish'.

10 Young, 'Butthole Surfers'.

11 Mark Sinker, 'Butthole Surfers: Riding the Shock Wave', NME (16 April 1988).

12 Jim Sullivan, 'The Butthole Surfers Ride a New Wave of Popularity', *Boston Globe* (19 July 1996).

13 Marc Rowland, 'In Conversation with the Biggest Weirdos in Rock, the Butthole Surfers', www.kerrang.com, 18 January 2018.

14 Daniel Dylan Wray, 'Butthole Surfers Were the Epitome of Every Hell-raising Rock'n'Roll Legend You Ever Heard', www.vice.com, 31 May 2016.

15 Young, 'Butthole Surfers'.

16 Ibid.

17 Azerrad, *Our Band*, p. 290.

18 John Lewis, 'An Audience with . . . John Paul Jones', www.uncut.com, 17 January 2014.

19 Zachary Leeks, 'Gibby Haynes Butthole Surfers Interview (The Lost Tapes from 2004)', www.caughtinthecrossfire.com, 8 February 2011.

20 Jason Cohen, 'The Butthole Surfers: In through the Back Door', *Rolling Stone* (24 June 1993).

21 Ibid.

22 Joshua Berger, 'Butthole Surfers: King Coffey's View', *Plazm*, 6 (1994).

23 Sullivan, 'The Butthole Surfers'.

24 Azerrad, *Our Band*, pp. 304, 310.

25 Kuipers, 'Texas Crude'.

26 John Jurgensen, 'An Aging Punk Star's Dilemma: Am I Too Old to Stage Dive?', www.wsj.com, 7 December 2017.

27 Lorraine Ali, 'Jesus Lizard: Punk and Disorderly', in *We Rock So You Don't Have To: The Option Reader #1*, ed. Scott Becker (San Diego, CA, 1998), p. 102.

28 Matt Golosinski, 'Apocalypse Yow: The Jesus Lizard, Lollapalooza's Surprise Darling, Sticks Out Its Tongue and Goes "Arrrgh"', *Phoenix New Times* (10 August 1995); Matthew Smith-Lahrman, 'Interview with Duane Denison, February 3, 1993', www.smithlahrman.blogspot.com, 30 January 2012.

29 Chuck Eddy, 'They Shoot Horses, Don't They?', *Spin* (October 1986).

30 Smith-Lahrman, 'Interview with Duane Denison'.

31 Ibid.

32 'The Jesus Lizard Orbit Room Dallas TX December 16 1994', www.youtube.com, accessed 23 January 2021.

33 David Yow, 'Memoir', www.magnetmagazine.com, 29 September 2007.

34 Jeff Kirby, 'Shirtless, Peerless: An Interview with David Yow of The Jesus Lizard', www.thestranger.com, 23 July 2009.

35 J. Bennett, 'Have You Seen David Yow's Balls? The Jesus Lizard Wrote a Book about Them & Some Other Stuff', www.vice.com, 26 February 2014.

36 Rafer Guzmn, 'The Lizard King', www.dallasobserver.com, 4 June 1998; Chris Ziegler, 'The Jesus Lizard: Obviously I'm Not a Pervert', www. larecord.com, 16 October 2009.

37 Allison Stewart, 'Alternative Nation's Last Stand: Lollapalooza 1995, an Oral History', www.washtingtonpost.com, 11 August 2015.

38 Golosinski, 'Apocalypse Yow'.

39 Kirby, 'Shirtless, Peerless'.

40 Matt Sullivan, 'Magnet Classics: The Making of The Jesus Lizard's *Liar*', www.magnetmagazine.com, 2 June 2014.

41 Greg Prato, 'David Yow of The Jesus Lizard', www.songfacts.com,
   31 July 2014; Sullivan, 'Magnet Classics'.

42 Eddy, 'They Shoot Horses'.

43 Matt Diehl, 'America, Welcome to The Jesus Lizard', *Rolling Stone*
   (10 August 1995).

44 Smith-Lahrman, 'Interview with Duane Denison'.

45 Bennett, 'Yow's Balls'.

46 The Jesus Lizard, *BOOK* (New York, 2013), p. 63.

47 Sullivan, 'Magnet Classics'.

48 Nick Hutchings, 'Constant vs. Variable: The Jesus Lizard Interviewed
   about *Down*', www.thequietus.com, 30 September 2014.

49 Thee Inspector, '*Blue* Customer Review', www.amazon.com,
   25 May 1998, accessed 23 January 2021.

50 Guzmn, 'The Lizard King'.

51 Mark Jenkins, 'The Jesus Lizard: *Blue*', *Washington Post* (15 May 1998).

52 Jane Dark, 'The Jesus Lizard: *Blue*', *Spin* (June 1998).

53 Jesus Lizard, *BOOK*, p. 152.

54 John Doran, 'Quietus Writers' Top 40 Noise Rock Tracks',
   www.thequietus.com, 29 March 2016.

55 Kirby, 'Shirtless, Peerless'.

56 Robert Christgau, 'Township Jive Conquers the World', *Village Voice*
   (3 March 1987).

57 Nick Soulsby, *Swans: Sacrifice and Transcendence, The Oral History*
   (London, 2018), pp. 118–19.

58 Kim Gordon, *Girl in a Band* (London, 2015), p. 168.

59 Mark Prindle, 'Shannon Selberg – 2002', www.markprindle.com,
   accessed 7 June 2019.

60 Ibid.

61 John Dougan, 'Cows: Biography', www.allmusic.com, accessed
   6 June 2019.

62 Michael H. Little, 'Graded on a Curve: Cows, *Cunning Stunts*',
   www.thevinyldistrict.com, 12 August 2013.

63 Azerrad, *Our Band*, 319.

64 Simon Reynolds, 'Steve Albini: Smoke 'Em If You Got 'Em', *Melody
   Maker* (21 November 1992).

65 Ibid.

66 Kory Grow, 'Big Black on *Songs About F—king* at 30: "We Wanted to
   Make Filthy Music"', www.rollingstone.com, 8 September 2017.

67 JR Moores, 'A Very Selfish Enterprise: The Strange World of . . . Shellac',
   www.thequietus.com, 3 August 2017.

68 Kevin Curtin, 'Playback: Cherubs Flit Back', www.austinchronicle.com,
   25 July 2014.

69 Theodore Sturgeon, 'On Hand: A Book', *Venture* (September 1957),
   p. 49.

70 Marah Eakin, 'Melvins' Buzz Osborne Picks Songs by "Bands That Were Good, But Blew It"', www.avclub.com, 7 January 2014.

71 Mark Prindle, 'Cows' (*Sorry in Pig Minor*), www.markprindle.com, accessed 14 June 2019.

9 Sabbath Phase II: Melvins' *Gluey Porch Treatments*

1 Adam Kivel, 'Three Bastards, 30 Years: An Oral History of The Melvins', www.consequenceofsound.net, 15 November 2013.

2 Steven Hyden, 'Melvins: *Everybody Loves Sausages* Review', www.pitchfork.com, 2 May 2013; Ned Raggett, '*Gluey Porch Treatments* Review', www.allmusic.com, 28 November 2018.

3 'Topic: Are the Melvins Closer to Punk or Metal?', www.themelvins.net, accessed 5 December 2018.

4 Michael Friedman, 'The Melvins are Not Screwing With You', www.psychologytoday.com, 26 September 2017.

5 'Why I Love Black Sabbath: King Buzzo', www.homeofmetal.com, 11 January 2017.

6 Harry Sword, 'Neanderthal Underswing', *Record Collector* (June 2014).

7 'Topic: *Colossus of Destiny*', www.themelvins.net, accessed 19 February 2019.

8 Matt Stocks, 'Buzz Osborne's Guide to the Greatest Melvins Albums Ever Made', www.loudersound.com, 28 June 2016.

9 Greg Prato, *Grunge is Dead: The Oral History of Seattle Rock Music* (Toronto, 2009), p. 188.

10 Phil Freeman, 'Amps of the Perverse', *The Wire* (December 2006).

11 Brad Angle, 'Kirk Hammett and Adam Jones: Bad Religion', *Guitar World* (April 2009).

12 Nick Richardson, 'Melvins Lite: Freak Puke Review', *The Wire* (June 2012).

13 Bruce Laidlaw, 'The Melvins', in *The Rough Guide to Rock*, ed. Peter Buckley (London, 2003), p. 664.

14 Brian Walsby, 'Massive Melvins Interview from the Pre-Stoner Witch Era', www.themelvins.net, accessed 5 December 2018.

15 Trevor Dunn, 'The Melvins 51 States in 51 Days Tour Diary, Days 19 and 20', www.spin.com, 26 September 2012.

16 Chris Ziegler, 'The Melvins: Judge Me by My Enemies', www.larecord.com, 27 January 2011.

17 Lucy Dayman, 'Buzz Osborne: The Top 5 People that Influenced my Career', https://tonedeaf.thebrag.com, 30 June 2014.

18 'Melvins Don't Need to Break Up to Be Relevant', www.ocweekly.com, 7 October 2010.

10 The Global Impact of Napalm Death's *Scum*

1 John Peel, 'Pop: John Peel Reports from Deepest Nottingham', *The Observer* (4 October 1987).
2 JR Moores, 'What's in Your Suitcase?: Buzz Osborne of Melvins', www.daily.bandcamp.com, 15 June 2016.
3 Steven Wells, 'Napalm Death, Extreme Noise Terror, Bolt Thrower: ULU, London', *NME* (11 March 1989).
4 Steven Wells, 'Napalm Death: End of an Earache', *NME* (4 January 1992).
5 Sheila Ravenscroft in John Peel, *Margrave of the Marshes* (London, 2005), p. 327.
6 John Peel, 'Introduction', in Albert Mudrian, *Choosing Death: The Improbable History of Death Metal and Grindcore* (Los Angeles, CA, 2002), p. 18.
7 'Five Records: The Eyes in the Heat', www.juno.co.uk, 1 October 2012.
8 Albert Freeman, 'Pan Sonics: Mika Vainio's Favourite Albums', www.thequietus.com, 1 September 2014.
9 Philip Sherburne, 'The Haxan Cloak: UK Producer Channels Demons, Curdles Blood', www.spin.com, 19 February 2013.
10 Russell Cuzner, 'A Sense for Contrast: The Strange World of Russell Haswell', www.thequietus.com, 20 March 2014.
11 Paul Régimbeau (aka Mondkopf), *I* by Extreme Precautions, https://inparadisum.bandcamp.com/album/i, accessed 15 February 2019.
12 Conversation with the author via Skype, 7 June 2017. All subsequent quotations from this source.
13 David Stubbs, 'Invisible Jukebox: Justin Broadrick', *The Wire* (September 2014); Matteo Uggeri, 'Darren McClure', www.concreteshelves.blog, 7 May 2019.

11 The Late 1980s and Early 1990s Pre-Grunge Underground

1 Jack Barron, 'Bad Brains: Brain Drain', *Sounds* (6 June 1987).
2 Dan Franklin, 'At the Extremities: Barney Greenway of Napalm Death Interviewed', www.thequietus.com, 15 January 2015.
3 Michael Azerrad, *Our Band Could Be Your Life: Scenes from the American Indie Underground, 1981–1991* (New York, 2001), pp. 78, 117, 145; Chuck Eddy, 'They Shoot Horses, Don't They?', *Spin* (October 1986).
4 Mark Yarm, *Everybody Loves Our Town: A History of Grunge* (London, 2001), p. 112; John La Briola, 'Here's Mud in Your Ear', www.westword.com, 16 August 2001.
5 Azerrad, *Our Band*, p. 214.
6 Jimmy McDonough, *Shakey: Neil Young's Biography* (London, 2002), p. 269.
7 Ibid., p. 270.

8 Ibid., p. 12.

9 Ibid., p. 77.

10 Joseph Yanick, 'J Mascis Can Play the Wimpiest Instruments Without Being a Total Wimp', www.vice.com, 26 August 2014.

11 François Ray Declercq, 'Greg Sage (Wipers) Interview', www.francoisraydeclercq.wordpress.com, 3 April 2015.

12 'Lou Barlow of Dinosaur Jr on Playing Bass with a Really Loud Guitarist', www.youtube.com, 14 November 2016, accessed 23 January 2021.

13 Azerrad, *Our Band*, p. 354.

14 Tzvi Gluckin, 'J Mascis Keeps It Loud!', www.premierguitar.com, 15 July 2016.

15 'Ernie Ball: String Theory Featuring J Mascis', www.youtube.com, 4 November 2016, accessed 23 January 2021.

16 Azerrad, *Our Band*, p. 353.

17 Gluckin, 'J Mascis'.

18 Ibid.

19 Sam Richard, 'J Mascis on the Guitarists you Really Must Hear', *The Guardian* (12 March 2011).

20 Gillian Watson, 'Dinosaur Jr: On the Couch with Lou Barlow', www.theskinny.co.uk, 19 June 2009.

21 Kory Grow, 'Hardcore Mettle: Bad Brains' Strange Survival Tale', *Spin* (29 November 2012).

22 Barron, 'Bad Brains'.

23 Ibid.

24 Vernon Reid, 'Brain Power', *Spin* (October 1990).

25 Al Quint, 'Bad Brains: An interview with HR', *Suburban Voice* (Winter 1987).

26 JR Moores, 'Taking Out the Thrash: Scott Ian of Anthrax's Top Albums from 1986', www.thequietus.com, 8 March 2016.

27 Azerrad, *Our Band*, p. 122.

28 Ibid., p. 384.

29 Alexandra Pollard, 'The Unlikely Renaissance of Slowdive', *The Guardian* (30 March 2017).

30 Yarm, *Everybody Loves Our Town*, p. 220.

31 Quoted in David Cavanagh, *Good Night and Good Riddance: How Thirty-Five Years of John Peel Helped to Shape Modern Life* (London, 2015), p. 523.

32 Yarm, *Everybody Loves Our Town*, p. 220.

33 Karen Schoemer, 'Post-Punk Angst of Babes in Toyland', *New York Times* (27 March 1992).

34 Ibid.

35 *Dinosaur Jr: Live in the Middle East* (DVD, Image Entertainment, 2007).

36 Kate Hutchinson, 'Riot Grrrl: Ten of the Best', www.theguardian.com, 28 January 2015.

12 TAD: The Heaviest and Least Celebrated Grunge Band

1 Jim Berkenstadt, 'The Vig Issue', *Vox* (March 1995).
2 Michael Azerrad, *Come As You Are: The Story of Nirvana* (London, 1996), pp. 162, 229.
3 David Hepworth, *Uncommon People: The Rise and Fall of the Rock Stars* (London, 2017), p. 382.
4 Michael Hann, '(13 On The) Wheels of Steel: Biff Byford of Saxon's Favourite LPs', www.thequietus.com, 13 February 2020.
5 Daniel Sarkissian, 'How Alice in Chains and Nirvana Changed MTV and Popular Music, ft. Jay Jay French (Twisted Sister)', www.youtube.com, 28 June 2020, accessed 23 January 2021.
6 Richard Bienstock, 'Kim Thayil on the Secrets behind His Tunings', www.guitarworld.com, 12 November 2012.
7 'Chris Cornell: The Difference between Hair-Metal and Grunge', www.youtube.com, accessed 23 January 2021.
8 *I'm Now: The Story of Mudhoney* (DVD, King of Hearts Productions, 2013).
9 *Leonard Cohen: Bird on a Wire* (DVD, Tony Palmer Films, 2010).
10 Conversation with the author via Skype, 25 June 2018. All subsequent quotations from this source.
11 Edwin Pouncey, 'Tad, Nirvana: Astoria, London', *NME* (16 December 1989).
12 Mark Yarm, *Everybody Loves Our Town: A History of Grunge* (London, 2001), p. 449.
13 https://twitter.com/HarrySword/status/1076596908179755009, accessed 22 December 2018.
14 Guy Oddy, '10 Questions for Musician Tad Doyle', www.theartsdesk.com, 21 March 2016.

13 Steve Albini: Heavy-duty Engineer

1 The Jesus Lizard, *BOOK* (New York, 2013), p. 35.
2 Stewart Lee, 'Steve Albini / All Tomorrow's Parties 2002', *Sunday Times* (10 March 2002).
3 Joe Matera, 'Steve Albini: "I Came to Respect Nirvana as Artists during the Making of *In Utero*"', www.ultimate-guitar.com, 25 July 2011.
4 Ibid.
5 Larry Crane, 'Steve Albini: Nirvana, Pixies, Stooges, PJ Harvey', www.tapeop.com, January–February 2012.
6 Steve Albini, 'The Problem with Music', *Maximumrocknroll*, 133 (June 1994).
7 Owen Murphy, 'The Jesus Lizard Regenerate Again', www.kexp.org, 26 September 2018.

8 Matthew Smith-Lahrman, 'Interview with Steve Albini, 1993', www.smithlahrman.blogspot.co.uk, 6 October 2010.

9 Gillian G. Gaar, *In Utero* (London, 2016), pp. 65–6.

10 Ibid., p. 69.

11 Ibid., pp. 73–4.

12 Ibid., pp. 43–4.

13 Crane, 'Steve Albini'.

14 Neil Macdonald, 'Fire Fighting: Steve Albini Interviewed', www.thequietus.com, 2 September 2013.

15 David Gedge, *Sleevenotes* (Keighley, 2019), pp. 23–4, 88.

16 *Pixies: Gouge* (Channel 4, 29 November 2001).

17 *120 Minutes* (MTV, 20 June 1993).

18 *Reeling with PJ Harvey* (VHS, PolyGram, 1994).

19 Because Slint singer and guitarist Brian McMahan never had much confidence in his own vocals, the band had placed an advert for 'interested female singers' in the liner notes to *Spiderland*. Polly Jean Harvey was one of the few listeners to respond. However, the band never made a follow-up album. Scott Tennent, *Spiderland* (New York, 2011), p. 130.

20 Martin Aston, 'PJ Harvey', *Puncture*, 32 (1991).

21 David Peisner, 'Let It Bleed: The Oral History of PJ Harvey's *Rid of Me*', www.spin.com, 1 May 2013.

22 Adrian Deevoy, 'PJ Harvey, Björk, and Tori Amos: Hips. Lips. Tits. Power.', *Q* (May 1994).

23 Robin Mills, 'Eva Harvey', www.marshwoodvale.com, 1 June 2010.

24 Barney Hoskyns, 'Angry Young Women', *Vogue* (1991).

25 JR Moores, 'A Very Selfish Enterprise: The Strange World of . . . Shellac', www.thequietus.com, 3 August 2017.

26 Camran Afsari, 'Chapter 9: Steve Albini – Nemesis of Corporate Rock', in *Music Producers: Conversations with Today's Top Hit Makers*, ed. Barbara Schultz (Emeryville, CA, 2000), p. 66.

27 Parker Langvardt, 'Interview: Steve Albini', www.epitonic.com, 7 December 2012.

28 *Long Distance* (2008) by Three Second Kiss being one example of such a find. Shellac's Bob Weston mastered the Albini-recorded LP, and the Italian trio's sound comes highly recommended for those in need of a fix of post- and math-rock brutalism in the long gaps between Shellac album releases.

29 Anne Hilde Nesset, 'Invisible Jukebox: Will Oldham', *The Wire* (December 2003).

30 Ian Christe, 'The Hard Golden Tone of Shellac: An Interview with Steve Albini', *Warp* (1994).

31 Unpublished excerpt from JR Moores, 'My Dad Wrote That Better: Andrew Falkous' Baker's Dozen', www.thequietus.com, 11 April 2018.

32 Ibid.

33 Jamie Coughlin, 'Russian Circles Interview', www.overblown.co.uk, 17 August 2016. Greg Norman is Electrical Audio's staff engineer and head technical officer. He has worked there since 1996, and in a salaried position since 1998. Reviewers have occasionally taken 'Greg Norman' to be one of Albini's mischievous pseudonyms. This is erroneous. There are two studios at Electrical Audio. Although he may work quickly and efficiently, Steve Albini does not possess the superhuman ability to record in two different studios at the same time. Greg Norman is a real person.

34 https://twitter.com/OozingWound/status/1101242028028018691, accessed 1 March 2019.

35 Vish Khanna, 'Inside the Making of METZ's *Strange Peace* with Steve Albini', www.exclaim.co.uk, 20 September 2017.

36 Jaime Lees, 'She's Crafty: The Breeders' Kelley Deal Talks Knitting, Nudity and Steve Albini's Bodily Functions', www.riverfronttimes.com, 7 May 2008.

37 Steve Albini, 'Eyewitness Record Reviews', *Forced Exposure*, 17 (1991).

38 '*Parallel Lines* by M. Chapman', www.youtube.com, accessed 23 January 2021.

39 Greg Milner, *Perfecting Sound Forever: The Story of Recorded Music* (London, 2010), p. 97.

40 John Tait, *Vanda & Young: Inside Australia's Hit Factory* (Sydney, 2010), pp. 165–6, 176–7.

41 Milner, *Perfecting*, pp. 130–31.

42 Vish Khanna, 'Ep. #453: Steve Albini', www.vishkhanna.com, 20 December 2018.

43 Quoted in Éamon Sweeney, 'The Steve Albini Interview', www.swench.net, 27 August 2016.

44 'The Wedding Present Re-record *George Best* with Steve Albini', www.scopitones.co.uk, September 2017.

45 Mitch Lafon, 'Full Box of Tricks in '04', www.bravewords.com, 29 June 2004, archived at www.web.archive.org, accessed 15 November 2019.

46 Matera, 'Steve Albini'.

47 Sweeney, 'Steve Albini Interview'.

14 Sabbath Phase III: Earth, Sleep, Electric Wizard and Other Assorted Stoners

1 G. K. Chesterton, 'A Romance of the Marshes', in Chesterton, *Alarms and Discursions* (London, 1910), p. 255.

2 JR Moores, 'Gnod is Sometimes Sludgy, Always Loud, and Never Bored on its New Album *Mirror*', www.vice.com, 29 March 2016.

3 Martyn Coppack, 'Gnod – *Infinity Machines*', www.echoesanddust.com, 20 April 2015.

4   Tom Breihan, '5-10-15-20: Earth's Dylan Carlson', www.pitchfork.com,
    2 February 2011.
5   Peter Silverton, 'Black Sabbath: Apollo Theatre, Glasgow', *Sounds*
    (27 May 1978).
6   T. J. Kliebhan, 'Rank Your Records: Dylan Carlson Revisits Earth's
    Pioneering Drone Albums', www.vice.com, 13 April 2018.
7   Sean McBurney, 'Interview – Dylan Carlson', www.brumlive.com,
    11 March 2015.
8   Breihan, '5-10-15-20'.
9   Edwin Pouncey, 'Unedited EARTH vs WIRE transcript via SAVX',
    www.ideologic.com, 23 October 2005.
10 Ibid.
11 Alex Needham, 'Earth: Godfathers of Drone Metal', www.theguardian.
    com, 21 June 2014; Robin Ono, 'Soundwaves to Landscapes: An
    Interview with Dylan Carlson of Earth', www.echoesanddust.com,
    26 April 2019.
12 Edwin Pouncey, 'Invisible Jukebox: Sunn O)))', *The Wire*
    (July 2004).
13 JR Moores, '20 Years of Southern Lord's Dark and Heavy Art',
    www.daily.bandcamp.com, 9 March 2018.
14 Kliebhan, 'Rank Your Records'.
15 McBurney, 'Interview – Dylan Carlson'.
16 'SUNN O)))', https://southernlord.com (2000), archived at
    www.web.archive.org, accessed 22 January 2021.
17 Mark Beaumont, 'Sunn O))) Review', www.theguardian.com,
    19 August 2015.
18 Alan Licht, 'Minimalist Top Ten III', *Volcanic Tongue* (10 June 2007),
    archived at www.diagonalthoughts.com, accessed 2 July 2019.
19 Tom Scanlon, 'Rocker Made Hard Choices, Is Back to Music and Life',
    www.seattletimes.com, 6 July 2007.
20 David Foster Wallace, *The Pale King* (London, 2012), p. 140.
21 'REM: Rough Cut (*Monster* Tour Documentary)', www.youtube.com, 16
    December 2016, accessed 22 January 2021.
22 Claire Biddles, 'Speaking in Tongues', *The Wire* (September 2019).
23 John McFerrin, 'REM', www.johnmcferrinmusicreviews.org, 2004.
24 Stuart Maconie, 'REM: *Monster* Review', *Q* (November 1994).
25 Joseph Heller, *Something Happened* (London, 1995), p. 33.
26 Erick Neher, 'In Praise of Boring Films', *Hudson Review*, LXVI/1
    (Spring 2013), p. 226.
27 Ibid., p. 227.
28 Ibid., p. 228.
29 Ibid., p. 232.
30 Needham, 'Earth'.
31 Mark Fisher, *The Weird and the Eerie* (London, 2016), p. 11.

32 Peter Cousaert, 'Earth', www.whiteheatmagazine.wordpress.com, 22 January 2011.

33 Briony Edwards, 'Dylan Carlson's Track-by-Track Guide to New Earth Album *Full upon Her Burning Lips*', www.loudersound.com, 24 May 2019.

34 Peter Toohey, *Boredom: A Lively History* (London, 2011), p. 175.

35 Wallace, *Pale King*, p. 463.

36 Ibid., p. 548.

37 Aaron Schmidt, 'Sleep Interview', www.thrashermagazine.com, 16 October 2018.

38 Kory Grow, 'Black Sabbath and Indica Weed: Inside the Grand Return of Stoner-Metal Heroes Sleep', www.rollingstone.com, 14 June 2018.

39 Matthew Tomich, 'Talking *Dopesmoker* with Sleep's Matt Pike', www.vice.com, 9 October 2017.

40 Joe Merrick, *Shane MacGowan: London Irish Punk Life and Music* (London, 2001), p. 75.

41 Marek Steven, 'Om – Interview with Al Cisneros', www.ninehertz. co.uk, 6 April 2007.

42 J. Bennett, 'High Times: The Making of Sleep's *Jerusalem*', in *Precious Metal: Decibel Presents the Stories Behind 25 Extreme Metal Masterpieces*, ed. Albert Mudrian (Cambridge, MA, 2009), p. 298.

43 Julian Cope, *Copendium: An Expedition into the Rock 'n' Roll Underwerld* (London, 2013), p. 367.

44 Max Burke, 'Sleep: Interview', www.prefixmag.com, 13 September 2010.

45 Bennett, 'High Times', p. 296.

46 Ibid., p. 294.

47 Frank Rini, 'Interview with Onslaught', www.allaboutherock.co.uk, 29 October 2013.

48 Bennett, 'High Times', p. 302.

49 Ibid., 298–9; Mikael Wood, 'High On Fire's Matt Pike: Drugs, Barbarian Metal "Trying to Find God" in Sleep', www.revolvermag.com, 1 November 2007.

50 Bennett, 'High Times', pp. 300–301.

51 Phil Alexander, 'Sleep – *Jerusalem*', *Kerrang!* (6 June 1998).

52 Moores, '20 Years of Southern Lord'.

53 Wood, 'High On Fire'.

54 Chris Kies, 'Matt Pike: Chug, Punch, and Sustain', www.premierguitar. com, 8 November 2018.

55 Grow, 'Black Sabbath'.

56 Dan Collins, 'Om: Ingesting that Sonic Food', www.larecord.com, 25 September 2009.

57 In reality, Osbourne did not spill any liquid. Rather unfairly, director Penelope Spheeris filmed a close-up of a male hand – one of the crew's – spilling the juice and cut that into the film so it seemed like Osbourne

was culpable, which gets a big laugh. Spheeris would go on to direct
Wayne's World.

58 Will Ashon, *Chamber Music: About the Wu-Tang Clan* (London, 2018),
pp. 234–41.

59 Barry Miles, *Paul McCartney: Many Years from Now* (London, 1997),
p. 190.

60 Dan Franklin, 'Review: Sleep, *The Sciences*', www.thequietus.com,
20 April 2018.

61 Joseph Stannard, 'Goat *Stonegoat/Dreambuilding* Review', *The Wire*
(June 2013).

62 Mike Liassides, 'Interview with Electric Wizard', www.doom-metal.
com, 20 February 2018.

63 Incidentally, while working on this chapter my dreams became more
vivid and memorable than usual. One of the most harrowing visions
involved most of my teeth falling out. Dream interpreters say such
dreams indicate anxiety and insecurity, but I blame Electric Wizard.
(I was not on drugs.)

64 John Doran, 'Electric Wizard: You Terrible Cult', *Stool Pigeon*
(November 2009).

65 Tim Bugbee, 'Electric Wizard: Interview', www.prefixmag.com,
26 January 2011.

66 Dan Franklin, 'Electric Wizard Talk New LP', www.thequietus.com,
20 January 2014.

67 Michael Friedman, 'Spitting at Mortality with Jus Oborn',
www.psychologytoday.com, 23 July 2018.

68 Bugbee, 'Electric Wizard'.

69 Ronnie Kerswell-O'Hara, 'Past Lives – Electric Wizard', *Terrorizer's
Secret History of Doom Metal* (April 2012).

70 '20 Great Black Sabbath Tracks Picked by the Stars', *Kerrang!*
(20 June 1998).

71 Andrew O'Neill, *A History of Heavy Metal* (London, 2018), p. 193.

72 Dan Franklin, 'Rise Above Records Turns 25: From Electric Wizard
to Iron Man', www.thequietus.com, 27 December 2013.

73 Malcolm Dome, 'The Story behind Electric Wizard: *Dopethrone*', www.
loudersound.com, 17 August 2011. Bagshaw and Greening would remain
in the line-up for one more album, 2002's *Let Us Prey*, before going on
to form Ramesses, another super-heavy unit, whose music, it ought to
be noted, contains scant debts to Stone Temple Pilots or Tupac Shakur.

74 Dom Lawson, 'Electric Wizard: "We had a fantasy we'd get busted for
having satanic sex orgies"', www.theguardian.com, 2 June 2015.

75 Franklin, 'Electric Wizard Talk'; Dome, 'The Story'; Klemen Breznikar,
'Electric Wizard Interview with Jus Oborn', www.psychedelicbabymag.
com, 1 March 2013.

76 'Jus Oborn shows us how to build one properly . . .', www.youtube.com,

accessed 23 January 2021; 'We Hate You + Barbarian – naff studio footage', www.youtube.com, accessed 23 Janaury 2021.

77 Dome, 'The Story'.

78 Stephanie Chen, 'Debunking the Myths of Columbine, 10 Years Later', www.edition.cnn.com, 20 April 2009.

79 Franklin, 'Electric Wizard Talk'.

80 Friedman, 'Spitting'.

81 '20/20 the Devil Worshippers – May 16, 1985', www.youtube.com, accessed 23 January 2021.

82 Dome, 'The Story'.

83 Brad Miska, '10 Favorite Horror Films of Electric Wizard's Jus Oborn!', www.bloody-disgusting.com, 23 November 2017.

84 Hugh Gilmour, 'Electric Wizard', www.gilmourdesign.co.uk, 2000.

85 For example: John Doran, 'The Twenty Heaviest (Metal) Records of All Time', www.nme.com, 4 May 2011 ('As a point of order I've kept this list down to one inclusion per band in case it just ended up looking like an Electric Wizard discography'); Nick Ruskell, 'Are These the 10 Heaviest Albums Ever Made?', www.theguardian.com, 10 November 2011; David89zemun, 'Friday Top: 25 Heaviest Albums Ever Made as Voted by UG community', www.ultimate-guitar.com, 7 December 2019.

86 Fred Pessaro, 'Electric Wizard on Sabbath Worship, Doom Domestic Bliss, Death of Rock', www.revolvermag.com, 12 October 2017.

87 Doran, 'Electric Wizard'.

88 Mörat, 'Blood on the Tracks', *Kerrang!* (29 July 2000).

89 J. Bennett, '1993: A Desert Odyssey: The Making of Kyuss' *Welcome to Sky Valley*', in *Precious Metal*, ed. Mudrian, p. 208.

90 J. J. Koczan, 'Interview with Brant Bjork: How the Former Kyuss and Fu Manchu Drummer came to Embrace the Classics', www.theaquarian.com, 14 April 2010; Jerry Ewing, 'My Life Story: Nick Oliveri', www.loudersound.com, 6 September 2016.

91 'Kyuss Interview, Toronto, The Rivoli, December 13, 1992', www.youtube.com, accessed 23 January 2021.

92 Chris Morris, 'Kyuss Lands on Its Feet', *Billboard* (15 January 1994).

93 Dom Lawson, 'Welcome to Sky Valley', *Kerrang!* (29 July 2000).

94 Tony Iommi with T. L. Lammers, *Iron Man: My Journey through Heaven and Hell with Black Sabbath* (London, 2012), p. 134.

95 Bennett, '1993', p. 211.

96 Damo Musclecar, 'Interview with Dave Wyndorf', www.longgoneloser.wordpress.com, 2 September 2011.

97 Joe Daly, 'Rock and Roll Coffee: A Conversation with Dave Wyndorf of Monster Magnet', www.theweeklings.com, 28 October 2013.

98 Valerie Siebert, 'Tailor Made for Worship: Dave Wyndorf of Monster Magnet's Favourite Albums', www.thequietus.com, 27 March 2014.

15 The Nadir: The Late 1990s and Early 2000s

1 '. . . And Now It's Oasis vs Limp Bizkit', *Melody Maker* (19 April 2000).

2 Greg Milner, *Perfecting Sound Forever: The Story of Recorded Music* (London, 2010), pp. 239–42.

3 Ibid., ch. 7.

4 John Harris, 'A Shite Sports Car and a Punk Reincarnation', *NME* (10 April 1993).

5 Adrian Deevoy, 'My Bloody Valentine's Kevin Shields: "I Play through the Pain"', *The Guardian* (3 October 2013).

6 John Doran, 'Why My Bloody Valentine's *MBV* has Come Too Late to Stop the End of the World', www.vice.com, 4 February 2013.

7 David Stubbs, 'The Pixies: *Death to the Pixies*', *Uncut* (November 1997).

8 Tom Sheehan, 'Blur: "Our Culture is Under Siege"', *Melody Maker* (25 September 1993).

9 Keith Cameron, liner notes to Dinosaur Jr, *Hand It Over* (Cherry Red, 2019).

10 Barney Hoskyns, 'The Alternative Metallica', *Mojo* (July 1996); Steffan Chirazi, 'Killed 'Em All', *Kerrang!* (10 January 1998).

11 Matthew Smith-Lahrman, 'Interview with Duane Denison, February 3, 1993', www.smithlahrman.blogspot.com, 30 January 2012.

12 Tom Connick, '20 Years of Nu-metal: The Rise, Fall and Revival of Rock's Most Maligned Offshoot', www.theguardian.com, 9 May 2017.

13 Mike Baker, 'Kittie Interview', *AntiMTV* (March 2000), archived at www.web.archive.org, accessed 22 January 2020; 'Kittie on Sexism in the Music Industry', www.youtube.com, 23 March 2018, accessed 22 January 2020.

14 Don Kaye, 'Faith No More / Limp Bizkit', *Kerrang!* (18 October 1997).

15 *Metal Evolution* (VH1, 2011).

16 'Popscene – All Shite!', www.nme.com, 24 October 2000.

17 Adrian Harte, *Small Victories: The True Story of Faith No More* (London, 2018), p. 128.

18 Ibid., pp. 224–6.

19 Sammy Maine, 'Alien Ant Farm + P.O.D. + Hoobastank Live Review', www.bristolinstereo.com, 22 May 2015.

20 '*Metal Hammer* Albums of 1999', www.rocklistmusic.co.uk, accessed 27 March 2018.

21 Bob Stanley, *Yeah Yeah Yeah: The Story of Modern Pop* (London, 2014), p. 714.

22 Paul Elliott, 'Manic Street Preachers: *This Is My Truth Tell Me Yours*', *Kerrang!* (12 September 1998).

23 Billy Corgan, 'Starcrossed, and Subsequently, a Door is Opened (1997)', https://billycorgan.livejournal.com, 7 June 2011.

24 JR Moores, 'Appetite for Self-destruction', *Record Collector* (May 2018).

25 Danilo Nikodinovski, 'Interview: Andy Cairns of Northern Irish Rockers Therapy?', www.musicexistence.com, 5 February 2019.
26 Stephen Hill and Remfry Dedman, 'Episode 02 – Testicular Embolisation, You First (feat. Andy Cairns from Therapy?)', www.riotactpodcast.com, 10 August 2018.

16 The 2000s Noise Scene

1 Marc Masters, 'Wolf Eyes: Ass Backwards into the Future', *The Wire* (May 2013).
2 Steve Appleford, 'Playlist: Henry Rollins' 5 Favorite Bands', www.spin.com, 2 March 2011.
3 Kim Kelly, 'Thurston Moore is the Patron Saint of Music Nerds', www.vice.com, 10 August 2016.
4 Michael Azerrad, *Our Band Could Be Your Life: Scenes from the American Indie Underground, 1981–1991* (New York, 2001), p. 255.
5 Paul Stokes, 'Q&A Thurston Moore', www.qthemusic.com, 13 July 2013.
6 Aaron Lake Smith, 'The Verge Q+A: Punk Pioneer Steve Albini on Music Festivals, the Future of Radio and Why He Wants *GQ* to Fail', www.gq.com, 29 September 2010.
7 'Sonic Youth: *SYR4 – Goodbye 20th Century* Album Review', www.nme.com, accessed 20 August 2018; Ashley Bird, 'Sonic Youth – *Goodbye 20th Century*', *Kerrang!* (18 December 1999); '50 Records of the Year', *The Wire* (December 1999).
8 Brent DiCrescenzo, 'Sonic Youth: *NYC Ghosts & Flowers* Album Review', www.pitchfork.com, 30 April 2000.
9 Mark Sinker, 'Invisible Jukebox: Sonic Youth', *The Wire* (February 1993).
10 David Kennan, 'Signal to Noise', *The Wire* (May 1997).
11 Greh Holger and Mike Connelly, 'Episode 1: *Tauromachine*', www.merzcast.bandcamp.com, 5 February 2019.
12 In Paul Hegarty, *Noise Music: A History* (New York, 2007), p. 156.
13 Ellen Carpenter, 'Thurston Moore and Kim Gordon of Sonic Youth Let Us Relax in Their Massachusetts Living Room', *Spin* (July 2009).
14 Joseph Stannard, 'Religious Knives: *The Door* Album Review', *The Wire* (November 2008).
15 Sylvie Simmons, 'Spotting a Star in the Texas Night', *The Guardian* (23 March 2007); Sam Richards, 'J Mascis on the Guitarists You Really Must Hear', www.theguardian.com, 12 March 2011.
16 Alexandra Pollard, 'NME Created an Indie Scene out of Thin Air in 2002 and Made It Stick', www.vice.com, 27 November 2017.
17 Tony Herrington, 'Fun from None: Live from the No Fun Fest 2004 & 2005 (DVD)', *The Wire* (February 2007).
18 https://twitter.com/HenryBlacker/status/1079486022713556994, accessed 23 January 2021.
19 Masters, 'Wolf Eyes'.

20 John Doran, 'Fuck Buttons: *Street Horrrsing* Album Review', www.thequietus.com, 20 March 2008.

21 Charlie Brigden, 'Why We Should Listen to Texas Chainsaw Massacre's Score as Musique Concrète', www.thequietus.com, 29 September 2017.

22 Jennifer Lucy Allan, 'Wolf Eyes on Detroit: 'You Can Walk a Block from Our Studio and See a War Zone', www.theguardian.com, 3 April 2017.

23 John Twells, '"A Healthy Supply of LSD – That was a Big Part of It": Nate Young on the Past, Present and Future of Wolf Eyes', www.factmag.com, 10 June 2013; David Sackllah, 'The Neverending Story of Wolf Eyes', www.consequenceofsound.com, 22 October 2015.

24 'The Self-titled Interview: Carlos Giffoni', www.self-titledmag.com, April 2011.

25 Robert Ham, 'William Bennett Explains His Career, from the Power Electronics of Whitehouse to the Rabid African Rhythms of Cut Hands', www.self-titledmag.com, 13 August 2015.

26 Matt Preira, 'Wolf Eyes' John Olson says Noise Music is Over: "Completely, 100 Percent"', www.miaminewtimes.com, 4 December 2013.

27 Masters, 'Wolf Eyes'.

28 Preira, 'Wolf Eyes'.

17 Post-rock and Post-metal

 1 Quoted in Jeanette Lynch, *Fearless: The Making of Post-rock* (London, 2017), p. 292.

 2 'Mogwai – "Blur: Are Shite"', www.nme.com, 7 June 1999.

 3 Ibid.

 4 Eamon Sweeney, 'Mogwai: "We Always Wanted to Get a Better Name than Mogwai but We Never Got Around to It', www.irishtimes.com, 12 June 2015.

 5 Stuart Braithwaite, 'Mixtape Monday: 10 Songs that Influenced Mogwai', www.drownedinsound.com, 4 February 2011.

 6 Keith Cameron, 'Mogwai: *Happy Songs For Happy People*', *Mojo* (July 2003).

 7 'Arab Strap's Aidan Moffat – The British Masters – Chapter 5', www.youtube.com, 7 March 2013, accessed 23 January 2021.

 8 Ben Thompson, *Ways of Hearing: A User's Guide to the Pop Psyche, from Elvis to Eminem* (London, 2001), p. 237.

 9 Ibid., pp. 235–6.

10 Lucy O'Brien, 'Live Report: Bardo Pond at the 100 Club', www.thequietus.com, 7 June 2018.

11 Paul Thompson, 'Bardo Pond: *Bardo Pond*', www.pitchfork.com, 13 January 2011.

12 JR Moores, 'Fugazi on Acid: The Cult of Bardo Pond',
     www.vice.com, 24 August 2015.
13 Ibid.
14 'Mogwai: Five Records', www.factmag.com, 15 February 2011.
15 Keith Cameron, 'For those about to Post-Rock . . .', *NME*
     (25 October 1997).
16 Simon Reynolds, 'Shaking the Rock Narcotic', *The Wire*
     (May 1994).
17 John Mulvey, 'Pet Shop Ploy', *NME* (November 1996), archived
     at www.youngteam.co.uk, accessed 6 December 2019.
18 Ben Myers, 'Irn Men', *Kerrang!* (17 April 1999).
19 Luke Turner, 'Luke Turner on Public Service Broadcasting's *Every
     Valley*', www.thequietus.com, 6 July 2017.
20 J. J. Anselmi, *Doomed to Fail: The Incredibly Loud History of Doom,
     Sludge and Post-metal* (Los Angeles, CA, 2020), p. 270.
21 Kory Grow, 'Neurosis on 30 Years of Finding "New Ways of Being
     Heavy"', www.rollingstone.com, 22 November 2016.
22 Anselmi, *Doomed*, pp. 270–71.
23 Ibid., p. 274.
24 Grow, 'Neurosis'.
25 Ibid.
26 Ibid.
27 Gavin Brown, 'Interview: Trevor de Brauw from Pelican',
     www.echoesanddust.com, 28 September 2019.
28 Lynch, *Fearless*, p. 308.
29 Stuart Berman, 'Metallica / Lou Reed: *Lulu*', www.pitchfork.com,
     1 November 2011.
30 Chuck Klosterman, 'Injustice for All: The Lou Reed/Metallica Album',
     www.grantland.com, 8 November 2011.
31 Quentin Bell, 'Bad Art', in Bell, *Bad Art* (Chicago, IL, 1989), pp. 11–12.
32 Andrew Massie, 'Hard Rock Interviews 2013 – Bardo Pond – Michael
     Gibbons', www.therockpit.net, 28 June 2013.

18 Sabbath Phase IV: Pigs Pigs Pigs Pigs Pigs Pigs Pigs and the Modern Heavy Underground

 1 Patrick Clarke, 'Porcine Pre-eminence: An Interview with Pigs Pigs Pigs
     Pigs Pigs Pigs Pigs', www.thequietus.com, 7 February 2017.
 2 Bekki Bemrose, 'A Demonic Fury: DiS meets Pigs Pigs Pigs Pigs Pigs
     Pigs Pigs', www.drownedinsound.com, 8 November 2018.
 3 Patrick Clarke, 'High on the Hog: An Interview with Pigs Pigs Pigs Pigs
     Pigs Pigs Pigs', www.thequietus.com, 16 April 2020.
 4 Luke O'Dwyer, 'Pigs Pigs Pigs Pigs Pigs Pigs Pigs – *Feed The Rats*',
     www.the-monitors.com, 14 February 2017.
 5 Matt Baty, interview with the author, 2020.

6 James Wadsworth, 'Interview: Pigs Pigs Pigs Pigs Pigs Pigs Pigs', www.underscorepart3.co.uk, 14 April 2019.

7 Jak Hutchcraft, 'Psych Noise Band Pigs Pigs Pigs Pigs Pigs Pigs Pigs on Heavy Music and Writing a Song about Greggs', www.vice.com, 26 May 2020.

8 Theo Kotz, 'Commanding Hellfire with Pigs Pigs Pigs Pigs Pigs Pigs Pigs', www.crackmagazine.net, 4 February 2018.

9 Wadsworth, 'Interview'.

10 Clarke, 'High on the Hog'.

11 John Peel, *The Olivetti Chronicles* (London, 2008), p. 32. As if to spite Peel, Butthole Surfers did sign to a major label in the early 1990s and scored a U.S. top-30 hit with 1996's Beck-ish single 'Pepper'.

12 Dave Simpson, 'Pigs Pigs Pigs Pigs Pigs Pigs Pigs: "When music is loud, niggling troubles just go"', www.theguardian.com, 9 April 2020.

13 Louise Brown, 'Columnus Metallicus: Your Month in Metal', www.thequietus.com, 6 June 2018.

14 JR Moores, 'Arson About: Burning Guitars with Mike Vest of 11Paranoias and Bong', www.thequietus.com, 25 April 2019.

15 Kotz, 'Commanding Hellfire'.

16 Joe Thompson, *Sleevenotes* (Keighley, 2019), p. 91.

17 Joe Thompson, *Dances/Curses*, press release, 2020.

18 Thompson, *Sleevenotes*, p. 222.

19 https://twitter.com/XeaglepissX/status/630414737550000130, accessed 23 January 2021.

20 Tom Pinnock, 'Richard Dawson's Favourite Albums', www.uncut.co.uk, 15 October 2019; Chris Waywell, 'Richard Dawson: One of the Most Original Voices in English Music', www.timeout.com, 5 June 2017.

21 Jennifer Lucy Allan, 'Dawn to Dusk: Richard Dawson's Favourite Albums', www.thequietus.com, 14 October 2019.

22 David Renshaw, 'Britain's Richard Dawson is the Empathetic Voice of a Divided Island', www.thefader.com, 14 October 2019; Allan, 'Dawn to Dusk'.

23 John Doran, 'A Mysore Masala Dosa and a Mango Lassi with Richard Dawson', www.vice.com, 27 October 2016.

24 Baty, interview with the author, 2020.

25 Ibid.

26 Ibid.

27 Ibid.

19 Never Say Die

1 Steve Albini, 'Big Black: Amen a Pen a Canal – Enema!', liner notes to Big Black, *Sound of Impact* (Not, 1986).

2 Max Pilley, 'Richard Dawson's New State-of-the-Nation Album

Refuses to Sugar-coat a Broken Society', *Loud and Quiet* (28 September 2019); Sam Sodomsky, 'Richard Dawson: *2020*', www.pitchfork.com, 17 October 2019.

3 Matt Baty, interview with the author, 2020.

4 Daniel Holland, 'Austerity Causes 1 Death Every Week in Newcastle, Warns "Chilling" New Evidence', www.chroniclelive.co.uk, 28 June 2019.

5 Sarah Neville, 'Gains in UK Life Expectancy Stall after Decade of Austerity, Report Says', www.ft.com, 25 February 2020.

6 Michael Marmot, 'Why did England have Europe's Worst Covid Figures? The Answer Starts with Austerity', www.theguardian.com, 10 August 2020.

7 Jak Hutchcraft, 'Psych Noise Band Pigs Pigs Pigs Pigs Pigs Pigs Pigs on Heavy Music and Writing a Song about Greggs', www.vice.com, 26 May 2020.

8 Daniel Boffey, 'Brexit Broadside: British Officials Bristle at Danish Scorn', www.theguardian.com, 14 June 2017.

9 Jeff McMahan, 'How Britain and the U.S. became Trapped in the Nationalism of Decline', www.newstatesman.com, 2 October 2020.

10 Christian Eede, 'Pigs x7 Share New Track, "Rubbernecker"', www.thequietus.com, 12 March 2020.

11 Steven Shaviro, *Doom Patrols: A Theoretical Fiction about Postmodernism* (London, 1997), available at www.shaviro.com, accessed 5 October 2020.

12 David Hepworth, *Uncommon People: The Rise and Fall of the Rock Stars* (London, 2017), p. 377.

FURTHER READING

Anselmi, J. J., *Doomed to Fail: The Incredibly Loud History of Doom, Sludge and Post-Metal* (Los Angeles, CA, 2020)

Azerrad, Michael, *Come As You Are: The Story of Nirvana* (London, 1996)

—, *Our Band Could Be Your Life: Scenes from the American Indie Underground, 1981–1991* (New York, 2001)

Bangs, Lester, *Psychotic Reactions and Carburetor Dung* (London, 1987)

Becker, Scott, ed., *We Rock So You Don't Have To: The Option Reader #1* (San Diego, CA, 1998)

Björnberg, Alf, and Thomas Bossius, eds, *Made in Sweden: Studies in Popular Music* (Abingdon, 2017)

Bolden, Tony, ed., *The Funk Era and Beyond: New Perspectives on Black Culture* (New York, 2008)

Cavanagh, David, *Good Night and Good Riddance: How Thirty-Five Years of John Peel Helped to Shape Modern Life* (London, 2015)

Chapman, Rob, *Psychedelia and Other Colours* (London, 2015)

Clerk, Carol, *The Saga of Hawkwind* (London, 2009)

Cope, Andrew L., *Black Sabbath and the Rise of Heavy Metal Music* (London, 2010)

Cope, Julian, *Copendium: An Expedition into the Rock 'n' Roll Underwerld* (London, 2013)

—, *Japrocksampler* (London, 2007)

Du Noyer, Paul, *Conversations with McCartney* (London, 2015)

Franklin, Dan, *Heavy: How Metal Changes the Way We See the World* (London, 2020)

Gaar, Gillian G., *In Utero* (London, 2016)

Gedge, David, *Sleevenotes* (Keighley, West Yorkshire, 2019)

Gordon, Kim, *Girl in a Band* (London, 2015)

Hanley, Steve, and Piekarski, Olivia, *The Big Midweek: Life Inside The Fall* (Pontefract, West Yorkshire, 2016)

Harte, Adrian, *Small Victories: The True Story of Faith No More* (London, 2018)

Haslam, Dave, *Sonic Youth Slept on My Floor* (London, 2019)

Hegarty, Paul, *Noise Music: A History* (New York, 2007)

Hepworth, David, *Uncommon People: The Rise and Fall of the Rock Stars* (London, 2017)

Iommi, Tony, with T. L. Lammers, *Iron Man: My Journey Through Heaven and Hell with Black Sabbath* (London, 2012)

The Jesus Lizard, BOOK (New York, 2013)

Jourgensen, Al, with Jon Wiederhorn, *Ministry: The Lost Gospels According to Al Jourgensen* (Boston, MA, 2013)

Lemmy, with Janiss Garza, *White Line Fever* (London, 2003)

Lynch, Jeanette, *Fearless: The Making of Post-Rock* (London, 2017)

McDonough, Jimmy, *Shakey: Neil Young's Biography* (London, 2002)

McIver, Joel, *Sabbath Bloody Sabbath* (London, 2014)

Miles, Barry, *Paul McCartney: Many Years From Now* (London, 1997)

Miller, Steve, *Detroit Rock City: The Uncensored History of Rock 'n' Roll in America's Loudest City* (Boston, MA, 2013)

Milner, Greg, *Perfecting Sound Forever: The Story of Recorded Music* (London, 2010)

Mudrian, Albert, *Choosing Death: The Improbable History of Death Metal and Grindcore* (Los Angeles, CA, 2002)

—, ed., *Precious Metal: Decibel Presents the Stories behind 25 Extreme Metal Masterpieces* (Cambridge, MA, 2009)

Needs, Kris, *George Clinton and the Cosmic Odyssey of the P-Funk Empire* (London, 2014)

O'Neill, Andrew, *A History of Heavy Metal* (London, 2018)

Peel, John, *Margrave of the Marshes* (London, 2005)

—, *The Olivetti Chronicles* (London, 2008)

Reynolds, Simon, *Rip It Up and Start Again: Post-Punk, 1978–1984* (London, 2019)

Rooney, James, *Bossmen: Bill Monroe and Muddy Waters* (New York, 1971)

Shteamer, Hank, *Chocolate and Cheese* (London, 2011)

Springsteen, Bruce, *Born to Run* (London, 2016)

Stanley, Bob, *Yeah Yeah Yeah: The Story of Modern Pop* (London, 2014)

Stubbs, David, *Future Days: Krautrock and the Building of Modern Germany* (London, 2017)

Sullivan, Paul, *Remixology: Tracing the Dub Diaspora* (London, 2014)

Tait, John, *Vanda and Young: Inside Australia's Hit Factory* (Sydney, 2010)

Thompson, Joe, *Sleevenotes* (Keighley, West Yorkshire, 2019)

Wall, Mick, *Black Sabbath: Symptom of the Universe* (London, 2014)

Wallace, David Foster, *The Pale King* (London, 2012)

Whiteley, Sheila, and Jedediah Sklower, eds, *Countercultures and Popular Music* (Farnham, 2014)

Yarm, Mark, *Everybody Loves Our Town: A History of Grunge* (London, 2001)

SELECT DISCOGRAPHY

AC/DC, *High Voltage* (Albert, 1975)
—, *Dirty Deeds Done Dirt Cheap* (Albert, 1976)
—, *Powerage* (Atlantic, 1978)
—, *Back in Black* (Atlantic, 1980)

Alice Cooper, *Love It to Death* (Straight/Warner Bros., 1971)
—, *Killer* (Warner Bros., 1971)
—, *School's Out* (Warner Bros., 1972)

Alice in Chains, *Facelift* (Columbia, 1990)

The Amboy Dukes, *Journey to the Center of the Mind* (Mainstream, 1968)
—, *Migration* (Mainstream, 1969)
—, *Call of the Wild* (DiscReet, 1973)
—, *Tooth, Fang & Claw* (DiscReet, 1974)

Amon Düül II, *Phallus Dei* (Liberty, 1969)
—, *Yeti* (Liberty, 1970)

Babes in Toyland, *Spanking Machine* (Twin/Tone, 1990)
—, *Fontanelle* (Reprise, 1992)

Baby Grandmothers, *Baby Grandmothers* (Subliminal Sounds, 2007)
—, *Merkurius* (Subliminal Sounds, 2018)

Bad Brains, *Rock for Light* (Passport, 1983)
—, *I Against I* (sst, 1986)

Bardo Pond, *Amanita* (Matador, 1996)
—, *Lapsed* (Matador, 1997)
—, *Record Store Day Trilogy* (Fire, 2015)

The Beatles, *Sgt. Pepper's Lonely Hearts Club Band* (Parlophone, 1967)
—, *The Beatles* (aka *The White Album*) (Apple, 1968)

Big Black, *Atomizer* (Homestead, 1986)
—, *Songs about Fucking* (Touch and Go, 1987)

Black Flag, *My War* (sst, 1984)

Black Sabbath, *Black Sabbath* (Vertigo, 1970)
—, *Paranoid* (Vertigo, 1970)
—, *Master of Reality* (Vertigo, 1971)
—, *Vol. 4* (Vertigo, 1972)
—, *Sabbath Bloody Sabbath* (Vertigo, 1973)
—, *Sabotage* (Vertigo, 1975)
—, *Technical Ecstasy* (Vertigo, 1976)
—, *Never Say Die* (Vertigo, 1978)

Blue Cheer, *Vincebus Eruptum* (Philips, 1968)

Brothers of the Sonic Cloth, *Brothers of the Sonic Cloth* (Neurot, 2015)

Budgie, *Budgie* (MCA, 1971)
—, *Squawk* (MCA, 1972)
—, *Never Turn Your Back on a Friend* (MCA, 1973)

Butthole Surfers, *Psychic . . . Powerless . . . Another Man's Sac*
    (Touch and Go, 1984)
—, *Rembrandt Pussyhorse* (Touch and Go, 1986)
—, *Locust Abortion Technician* (Touch and Go, 1987)
—, *Hairway to Steven* (Touch and Go, 1988)
—, *piouhgd* (Rough Trade, 1991)
—, *Independent Worm Saloon* (Capitol, 1993)

Cabaret Voltaire, *2x45* (Rough Trade, 1982)

Can, *Monster Movie* (Music Factory/Liberty, 1969)
—, *Tago Mago* (United Artists, 1971)
—, *Ege Bamyası* (United Artists, 1972)

Captain Beefheart & His Magic Band, *Trout Mask Replica*
    (Straight, 1969)
—, *The Mirror Man Sessions* (Buddha, 1999)

Cherubs, *Heroin Man* (Trance Syndicate, 1994)

Cows, *Taint Pluribus Taint Unum* (Treehouse, 1987)
—, *Cunning Stunts* (Amphetamine Reptile, 1992)
—, *Sorry in Pig Minor* (Amphetamine Reptile, 1998)

Betty Davis, *Betty Davis* (Just Sunshine, 1973)
—, *They Say I'm Different* (Just Sunshine, 1974)
—, *Nasty Gal* (Island, 1975)

Miles Davis, *Agharta* (Columbia, 1975)
—, *Pangaea* (Columbia, 1976)
—, *Dark Magus* (Columbia, 1977)

Richard Dawson, *2020* (Domino, 2019)

Deftones, *Around the Fur* (Maverick, 1997)
—, *White Pony* (Maverick, 2000)

Depeche Mode, *Black Celebration* (Mute, 1986)
—, *Ultra* (Mute, 1997)

Dinosaur Jr, *You're Living All Over Me* (SST, 1987)
—, *Bug* (SST, 1988)

Earth, *Earth 2: Special Low Frequency Version* (Sub Pop, 1993)
—, *Phase 3: Thrones and Dominions* (Sub Pop, 1995)
—, *Pentastar: In the Style of Demons* (Sub Pop, 1996)
—, *Hex; or Printing in the Infernal Method* (Southern Lord, 2005)
—, *Primitive and Deadly* (Southern Lord, 2014)

Einstürzende Neubauten, *Kollaps* (ZickZack, 1981)

Electric Wizard, *Come My Fanatics...* (Rise Above, 1997)
—, *Dopethrone* (Rise Above, 2000)

Evil Acidhead, *In the Name of All That Is Unholy* (Agitated, 2015)

Faith No More, *Angel Dust* (Slash/Reprise, 1992)

The Fall, *Hex Enduction Hour* (Kamera, 1982)
—, *Perverted by Language* (Rough Trade, 1983)
—, *Re-Mit* (Cherry Red, 2013)
—, *New Facts Emerge* (Cherry Red, 2017)

Faust, *Faust* (Polydor, 1971)
—, *Faust So Far* (Polydor, 1972)
—, *The Faust Tapes* (Virgin, 1973)
—, *Faust IV* (Virgin, 1973)

Flower Travellin' Band, *Anywhere* (Philips, 1970)
—, *Satori* (Atlantic, 1971)

Fugazi, *Repeater* (Dischord, 1990)
—, *In on the Kill Taker* (Dischord, 1993)
—, *The Argument* (Dischord, 2001)

Funkadelic, *Funkadelic* (Westbound, 1970)
—, *Free Your Mind . . . and Your Ass Will Follow* (Westbound, 1970)
—, *Maggot Brain* (Westbound, 1971)
—, *America Eats Its Young* (Westbound, 1972)
—, *Cosmic Slop* (Westbound, 1973)
—, *Standing on the Verge of Getting It On* (Westbound, 1974)
—, *Let's Take It to the Stage* (Westbound, 1975)

Future of the Left, *The Peace & Truce of Future of the Left*
    (Prescriptions, 2016)

Gang of Four, *Entertainment!* (EMI/Warner Bros., 1979)

Godflesh, *Streetcleaner* (Earache, 1989)
—, *Love and Hate in Dub* (Earache, 1997)

Godspeed You! Black Emperor, *Yanqui u.x.o.* (Constellation, 2002)

Michael Hampton, *Heavy Metal Funkason* (P-Vine, 1998)

Harvester/International Harvester, *Remains* (Silence, 2018)

PJ Harvey, *Rid of Me* (Island, 1993)

Hawkwind, *In Search of Space* (United Artists, 1971)
—, *Doremi Fasol Latido* (United Artists, 1972)
—, *Space Ritual* (United Artists, 1973)

Heldon, *Un rêve sans conséquence spéciale* (Cobra, 1976)
—, *Interface* (Cobra, 1977)
—, *Stand By* (Egg, 1979)

Hey Colossus, *Dances/Curses* (Wrong Speed, 2020)

Hole, *Pretty on the Inside* (Caroline, 1991)
—, *Live through This* (dgc, 1994)

Howlin' Wolf, *Moanin' in the Moonlight* (Chess, 1958)
—, *Howlin' Wolf* (aka *The Rockin' Chair Album*) (Chess, 1962)

Iron Butterfly, *In-A-Gadda-Da-Vida* (Atco, 1968)

Isis, *Oceanic* (Ipecac, 2002)

Jefferson Airplane, *Surrealistic Pillow* (RCA Victor, 1967)

Jesu, *Jesu* (Hydra Head, 2004)

The Jesus Lizard, *Goat* (Touch and Go, 1991)
—, *Liar* (Touch and Go, 1992)
—, *Down* (Touch and Go, 1994)

The Jimi Hendrix Experience, *Are You Experienced?* (Track, 1967)
—, *Axis: Bold as Love* (Track, 1967)
—, *Electric Ladyland* (Reprise, 1968)

Joy Division, *Unknown Pleasures* (Factory, 1979)
—, *Closer* (Factory, 1980)

Kandodo/McBain, *Lost Chants/Last Chance* (Rooster Rock, 2016)

Khünnt, *Failures* (Riot Season, 2016)

Killing Joke, *Killing Joke* (E.G., 1980)

King Crimson, *In the Court of the Crimson King* (Island, 1969)
—, *Red* (Island, 1974)

The Kingsmen, 'Louie Louie' (Jerden, 1963)

Kittie, *Oracle* (Artemis, 2001)

Kyuss, *Blues for the Red Sun* (Dali, 1992)
—, *Welcome to Sky Valley* (Elektra, 1994)

L7, *L7* (*Epitaph*, 1988)
—, *Smell the Magic* (Sub Pop, 1990)

Lana Del Rabies, *Shadow World* (Deathbomb Arc, 2018)

Les Rallizes Dénudés, *Heavier than a Death in the Family*
    (Phoenix, 2010)

Liars, *They Were Wrong, So We Drowned* (Mute, 2004)
—, *Drum's Not Dead* (Mute, 2006)

Magik Markers, *Boss* (Ecstatic Peace/Arbitrary Signs, 2007)

Magma, *Magma* (aka *Kobaïa*) (Philips, 1970)

The Maze, *Armageddon* (MTA, 1969)

MC5, *Kick Out the Jams* (Elektra, 1969)
—, *Back in the USA* (Atlantic, 1970)
—, *High Time* (Atlantic, 1971)

Mclusky, *Mclusky Do Dallas* (Too Pure, 2002)
—, *The Difference between Me and You is that I'm Not on Fire* (Too Pure, 2004)

Melvins, *Gluey Porch Treatments* (Alchemy, 1987)
—, *Bullhead* (Boner, 1991)
—, *Lysol* (1992)
—, *Houdini* (Atlantic, 1993)
—, *Stoner Witch* (Atlantic, 1994)
—, *Stag* (Atlantic, 1996)

Merzbow, *Venereology* (Release, 1994)

Metallica, *St. Anger* (Elektra, 2003)

Ministry, *The Land of Rape and Honey* (Sire, 1988)
—, *The Mind is a Terrible Thing to Taste* (Sire, 1989)
—, *ΚΕΦΑΛΗΞΘ* (aka *Psalm 69: The Way to Succeed and the Way to Suck Eggs*) (Sire, 1992)
—, *Filth Pig* (Warner Bros, 1996)

Mogwai, *Young Team* (Chemikal Underground, 1997)
—, *Come On Die Young* (Chemikal Underground, 1999)
—, *Mr Beast* (pias, 2006)

Monster Magnet, *Spine of God* (Glitterhouse, 1991)
—, *Tab* (Glitterhouse, 1991)
—, *Powertrip* (A&M, 1998)

Moor Mother, *Fetish Bones* (Don Giovanni, 2016)

The Mothers of Invention, *Freak Out!* (Verve, 1966)

Motörhead, *Overkill* (Bronze, 1979)
—, *Bomber* (Bronze, 1979)
—, *Ace of Spades* (Bronze, 1980)

Muddy Waters, *At Newport 1960* (Chess, 1960)
—, *The Real Folk Blues* (Chess, 1966)
—, *More Real Folk Blues* (Chess, 1967)

Mudhoney, *Superfuzz Bigmuff Plus Early Singles* (Sub Pop, 1990)

My Bloody Valentine, *Loveless* (Creation, 1991)

Napalm Death, *Scum* (Earache, 1987)
—, *Apex Predator – Easy Meat* (Century Media, 2015)

Necro Deathmort, *The Colonial Script* (Distraction, 2012)

Neurosis, *Through Silver in Blood* (Relapse, 1996)

The New Blockaders, *Das Zerstoren, Zum Gebaren* (Blossoming Noise, 2007)

Nine Inch Nails, *The Downward Spiral* (Nothing/Interscope, 1994)

Nirvana, *Nevermind* (DGC, 1991)
—, *In Utero* (DGC, 1993)

Nyl, *Nyl* (Urus, 1976)

Pärson Sound, *Pärson Sound* (Ti'llindien/Subliminal Sounds, 2001)

Pelican, *Australasia* (Hydra Head, 2003)

Pigs Pigs Pigs Pigs Pigs Pigs Pigs, *Feed the Rats* (Rocket, 2017)
—, *King of Cowards* (Rocket, 2018)
—, *Viscerals* (Rocket, 2020)

Pixies, *Surfer Rosa* (4AD, 1988)

The Pop Group, *Y* (Radar, 1979)

Public Image Ltd, *Public Image: First Issue* (Virgin, 1978)
—, *Metal Box* (Virgin, 1979)
—, *The Flowers of Romance* (Virgin, 1981)

Rage Against the Machine, *Rage Against the Machine* (Epic, 1992)

Lou Reed, *Metal Machine Music* (RCA, 1975)

Lou Reed and Metallica, *Lulu* (Warner Bros./Vertigo, 2011)

REM, *Monster* (Warner Bros, 1994)

Sex Pistols, *Never Mind the Bollocks, Here's the Sex Pistols* (Virgin, 1977)

Shellac, *At Action Park* (Touch and Go, 1994)
—, *Terraform* (Touch and Go, 1998)
—, *1000 Hurts* (Touch and Go, 2000)
—, *Excellent Italian Greyhound* (Touch and Go, 2007)
—, *Dude Incredible* (2014)

Sleep, *Sleep's Holy Mountain* (Earache, 1992)
—, *Dopesmoker* (Southern Lord, 2012)
—, *The Sciences* (Third Man, 2018)

The Slits, *Return of the Giant Slits* (CBS, 1981)

Sly & the Family Stone, *Stand!* (Epic, 1969)
—, *There's a Riot Goin' On* (Epic, 1971)
—, *Woodstock Sunday August 17, 1969* (Epic, 2019)

Soft Machine, *The Soft Machine* (Probe, 1968)
—, *Volume Two* (Probe, 1969)
—, *Third* (CBS, 1970)

Soundgarden, *Louder than Love* (A&M, 1989)

Bruce Springsteen, 'Born in the USA / Shut Out the Light'
     (Columbia, 1984)

The Stooges, *The Stooges* (Elektra, 1969)
—, *Fun House* (Elektra, 1970)
—, *Raw Power* (as Iggy & the Stooges) (Columbia, 1973)

Sunn O))), *The Grimmrobe Demos* (Hydra Head, 1999)
—, *Monoliths & Dimensions* (Southern Lord, 2009)

Swans, *Filth* (Neutral, 1983)

TAD, *God's Balls* (Sub Pop, 1989)
—, *Salt Lick* (Sub Pop, 1990)
—, *8-Way Santa* (Sub Pop, 1991)
—, *Inhaler* (Giant/Warner Bros.)
—, *Infrared Riding Hood* (EastWest, 1995)

Sister Rosetta Tharpe, *Precious Memories* (Savoy, 1968)

Therapy?, *Troublegum* (A&M, 1994)
—, *Suicide Pact – You First* (Ark 21, 1999)

Träd, Gräs och Stenar, *Träd, Gräs och Stenar* (Anthology, 2016)

The Troggs, *From Nowhere* (Fontana, 1966)
—, *Trogglodynamite* (Page One, 1967)

Unsane, *Sterilize* (Southern Lord, 2017)

Vanilla Fudge, *Vanilla Fudge* (Atco, 1967)
—, *The Beat Goes On* (Atco, 1968)
—, *Renaissance* (Atco, 1968)

Various artists, *Nuggets: Original Artyfacts from the First Psychedelic Era,
    1965–1968* (Elektra, 1972)

The Wedding Present, *Seamonsters* (RCA, 1991)

Ween, *The Pod* (Shimmy Disc, 1991)

The Wildhearts, *Endless, Nameless* (Mushroom, 1997)

Wipers, *Youth of America* (Park Avenue, 1981)

Wolf Eyes, *Burned Mind* (Sub Pop, 2004)
—, *Human Animal* (Sub Pop, 2006)
—, *No Answer: Lower Floors* (De Stijl, 2013)

Link Wray, *Early Recordings* (Chiswick, 1978)

Neil Young & Crazy Horse, *Everybody Knows This Is Nowhere*
    (Reprise, 1969)
—, *Zuma* (Reprise, 1975)
—, *Weld* (Reprise, 1991)
—, *Year of the Horse* (Reprise, 1997)

ACKNOWLEDGEMENTS

First and foremost I thank my editor, Dave Watkins, for all of his encouragement and guidance. Without him this book would not exist. Thanks to everyone else at Reaktion Books who worked hard to bring this book to fruition, and especially copy-editor Aimee Selby, whose thorough reading improved the text immeasurably.

Eternal gratitude to my parents for all their love and support, and also for keeping hold of all those old copies of *Kerrang!* and other magazines that were collected during my misspent youth. Those dusty boxes in the attic finally proved useful. My siblings, Chris and Kate, and their partners, Jane and Neil, have always been wonderfully encouraging. My grandmother, known to the family as Bubbles, has been a constant inspiration, even if she does keep asking my friend Dean, who drives the mobile library, when I intend to get a proper job.

My incredible partner Stephanie, to whom this book is dedicated, gave endless love, support and practical advice. Thank you for putting up with me asking 'Is so-and-so heavy? What about such-and-such? Is that heavy? Are they heavy? WHAT IS HEAVY?' for longer than can reasonably be expected.

John McCready regularly boosted my efforts with his enthusiasm, recommendations and cups of coffee, pointing me in the direction of Magma and firing over some heavy dub playlists (a fantastic accompaniment to the writing process). Various conversations with other colleagues and students at the Manchester arm of the BIMM Institute and the University of Huddersfield also helped to get the mental cogs whirring. With good reason, Mario Gregoriou insisted on the inclusion of Pärson Sound and associated Swedes. He also proposed a section on the late 1960s bagpipe-wielding weirdoes Cromagnon, but I didn't manage to squeeze that in. Sorry, Mario, maybe next time.

Matthew Huxford accompanied me when I reported on the festival mentioned at the beginning of Chapter Two. He also did the driving, which is always appreciated, and kept the spirits up during the weekend's regular downpours. This more than makes up for his habit of leaving all the tent pegs at home. Another regular spirit-raiser is Colin Yardley. I expect he'd have liked to hear more about early Smashing Pumpkins. For this I can only apologise.

John Doran was happy to be 'immortalized' in book form as a 'recovering chronic alcoholic' and suggested I changed the wording of the relevant passage only slightly. ('If anything you don't go far enough . . .') He and Luke Turner have been exemplary editors and allies since I began writing for *The Quietus* in 2013. It is always a pleasure to bump into them at festivals (Birmingham's Supersonic, in particular) or on my occasional trips down to gigs and *tQ* shindigs in 'that London'. This book wouldn't exist, either, if those two hadn't taken a punt on letting me contribute to their phenomenal website. Long may it run.

As well as all the articles by other writers on *The Quietus*, the online back issues of *The Wire* are a ridiculously rich resource for anyone wanting to research decent music. The *Rock's Backpages* archive also proved extremely useful, along with the collections held at Manchester Central Library and the University of Huddersfield Library. I thank all the writers whose work is drawn upon.

Three of the chapters were adapted from previously published pieces: 'Cult heroes: Melvins, the dadaist rock outsiders who changed everything' (*The Guardian*, 2015); 'The Chaotic Evolution of Napalm Death's Scum, the World's First Grindcore Album' (*Noisey*, 2017); and 'TAD: "We destroyed every night"' (*Record Collector*, 2018). Thanks to Guardian News & Media, Vice/Noisey and Metropolis International/Diamond Publishing for their permission to extend, adjust and reuse that material.

Some of the thoughts, ideas and arguments expressed elsewhere will have been raised initially in reviews and other bits and pieces I've written for *Record Collector*, *Vinyl Me Please*, *Drowned in Sound*, *Bandcamp Daily*, *The Quietus* and in my liner notes for Richard Pinhas/Heldon reissues on Bureau B, although usually in different and probably fewer words. I am grateful to the staff at those places and all the other editors who have commissioned words from me over the years.

I am indebted to all the endlessly cooperative PR people who regularly send me heavy music, arrange interviews with musicians, put names on guest lists and help writers out in all sorts of other ways. I would like to give a special shout-out to Lauren Barley of Rarely Unable, who invariably has the finest collection of high-quality heavy music on her roster at any given time. Ryan Oxley of Sub Pop was very helpful and patient when I needed to source pictures and get hold of contact details for photo permissions. Thanks to Dylan Carlson and Thomas Doyle for their speedy approvals, and to Mackie Osborne for sending over some vintage pictures of Buzz. Cory Rayborn of Three Lobed Recordings and Michael Gibbons of the mighty Bardo Pond fired over their images and permissions with generous haste. What a band and what a label.

Take note, fellow journalists, because Andrew Falkous is the best interviewee anyone could ever hope for (at least this side of Steven Albini – ha ha). Matt Baty was most obliging with his time and openness. It was

Grainne Wood who asked whether Pigs Pigs Pigs Pigs Pigs Pigs Pigs were a Christian rock band.

Les Hall (aka Rolex Tharsus) did some deep Googling while 'stuck on a really boring conference call', managing to track down a serviceable image of Fred Durst. That goes far beyond the call of duty, if you ask me. Steve Pringle is the person to contact if you ever need to know or double-check anything about The Fall.

My sincere apologies to those who I have inevitably and unforgivably neglected to mention here. It is no excuse, but writing a book this long about music this heavy can occasionally cloud the brain.

Last but not least, thank you to all the bands and musicians whose heaviness genuinely keeps their listeners going in times of need. While this book was being completed the outbreak of COVID-19 put a halt to gigs, and there are no words to describe how much I have missed watching brilliant bands play heavy music at loud volume. I hope to see and hear you all again soon.

Praise Sabbath!

PHOTO
ACKNOWLEDGEMENTS

The author and publishers wish to express their thanks to the below sources of illustrative material and/or permission to reproduce it. Every effort has been made to contact copyright holders; should there be any we have been unable to reach or to whom inaccurate acknowledgements have been made, please contact the publishers, and full adjustments will be made to subsequent printings.

Photo Bob Agee/Wikimedia Commons: p. 31; photo Piers Allardyce/Shutterstock: p. 345; photo Art Aubrey, supplied by Sub Pop, with permission from Dylan Carlson: p. 296; reproduced with permission from Michael Gibbons: p. 382; reproduced with permission from Stephanie King: p. 402; photo Phil Nash/Wikimedia Commons: p. 18; reproduced with permission from Mackie Osborne: p. 214; photo Charles Peterson, supplied by Sub Pop, with permission from Thomas Doyle: p. 257; photo Daniel Souza Luz/Creative Commons: p. 272.

INDEX